The
Time-Life
Family
Legal Guide

TIME
LIFE
BOOKS ®

LIFE WORLD LIBRARY

LIFE NATURE LIBRARY

TIME READING PROGRAM

THE LIFE HISTORY OF THE UNITED STATES

LIFE SCIENCE LIBRARY

GREAT AGES OF MAN

TIME-LIFE LIBRARY OF ART

TIME-LIFE LIBRARY OF AMERICA

FOODS OF THE WORLD

THIS FABULOUS CENTURY

LIFE LIBRARY OF PHOTOGRAPHY

THE TIME-LIFE ENCYCLOPEDIA OF GARDENING

●

FAMILY LIBRARY
   THE TIME-LIFE BOOK OF FAMILY FINANCE
   THE TIME-LIFE FAMILY LEGAL GUIDE

The Time-Life Family Legal Guide

TIME-LIFE BOOKS, NEW YORK

TIME-LIFE BOOKS

EDITOR: Jerry Korn
EXECUTIVE EDITOR: A. B. C. Whipple
PLANNING DIRECTOR: Oliver E. Allen
TEXT DIRECTOR: Martin Mann
ART DIRECTOR: Sheldon Cotler
CHIEF OF RESEARCH: Beatrice T. Dobie
DIRECTOR OF PHOTOGRAPHY: Melvin L. Scott
ASSOCIATE PLANNING DIRECTOR: Byron Dobell
ASSISTANT TEXT DIRECTORS: Ogden Tanner, Diana Hirsh
ASSISTANT ART DIRECTOR: Arnold C. Holeywell
ASSISTANT CHIEF OF RESEARCH: Martha T. Goolrick

PUBLISHER: Joan D. Manley
GENERAL MANAGER: John D. McSweeney
BUSINESS MANAGER: John Steven Maxwell
SALES DIRECTOR: Carl G. Jaeger
PROMOTION DIRECTOR: Paul R. Stewart
PUBLIC RELATIONS DIRECTOR: Nicholas Benton

The Time-Life Family Legal Guide

EDITOR: John Dille
ASSISTANT TO THE EDITOR: Patricia Mohs
DESIGNER: Edward Frank
TEXT EDITORS: Jay Brennan, Betsy Frankel, David S. Thomson,
L. Robert Tschirky
STAFF WRITERS: Sam Halper, John von Hartz
RESEARCHERS: Mary Kay Moran, Diana Sweeney, Timberlake
Wertenbaker, Linda Wolfe, Nancy Jacobsen
ART ASSISTANT: Lee Wilfert

EDITORIAL PRODUCTION
PRODUCTION EDITOR: Douglas B. Graham
QUALITY DIRECTOR: Robert L. Young
ASSISTANT: James J. Cox
COPY STAFF: Rosalind Stubenberg, Susan B. Galloway,
Bobbie Berry, Florence Keith
PICTURE DEPARTMENT: Dolores A. Littles

Valuable assistance was provided by the following departments and individuals
of Time Inc.: Editorial Production, Norman Airey, Margaret T. Fischer;
Library, Peter Draz; TIME-LIFE News Service, Murray J. Gart;
Correspondents Joyce Leviton (Atlanta); Sally O'Quin (Los Angeles); Sue
Wymelenberg (Boston); Harriet Mechling (Chicago); Margot Hapgood
(London); Don Davies (Madison); Richard Harnett (San Francisco); Dean
Fischer (Washington, D.C.).

CONTENTS

THE AUTHORS

JAY BRENNAN is an editor on the staff of TIME-LIFE BOOKS.

FRED P. GRAHAM, legal writer for *The New York Times,* is the author of *The Self-Inflicted Wound.*

BERKELEY RICE, a freelance journalist, is the author of *The Other End of the Leash, Enter Gambia* and *The C-5A Scandal.*

DON A. SCHANCHE served as editor-in-chief of *Holiday* and managing editor of the *Saturday Evening Post.* Among his books is *The Panther Paradox: A Liberal's Dilemma.*

CARLTON SMITH is coauthor of *The TIME-LIFE Book of Family Finance* and, since 1966, coauthor of the nationally syndicated newspaper column "Your Personal Finance."

DAVID S. THOMSON is an editor on the staff of TIME-LIFE BOOKS.

ROBERT G. WERNICK, a freelance writer, was a staff writer for LIFE magazine for many years.

LINDA WOLFE, a member of the editorial staff of TIME-LIFE BOOKS, is the author of *The Cooking of the Caribbean Islands* in the Foods of the World series, and of *The Literary Gourmet.*

Research consultant: JEREMY WIESEN
Illustrations by LARRY ROSS

1
The law

What it is, where it
comes from
and how to use it

One of America's wisest jurists, Judge Learned Hand, once observed that the worst misfortune anyone can suffer—next to a lengthy illness in the family—is to become involved in a serious lawsuit. Either kind of crisis can lead to an enormous drain on a family's financial and emotional resources. And because each of these problems can arise suddenly, without warning, it is vital for a family to be prepared for both of them. Nearly everyone, of course, has a doctor in mind for unforeseen emergencies that could affect his health. And most people make a point of knowing how to recognize dangerous symptoms in order to take proper precautions until the doctor comes. In medical matters they can, at least temporarily, fend for themselves fairly well.

But what about matters of law? Each person is a potential legal case from before birth (an unborn child has legal rights to his parents' resources) until after death (when his will is being probated). And yet it is the rare individual who has more than a glimmering of the great mass of statutes, decrees, decisions and precedents that govern his conduct, protect his rights and define his responsibilities in almost everything he does—including starting a family, caring for the children, driving down the street, dealing with a merchant or a contractor, buying or selling a house, renting an apartment, paying taxes.

Most people know little about their legal rights and obligations simply because they are leery of the subject. For the law does seem remote, awesome, confusing and forbidding. It is based on centuries of accumulated theories and customs. It is couched in language that is all but unintelligible to a nonlawyer. New statutes are constantly being piled on top of old ones, and then interpreted, reinterpreted and altered so often in the courts that not even the most conscientious judge can always keep up with them. As for the courts themselves, the elaborate rituals that take place in these sometimes dark and musty places may appear boring or irrelevant, or both. The result is that many people shy away from the law—and from lawyers—in the belief that there is no hope of understanding so difficult a subject.

There are two things wrong with this attitude. First, it may be risky not to know what the law can do, both for you and to you. Many people suffer loss and inconvenience simply because they are unaware of their legal rights or responsibilities in a specific situation.

Second, the law is not really so mysterious. Most laws are based on common sense. And the legal system does work. It is not perfect; mistakes are sometimes made; a court calendar may be so crowded that a case can take years to be resolved. But it is the rule of law—personified by policemen on the beat, prosecutors investigating reported wrongdoing, lawyers representing clients, juries weighing testimony and judges handing down decisions—that enables a complex society to function with a maximum of order and a minimum of injustice.

The purpose of this book is to explain how this legal system works. The law, like medicine, exists for your benefit. Lawyers, like doctors, are in business to help solve your problems. Courts, like hospitals, are there to perform the intricate operations necessary to remove obstacles to your well-being or to bring relief when you are in trouble. But just as your doctor must rely to some extent on your own recognition of your symptoms—and on the intelligence with which you carry out his instructions—so does a lawyer need your cooperation when you sit down to discuss a legal matter. It is distinctly to your advantage that you come to a lawyer with some realization of your legal rights and responsibilities, with some grasp of the legal principles involved in the matter under discussion and with a clear notion of what the lawyer can—or cannot—do for you. Most important, an understanding of the law can keep you from getting into the kind of situation that makes you need a lawyer. Such knowledge must start with a grasp of some basic ideas about the law. What is it, how is it made, how does it work, how can you use it?

A LAND OF LAW AND LAWYERS

To begin with, the United States has more laws—and more lawyers —than any other nation in the world. Its overlapping system of federal, state, county and municipal jurisdictions produces hundreds of fresh volumes of new statutes and decisions each year. To deal with this formidable web of law, there are about 250,000 lawyers engaged in private practice—one for every 800 men, women and children in the nation. And the lawyers have plenty of work to do, for about half of the adults face some sort of legal problem each year. Whether the problem is large or small, it more often than not arises because one of the parties involved has done something he should not have done or has neglected to do something he should have done. He may have been unaware that the law he became involved with even existed; or he may not have understood how he could have achieved his end within the law. In one way or another, he has run afoul of the system of rules by which society regulates its affairs.

The kinds of legal predicaments people can inadvertently get themselves into are remarkably varied:

■ The Jones family is moving into a house it has recently bought. On moving day Mrs. Jones finds that the previous owner—without prior mention to her or her husband—is preparing to remove an expensive antique chandelier from the dining room. What is the law?

(The seller of the house has no right to remove anything that is an integral part of the property—like a lighting fixture—unless the sales agreement specifies he can. *See Chapter 4.*)

■ Kathy and Bob decide in a moment of panic to get married because she is pregnant; at the time, they agree to get a divorce as soon as the child is born. After the baby arrives, Kathy refuses to consent to a divorce. What is the law? (It varies from state to state in this as in many other matters, but most courts would not honor a premarital agreement made in haste and under tension. Kathy is not legally bound to go through with the promised divorce. *See Chapter 3.*)

■ Paul has an automobile accident and immediately jots down the remarks of a witness who assures Paul that he was clearly not at fault. But when the suit for damages finally comes to trial three years later, the witness testifies under cross-examination that he cannot remember what he said. What is the law? (Paul—or his attorney—should have obtained a signed statement from the witness as soon as possible after the accident. A mere note or memorandum of what the witness said may be admitted as evidence but is not nearly as persuasive as a signed statement. *See Chapter 5.*)

Ignorance of the law often extends to common financial transactions. For example:

■ A housewife did not realize that she had to pay Social Security taxes on the wages she paid her maid. The maid worked two days a week for two years and earned $26 each week. Seven years later, when she reached 65 and applied for the retirement benefits she legally had coming to her, the government discovered that the housewife had not paid the required taxes. Her husband had to dig up $269 for back taxes, interest and penalties *(Chapter 6)*.

■ The friend of a businessman who was forming a new company allowed his name to be included on the firm's letterhead, apparently unaware that he might thereby become legally liable for some of the firm's debts. A creditor later claimed that he had agreed to extend credit to the company because of the friend's supposed participation in the business. When the creditor sued to collect his money, the unwary friend had to pay his share.

■ A wealthy man drew up a will that would have provided financial security not only for his wife and children but also for a favorite nephew. But he made the mistake of asking only one person to witness the document, rather than the two required by the law of his state. After his death the will was declared invalid, and not a penny of his estate went to his nephew *(Chapter 12)*.

In each of these cases, a disappointment or monetary loss was suffered because someone did not know or understand a law that was involved. In none of these cases was the law seeking to punish anyone. Although punishment is also one of its functions, the law is basically intended to regularize dealings between individuals, and between society as a whole and its individual members. The law is, in effect, a body of precise rules that have been painstakingly developed and tested in order to protect everyone's rights, make every person carry out his legal responsibilities and resolve controversies that may arise over these rights and responsibilities. In a democracy these rules must be applied and administered by the courts with as much uniformity as possible and with total impartiality toward all parties.

Justice Oliver Wendell Holmes summed up these principles one morning as he was entering the Supreme Court building in Washington for the day's duties. A friend who had walked to work with him said, "Goodbye—do justice."

"That is not my job," Holmes replied. "My job is to play the game according to the rules."

The American legal system works best for those who understand the rules; and it may penalize or discomfort those who do not. The logical reasoning behind the old Latin maxim that "Ignorance of the law is no excuse" is that if everyone were allowed to excuse his conduct by claiming he did not know the rules, there would soon be no law and anarchy would result. One way the law seeks to provide justice and maintain order is by giving fair warning of what the rules are and thereby affording a degree of predictability to a man's affairs. To those who do not recognize the law's warnings, it may seem unfeeling. But the law is not a mean beast. As you read this book, you will find that much of what the law says is simply what any thoughtful, fair-minded person could normally figure out for himself.

THE DANGERS OF DO-IT-YOURSELF

The fact that the law is generally logical and reasonable does not mean that anyone who learns the rules can practice law, or that you or anyone else should view this book as a do-it-yourself guide. Neither this nor any other book on the subject—nor an entire library full of law books, for that matter—can provide the specialized information, background or techniques you would need to handle a complex matter of law all by yourself. You should no more consider trying to take on an intricate law case of your own than you would think of trying to take out your own appendix. Trained doctors take care of medical problems; trained lawyers handle legal problems.

Indeed, some areas of the law can be so complicated and tricky that even the most experienced lawyers find it necessary to turn for help—as doctors do—to specialists outside the field. A lawyer who is handling a case involving a car collision, for example, may bring in a medical expert to examine his client and testify concerning the injuries sustained, an automotive expert to examine the wreckage and determine whether or not a mechanical flaw might have contributed to the accident, and a highway safety engineer to determine traffic conditions at the time of the accident. It is only after a lawyer has digested all of this information that he can prepare his case and present it effectively in court. There his training and experience must continue to come into play as he plans his strategy, sizing up the temper of the jury he wishes to impress, even deciding the order in which his expert witnesses should appear in order to build the strongest case. He will also have to cope with interruptions from the opposing counsel and with procedural instructions from the judge. The law is definitely not a game for amateurs. As another old saying puts it, a layman who insists on handling his own legal problems has a fool for a client.

WHAT LAW IS MADE OF

Another reason a lawyer's task is complicated is that the sources of our law are so enormously varied. Much of it is still based on legal principles that were in effect under English rule before the American Revolution and are referred to as common law. Much of English law, in turn, was influenced by ancient Roman law. French law, too, has left its traces in the nation, particularly in the case of the state of Louisiana; as a former French colony, it still bases a great deal of its law on the so-called Napoleonic Code, which was put into effect by the French

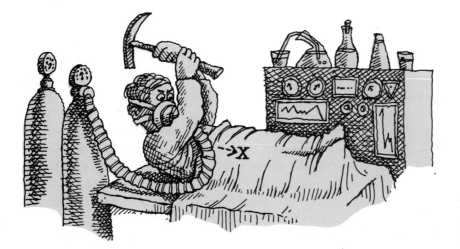

Trying to handle intricate legal cases yourself is like trying to take out your own appendix.

emperor at the peak of his power at the beginning of the 19th Century.

On this base of borrowed and inherited law, the United States has built its own structure, composed of three layers: first, the fundamental law laid down in the constitutions of the federal government and of the 50 separate states; second, the mass of statutes—the laws made by legislators—that have been enacted by Congress as well as by the 50 state legislatures; third, the court decisions, handed down over the years, that interpret laws and modify them as circumstances change. This three-layered structure, it should be noted, applies to civilians. A specialized code of military criminal justice deals with legal situations involving military personnel on active duty and does not fall within the scope of this book.

Because the federal and state constitutions lay down the general principles, and because amending a constitution is a cumbersome process, it cannot always satisfy specific needs that change as time goes by. The task of enacting laws to meet new problems and new situations is left largely to Congress and the state legislatures. Take, for example, the growing public demand for consumer protection. Until recently, the old Roman maxim *caveat emptor* (let the buyer beware) still held true in the world of commerce. It required a customer to put up with almost any purchase he made, no matter how unsatisfactory the item turned out to be after he got it home. With increasing frequency, however, state legislatures have passed laws that give the consumer more say in the matter and even provide a cooling-off period that allows a dissatisfied buyer to back out of a purchase he might have been fast-talked into by a high-pressure salesman *(Chapter 7)*.

But even new statutes are not always flexible enough to meet new situations or precise enough to make clear what a particular law means in every respect. This is where the courts enter the picture. When a law turns out to be ambiguous, or when a reasonable appeal is made to challenge its validity, the courts are obliged to render their opinions on these matters. These judicial decisions become what are known as precedents, and they are binding upon all citizens until either the lawmakers or the courts decide to change the law again. Sometimes, as in the field of civil rights, these changes can take place so rapidly—even from month to month—that keeping up with them is a task only a professional can tackle.

While federal law is uniform across the land, the state laws on any given subject can vary widely from one state to another. In some states, for example, an unwitnessed handwritten will would be adequate to dispose of even a millionaire's fortune, while in others such a will could not be relied on to bequeath so much as an old watch.

In some states the law requires a person seeking to dissolve a marriage to provide proof of a mate's cruelty or adultery, while California permits dissolution of a marriage whenever it can be shown that the marriage has simply not worked out.

Just as there can be important differences between the laws of one state and another, so there can be differences in the laws within a single state: from one county to another, or between cities and towns that lie within the same county. Local laws—called ordinances—that your municipal government is empowered to make can sometimes affect your life more directly than the U.S. Bill of Rights or any acts of Congress, simply by regulating such matters as where and how you build your house, the types of business enterprises that are allowed in your neighborhood and the hours in which you can be served a drink at your favorite tavern—or whether you can be served a drink at all.

CRIMINAL LAW AND CIVIL LAW

There are two major kinds of law: criminal and civil. Criminal law deals with acts that society deems so harmful to the public welfare that the government takes the responsibility for prosecuting and punishing the perpetrators *(Chapter 9)*. The act may be as major as murder or as minor as jaywalking (a jaywalker may snarl traffic and thus endanger public safety as well as his own). But all criminal offenses are alike in that the offenders are prosecuted in the name of society as a whole, whether or not a victim of a crime comes forward to demand prosecution (and whether or not there is even a victim).

You are much less likely to come into direct contact with criminal law than with civil law. Whereas criminal law is designed to protect the public at large, civil law is designed to protect you as a private individual in your legal relationships with others. Marriage, divorce, dealings with merchant or customer, any contracts you make, certain "wrongs" you think have been done to you or to your property—all these matters are governed by civil law. And while under criminal law it is the government that starts legal proceedings and seeks redress, under civil law it is you, the individual, who must do so.

Relatively speaking, the government has an easier time of it, for the route from crime to punishment is fairly straightforward. The average person who contemplates taking some action under civil law —or who finds himself the target of such an action—is usually uncertain of the course he should follow and unfamiliar with his rights and responsibilities in the matter. Some of the mystery is dispelled once you understand that by far the largest number of civil lawsuits arise from only two broad areas of civil law: contracts and torts.

A contract is an agreement under which people arrange specific affairs by making certain promises to each other. In effect, they create a situation of law between themselves. A contract does not always have to be written to be binding, and a basic premise of contract law is that any sane adult who enters into an agreement can be held to his promises. (He also has to be sober; one man-about-town who proved that he was falling-down drunk when he signed a lease on a Chicago penthouse apartment was able to get out of the commitment.) If necessary, a court can compel a party to an agreement to honor it, either by carrying out his promises to the full or by paying damages for his failure to do so. Yet each day countless numbers of people blithely enter into contractual commitments of all kinds—not only signing leases, but also buying on credit, borrowing money, taking out insurance, hiring workers—without fully understanding the possible legal consequences of their actions. And very often a person who makes a contract will break it without intending to do so, simply through inattention or negligence *(Chapter 6)*.

A tort (the word comes from the Latin *tortus,* meaning twisted) is a wrong or injury for which the injured person can collect monetary damages from the person who inflicted the harm. Some tort cases result from criminal actions that are regarded as harmful to the public welfare and are punishable by the government; among these are assault and battery, the legal terms for physical attacks upon a person. But for the most part, torts are wrongs of a private sort, damaging not to the public at large but to a particular individual. Among these are libel, slander, invasion of privacy and injuries to the individual or to his property that are brought about through negligence.

A MATTER OF FORMS

The making of contracts has become so routine that many are executed simply by signing a preprinted form. The ubiquitous bank check is one example. Today approximately 63 million checks are signed every day, yet a little more than a century ago bank checks were considered such complex legal documents that only experienced lawyers were believed qualified to draft them. Bank checks are still legal documents, of course; the signer of a check is ordering the bank to pay a certain amount of money to the recipient and is placing the responsibility on himself for ensuring that his checking account will cover the payment. People also affix their names to all kinds of other preprinted legal documents—a contract to buy a refrigerator with 18 months to pay, an application for a credit card, a promissory note at the bank, a lease for an apartment.

In some instances, the wide use of these standardized legal forms has created the impression that they cannot be altered in any way —that the signer must sign on a take-it-or-leave-it basis. This is not always so, although one or the other party to the deal often benefits from the assumption that it is. A standard contract may be unabashedly loaded in favor of the businessman who is trying to get your signature on it—a seller who is pushing expensive goods, a lender who wants to collect your interest, a landlord who hopes to control his tenants' actions. If you walk into a printing shop or stationery store specializing in legal forms and ask, for example, for a standard lease, you may be confronted with a bewildering variety. One type is crammed with detailed clauses designed to protect the landlord against every imaginable problem—hence it is, in effect, a landlord's lease. But you may also find what can be described as a tenant's lease, a much briefer document that obligates the tenant to not much more than paying his rent at regular intervals. (For an illustration of two such leases, see the following page.)

Moreover, not every clause in the standard landlord's lease is sacred. If you are preparing to sign such a document, you can seek to strike out any provision you really object to, such as one that gives the landlord the right to enter and inspect your apartment at any hour he chooses. Landlords are sometimes willing to omit such provisions. Similarly, if you are preparing to sign a printed form used by money lenders, there are clauses in it, too, that you may want to strike out. By one such clause, the borrower gives up his right to receive fair notice of any suit brought against him by the creditor because of a default in payments; another requires the debtor to pay the creditor's legal fees in the event of such a suit. Eliminating these clauses calls for bargaining; but if the money lender wants the business badly enough, he may agree to delete these sections.

IMPERFECTIONS IN THE LEGAL SYSTEM

Legal forms provide tested ways to meet specific situations and problems. Yet despite their usefulness and the care with which statutes generally have been conceived and written, the law cannot always guarantee that your rights will be protected. Sometimes it is helpless to do the job for which it was designed. Consider, for example, a wholesaler who has a contractual claim against the corner grocer for unpaid bills. The claim is airtight, but the wholesaler may not be in a practical position to sue for his money—a suit might drive the grocer into bankruptcy and thus effectively deprive the wholesaler of any hope of recovering the amount owed. Or consider a movie producer who is

A contrast in two leases

"Standard" legal forms are not all that standard. How much they may vary, to benefit one party or the other, is indicated by the parallel clauses excerpted below from two of many lease forms sold in legal stationery stores. If you are a tenant, you would doubtless prefer lease 1 (but might have difficulty getting a landlord to agree to it). If you are a landlord, your interests are better protected by lease 2.

Lease 1

■ The Tenant will take good care of the leased premises, fixtures and appurtenances, and suffer no waste or injury; make all repairs to the leased premises, fixtures and appurtenances necessitated by the fault of the Tenant.

■ The Landlord shall furnish, insofar as the present facilities provide; a) Elevator service; b) Hot and cold water in reasonable quantities; c) Heat at reasonable hours during the cold seasons of the year; d) Air-conditioning during the warm seasons of the year.

■ If the Tenant defaults in the performance of any of the covenants herein contained, other than the covenants to pay rent . . . the Landlord may give to the Tenant ten days' written notice thereof, and if such default has not been cured within said period, then the Landlord may give the Tenant five days' notice of the termination of this lease . . . and the Tenant shall then surrender the leased premises.

■ The Landlord covenants that the Tenant, on paying the rent and performing the covenants hereof, shall and may peaceably and quietly have, hold and enjoy the leased premises for the term . . . mentioned.

Lease 2

■ The Tenant shall take good care of the apartment and its fixtures, and suffer no waste or injury, shall not drive picture or other nails into the walls or woodwork of said premises, nor allow the same to be done.

■ It is expressly agreed that if the operation of the elevators, the furnishing of heat or of any service, shall cease by reason of accident, strike, repairs, cleaning out boilers, alterations or improvements to be made . . . the obligations of the Tenant under the terms of this lease shall not be affected thereby.

■ It is agreed by the Tenant that upon default made in any of the covenants, agreements and conditions, or of the rules and regulations herein, that then this lease at option of the Landlord after five days' notice of such option in writing served upon the Tenant, shall expire immediately at the expiration of such notice, and the Landlord shall be entitled to immediate possession of said premises and to institute summary proceedings against the said Tenant.

A "landlord" lease often contains a number of stipulations that are rarely included in "tenant" leases:

■ The Tenant shall . . . use only such shades in the front windows of said apartment as are put up or approved by the Landlord.

■ The halls . . . fire escapes or roof of the building shall not be used as playing grounds for children.

■ The waterclosets and water apparatus shall not be used for any purpose other than that for which they were constructed and no sweepings, rubbish, rags or other articles, shall be thrown therein.

■ All kitchen and market supplies, bundles, parcels, furniture and baggage shall be delivered through the basement and conveyed by the dumbwaiter or freight elevator, but at the Tenant's risk.

■ Talking by servants or employees through elevator, dumbwaiter or vent shafts is strictly prohibited.

■ The Landlord reserves the right to make such additional rules from time to time as shall in the opinion of the Landlord be necessary for the safety and good order of the premises.

having trouble with a temperamental leading lady. He has a contract that guarantees her prompt appearance each morning on the set, yet she seldom shows up before noon. He could sue for breach of contract, but he also knows the lady might retaliate by succumbing to hiccups during crucial scenes and thus cause even greater damage. So he decides to grin and bear it.

Recourse to the law in such cases is futile, and people who ignore that harsh reality can be frustrated figures indeed. For there is often a gap between what the law actually requires and the ability of the courts to enforce that requirement. Judges have only a few ways to make people obey the law: In the case of a criminal conviction they may impose a jail sentence or a fine or place the guilty person on probation; in the case of civil suits they may award monetary damages or issue a court decree ordering strict compliance with the terms of a contract. On the surface, it might appear that these means should suffice to give an individual satisfaction for any wrong he has suffered. But often, in actual practice, such remedies fail to work and thus fall short of achieving adequate justice.

In certain kinds of situations that are heavily charged with passion and emotion, such as family conflicts or squabbles between neighbors, the losing party may be so defiant that the law is placed in the position of struggling with a shadow. A California judge once issued a decree forbidding a man to continue molesting his estranged wife. The order so enraged the husband that he shot and killed the woman's boyfriend and then threatened to do the same to her. The man was eventually convicted of murder; but meanwhile he had made a mockery of the principle that a court decree can preserve the peace. Some states have attempted to solve such problems by means of a peace bond, which requires a person who has been brought before a court for threatening others to put up a sum of money as a guarantee that he will behave; the alternative to posting the bond is to be sent to jail. The difficulty with this approach is that the people who face such a choice are usually too poor to put up the bond; moreover, the complainants are usually relatives who do not wish to see them sent to jail. As a result, no action is taken, and the peace bond—while theoretically a useful device—often lies dormant on the statute books, another testimonial to the imperfections of the law.

THE DOCTRINE OF FAIRNESS

One major way in which the law has sought to correct its own failings has been to develop, over the years, doctrines of "equity," or fairness. These are intended to prevent economic power or special knowledge

The law is not easily fooled

The scene is a secluded spot at the state line, near a popular lovers' lane. A car stops just short of the line. A woman hops out, walks across the line and climbs back into the car after it has crossed the border without her. The driver is confident he has thus thwarted the Mann Act, a federal law that makes it illegal to transport a woman across state lines for immoral purposes. But if state troopers had witnessed the driver's maneuver, the law would hold that he had proved his *intent* to transport the woman across the border and had therefore done so, whether she walked the last few feet or not.

from giving one class of people undue advantages over another. A good example is the work done on both state and national levels to protect the legal rights of consumers, who may find themselves at the mercy of sharp or downright dishonest businessmen.

One woman on welfare, the mother of seven children, bought a $514 stereo set from a "buy now, pay later" furniture dealer in Washington, D.C. She signed an installment contract that was written in language so complicated and abstruse it would have boggled the mind of a corporation lawyer. When stripped of all its verbiage, the contract turned out to provide that if the woman missed a single payment on the stereo set, the store could repossess not only the set but all other items of furniture she had purchased on time from the same store over the previous five years.

After about a month the woman decided that such costly musical culture was not for her and returned the stereo without having made any payment for it. The store quickly sent a team of men to clean out her apartment. The woman was over 21; she was not illiterate; and by the standard rules of commercial contracts, she could have been held strictly to the terms of the agreement she had signed. But when she went to court to protest the seizure of her other property, the judge ruled that the store had made an "unconscionable bargain"—one so unscrupulous that no person could be forced to accept it and that no honest and fair person should have proposed it in the first place. The stereo transaction was canceled; and the store was required to return the items it had repossessed.

In many jurisdictions across the United States *any* contract that is unreasonable to the point of being unconscionable will be thrown out of court. When a used-car salesman assured a college student that the red convertible he was selling him had a perfectly sound top (while knowing all the time that the roof leaked), he made a sale that a court undid after the first hard rain. Anytime lies are told to induce a buyer to sign a contract—and he can prove it—the courts will not enforce that contract. They will also dissolve a contract whenever a person can prove he has been forced into an unsound bargain under a threat. A young man quarreled bitterly with an uncle who had lent him money to purchase a drugstore; the uncle promptly retaliated by threatening to foreclose the mortgage he held on the store unless he were paid exorbitant monthly sums. The court forced the irascible uncle to back down and, moreover, to repay the monthly overcharges he had already collected from his nephew.

WHEN TO CALL A LAWYER

Whether or not you ever make an unsound deal, under pressure or otherwise, the chances are that some occasion will arise when you will want to seek a lawyer's advice. It is not always easy to know when to seek it. Some situations—for example, those involving the use of such standardized legal forms as a lease or a loan agreement—are often so simple that most people would feel foolish asking a lawyer to handle these matters. In some cities you do not need a lawyer even to settle some disputes that require a judge's decision. These minor business controversies can be taken to a Small Claims Court *(Chapter 10),* where the routine is so simple that a lawyer's presence is not required and in some instances is even forbidden. Moreover, the sums at stake (usually $100 or less) would not normally warrant paying a lawyer for his time. Instead, each party handles his own case, with a little help from the judge when needed.

At the other extreme, however, are situations so bristling with legal complexities that anyone who tries to get along without professional assistance almost invariably finds he has blundered into even more serious trouble. Usually, in the end, he is obliged to retain a lawyer to help extricate him, and in some cases the ultimate costs are higher than if a lawyer had been hired in the first place.

Between these two poles—the routine legal transaction that normally requires no expert assistance and the tangled situation that should never be approached without experienced counsel—there lies a broad spectrum of situations in which it is unclear to many people whether they should try to go it alone or not. This question can be a subtle one to answer, for legal services are often expensive, and people differ in their ability to deal with intricate business matters. There is only one good general rule to go by, and that is: "Whenever you are in doubt about some legal problem, see a lawyer." There are, however, some specific guidelines that are helpful.

Consult a lawyer before you sign anything that you do not fully understand. No matter how innocuous a document seems, always ask yourself—before signing it—if there is anything at all in the fine print that is not completely clear to you. If the answer is "yes," you should at least ask for time to study the document before signing it. If the person who wants your signature seems overanxious to procure it immediately, then insist on a delay and start looking up your lawyer's telephone number before you proceed any further.

You have a right to take your time. Obviously, you can do a better job of analyzing a document if you are out of the immediate presence of the person whose interests may conflict with yours. You might merely go to the next room or ask for enough time—overnight or longer, if necessary—to consult a friend or an attorney. There is a saying among lawyers that you should always read a legal document the way porcupines make love—very carefully. If you do not understand each word and phrase in a document you have been asked to sign, you may come in for some unpleasant surprises:

■ When Alfred took a desk job in a large corporation, he was visited by representatives of the clerical workers' union, urging him to join it. Alfred had had no previous contact with unions but had come to admire many of their objectives. So he signed a card entitled "Application for Membership." It turned out to be a contract, although that word did not appear on the card. What did appear was a statement that membership would continue "in accordance with Paragraph 13(c) of the Agreement" between the union and the company. Alfred learned only later that Paragraph 13(c) provided that once an employee joined the union, he could not resign so long as he worked for the company. As it turned out, Alfred was soon transferred to a branch in another city where the union was not so active and few workers belonged. Over the years the amount deducted each month from his paycheck for union dues continued to grow. Because he could see

There is a saying among lawyers
that you should always read a
legal document the same
way porcupines make love—
very carefully.

little benefit from his membership, Alfred had reason to regret his off-hand signing of an "application" without checking out its full meaning. He might not have needed a lawyer—Paragraph 13(c) might have been quite clear—but he should have read the application more carefully and consulted a lawyer if any part was unclear.

■ The standard lease used in the Richmond, Virginia, area contains a paragraph 2(k), which commits the tenant and his family to "comply with the rules and regulations set forth herein and such rules should be considered as a part hereof, just as though they were set forth *in haec verba* and the Lessor may from time to time, after reasonable notice to the Lessee, impose such additional rules as he may deem expedient." It will never be known how many people have signed this lease without the faintest notion of the meaning of the Latin phrase *in haec verba*. What they were agreeing to was to abide by 12 rules as if they were printed here word-for-word in paragraph 2(k)—though in reality the rules were tacked on at the very end of the three-page lease. Thus the signers agreed, among other things, that they would not keep a dog, canary or any other pet in their new quarters; that when they entertained they would not include on the guest list people who might be considered "of a bad or loose character, or of improper behavior"; and that the landlord could add any other such rules as occurred to him. An alert lawyer looking over the lease would spot the Latin words and at least warn his clients about the rights they were signing away.

Consult a lawyer before you sign an agreement involving a large sum of money or a long-term commitment. Such agreements are signed every day without legal advice, and in many instances nobody is harmed. But if a mistake is made, it could be costly. You should certainly consult a lawyer whenever you invest in a business or sign an extended lease. In such matters the price of being sure (that is, having a lawyer) is less than the possible cost of being wrong (not having one).

Consult a lawyer before you agree to settle an accident case that involves a possibility of anything more than minor property damage. After an automobile accident, the driver who was clearly in the right

You have a right to take your time when you analyze a document someone wants you to sign. Going to the next room takes the pressure off you.

Always consult a lawyer of your own if the other party to a contract has one. His lawyer can't help you: a lawyer may advise only one side to a particular legal transaction—and must do his best to represent that side.

is often tempted to settle quickly with the other party's insurance company. An insurance adjuster may call on him immediately, offer to pay damages, get his signature on a release stipulating that all claims have been settled and close the file. Even if only minor property damage is involved, the driver should first have his doctor check him out. If the doctor gives him a clean bill of health, it is usually to his advantage to settle the matter without employing a lawyer, whose fee could be a fairly generous percentage of the settlement. If the other driver has conceded his fault, and if the amount of damages will be determined automatically from estimates furnished by a repair shop, there is very little for an attorney to do. But all too often the wronged driver does not consult a doctor and discovers later that he has sustained serious physical injuries. The sad case of a West Coast woman is typical. After her car was struck from the rear by a panel truck that had made an illegal U-turn, she felt no pain and assumed that she was unhurt. The next day she accepted an insurance adjuster's offer of $200 to satisfy all claims. Two months later she was stricken with pain in her arm and back caused by the dislocation of two spinal disks in the impact of the collision. She had a long and costly recuperation. By failing to exercise caution at the outset—as a lawyer would undoubtedly have suggested—she missed her chance to collect full damages from the insurance company.

Consult a lawyer whenever you are faced with a major domestic problem. A couple whose marriage is breaking up, for example, may wait until they have discussed all the details of separation or divorce before deciding to ask for outside advice. While theoretically it is possible to obtain a divorce without legal counsel, it is not only extremely risky but also foolhardy. A marriage is a complex legal arrangement, involving mutual rights and responsibilities that are difficult to untangle. The problem is particularly complicated when children are involved, for the court will want to supervise any agreements that are made concerning custody, support and visitation rights. Complications can also arise when a happily married couple wish to adopt a child; they, too, should contact a lawyer, for if precise legal procedures are not followed, frustration and sometimes tragedy may result.

Consult a lawyer whenever you are implicated in any crime more serious than an ordinary traffic offense. At a time like this, your good name, your career and even your freedom can be at stake. Your course here is obvious: you should employ a lawyer immediately, preferably one who has had special experience in handling criminal cases. The principle of having a lawyer on hand in this kind of situation is so basic that all 50 states are required to provide free legal services for suspects in felony cases who are unable to afford their own attorneys.

Consult a lawyer of your own if you are implicated with others in a criminal action. An example of the complications that can arise when a lawyer tries to represent more than one client in the same case occurred when three college students were arrested on drug charges while on an automobile jaunt away from home. The father of one boy rushed a leading local lawyer to the scene, and he took over the defense of all three boys. After a few anxious days, the parents of the other two boys discovered that only the boy whose father had hired the lawyer had actually been caught in possession of the drugs. The other two might have gotten off lightly, but the lawyer was attempting to negotiate a joint disposition of all three cases. He was not trying to be unfair to the other two boys; but he was employed to represent the third, and his best chance to get a suspended sentence for his primary client was to have all three boys dealt with on the same basis. When the parents of the other two boys finally grasped the situation, they promptly hired separate lawyers to represent their own sons: each got a suspended sentence, while the boy in possession of the drugs—a first offender—received a sentence of six months in jail.

Consult a lawyer of your own if the other party to a contract or dispute has one. In the United States, court trials are conducted under an "adversary" procedure, with one party and his witnesses trying to prove the facts essential to his case, while the other party tries to disprove these same facts. A corollary of the adversary system is that a lawyer may advise only one side to a particular legal transaction—and must do his best to represent that side. He cannot provide advice to both sides. Thus, when a businessman with whom you are about to enter an agreement tells you, "I'll have my lawyer draw up the contracts," remember that his lawyer is obligated to draft the documents with an eye toward protecting his client. Your response should be: "Fine, I'll have *my* lawyer look them over before we sign."

There will almost certainly be times in your life when it will be a good idea for you to consult a lawyer for yourself or some member of your family. How do you go about finding one? What are lawyers like, and how do they work? How much do they charge? You will find the answers to these and other questions in the following chapter.

By **FRED P. GRAHAM**
ERNEST C. FRIESEN, Consultant

2
Finding a lawyer

His skills, his specialties,
his fees

When you need to consult a lawyer, it is useful to be armed with some understanding of how lawyers go about their business and what sort of people, in general, they are. You may already have some preconceptions of what to expect. But the practitioners of law differ from one another widely. Many are as shrewd as Perry Mason and as honest as Abe Lincoln. Some are only marginally competent, able to handle just the most routine matters. And some are struggling so hard to make ends meet that they are more concerned about their fees than about their clients' welfare. The American Bar Association, which sets standards for the U.S. legal profession, once described the typical American lawyer as "a crusader in the noblest quest of our times —peace through law." That characterization was perhaps immodest, but by no means entirely incorrect. Yet, over the years, the reputation of lawyers as a tricky group has persisted. Many people have concurred with poet Carl Sandburg's biting lines:

Why is there always a secret singing
When a lawyer cashes in?
Why does a hearse horse snicker
Hauling a lawyer away?

Most American lawyers can be found somewhere between the crusader and the tricky operator. They may range from lazy to hyperactive, from inept to brilliant, from idealistic to self-serving. Yet there are certain attributes that run through the entire profession. One mark of lawyers today is that they are well educated. The man who never finished high school but who "read law" in his spare time and went on to glory in the courtroom has virtually passed into the realm of folklore. A minimum of six years of higher education (three in college and three in law school) is now required before a potential lawyer may take the bar examination and be licensed to practice.

A lawyer's schooling and his first few years in practice combine to instill in him the essential quality that sets his profession apart from all others—a quality that is summed up in the phrase "to think like a lawyer." The experienced lawyer's special way of thinking is a highly rational, abstract process that enables him to sort out all the facts in a tangled situation, ignore those that are legally irrelevant and decide on the most promising legal techniques for solving the problem. Take a case in which a man was injured after he tripped over a lunch box at a construction site. Most people would probably be impressed by testimony that the lunch box had fallen open to reveal some heroin inside. This fact somehow seems to make the injury worse. But the presence of heroin is totally irrelevant. An experienced lawyer would know that the lunch box might just as well have been packed with bananas for all the legal difference it made in adjudicating the claim for damages.

HOW LAWYERS WORK

A good attorney is likely to be a cool, analytical person who is impressed only by hard, cold facts, largely unmoved by external or emotional considerations, and not given to raising his client's hopes with wishful thinking or dramatic poses. In his personal manner he may be informal and sympathetic; on the other hand, some lawyers carry the pose of cool detachment to such an extreme that they appear almost Olympian in their manner and attitude. A study made of lawyer-client relationships by a group of law school professors disclosed that many clients were shocked and disappointed to find their lawyers so aloof when discussing their problems.

One reason for this reaction among clients may well have been that the practice of law does not always lend itself to a cozy, reassuring approach. When a client first enters a lawyer's office, he may indeed need reassurance, but a careful professional is not inclined to give it until he has all the facts. And a lawyer's office is not exactly a homey place at best, especially if you look into his library with all those imposing tomes. But these books are the lawyer's tools—the collection of statutes and decisions, precedents and case histories that he must refer to in order to find legitimate, practical ways to remedy his client's problems.

Lawyers range from lazy to hyperactive, from inept to brilliant, from idealistic to self-serving.

Moreover, the language of law usually sounds odd and stilted (*Glossary*). The phrases in the contract you are about to sign—"party of the first part," "hereinafter known as" and "the declarations applicable hereto" are likely to make you think you need the services of a translator as well as an adviser and counselor. But this formal language has its purpose. A common language of precise, standardized terms is necessary; otherwise, the rules of conduct that the terms describe could not be applied impartially to everyone concerned. Of course, a good lawyer should be able to explain the more formidable terminology or, at least, translate those parts of it that affect you.

LAWYERS AS ADVERSARIES

The layman is also apt to be puzzled and confused by the way lawyers conduct themselves under the adversary process. This system of pleading cases calls for a lawyer to act as an aggressive advocate for his client's position, arguing and disputing and challenging as much as he feels is necessary in order to establish that position. The adversary role lawyers assume is especially noticeable in courtroom situations, where the verdict may very well depend on which of the opposing attorneys can make the more lasting impression on a judge or a jury. In court, lawyers will sometimes pull out all stops, needling the opposition, snapping out objections, seeming to joust with each other in order to give their respective clients the best representation possible. All this is a proper part of the game. Indeed the rules even encourage it. The American Bar Association's "Code of Professional Responsibility,"

Lawyers' hide-and-seek

The main reason lawyers are so hard to find is not that they are scarce but that the rules of their profession limit what they can do to make their presence known. An attorney cannot advertise in the local paper. He cannot put up a shingle in front of his home to announce that a lawyer lives there. His office sign must be simple and dignified; he cannot, for instance, emblazon his name in neon lights. He is not even allowed to advertise himself to other lawyers. He can list his name, address and telephone number in certain approved law journals and in directories that other lawyers refer to, such as the *Martindale-Hubbell Law Directory, Best's Recommended Insurance Attorneys, Sullivan's Probate Directory* and *Markham's Negligence Counsel*. But he is not allowed to boast of any special expertise or even to state how many years he has been in practice. No scrambling for clients is the rule—but this adds to the job of finding the lawyer you need.

which all lawyers are expected to obey, includes an admonition that "The duty of a lawyer, both to his client and to the legal system, is to represent his client zealously within the bounds of the law."

In television dramas—and sometimes in real life—a lawyer may demonstrate a little more zeal than seems to be absolutely necessary. Some lawyers do make frequent use of an emotional or bombastic style, and when this style happens to fit the nature of the case, they often succeed. But by and large most successful lawyers play a quietly controlled role in the courtroom and win their cases by thorough preparation, skillful marshaling of the evidence and expert presentation of it, rather than by dazzling dramatics or legal sleight of hand.

Furthermore, lawyers are expected at all times to maintain the dignity of the profession; this requirement is impressed on them both in law school and in the courtroom. A lawyer, like the judge he faces and the bailiff who swears in witnesses, is an officer of the court—he is required to uphold the law as well as aid his client, and his duty to the law comes before his duty to his client. He must be granted permission to practice by the courts in which he appears, and he is sworn to uphold the Constitution of the United States as well as the laws of the state in which he practices. And so, no matter how vigorously a lawyer may do battle on his client's behalf, he cannot make a mockery of the law and get away with it. At the very least, the judge can keep him in line by overruling him and, if necessary, by holding him in contempt of court, a punishable offense. If his conduct seriously violates professional ethics, he can be disbarred, that is, deprived of his legal status as an attorney, and prevented from further practice.

FINDING THE RIGHT LAWYER

Selecting a lawyer is far from easy, particularly for the vast majority of Americans who are neither rich nor poor. People who are affluent rely on lawyers so much in the management of their affairs that they seldom need to search; they retain lawyers as a matter of course. Poor people can make use of a relatively new breed of public-spirited younger attorneys who, with financial backing from various sources, set up offices in city slum neighborhoods or in economically depressed rural areas and offer free advice on domestic and other problems. The Legal Aid Society offices in major cities across the nation also provide free legal advice for clients who cannot pay for it; the societies are forbidden, under their charters as nonprofit organizations, to make their services available to those able to pay. Americans of moderate income —who constitute the bulk of the population—are on their own.

The major difficulty involved in locating a lawyer is that he is not permitted, under the code of ethics of his profession, to advertise himself or otherwise solicit your business. A long-cherished assumption of the profession has been that a respectable lawyer obtains his clients as a result of his own reputation for competence and not by moving about in public looking for customers. Client-hunting, the profession maintains, would tarnish the entire legal calling and would, moreover, result in a stirring up of litigation that could further clog the already crowded courts. Some lawyers argue that it is more important for the profession to make its services readily available to the public at large than to abide by old traditions, and some efforts are being made to loosen up the system. Meanwhile, lawyers are not allowed by the strict code of their profession to come to you; you must go to them. And since you are probably looking for the kind of lawyer who, among other qualities, abides by his profession's rules of conduct, you will want to take the initiative.

Most people seeking a lawyer first turn to friends for recommendations. This method can be useful but it requires caution. If your neighbor knows the lawyer only socially, he may be unaware of his professional qualifications. The attorney in question may talk a good lawsuit but fumble in court.

If your friend has actually employed the lawyer—or at least knows someone who has—the recommendation may be worth further checking. The next questions to ask would be: What type of case did the lawyer handle for your friend? Was the client satisfied? Did the lawyer keep him abreast of developments as the case progressed? Did the lawyer avoid delay and do his work efficiently? Was his fee reasonable? Did he win the case?

Another source of recommendations, at least for people who work for fairly large firms, is the company lawyer. He is probably in no position to take on outside work or give you legal advice; but he may be able to suggest other lawyers who might help with your case.

THE LAWYER REFERRAL SYSTEM

In an attempt to make it somewhat easier for people to get legal advice, many state and local bar associations have established Lawyer Referral Services, which operate in some 250 communities around the country. The system varies somewhat from city to city, but in general it works this way. If you need legal advice, you first telephone the Lawyer Referral Service (if it is not listed in the telephone directory, call the local bar association). After you state your problem, the referral service either gives you the name and address of a local lawyer to contact, or it arranges an appointment for you. The lawyer involved has voluntarily placed his name on a list of attorneys who agree to give preliminary advice to prospective clients at a modest fee. The fees vary, but $10 for a half-hour interview in the lawyer's office is typical. If after that first talk you decide that you require additional advice—and the lawyer agrees to take your case—you are then free to work out further consultations at his regular fee. The Illinois State Bar Association, which has pioneered in this field, operates the largest referral plan, a statewide service under which any resident can telephone the central referral office toll-free from anywhere in the state and receive the name and address of the nearest available lawyer.

BUT WHAT KIND OF LAWYER?

One drawback to the referral system is that the local office is usually equipped only with a single list of lawyers who have agreed to serve. Their names rotate on this list; when you call you are given the name of the attorney who happens to be at the top of the list at the moment, regardless of how competent he may be or whether he has the training and experience necessary to handle your specific problem. In some areas—notably Detroit and Los Angeles—the system has been refined by breaking up the master list into sublists according to specialties. Thus, if you telephone the service because you are about to be sued by an irate neighbor whose child just fell out of your tree, you will not be put in touch with a nice, elderly gentleman who specializes in drawing up wills or an attorney whose chief experience is in processing divorces.

The bar associations are endeavoring to improve the referral system and raise its standards by encouraging local groups not only to divide their lists into specialties but also to develop some way of keeping marginal performers off their lists entirely. In order to weed the lists, some local referral services follow up on their initial recommendations and ask the clients to report on the quality of assistance they received. Many lawyers resent being rated in this way, however, and prefer to remain off the lists entirely.

Obviously a quality-conscious referral service is to be preferred. When telephoning for a referral, ask how the service operates even before you state your problem and request a lawyer's name. After all, it is your problem and your money, and you have a right to inquire about the kind of service you will be getting. The first question to ask: "Is your list divided into specialties so I know I will be getting someone qualified to handle my case?" The second question: "Is there some system for rating the lawyers on your list so I know I will be getting someone who is competent?" If the answer to both questions is "yes," you may find the referral service a good way to get in touch with a lawyer. If the answer to either question is "no," then it might be better to stick with the recommendations of your friends.

One way you should not choose a lawyer is to take one who has been suggested to you in the midst of an emergency by a hospital attendant, ambulance driver, insurance adjuster, bail bondsman or policeman. A person who has suffered a serious injury for which someone else is responsible (or who is suddenly placed under arrest for some reason) does, of course, need a lawyer's services rather quickly. But it is not necessarily wise to accept the services of the first lawyer to rush to the rescue. Although very few lawyers chase after ambulances in person, some do offer kickbacks to hospital attendants, or to other personnel who deal with emergency situations, for every client they "deliver." This grossly unethical practice says a good deal about the professional ethics of the lawyers who indulge in it. So beware of the rare lawyer who actively seeks you out.

CHOOSE A LAWYER NOW?

As you read on in this book and discover some of the kinds of legal problems you or members of your family might face, you may decide that it would be prudent to begin your search for a good lawyer soon. In this way you can avoid having to cast about frantically when a legal crisis arises. You might begin by calling on a lawyer whom you know to be reputable and telling him that you have no pressing legal problems at the moment but wonder if he would be available should a problem crop up. You are simply a prospective client. A good lawyer would not charge you for this sort of brief, informal visit; he understands that you are sizing him up and that you may never return. But if you like him, and if he agrees to be on tap for whatever problems you may have, you will get a feeling of at least initial security by jotting down his home and office telephone numbers and keeping them as handy as your doctor's numbers. In fact, the American Bar Association has suggested that every family should equip itself with a family lawyer, just as it has a family doctor, to handle the family's legal problems both in and out of emergencies, and even to give the family an annual legal "checkup," including a review of wills, deeds, contracts and other legal matters.

THE PROBLEM OF SPECIALTIES

There is a drawback to the idea of a family lawyer: not all lawyers are equally competent in all branches of the profession. Like medicine, the law has become increasingly specialized. The family doctor, who is usually a general practitioner, refers a pregnant woman to an obstetrician or brings in a surgeon to perform an operation; similarly, the family lawyer is limited in what he is trained or able to do. Legal procedures have become so complex that many lawyers find it more efficient and profitable to practice in one field rather than across the board. The choices open to them—and thus the choices you have to make in selecting a lawyer—are considerable.

Specialization presents a unique complication. Not only are lawyers forbidden to advertise their availability; they—unlike physicians—cannot even announce themselves as specialists. The only exceptions to this rule are attorneys who practice in the rather narrow fields of maritime or patent and trademark law. Divorce lawyers, real estate lawyers, criminal lawyers, tax lawyers and other specialists must keep their fields of expertise a secret from the public. You must search the specialists out.

One man who learned this lesson the hard way was an enterprising grocer who had developed a thriving side line in frozen dinners. He decided to incorporate his business and sell stock in order to raise additional capital. Instead of looking for a specialist in corporation law, the grocer retained the attorney who had drawn up his mother's will. This man was capable, but he had little experience beyond probate and real estate law. After much preparation, he finally registered the new corporation's shares. But the long hours he had to spend trying to master unfamiliar securities regulations delayed the issuance of the stock, and the grocer had to pay a large fee for the extra time spent. A corporate specialist could have breezed through the transaction using standard procedures he had relied on many times before and at a lesser fee.

Thus, if your legal problem is a rather complicated one, you would be wise to ask among your friends and colleagues for the name of an attorney they might know who has handled your kind of problem. If there is a Lawyer Referral Service in your community, you should inquire if it can supply you with the name of a specialist. If you already have a lawyer, do not be abashed to ask about his experience with cases such as yours; he should be able to refer you to a colleague he knows by reputation who could take on a case that he does not feel qualified to handle himself.

HOW LAWYERS FIND LAWYERS

Interestingly enough, even lawyers have trouble finding lawyers. Sometimes they need another lawyer to take on a case because they are unfamiliar with the specialty involved, or because the client lives

A swarm of specialties

The law has become so complicated that no one attorney, no matter how experienced he is, can handle all of your possible legal affairs with equal skill or answer all the questions you may raise. A family lawyer, like a family physician, will often refer his clients to specialists who restrict their practice to particular types of cases. A few of their specialties are narrow indeed—there are some lawyers who spend all their time handling intricate tax cases. The most important specialties cover broader fields of law and are listed below.

Domestic relations

Advice and legal representation involving family matters such as divorce, adoption, guardianship, juvenile delinquency, rights and problems of the aged.

Personal injury

Civil suits arising out of damage claims for accidents, mainly those involving automobiles but also including home and industrial accident cases and medical malpractice suits.

Crimes

Arrests; any case involving a client with criminal, rather than civil, law.

Civil liberties

Defense of constitutional rights to freedom of speech and assembly; cases involving religious and racial discrimination.

Taxes

Dealings with the Internal Revenue Service and other tax agencies; cases brought to tax courts; financial advice that helps clients comply with the tax laws in ways most advantageous to themselves.

Trusts, estates and probate

Preparing wills, planning estates and setting up personal trusts.

Corporations

Advice on licenses, partnerships, incorporation papers, stock issues, stockholders' agreements, corporate taxes, employment contracts; lawsuits involving corporations.

Administrative agencies

Cases involving social security, welfare, workmen's compensation and veterans' rights.

Real estate

The drawing up of sales agreements, deeds, leases, mortgages; litigation over zoning ordinances; condemnation proceedings and disputes between landlords and tenants.

Libel

Cases involving alleged damage to someone's reputation by something printed in a publication or broadcast by a radio or TV station.

Bankruptcy

Dealings between creditors and debtors; financial advice to debtors; cases in bankruptcy court.

Patents and copyrights

Protection of the rights of inventors, authors, composers and artists to control their works.

in another part of the country. To be sure, lawyers do have access to sources of information not available to the public. Among these are directories and lists of lawyers that are kept on file in law offices and libraries. But while some of these lists may indicate which lawyers are trained in specialized fields, the directories do not provide details concerning a lawyer's special talents or abilities. As a result, lawyers themselves resort to the same tactic everyone else uses when he needs an attorney: They check around among their friends for the name of a good lawyer whom someone knows and has seen in action.

GETTING TOGETHER WITH A LAWYER

Once you find a lawyer—and he has agreed to discuss your problem with you—do not be surprised if he does not exactly jump at the chance to represent you. Like any professional, a lawyer hopes to get new business and add to his income. But any kind of litigation takes careful preparation and a good deal of time—and time means money to a lawyer. The matter of time can be especially critical if a new case involves the probability of a trial. Several months may be required to collect and prepare all the evidence, and—because the courts are often crowded—additional months may be spent waiting to get on the docket (the list of pending cases). Therefore, unless a lawyer is fairly certain that you have a strong case, with a preponderance of evidence and legal rights on your side, he may decide that neither he nor you can afford to devote the time and effort needed to take it to court; he will then refuse the case and turn you down as his client.

He may also inform you—perhaps to your annoyance—that you do not even have a case. Let's assume, for example, that you have been injured while riding as a passenger in a neighbor's automobile. The neighbor was careless; you know that he is adequately covered by insurance; and you therefore assume you can sue him for damages. But the lawyer you talk to points out that you live in a state that has a "guest statute" that prohibits such suits unless you can prove "gross" or "wilful" negligence on your neighbor's part *(Chapter 5)*. But there is no proof at all, he explains, that your neighbor was that negligent. The court, therefore, would not give much credence to such a suit, much less find in your favor.

Simply finding out whether a lawyer will accept you as a client may take a bit of time and money. And whatever your legal problem the lawyer may question you so strenuously about it that you start to feel uncomfortable. But he has a purpose in doing this. He may conclude that he needs to study the problem and collect more facts before he can make a decision. He is justified in charging you for this

extra study and research as well as for the time taken up by the preliminary consultation. Even if he eventually turns down your case on
legal grounds, he will probably bill you for the time he spent considering your problem. He will not feel abashed, and you should not
feel put upon. For when you walked into his office to consult with
him, you were in effect indicating that you were willing to pay for his
judgment. The time he spent on your case could have been devoted
to another, more profitable one. And just by hearing you out, the lawyer may have helped you to settle your problem. For if he manages to
save you additional time, money and nervous energy merely by bringing you down to earth, he has performed a useful service and earned a
reasonable fee.

THE FEE

If the lawyer agrees that you have a case—and is willing to take you
on as his client—the next thing to do is to come to terms on the fee he
will charge you, as well as the method of payment. It is always better
to settle these matters in advance, in order to avoid future controversy. The lawyer will probably take the initiative in discussing terms.
If he does not, bring up the subject yourself.

Lawyers are not always able to predict with any degree of accuracy exactly what their final fee will be, for they cannot pinpoint at
the outset how much expense a case will entail. Still, a good lawyer
can usually provide some sort of estimate. Among the factors he considers are: the time to be spent on your case, its complexity and the difficulties he anticipates in handling it, the going rate that other lawyers
charge for similar cases in the community, the actual amount of money at stake in your case, and the benefits that will accrue to you if you
win it. If you are a new client, he may charge you slightly more for a
certain service than he would a regular client who gives him steady
business. And he will also take into account, as he estimates his total
fee, the method of payment you and he have decided on.

Lawyers ordinarily bill their clients in one of four different ways:
(1) by charging a flat rate for a routine job, such as drawing up a
will or handling a fairly straightforward, uncontested divorce; (2) by
collecting a contingency fee—a percentage of the actual amount
awarded by the jury—in cases involving damages and personal injury; (3) by collecting a percentage of the total amount involved in
such legal transactions as settling an estate or buying and selling property; or (4) by charging an hourly rate.

The spectacle of lawyers scrambling for business by undercut-
ting one another's fees is a nightmare that haunts professional groups.

To prevent price wars, most local bar associations publish a schedule of minimum fees for various kinds of legal services. However, lawyers are free to charge less than these minimum rates, and under certain circumstances it is possible for you to bargain over the fee—or at least its method of payment. Some lawyers lower their standard fees for clients who simply cannot afford to pay them and make up some of the loss on other clients who can. (A busy Western lawyer, who normally handles only expensive damage suits and collects contingency fees as high as $100,000, once accepted a total payment of two smoked salmon from a tribe of Indians whose fishing rights he had defended.)

In an experiment that could prove of enormous value to millions of Americans of moderate means, local bar associations are cooperating with labor unions to set up a system of prepaid legal services for the union members, financed in part out of their dues. This, in effect, is a group legal policy akin to the group health policies so prevalent today, and other organizations, such as credit unions, are studying the plan with interest. While its purpose is to lessen the burden of legal costs, it has already turned up another benefit: In one Louisiana community, the usual run of harassment actions and bill-collecting suits leveled against members of a local union by small loan companies began to let up when word got around that the local had its own attorneys ready to defend its members.

When you are dealing with a lawyer on your own, you can sometimes save on legal expenses by careful choice of the basis on which fees are charged—contingency, hourly rate, flat sum or percentage. The lawyer's fee for administering an estate, for example, is customarily based on a percentage of the estate's total value. But if the work involved on a small estate is fairly routine, a lawyer may agree to charge you a flat hourly rate—which will usually come to less than a percentage fee. It is not unusual for a lawyer who has won a difficult case to feel at the end that he has earned a little extra and reopen the question of the fee. On the other hand, a lawyer who has lost a case may decide to translate his embarrassment into a slightly lower fee.

In some instances, the lawyer may require a partial payment of his fee in advance. This is known in the trade as a retainer. A retainer is especially common in the kind of case that, by its very nature, could leave the lawyer without any payment at all if he waited until after it was settled to bill the client. In criminal cases, for example, or bankruptcy proceedings, in which a client could wind up either in jail or broke, an experienced lawyer would probably arrange for at least a portion of his fee to be paid in advance.

Sometimes fees can be paid on the installment plan. Several local bar associations permit lawyers to have their clients sign promissory notes, which are then sold to banks that collect the debt from the client in regular payments.

If, when your legal problem has been taken care of and the bill has been presented, you honestly feel that you have not received your money's worth from the lawyer, you should frankly say so. Most lawyers place a high value on their reputation for fair dealing and would rather work out a quiet compromise than let a dispute turn into a public squabble. If the lawyer will not agree to a compromise—and you have good reason to criticize his work—you can file a grievance against him with the local city or county bar association. Unfortunately, many of these groups seem to be timid and slow about disciplining their dues-paying members and tend to be overly protective of them. Sometimes the groups fail to act for months, then exonerate the lawyer without offering a satisfactory explanation of their action.

The legal profession as a whole is aware of this problem—and of the poor impression such episodes make if they are not resolved. In an effort to arrive at a partial solution, some local bar associations assess money from their members to set up "client security funds." If a

How much do lawyers charge?

There is no standard price list for lawyers' services. Their fees vary according to the locality, the nature of the case—and sometimes the ability of a client to pay. The figures given here, based on surveys by the American Bar Association, show the wide range even among minimum fees that lawyers charge for various kinds of work.

TRIAL PRACTICE. For representing a client in court, $25 to $300 per day.

OFFICE WORK. For drawing up documents and handling other legal matters in the lawyer's own office, $10 to $50 per hour.

UNCONTESTED DIVORCE. For cases in which the custody of children or a property settlement is not a question, $75 in some states to $1,000 in California.

CONTESTED DIVORCE. For cases involving alimony or custody problems, several hundred dollars to several thousand.

DRAFTING A WILL. For drawing up a simple will, $10 to $50.

ADOPTION CASES. For completing a normal, uncontested adoption, $30 in some states to $350 in others.

Many kinds of legal work, such as settling an estate, collecting debts and handling damage suits, are paid for on a contingency basis. Here, the lawyer takes a certain percentage of the money his client is awarded or collects. The usual fee for winning an automobile injury suit, for example, is one third of the damages awarded to the client.

disappointed client can demonstrate to the trustees of the local fund that he suffered monetary loss because of an inept or otherwise unacceptable performance by his lawyer, the trustees reimburse the client with money from the security fund.

Occasionally a client loses so much confidence in his attorney that he wants to change lawyers before the case is finished. As a rule, it does not pay to switch. If, however, you become convinced that your interests will suffer materially if you let your lawyer continue to represent you, you should inform him of your decision and tell him that you intend to get someone else. After you retain your new attorney, you can let him work out the details of the transfer with the original lawyer. You will have to pay the first lawyer for the time he spent on your problem; he, in turn, will have to return all of the papers you gave him concerning the case, plus any other materials that he developed while representing you.

BE HONEST WITH YOUR LAWYER

If laymen occasionally distrust lawyers, lawyers sometimes have cause to take a dim view of their clients. One frequent criticism leveled by lawyers is that many a client is reluctant to relax, take his lawyer into his confidence and communicate with him fully and truthfully. Some clients try to hide part of the truth from their lawyers or at least put a

Whatever you tell your lawyer
will be held in confidence,
for the law regards
your conversations with him as
privileged—he cannot
be required to divulge them.

better face on it. For example, a landlord who has been repeatedly warned by building inspectors for infractions of the building code, and who has finally been handed a summons, may neglect to tell his lawyer the full story of the earlier warnings. His failure to come clean will complicate matters when the inspectors tell their side of the story in court, for a lawyer who has not been thoroughly briefed by his client can hardly be in a position to put up the best defense.

There is another good reason for telling the whole story to your lawyer. You can be sure that whatever you tell him will be held in confidence, for in order to promote the freest possible discussion between lawyers and clients, the law has made the relationship between them privileged. A lawyer, although a sworn officer of the court, can never be compelled to reveal any of his client's confidences in that court; and he risks the charge of unethical conduct—and even censure by his local bar association—if he reveals them in private conversation.

It is essential for the proper handling of your problem not only that you tell your lawyer everything about it, but also that you take to his office any records bearing on the problem—insurance policies, receipts, canceled checks, letters, diaries, photographs. It is no less crucial that you relate the facts to him as calmly and unemotionally as you can. This, in turn, will make it easier for him to get at the legal substance that lies at the core of your problem, and hence make it easier for him to do a better job for you.

THE LAW IS MORE THAN LAWYERS

One final and all-important point to keep in mind about your lawyer is that the law does not begin or end with him. He may have furnished you with the immediate advice you needed; he may have searched through dozens of thick volumes to find precedents on which to base your case; he may have made numerous late-night telephone calls to prospective witnesses on your behalf; and he may have argued your case in court with skill and the warmest of zeal. But the chances are that your opponent's lawyer did all of those things, too. And so, after the two adversaries have done their work, another element—neutral and dispassionate—takes over to decide the issue.

This element may be a judge, steeped in the law, an imposing symbol of its majesty; or it may be a jury of ordinary men and women whose task it has been to hear the evidence, sort out the arguments and render a verdict. In the end, our system of law depends heavily on the judgment and understanding of average citizens like yourself.

By **FRED P. GRAHAM**
ERNEST C. FRIESEN JR., Consultant

3
The family

Marriage and divorce,
children
and the elderly

That most personal and private of relationships, marriage, is anything but private in the eyes of the law. Great numbers of statutes and court rulings surround and control it. Poets may hail it as a union made in and answerable only to heaven; the law takes an earthier view. As one legal definition prosaically puts it, marriage is "a mutually accepted agreement between a man and a woman to cohabit and to accept certain interrelated rights and duties." It is, in short, a contract that is even more binding than any undertaken by two corporate giants—and just as enforceable by law.

The law's lively interest begins before the wedding ceremony and persists after the marriage ends. It specifies the age below which you may not marry; it may require you to apply for and receive a license to marry; it may compel you to take a premarital blood test for venereal disease. The wedding itself has legal sanction; if you choose to have a civil ceremony, you are married by a representative of the state, and if a clergyman performs the rites, he does so through a power vested in him by state law. If you have children, the law does not ignore their upbringing. You are required to provide them with proper care, including the food, clothing, medical attention and education that they have a right to expect. As your children mature and you get on in years, they may face certain legal responsibilities for you, just as you may for aged parents of your own. And if, at any time during the course of your marriage, you should decide to call it quits, you may do so only in ways specified by law.

Each state makes its own laws governing marriage and divorce, and as result they vary markedly (*charts, pages 46-47 and 58-59*). But behind them all is a single sweeping purpose: to safeguard society's basic structural unit, the family. The requirement of a waiting period between the application for and issuance of a marriage license no doubt irks hot-headed lovers, but it is essentially intended to fend off the ills that may come of a hasty marriage. The cooling-off period usually required before a divorce is intended to encourage a couple to reconsider and perhaps salvage their life together. Society's desire to protect and preserve the family is what, in fact, motivates the entire broad field of so-called domestic relations law, which includes the relations not only between husband and wife, but between parents and children and between the family unit and the community at large. Domestic relations law rarely affects directly the daily activities of the average, reasonably contented household; normally it steps in only when there is serious family trouble of some sort. But it stands by to be ready if it is needed.

So inclusive is the law's coverage in the field of domestic relations that its long arm sometimes reaches out to those who change their minds about marrying. A proposal of marriage, and its acceptance, constitutes a kind of contract. If it is broken by one party to it, the other can sue for damages for breach of promise.

It should be quickly noted, however, that this type of legal recourse is not available countrywide. Many states have outlawed such suits and most others discourage them. One reason is a shift in social attitudes; a jilted woman—women have been preponderantly the plaintiffs in such actions—is no longer regarded as having suffered particularly grievous damage. Another reason is the potential for blackmail. The threat of a breach of promise suit, with its likely revelations in court of the intimate details of a courtship, has led many a man to pay off to silence a girl he has spurned.

Nevertheless, a few years ago a young woman in Hawaii successfully sued a young man who had promised to marry her, then seduced her, then returned to the mainland, where he promptly married another girl. Although seduction itself does not constitute a promise to marry, the jury awarded the plaintiff some $5,000 for expenses she had incurred during the courtship and then underscored its opinion of her ex-fiancé by tacking on almost $6,000 in punitive damages.

Although jilted men who sue are few and far between, the law offers them some tangible consolation. If a spurned fiancé lives in a state where breach of promise actions are allowed, he can recover the engagement ring he gave his bride-to-be and his share of a joint savings account they set up in anticipation of furnishing an apartment. These are what the law calls conditional gifts—offered in the expectation that the marriage will take place. The plaintiff cannot, however, recover a hi-fi set he gave his fiancée as a Christmas gift; this was not conditional on the marriage—it was an absolute gift.

Recovery of property is also possible, although more difficult, in states whose courts will not entertain breach of promise suits. In some states—California and New York are two—special statutes provide for the return of engagement rings and other conditional gifts. The ring does not really belong to the girl until she goes through with her promise to marry the donor. The recovery laws are considerably less accommodating to a man who has done the jilting. Only one state, Louisiana, allows him to get back the engagement ring.

Getting married: who can and who can't

Assuming that all goes well en route to the altar, the final few steps to it are still subject to legal scrutiny. All but 10 states require a waiting period of two to five days between the application for and granting of a marriage license, or between issuance of the license and the ceremony. But the law is not unyielding on this score. A soldier on home leave may receive a waiver of the waiting period, and so may others who can show that the wait will pose special difficulties.

These exceptions, however, do not lessen the law's interest in discouraging quick-and-easy marriages. Its interest in preventing potentially unstable or unsuitable marriages is even stronger. Every state has a statute specifying the minimum age of a prospective bride and groom, and most states require a blood test of each partner before issuing a license. What happens if the test turns up evidence of venereal disease differs from state to state. Some automatically deny the license; others grant it if the disease is in a nontransmittable stage or if the infected person promises to undergo treatment. And some states will refuse a license if either prospective partner is a drug addict, a chronic alcoholic or a mental retardate.

Some couples are not allowed to marry under any circumstances —regardless of how long they are willing to wait and how fully they might comply with age and medical requirements. All states forbid close blood relatives to marry; some states also extend this ban to first cousins; many will not permit a woman to marry her brother-in-law or a man to marry his sister-in-law. Until recently, interracial marriage was prohibited in many jurisdictions; but in a landmark decision of 1967 the Supreme Court struck down all laws forbidding such marriages. No state, wrote Chief Justice Earl Warren, could enforce a law that arbitrarily restricted a basic freedom of any citizen or group of citizens, including the freedom to marry.

Common law marriages

It is possible for a couple with marriage in mind to bypass the blood test, the license, even the ceremony, and still get themselves legally married if they live in one of the states *(chart, pages 46-47)* that recognize a time-honored legal concept, the common law marriage. The only requirements are that the couple be free of other marital ties and that they make an informal but definite agreement to consider themselves husband and wife. They do not even have to live together for any specific time for their private vows to be legally valid; 10 minutes of cohabitation can precede the vows, or 10 years.

Some of the states recognize common law marriage only if the couple acknowledge their status in some public fashion—for example, by letting it be known among the neighbors that they are married or by opening joint charge accounts as "Mr. and Mrs. Jones." Mrs. Jones, by proving that she and Mr. Jones had taken some definite action to in-

TEXT CONTINUES ON PAGE 48

REQUIREMENTS FOR MARRIAGE
STATE BY STATE

U.S. marriage laws basically reflect society's desire to ensure family stability by preventing hasty or unsuitable marriages, chiefly—as the chart below shows—by requiring a couple to be of a minimum age, to wait a specified period before the ceremony and to take some sort

STATE	MINIMUM AGE FOR MARRIAGE[a]				WAITING PERIOD BEFORE MARRIAGE (Days)[b]	COMMON LAW MARRIAGE RECOGNIZED	MEDICAL TEST REQUIRED
	With parents' consent		Without parents' consent				
	BRIDE	GROOM	BRIDE	GROOM			
ALABAMA	14	17	18	21	0	YES	YES
ALASKA	16	18	18	21	3	NO	YES
ARIZONA	16	18	18	21	3	NO	YES
ARKANSAS	16	18	18	21	2	NO	YES
CALIFORNIA	16	18	18	21	0	NO	YES
COLORADO	16	18	18	21	0	YES	YES
CONNECTICUT	16	16	21	21	4	NO	YES
DELAWARE	16	18	19	19	1	NO	YES
DIST. OF COL.	16	18	18	21	3	YES	YES
FLORIDA	16	18	21	21	3	NO	YES
GEORGIA	16	18	19	19	3	YES	YES
HAWAII	16	18	18	20	0	NO	YES
IDAHO	16	18	18	21	3	NO	YES
ILLINOIS	16	18	18	21	0	NO	YES
INDIANA	16	18	18	21	3	NO	YES
IOWA	16	18	18	21	3	YES	YES
KANSAS	18	18	18	21	3	YES	YES
KENTUCKY	16	18	18	21	3	NO	YES
LOUISIANA	16	18	21	21	3	NO	YES
MAINE	16	16	18	21	5	NO	YES
MARYLAND	16	18	18	21	2	NO	NO
MASSACHUSETTS	16	18	18	21	3	NO	YES
MICHIGAN	16	18	18	18	3	NO	YES
MINNESOTA	16	18	18	21	5	NO	NO
MISSISSIPPI	15	17	21	21	3	NO	YES
MISSOURI	15	15	18	21	3	NO	YES

(a) Some states make special provision to permit marriages at younger ages under special circumstances—most commonly, when the bride is pregnant. In some states both the parents' consent and the permission of a judge are required for one or both of the parties for a valid marriage to be contracted at or below the ages listed.

of premarital medical examination. While most marriages are contracted by formal ceremony, 13 states and the District of Columbia still sanction the "common law" marriage, which needs neither a license nor witnesses to be valid. But the partners must, as in a solemnized marriage, be of legal age, of sound mind, not of a kinship prohibited by law and free of existing marriage ties. In both types of union the man and woman must, in some fashion, promise to take each other as husband and wife for life.

STATE	MINIMUM AGE FOR MARRIAGE[a]				WAITING PERIOD BEFORE MARRIAGE (Days)[b]	COMMON LAW MARRIAGE RECOGNIZED	MEDICAL TEST REQUIRED
	With parents' consent		Without parents' consent				
	BRIDE	GROOM	BRIDE	GROOM			
MONTANA	16	18	18	21	5	YES	YES
NEBRASKA	16	18	21	21	0	NO	YES
		18	18	21	0	NO	NO
		14	18	20	5	NO	YES
		18	18	21	3	NO	YES
		18	18	21	3	NO	YES
		16	18	21	1	NO	YES
		16	18	18	0	NO	YES
		18	18	21	0	NO	YES
		18	21	21	5	YES	YES
		18	18	21	0	YES	YES
		18	18	21	7	NO	YES
		16	21	21	3	YES	YES
		18	21	21	0	YES	YES
		16	18	18	1	YES	NO
		18	21	21	0	NO	YES
		16	21	21	3	NO	YES
		16	18	19	0	YES	YES
		16	18	21	0	NO	YES
		18	18	18	0	NO	YES
		18	21	21	0	NO	YES
		17	18	21	3	NO	YES
		18	21	21	3	NO	YES
		18	18	21	3	NO	YES
		18	21	21	0	NO	YES

depending on the state in ... rried. In some states the wait- ... he time between application for a marriage license and its issuance. In other states the bride and groom must wait a specified period of time between issuance of the license and the marriage ceremony.

dicate their status to others, would be able to assert her right to Social Security or veterans' benefits if she became widowed, as well as her rights to any estate Mr. Jones had left. In most states that recognize common law marriages she would find it difficult to convince a court that she was legal heir to his estate by asserting that she and Mr. Jones had exchanged secret vows of marriage. But if she could supply proof of their arrangement and the date it began, her chances would be better—even if another Mrs. Jones, armed with a later marriage certificate, showed up to contest the claim.

The law and the wedding ceremony

The overwhelming majority of Americans who marry do so by the conventional means of a civil or religious ceremony. At this point, if they have chafed at the preliminary requirements imposed on them by law, they are in for an agreeable surprise. For usually, only two elements are essential to legalize a marriage: the presence of witnesses, one of whom must be either a clergyman or a state official, and the declaration by the bride and groom of their intention to take each other as husband and wife for life. The law is entirely flexible about details. The Quaker wedding ceremony, in which the bride and groom exchange vows without an ordained clergyman present, has long been sanctioned by special statute, and indeed the marriage rites of any bona fide religious sect are recognized as valid by virtually all states.

Beyond the two elements cited, the law has no concern with the form of the proceedings. They may be brief or lengthy, heavy with ritual or devoid of it, traditional or exotic. How the couple verbalize their vows is their own affair. They may adhere to a time-honored service or choose to compose their own; the bride may or may not promise to obey. For years one New York judge bound couples with two brief questions and one quick statement: "Do you want to marry her?" "Do you want to marry him?" "You're married."

DISSOLVING A MARRIAGE

To go immediately from discussing the solemnization of a marriage to discussing its possible smashup may seem cynical, but the fact is that about one out of every four marriages contracted in the United States ends in divorce and the number is on the rise; over 700,000 marriages foundered in 1970 alone.

And so the law must necessarily look upon divorce as a fact of life for all too many Americans. It is not, however, the sole way in which married people can be legally parted. Two other forms of recourse are open to them. One is a legal separation, which stops short

FORM NO. VS-20
30M - REV. 12-68

STATE OF WISCONSIN
DIVISION OF HEALTH
CERTIFICATE OF MARRIAGE

STATE FILING DATE

STATE NO.

GROOM

GROOM - NAME	FIRST	MIDDLE	LAST	SOCIAL SECURITY NO.
1a.				1b.

PLACE OF RESIDENCE: STATE	COUNTY	☐ CITY ☐ VILLAGE ☐ TOWNSHIP	INSIDE CITY OR VILLAGE LIMITS
2a.	2b.	2c.	2d. ☐ YES ☐ NO

MAILING ADDRESS	STATE OF BIRTH (IF NOT IN U.S.A., NAME COUNTRY)	DATE OF BIRTH — MONTH DAY YEAR	AGE
2e.	3.	4.	

FATHER - NAME	STATE OF BIRTH (IF NOT IN U.S.A., NAME COUNTRY)	MOTHER - MAIDEN NAME	STATE OF BIRTH (IF NOT IN U.S.A., NAME COUNTRY)
5a.	5b.	6a.	6b.

BRIDE

BRIDE - NAME	FIRST	MIDDLE	LAST	MAIDEN NAME IF DIFFERENT	SOCIAL SECURITY NO.
7a.				7b.	7c.

PLACE OF RESIDENCE: STATE	COUNTY	☐ CITY ☐ VILLAGE ☐ TOWNSHIP	INSIDE CITY OR VILLAGE LIMITS
8a.	8b.	8c.	8d. ☐ YES ☐ NO

MAILING ADDRESS	STATE OF BIRTH (IF NOT IN U.S.A., NAME COUNTRY)	DATE OF BIRTH — MONTH DAY YEAR	AGE
8e.	9.	10.	

FATHER - NAME	STATE OF BIRTH (IF NOT IN U.S.A., NAME COUNTRY)	MOTHER - MAIDEN NAME	STATE OF BIRTH (IF NOT IN U.S.A., NAME COUNTRY)
11a.	11b.	12a.	12b.

GROOM - SIGNATURE	DATE SIGNED	BRIDE - SIGNATURE	DATE SIGNED
13a.	13b.	14a.	14b.

CERTIFICATION OF OFFICIANT

I, _____ (TYPE OR PRINT NAME OF OFFICIANT) OF _____ (MAILING ADDRESS OF OFFICIANT (STREET OR RFD, CITY OR VILLAGE, STATE)), HEREBY CERTIFY THAT THE ABOVE NAMED GROOM AND BRIDE WERE BY ME UNITED IN MARRIAGE AS AUTHORIZED BY A MARRIAGE LICENSE ISSUED FOR THAT PURPOSE BY _____ (NAME OF COUNTY CLERK) OF _____ (NAME OF COUNTY), STATE OF WISCONSIN

MARRIAGE LICENSE NUMBER _____ EFFECTIVE DATE OF MARRIAGE LICENSE _____, A.D., 19____

MY CREDENTIALS ARE FILED IN THE OFFICE OF CLERK OF CIRCUIT COURT _____ COUNTY, STATE OF WISCONSIN

DATE OF MARRIAGE	MONTH	DAY	YEAR
15a.			A.D., 19

PLACE OF MARRIAGE	CHURCH, ETC.	CITY OR VILLAGE (IF NEITHER, NAME TOWNSHIP)	COUNTY	STATE
15b.				15c.

OFFICIANT - Enter Signature	DATE SIGNED — MONTH DAY YEAR	OFFICIANT
15d.	15e.	15f. ☐ RELIGIOUS ☐ CIVIL OFFICIAL

WITNESS

WE, THE UNDERSIGNED ADULT WITNESSES, WERE PRESENT AT THE MARRIAGE OF THE ABOVE NAMED GROOM AND BRIDE, AS SET FORTH IN THE FOREGOING CERTIFICATE, AT THEIR REQUEST AND HEARD THEIR DECLARATIONS THAT THEY TOOK EACH OTHER FOR HUSBAND AND WIFE.

WITNESS - SIGNATURE	WITNESS - SIGNATURE
16a.	16b.

LOCAL OFFICIAL, MAKING RETURN TO STATE HEALTH DEPARTMENT	SIGNATURE AND TITLE	DATE RECEIVED BY LOCAL OFFICIAL — MONTH DAY YEAR	LOCAL REGISTER NO.
17a.		17b.	17c.

CONFIDENTIAL INFORMATION

GROOM

RACE - WHITE, NEGRO, AMERICAN INDIAN, ETC. (SPECIFY)	NUMBER OF THIS MARRIAGE (CHECK ONE)	LAST MARRIAGE ENDED BY (CHECK ONE)	DATE LAST MARRIAGE ENDED — MONTH YEAR
18.	19. ☐ FIRST ☐ SECOND ☐ THIRD	20a. ☐ DEATH ☐ DIVORCE ☐ ANNULMENT	20b.

USUAL OCCUPATION	KIND OF BUSINESS OR INDUSTRY	WAS GROOM EVER IN U. S. ARMED FORCES? (IF YES GIVE WAR OR DATES OF SERVICE)
21a.	21b.	21c. ☐ YES ☐ NO

BRIDE

RACE- WHITE, NEGRO, AMERICAN INDIAN, ETC. (SPECIFY)	NUMBER OF THIS MARRIAGE (CHECK ONE)	LAST MARRIAGE ENDED BY (CHECK ONE)	DATE LAST MARRIAGE ENDED — MONTH YEAR
22.	23. ☐ FIRST ☐ SECOND ☐ THIRD	24a. ☐ DEATH ☐ DIVORCE ☐ ANNULMENT	24b.

USUAL OCCUPATION	KIND OF BUSINESS OR INDUSTRY	WAS BRIDE EVER IN U. S. ARMED FORCES? (IF YES GIVE WAR OR DATES OF SERVICE)
25a.	25b.	25c. ☐ YES ☐ NO

BRIDE'S COPY

Making a marriage official

Besides getting a marriage license, a bride and groom must see to it that proof of their marriage is put on file with the state. Such a marriage registration (*above*) must be filled in after the ceremony. Most simply ask for the pertinent facts —names, date, place—although some, like Wisconsin's, also provide space for confidential information about race and employment.

of divorce but is often a prelude to it. The other is an annulment, which, in the eyes of the law, simply cancels a marriage ceremony, as though it had never taken place.

Annulment—ending a marriage that never was

An annulment is, in essence, a court decision saying that some obstacle made the marriage invalid from the start. The law distinguishes two kinds of obstacles. The first, and more serious, sort makes a marriage "void" automatically; an incestuous marriage and a marriage contracted by a person who is already married come under this category. The second sort of obstacle makes a marriage not void but "voidable." Among the grounds for annulling a marriage under the voidable category are the following:

■ Underage (technically, nonage). If either husband or wife was below the age for marriage set by law in their state, parents can bring suit on behalf of their minor child for an annulment. But such a suit is not inevitably successful. In a few states judges may refuse to grant an annulment if they believe that the youngsters are mature enough emotionally to make a go of marriage.

■ Sexual impotence. If either partner proves physically or psychologically incapable of intercourse from the very start of the marriage, it can be annulled in most states.

■ Lack of "true consent." The validity of a marriage may come into question, for example, if a couple get married on a lark with no real intention of creating a lasting relationship, or if either partner is of unsound mind, or if either has married against his or her will—in legal terminology, under duress. In this context duress is a polite synonym for a shotgun wedding, but it need not take the traditional form of an angry father pointing a loaded firearm at his daughter's betrayer. One New York girl went through a wedding ceremony with a young man she detested after his clannish and violence-prone family threatened to kidnap her, disfigure her and blow her father's house to pieces. To say the least, true consent was absent in this case, and the girl got an annulment.

■ Fraud. Courts take a serious view of concealments and misrepresentations that strike at the fundamentals of the marriage relationship. Annulments have been granted for hiding a history of mental disorder, serious illness or "important information" about a previous marriage. One man married an apparently amiable divorcee who told him she had divorced her previous husband for cruelty. When the woman began to display a ferocious temper, the alarmed husband checked into her past and learned that not she, but her ex-husband,

had sued for divorce for cruelty; she had, in fact, attacked him with a knife. The woman's duplicity won her new groom an annulment.

More frequent causes for annulment on the basis of fraud are concealment by the bride of her pregnancy by a man other than her husband and lying by either partner about a desire to have children. If, during courtship, the man or the woman expounds on the joys of parenthood and then, after the ceremony, reveals that the mere thought of children is repulsive, the spouse can sue for annulment.

On the other hand, there are some concealments that the courts regard indulgently. The law attempts to distinguish between serious frauds and relatively harmless falsehoods. If a man exaggerates his financial status to his fiancée—weaving a tale about the large house they will live in but later carrying her across the threshold of a simple cottage—she cannot get an annulment. Nor can a man get one if he discovers after marriage that his bride has fibbed about her age or that her captivating figure is largely padding.

Legal separations

When annulment is impossible, a divorce must end the marriage. A halfway step is a judicial separation. It is a way out chosen by couples who decide that they can no longer live together but who, for some reason, shy away from divorce. The proceeding requires an appearance by one or both parties in court and proof that one has been guilty of some offense that strikes at the marriage relationship. They then receive what is called a decree of "divorce from bed and board." But even before this judicial separation or, in fact, prior to a suit for absolute divorce, most estranged couples choose to work out separation agreements. The agreement settles the same practical issues that arise in a divorce—custody of children, financial support, division of property—and it is initiated in much the same fashion as a divorce.

The husband goes to one lawyer, the wife to another. The husband tells his lawyer what money and property he can afford to give his wife and, if there are children, what his wishes are concerning their custody. The wife tells her lawyer what money she needs to live on each month and what her desires are about child custody and support. Then the lawyers negotiate until they work out an agreement. If both husband and wife accept it, they simply sign copies of the document in their respective lawyers' offices, and they then have what is known as a voluntary separation, which need not go through a court.

Separation does not wholly free a couple of the rights and obligations of marriage. Both, for example, are barred from engaging in adulterous conduct, and the husband is still obligated to support his wife. Provisions of a voluntary agreement are difficult to enforce. But if the terms of the separation are stipulated by a court, the court can punish violations of the agreement by holding the offending party in contempt, with a possible jail sentence to follow.

Again because of the court's role, a judicial separation takes more undoing if the couple become reconciled. If their separation was voluntary, they simply tear up their agreement to live apart; in the case of a judicial separation they must petition the court to revoke it. In many states, if a couple with a separation do not become reconciled within a specified period—usually one to five years—either partner can obtain a divorce from a court simply by applying for one.

Divorce American-style

For people bent on divorce without stopping for a separation, state laws provide a variety of grounds *(chart, pages 58-59)*. But by far the most frequently used ground is cruelty, mental or physical. More than 60 per cent of all U.S. divorces are granted for this reason.

Physical cruelty is what it sounds like: One spouse inflicts some sort of bodily harm upon the other. Contrary to what might be supposed, the man is not always the aggressor. In one Pennsylvania case, the court record awarding the divorce to the husband reads: "The plaintiff carries a scar where his wife hit him across the face with a piece of Masonite; she hit him on the ankle with an ash tray, so injuring him that he could not walk for weeks; she hit him over the head with a baseball bat; she hit him with a brick; she threw books at him . . . she dumped a plate of spaghetti over his head."

Mental cruelty is less easily defined. In essence, the law accepts it as meaning that one spouse has behaved or spoken in such a way as to make the other so miserable that the marriage becomes intolerable. It includes what lawyers call indignities—things one spouse does that insult and humiliate the other. One insult, however, does not make for mental cruelty; the insulting behavior must be persistent, malicious in intent and destructive of the marriage relationship.

Two recent cases illustrate what has and has not been judged mental cruelty. A wife sued for divorce on the complaint that her hus-

SUPERIOR COURT OF CALIFORNIA, COUNTY OF LOS ANGELES

In re the marriage of

Petitioner:

        and

Respondent:

CASE NUMBER

☐ **PETITIONER'S**   ☐ **RESPONDENT'S**
CONFIDENTIAL QUESTIONNAIRE (MARRIAGE)

The information supplied by you in this questionnaire is strictly confidential and may be used only by the court. Answer all the questions and be as fair and impartial as possible. (You may answer questions 1 through 29 by attaching a copy of Bureau of Vital Statistics Form VS-243A as filed with the court.)

☐ A copy of Form VS-243A is attached.

1. Type of proceeding _____

MARRIAGE AND FAMILY INFORMATION

24. Place of marriage _____ (City) (County) (State or Country) 25. Date of marriage _____

26. Number of children of this marriage _____ 27. Ages of these children _____

28. Are you living together now? _____ 29. If not, when did you separate? _____

30. Husband's age at time of this marriage _____ 31. If previously married give the age at the time of each _____

32. Wife's age at time of this marriage _____ 33. If previously married give the age at the time of each _____

34. The children of this marriage are now living with _____

35. Are there children not of this marriage? _____ (yes / no)

    a. Husband's children: _____ (Number) (Ages), now living with _____

    b. Wife's children: _____ (Number) (Ages), now living with _____

36. Are the children now living with the husband or wife aware of your difficulties? _____

37. Is the wife pregnant now? _____

38 When you were growing up did your (or your spouse's) parents or step-parents have any serious marital difficulties? _____

39. Did they ever separate or get a divorce? _____

40. If so, how old were you (or your spouse) at the time? _____

41. Who was the first person other than your spouse with whom you discussed your marital problems (parents, relative, minister, attorney, doctor, neighbor, etc.)? _____

42. Have you or your spouse ever sought professional counseling for this marriage? _____ (yes/no) If so, specify from whom (psychiatrist, psychologist, clergyman, licensed marriage counselor, social worker) _____

43. For how long? _____

44. What do you feel is wrong with this marriage? _____

_____

45. Would you like counseling? _____ (yes / no)

Date _____ _____ (Petitioner/Respondent)
                           (Signature)

Trying to save a marriage

The form at left shows how the courts attempt to preserve marriages in California, where they are simple to dissolve (one of the state's two grounds for dissolution is "irreconcilable differences" between the partners). The form is designed to elicit answers that will draw a profile, so to speak, of the marriage and pinpoint some of the reasons for its troubles. A key question is number 45, "Would you like counseling?" If the answer is "yes," the court schedules a meeting between the troubled husband and wife and a marriage counselor in the hope that such aid will enable the couple to resume life together.

band drank, stayed out late and verbally abused both her and the children. The husband denied that he had done any of these things often or that he meant to be cruel. The judge found that while the husband's behavior was far from ideal, it was not maliciously intended, and the suit was dismissed. In the other case, a husband won a divorce when he produced as evidence a number of lengthy notes his wife had written him over a period of five years. These communications were, in the words of his complaint, "vituperative" and "couched in terms of vulgarity." Had the notes been written in "hot blood," the judge said, they would have been a less serious matter; but since they had been written with obvious deliberation, at length and over a period of years, they indicated, on the wife's part, "such utter contempt for her husband as to constitute an indignity."

Another ground for divorce that virtually all states recognize is adultery. Circumstantial evidence of the defendant's guilt is usually sufficient. The courts apply a test for "inclination and opportunity." If a detective hired by a suspicious wife testifies that he saw her husband meet another woman in a hotel, that they registered as man and wife, and that he watched them go to a room they did not leave until the next morning, this testimony would very likely convince the judge that the husband had not been playing checkers.

The husband has several possible defenses. One is to deny the allegation. If, in fact, he had been in another city on the night in question and if he can produce a receipted hotel bill and perhaps a sworn statement from a business associate in that city, he can probably persuade the judge that the detective had followed the wrong man.

His second defense, if circumstances warrant it, can be something the law calls condonation. Suppose he had previously committed adultery and his wife knew it but nevertheless had allowed him back into their home and indeed into her bed. Such forgiveness rules out a divorce for adultery suit. "You may not copulate by night and litigate by day" is the way one judge summed up the law's attitude toward a spouse who condoned misconduct.

Condonation is one of four ways by which, in most states, a divorce action may be stopped. The other three are:

■ Connivance. One spouse may not deliberately plot to create grounds for a divorce action against the other. A husband who hired a detective and connived with him not just to shadow his wife but to seduce her, and who then sought to divorce her for adultery, would have his case tossed out of court.

■ Recrimination. If a husband and wife are equally guilty of misbehavior, neither can get a divorce. Suppose he has treated her so badly over the years that she seeks solace with another man. Learning of the adultery, the husband sues for divorce. But the wife does not want a divorce and fights back, offering proof of his cruelty to her, saying, in effect, "If I'm guilty, so is he." She is thus recriminating—accusing in return. Theoretically, this case, too, would get short shrift from a court. In many states, however, a judge may weigh guilt and decide in favor of the spouse more harmed.

■ Collusion. A judge can dismiss a divorce action—whatever the grounds on which it is brought—if he has valid reasons to believe that the couple before him have conspired to proffer false evidence.

As a practical matter, none of these four bars to divorce action is raised very often. Judges increasingly refuse to apply the doctrine of recrimination, for example, because they tend to regard as barbaric the notion of keeping two people locked in a marriage so empty that it has led both to misbehave.

But the principal reason these bars to divorce are not invoked very often seems to be that they are seldom necessary. If either spouse wishes to block a divorce, he or she can raise formidable obstacles (and gain considerable bargaining power) simply by refusing to cooperate in the action. In a broad sense, therefore, all U.S. divorces can be said to fit into one of two categories: hard or easy, depending on whether the partners decide to clash or cooperate.

The uncontested divorce

Usually, an uncontested divorce suit will glide through its day in court without so much as a ripple. Take, for example, the case of Greta and Bill. Both are achingly unhappy in their marriage. What sexual attraction they had for each other in their early years together has long since faded; they have few interests in common. Worse still, everything one of them does irritates the other, and this mutual rubbing-raw has erupted from time to time in vicious verbal battles. Twice Bill, in his fury and frustration, has slapped Greta.

Life together has become a torment, and they decide to get a divorce. Their respective lawyers draw up a settlement that satisfies them both, and they sign it. The lawyers then huddle to decide on the next step: Who will divorce whom and on what grounds? Greta and Bill live in a state where the legal grounds for divorce are incurable insanity, long-term imprisonment, desertion, adultery, and physical or mental cruelty. Neither Greta nor Bill is insane or in jail, neither has run off for a year (the period that usually constitutes legal desertion) and neither has committed adultery. So the ground of cruelty is left. Will it be physical or mental?

The lawyers mull this over. Mental cruelty is plausible; Greta and Bill did say some cruel and cutting things in those verbal battles. But the lawyers are aware that many judges remain unmoved by a plea of mental cruelty unless it is backed up by strong evidence, such as a doctor's testimony that the stress produced by the cruelty has brought on some nervous disorder. Greta and Bill are indeed depressed and jumpy, but neither is certifiably ill. So the lawyers settle on physical cruelty—those hard slaps Bill gave Greta. This means, of course, that she will be the one to sue for divorce.

When the day arrives for the hearing before a judge, Greta's lawyer rises and asks her a series of questions, eliciting the information that her husband "struck her repeatedly and viciously," that these blows caused her both physical pain and great mortification, and that they also caused her to be temporarily disfigured, her face having been badly swollen. The lawyer elicits a further statement from Greta that Bill's violent temper makes her afraid to go on living in the same house with him. The lawyer then calls a witness, Greta's next-door neighbor and best friend. Responding to questions, this woman states that she was aware that Bill and Greta fought—she could hear their arguments—and that she also knew that Bill had struck Greta.

All these statements by Greta and her witness are phrased in a way to make Bill seem far more a villain than he really is. But he and his lawyer offer no challenge to Greta's case. And this is the key to the proceeding. Because Bill remains silent, the judge is obliged to base his ruling on Greta's statements. And what she has charged does constitute cruelty: Legally it is cruelty for a husband to strike his wife. So the judge enters a decree of divorce and Greta and Bill are legally parted. The hearing has lasted only about half an hour.

This proceeding seems absurdly easy and even a bit shady. Bill and Greta, as well as their lawyers, know that it was not Bill's slapping of Greta that caused the marital breakdown, but a subtle tangle of emotional maladjustments, to not one of which a label like cruelty could honestly be attached. But this is the way the law works in those states—most of the 50—where divorce is still regarded as an adversary procedure, with the "innocent" party accusing the "guilty" party of some legally recognized form of marital wrongdoing.

The contested divorce

The ease with which Greta and Bill shed their marital ties is in sharp contrast to the difficulties that beset another couple, Frances and Tom, in a typical case of contested divorce.

Frances and Tom are also unhappy in their marriage. As she sees

it, he is lazy, never helps around the house, spends all his spare time drinking with friends or playing golf; even more, she resents Tom's mother, a natural busybody who has turned into a nosy mother-in-law. Tom, for his part, cannot bear his wife's outbursts of temper; he feels so wretched that he seeks psychiatric help. In time the situation at home deteriorates to the point that Tom moves out, hires a lawyer and prepares to sue for divorce.

Frances believes a divorce is necessary, but she is determined to protect her own interests. She, too, gets a lawyer, and tells him she would need at least $10,000 a year to support herself and their four-year-old son; she also wants a guarantee that when the boy reaches school age Tom will pay the tuition at a private school. Her lawyer communicates these terms to Tom's lawyer, who is then told by Tom that he makes about $16,000 a year after taxes and that he can afford to give Frances at most about $7,000. He points out that she has had a college education and can work and earn. He also says that he cannot guarantee his son's tuition at today's private school costs. The child will have to go to public school.

The two lawyers try to arrive at a compromise, but Frances sticks to her figure of $10,000, saying that she will not cooperate in getting a divorce unless Tom gives in. And here is the crux of the matter: Her threat to contest the suit before a judge is enough to stymie the whole process. Tom does not have good enough legal grounds for a divorce if Frances chooses to fight the case in court. It was Tom who moved out of the house, so Frances has as much right to obtain a divorce as Tom does. He might use the ground of mental cruelty, pleading that her temper tantrums drove him to a psychiatrist, but most judges would not sustain this charge unless Frances did not answer it.

The case, obviously, is at an impasse without even having gone to court. But what if the circumstances were slightly different and the matter did reach court? Suppose that Frances not only had occasional fits of temper but also insulted Tom in public; threw plates and cups at him, once gashing him on the forehead; and drove him to such depression that his doctor had feared he might commit suicide. If all

Divorce through "cruelty"

If a wife claims to her lawyer that her husband beat her, and the husband and his lawyer agree not to contest her claim, the courts in most states will award the wife a divorce. It does not matter if the wife is built like a lady wrestler and the husband is a milquetoast. Such uncontested divorces on the ground of cruelty, either physical or mental, make up the great majority of all the divorces awarded in the United States.

TEXT CONTINUES ON PAGE 60

A GUIDE TO DIVORCE LAWS

The legal conditions for terminating a marriage vary confusingly from state to state. As the table below shows, almost all states grant divorces for adultery, but only three recognize attempted murder of a spouse as adequate grounds. Most states insist that one partner

STATE	Residence requirement (a)	Sexual incapacity	Adultery	Cruelty	Habitual drunkenness or drug use	Nonsupport	Desertion	Conviction of a felony	Life imprisonment	Postmarital insanity	Lengthy separation	Some other grounds for divorce
ALABAMA	1 year	●	●	●	●	●	●	●	●	●		Wife pregnant at marriage by another man without husband's knowledge
ALASKA	1 year	●(b)	●	●	●	●	●	●		●		Incompatibility
ARIZONA	1 year	●(b)	●	●	●	●	●	●			●	Wife pregnant at marriage by another man without husband's knowledge; willful neglect
ARKANSAS	3 months	●(b)	●	●	●	●	●	●	●	●	●	Bigamy
CALIFORNIA	6 months	California has replaced divorce with "Dissolution of Marriage." The only ground besides postmarital insanity is "irreconcilable differences."										
COLORADO	1 year	●(b)	●	●	●	●	●	●		●	●	
CONNECTICUT	1 year		●	●	●		●		●	●	●	Fraud in obtaining marriage
DELAWARE	2 years		●	●	●	●	●	●	●	●	●	Incompatibility; bigamy; either partner underage at marriage
DIST. OF COL.	1 year		●				●	●			●	
FLORIDA	6 months	Florida has replaced divorce with "Dissolution of Marriage," which is granted when the marriage is irretrievably broken, or one of the partners is mentally incompetent for three years.										
GEORGIA	6 months	●(b)	●	●	●		●	●		●		Wife pregnant at marriage by another man without husband's knowledge; use of fraud or duress in obtaining marriage
HAWAII	1 year		●	●	●	●	●		●	●	●	Expiration of separate maintenance decree without reconciliation
IDAHO	6 weeks		●	●	●	●	●	●		●	●	Willful neglect for one year
ILLINOIS	1 year	●	●	●	●		●	●				Veneral disease; bigamy; attempt to take life of spouse with poison or some other means showing malice
INDIANA	1 year	●(b)	●	●	●	●	●	●		●		
IOWA	1 year	Iowa has replaced divorce with "Dissolution of Marriage," which is granted when the marriage relationship has broken down and there is no reasonable likelihood that it can be restored.										
KANSAS	6 months		●	●	●	●	●	●	●	●		Gross neglect; incompatibility
KENTUCKY	1 year	●	●	●	●		●	●		●	●	Wife pregnant at marriage by another man without husband's knowledge; use of force or duress in obtaining the marriage
LOUISIANA	2 years		●				●			●		
MAINE	6 months	●	●	●	●	●	●		●			
MARYLAND	1 year	●(b)	●				●	●		●	●	Marriage invalid because of bigamy, incest or similar reason
MASSACHUSETTS	2 years	●	●	●	●	●	●	●	●			
MICHIGAN	1 year	As of January 1, 1972, the sole ground for divorce in Michigan is proof that the marriage has broken down and there is no reasonable likelihood that it can be restored.										
MINNESOTA	1 year	●	●	●	●		●		●	●	●	
MISSISSIPPI	1 year	●	●	●	●		●		●	●		Wife pregnant at marriage by another man without husband's knowledge; mental incapacity at marriage; bigamy
MISSOURI	1 year	●(b)	●	●	●		●	●				Wife pregnant at marriage by another man without husband's knowledge; personal indignities; vagrancy of husband; bigamy

prove the other guilty of a specific fault, such as desertion, cruelty or drunkenness, while a few allow the broad ground of incompatibility. And several have gone all the way in adopting liberal "no-fault divorce" laws, under which no wrongdoing need be proved in order to dissolve a marriage. Even where the acceptable grounds are similar, the details vary—lengthy separation can lead to divorce in many states, for instance, but the required duration is one year in the District of Columbia, 10 years in Rhode Island.

STATE	Residence requirement (a)	Sexual incapacity	Adultery	Cruelty	Habitual drunkenness or drug use	Nonsupport	Desertion	Conviction of a felony	Life imprisonment	Postmarital insanity	Lengthy separation	Some other grounds for divorce
MONTANA	1 year		•	•	•	•	•	•		•		Willful neglect for one year
NEBRASKA	2 years	•(b)	•	•	•	•	•		•	•		
NEVADA	6 weeks	•(b)	•	•	•	•	•	•		•	•	Incompatibility
NEW HAMPSHIRE	1 year	•	•	•	•	•	•	•		•		
NEW JERSEY	1 year		•				•			•		Incompatibility
NEW MEXICO	1 year	•	•	•	•	•	•	•		•		Wife pregnant at marriage by another man without husband's knowledge; incompatibility
NEW YORK	2 years		•	•			•	•			•	
NORTH CAROLINA	6 months	•(b)	•						•	•	•	Wife pregnant at marriage by another man without husband's knowledge
NORTH DAKOTA	1 year	•	•	•	•	•	•	•		•		Willful neglect for one year
OHIO	1 year	•	•	•	•	•		•			•	Fraud; bigamy
OKLAHOMA	6 months	•	•	•	•	•	•	•		•		Incompatibility; wife pregnant at marriage by another man without husband's knowledge; fraud
OREGON	1 year	•(b)	•	•			•	•		•		
PENNSYLVANIA	1 year	•(b)	•	•			•	•				Sterility; fraud; bigamy; use of fraud or duress in contracting marriage; personal indignities
RHODE ISLAND	2 years	•(b)	•	•	•	•	•		•		•	Marriage invalid because of bigamy, incest or similar reasons
SOUTH CAROLINA	1 year		•	•	•		•	•			•	
SOUTH DAKOTA	1 year		•	•	•	•	•	•				Willful neglect for one year
TENNESSEE	1 year	•(b)	•	•	•	•	•	•			•	Wife pregnant at marriage by another man without husband's knowledge; bigamy; attempted murder of spouse
TEXAS	1 year		•	•			•	•		•	•	Divorce granted without regard to fault when marriage has become insupportable
UTAH	3 months	•(b)	•	•	•	•	•	•		•	•	Willful neglect
VERMONT	6 months		•			•	•	•		•	•	Intolerable severity
VIRGINIA	1 year	•(b)	•				•	•	•		•	Wife pregnant at marriage by another man without husband's knowledge; sexual perversion
WASHINGTON	6 months	•	•	•	•	•	•	•		•	•	Mental incapacity at marriage; fraud; use of force or duress in obtaining marriage; either partner underage at marriage
WEST VIRGINIA	2 years		•	•	•		•	•		•		
WISCONSIN	2 years		•	•	•	•		•			•	
WYOMING	60 days	•(b)	•	•	•	•	•	•		•	•	Wife pregnant at marriage by another man without husband's knowledge; personal indignities; vagrancy of husband

(a) Requirements may be altered in some states, depending on grounds for divorce and where the couple were married.

(b) This ground is accepted only if the condition existed at the time of marriage.

this were true, Tom would seem to have firm grounds for divorce. He and his lawyer would therefore go to court and present these charges of physical and mental cruelty. But Frances and her lawyer would also appear in court; they would present evidence and witnesses not only to refute Tom's charges but to show that the marriage had gone on the rocks because of his behavior rather than his wife's.

What would be the outcome? It would depend on the judge and his evaluation of the evidence. If the judge concluded that Tom had proved his case, Tom would get a divorce. Otherwise—no divorce.

The migratory divorce

Many people, impatient with the difficulties of divorce procedures at home, have sought quick release from unhappy marriages by obtaining migratory divorces in other countries or other states. The Mexican divorce mills were shut down in 1970 by the national government, but their place was quickly taken by complaisant courts in Caribbean countries. And three of the 50 states—Nevada, Idaho and Wyoming—have rather relaxed divorce laws. In these states the statute most alluring to incoming divorce-seekers is the brief residency requirement. A newcomer need live for only six weeks in Nevada and Idaho, only 60 days in Wyoming, to qualify as a legal resident and thus acquire the right to bring a divorce suit in a local court; the judge will usually hand down the divorce decree as soon as the residency requirement has been fulfilled.

Speed and simplicity are the principal advantages of the migratory divorce. Anyone using it faces the same legal perils that exist in the home state if the partner to the divorce fails to cooperate. Assume that a wife goes to Nevada, stays for six weeks, swears that she intends to settle in the state, and takes all the other necessary legal steps to a divorce. Her husband does not want a divorce, but he neither appears in the Nevada court to contest the case nor hires a Nevada lawyer to appear on his behalf. When the time comes for the decree, the judge hands it down to the wife alone. The result is that she possesses a so-called ex parte, or one-sided, divorce. The danger of such a decree is that her husband can ask a court in their home state to set aside the divorce; the court may do so if he can prove that his wife's claim of legal residence in Nevada was not valid. In short, an ex parte decree may be worthless if challenged in a court of the home state.

But if there were cooperation between the husband and wife, a valid out-of-state decree could be obtained. The husband in this case would have to be persuaded to sign a paper indicating that he recognizes and submits to the Nevada court proceedings. If he signs this agreement, he could not later move to invalidate the divorce decree, since he had participated in the divorce proceeding, even if his only participation was a written statement.

The movement for divorce reform

In 1969 California and Iowa chose to cut through many of the legal complications that attend divorce elsewhere and instituted the so-called no-fault divorce. Since then other states have followed their lead and reformed their divorce laws along similar lines.

California actually banished the word divorce, replacing "divorce decree" with "dissolution of marriage decree." And it reduced the grounds for dissolving a marriage to only two: incurable insanity and, to quote the state's Civil Code, "irreconcilable differences, which have caused the irremediable breakdown of the marriage." When one partner in a marriage in California wants a divorce, there is no longer any need for the process in which one spouse accuses the other of having been guilty of cruelty, adultery or other wrongdoing. One party merely asserts—or both assert—that there are "substantial reasons for not continuing the marriage." No fault of any sort need be proved.

TWO MAJOR CONSEQUENCES OF DIVORCE

Two basic questions usually arise in the course of a marital breakup: Who is to get the custody of the children, and how much money is the husband to pay to support them and their mother? The resolution of these issues is likely to follow the pattern of the breakup itself. They may be settled amicably, at the time of a legal separation or a divorce, if the couple are cooperative. If there is an argument or if the terms seem unfair, the issues are adjudicated in court. Occasionally they engender enough bitterness to last well beyond the granting of the divorce decree, in some cases entailing years of wrangling and litigation.

Custody arrangements

The laws that concern custody and support are less the doing of legislators than of judges deciding individual cases on their own merits. Usually the care of the children—especially if they are young—is entrusted to the mother. The exceptions occur in cases in which the mother simply does not want to care for the children; in which she is physically or mentally incapable of doing so; or in which the father can prove, to the court's satisfaction, that she is morally unfit to do so. Splitting custody rights between the parents, when several children are involved, is seldom approved by the courts. They usually decline further to divide a family that is already breaking up.

Not only does the mother generally win custody of all the children, she is also usually awarded sole control of them, on the theory that it is better for them to have a single source of day-to-day authority. Sometimes, however, through a compromise the mother gets control of routine affairs but agrees to consult with the father on such major matters as a choice of schools. Sometimes, too, an arbitration clause is added, providing that when the parents cannot agree on a major decision, a neutral party—the family doctor, perhaps, or an old friend—has the power to step in and settle the question.

The father is customarily awarded visitation rights. Legally he has the right to be with his children at regular intervals. Fathers who live near their children usually have the right to their company on either Saturday or Sunday of every weekend, as well as on some holidays and for a modest amount of summer vacation time. Fathers who live at a distance may arrange instead for a summer-long holiday with the youngsters.

Financial settlements

A few states will force a wealthy woman to pay alimony to her ex-husband if he is disabled. Such action is the exception. Everywhere but in a few states the man can be required to pay his ex-wife alimony if she demands it, whether or not they have children. If they do have children, he must provide added sums for their support. How much he pays varies with the circumstances; generally, however, courts decline to order a man to give his ex-wife and children more than half of his income. He must provide some measure of alimony and support even if the ex-wife has considerable inherited wealth, or if she is employed and earning a good salary. By getting married, the courts have ruled, the man undertook the duty of support, and he cannot evade the obligation by getting divorced. Moreover, many alimony agreements contain an "escalator clause." If a man's salary goes up significantly, his ex-wife receives a specified percentage of the increase. Recently, however, judges have tended to award smaller amounts of alimony than formerly if the woman involved is wealthy or able to work. Today the women's liberation movement has influenced increasing numbers of ex-wives to refuse any alimony at all on the ground that it would keep them in a dependent status.

Alimony usually ceases if the woman remarries; support of children does not. The father must continue to send whatever money he guaranteed them until they reach 21, or, as this clause often reads, until they achieve "the B.A. degree."

But many states also allow the payment of a lump sum in lieu of alimony. Women with children sometimes take the family home and forego alimony. This kind of arrangement may cover not only the house, but also the car, furniture, stocks and bonds—any material goods. In the case of objects that both partners want to keep, lawyers usually arrange a compromise: The controversial item is sold and the proceeds are split. Such settlements are always made in the eight states with community property laws. In these states—Arizona, California, Idaho, Louisiana, Nevada, New Mexico, Texas and Washington—all the property a husband and wife together have accumulated while married is split 50-50 (for more on community property, see Chapter 12). Settlements have been known to include clauses specifying that the woman will keep the family dog, while the man retains the right to a pair of hard-to-get season tickets to pro football games. Judges care little, however, for these details. The main concern of the law is to see to it that the woman and children, if any, live in reasonable comfort, while the man retains enough possessions, savings and income to maintain himself properly.

What happens if the man refuses to pay alimony or any of the sums he has promised in a financial agreement? His ex-wife has several recourses. She can garnish the husband's salary—that is, secure a court order to have part of his salary paid to her. Or if he defaults on a court-arranged settlement she can ask the court to issue a contempt citation against him. The ex-wife also has a weapon if the man goes to another state and stops sending her support. This weapon is the Uniform Reciprocal Enforcement of Support Act, adopted in some form by all the states. The woman goes to court in her home state and complains of the ex-husband's failure to pay. The court then gets in touch with officials in the state where the man now lives. They in turn track him down; if he does not send the funds he owes his ex-wife, he can be held in contempt of court.

THE RIGHTS AND DUTIES OF HUSBANDS AND WIVES

It sometimes seems that society focuses its attention on the family unit only when a family is in the process of dissolving. But society —and hence its legal system—maintains a keen interest in families that do not have the slightest intention of breaking up. How husbands and wives behave toward each other, what obligations they owe each other—these and a number of related matters are set out in a large sector of the field of family law.

On many aspects of home life, the law has little to say. How you pass your time, how you spend or save your money, what religion (if any) you practice—all these matters are very much your own business. But when major domestic difficulties arise, the law may find it necessary to step in to help resolve them.

A husband and wife are expected to live in the same house, and under normal circumstances it is the husband who has the right to decide where they will live. If a husband's firm assigns him to a branch office in Amsterdam, his wife has a legal duty to accompany him even if she detests the prospect of trying to run an American household in Europe. If she refuses to go along, she is guilty of desertion. The law, however, is not inflexible. If she bases her refusal on solid grounds such as health—her doctor testifying, for example, that Amsterdam's damp climate would aggravate an already painful sinus condition—she need not accompany her husband. Moreover, a husband cannot force his wife to move to a completely alien environment. If he suddenly chooses to throw up his job and insists on moving the family from Chicago to a fisherman's shack in the Louisiana bayous or an igloo in the frozen north, he may be the one charged with desertion. A wife need not submit to an unreasonable shift in the family's way of life.

Wherever the home is located, the wife is its undisputed mistress. The husband cannot move his mother in and allow her to dominate the household. Should he do so, the wife can move out without risking a charge of desertion. The husband also has no legal right to compel his wife to move in with his parents simply because he thinks it is a good way to save money. If he is financially able to provide it, she can insist on a home of her own.

Supporting her in the style . . .

Perhaps the most fundamental of all laws governing the family is that a husband must support his wife. He must provide food, clothing, shelter and, when needed, medical care. If a husband refuses to do so and

A husband normally decides where a family will live—but he cannot force his wife to move to an alien environment. If he gives up his job and heads for an igloo in the frozen north, his wife can refuse to go.

Though a wife is entitled to receive financial support from her husband, she may not go through his pockets to get it—or so the law says.

is not himself destitute, the wife may get a court to force him to furnish these essentials. (She cannot, however, go through his pockets and help herself to his money.)

Not only must the husband provide, but he must do so to the best of his ability. A man who is manifestly well off must provide a more comfortable life for his wife than a man of meager means. To measure the required degree of comfort, lawyers and judges employ the term necessaries, which depend on social and economic position. The necessaries called for by a husband's particular station in life are what he must legally provide.

Two actual cases will illustrate how judges interpret this concept. A New York millionaire concluded that it would be best for his children if he adopted a spartan mode of life. He installed his family in a modest apartment in a decent but unfashionable part of the city. He refused his children riding and dancing lessons and sent them to public rather than to private school. Life seemed so austere, considering his wealth, that in time his wife sued to force him to provide her and the children with a more stylish and expensive residence. She lost her case. The court maintained that no matter how rich a husband may be, he is not required to give his family a luxurious existence so long as the comforts he does provide are in keeping with the mode of life he has chosen. In the second case, the man's own living style was different—and so was the judge's decision. This man belonged to several swank clubs and also entertained frequently in his lavish 20-room house. Furs and jewels, the court decided, were necessaries for the wife of someone who maintained such a station in life, and the judge ordered the husband to pay for a diamond necklace and a mink coat his wife had bought.

The right to consortium

In the complex relationship between husband and wife there is no more important mutually enjoyed legal right than what is referred to in legal parlance as consortium, the conjugal fellowship of husband

and wife. It gives one spouse the right to "the person, affection, society and assistance" of the other spouse—the mixture of romantic and practical attention that most husbands and wives expect from each other. But consortium has precise legal applications.

First, a husband is as legally entitled to the domestic services of his wife as he is to her "affection and person." She is responsible, on a day-to-day basis, for seeing to the cooking, the dish-washing, the cleaning, the bed-making and so on. The husband is not obliged to pay his wife for performing these tasks. This point of law is so firmly established that courts will not honor even a voluntary agreement by a husband to pay his wife for housework. A Texan promised to leave his wife an extra $5,000 in his will—over and above the half of the estate she was entitled to by state law—if she would continue to do all the usual household tasks until his death. She complied and after his death sued his estate for the additional money he had promised her. The court, however, held that the contract was unenforceable because the law did not require remuneration for duties the wife was legally expected to perform anyway.

A husband's right to his wife's consortium is so basic that he may institute legal proceedings against any third party who, even inadvertently, deprives him of her company and services. Let us say that Mrs. Anderson is seriously injured as the result of an automobile accident caused by another driver's negligence. The negligent driver is liable for the harm he has done Mrs. Anderson. But he may also be liable for damages to her husband. Even though Mr. Anderson was not hurt, he can expect to be reimbursed for the loss of his wife's consortium. He now needs a housekeeper to do the normal chores that Mrs. Anderson cannot do while she is recuperating. And he may also be able to place a monetary value on his own "anguish" and "inconvenience," as well as on the loss of his wife's physical companionship—a factor in consortium—and add this sum to the damages.

Until recently consortium suits were brought only by husbands. Increasingly, however, the law has tended to recognize the wife's equal right in this regard. A New York court, for example, awarded a wife damages for loss of consortium after her husband had been paralyzed from the waist down in an elevator accident.

The duties and rights of a working wife

A husband who owns a small business can ask his wife to work for him —and without salary, for the law considers it part of her duty to pitch in and help. The husband would, however, be far wiser if he paid his wife a salary, and not just to ensure family harmony. Should she be in-

A wife has the right to any money she earns working at an outside job and can save or spend it as she wishes. A husband, of course, remains legally obliged to support his wife even if she does work.

jured while working for her husband, she would not be able to collect disability payments under the Workmen's Compensation Act or under the Social Security Act—unless she were a salaried employee.

While a husband can ask his wife to work in his business without pay, he has no claim on money she earns from an outside job. Under law the paycheck is hers, to save or spend as she sees fit.

A wife's property

Just as a wife has a right to her outside earnings, so she has a right to own and control her own property. This may seem an outrageous statement of the obvious in an era in which the issue of women's equality has flared anew, but it was not always true. In times past, a woman who married automatically gave over her property to her husband, in return for his support; in this sense she was at a clear disadvantage compared to an unmarried sister, who—simply because she did stay single —was permitted to hang on to her share of a parental inheritance and any other assets she had.

Although many aspects of common law have stood the test of time, this one has not. During the 19th Century every state in the union passed a series of Married Women's Property Acts, allowing a wife to retain ownership of any property she possessed before she married; in most states a woman also owns outright any property she acquires while married; however, in community property states all property acquired during a marriage by husband and wife together belongs equally to both. The Married Women's Property Acts were the first great milestones on the road to women's equality, precursors both of the constitutional amendment of 1919, which gave women the right to vote, and of the 1964 Federal Civil Rights Act, which forbade any form of discrimination against them because of their sex. By a curious turn of events, the fact that a wife has full ownership and control of her own property is now being used by more militant women's liberationists as an argument for relieving a husband of his legal obligation of support—an argument in which some legal experts concur. As one scholar puts it, the husband is now deprived of the "ancient cloak" provided by his wife's property but still has "the same stony road to traverse."

However this argument may ultimately be resolved, the Married Women's Property Acts inspired a number of laws and court decisions that granted a wife a broad variety of rights—the right to make contracts, engage in business, be employed, keep outside earnings —and legal independence as well. She can sue, or be sued, on her own. If she wins a suit, whatever money she recovers is hers. If she loses a suit, any damages the court orders her to pay must come from her own bank account. Moreover, a husband is not liable for damage judgments against his wife unless the harm done was partly his fault.

Since a wife's property is strictly her own, it remains beyond the reach of her husband's creditors. If he runs into financial difficulties, they can attach his assets—his bank account, his stocks and bonds, even his house. But they cannot touch his wife's property; it is for this reason that husbands—particularly those who are in businesses that make them vulnerable to large damage suits—sometimes transfer substantial amounts of family assets from their personal ownership to their wives'. Obviously, however, the transfer must be made before a suit appears likely or the court may suspect fraud.

A wife may "convey" her own property in any way she chooses; that is, she can sell it, leave it in a will or give it to her child, friend or anyone else. But she cannot turn it over temporarily to her husband —and always be sure of getting it back. The reason becomes clear if we take a simple example. Mary transfers a considerable amount of her property to her husband John so that he can invest her money wisely and generally look after her financial interests. Then John dies suddenly, without having had a chance to transfer Mary's property back to her, and without having executed a will. Under the laws of their state, Mary would inherit only a third of the estate. But two thirds of the property in John's name was really Mary's to begin with. If Mary had evidence that she had transferred the property to her husband only so that he could act as a trustee of it, the court might set aside the transfer. However, if her evidence were not convincing—for example, if only an unwitnessed oral agreement existed between them—the property might well be considered an outright gift.

Can husbands and wives sue each other?

At one time a wife could not sue her husband for damages, nor could he sue her. While a hired workman who tripped on a loose step in their house and fell down the cellar stairs had a good case against the husband for his negligence in failing to repair the faulty step, the wife injured in exactly the same way could not sue. The legal principle dates back to the era when the law accepted the Judeo-Christian concept that a man and woman become one flesh when they marry; if they were one flesh, then they were a single person—and no person can sue himself. The principle has survived partly because of the belief that suits between husbands and wives would lead to bitterness and breakups, but it is now often ignored.

A similar legal principle that has developed over the centuries holds that husbands and wives cannot be compelled to testify against each other in court. Many states regard private communication between husbands and wives as privileged—legally exempt from being divulged—and so no court can order a husband or wife to reveal something one learned from the other. But of course either can testify in court in support of a suit the other has brought—for example, to confirm an account of an accident in which their car was damaged.

The right not to have children
Beyond the rights and duties of husbands and wives toward each other are the responsibilities they take on when they raise a family, for the law has a good deal to say about how parents must treat their children. It has also begun, in recent years, to express itself on the problems of couples who may want children—but not just yet.

In 1965 the Supreme Court ruled that no state had the right to tell husbands and wives that they could not use artificial contraceptive devices; in every state, married people can now buy contraceptives, use them and obtain advice from doctors or clinics on the most suitable and reliable kinds, without incurring the danger of running afoul of the law.

As to abortion, however, the legal situation is far from uniform. Controversy still rages—not only among churchmen but among state lawmakers—over the question of whether a woman should be permitted to get an abortion when she wants one. As of 1971, two states —New York and Hawaii—had concluded that she should be. Hawaii's law stipulates that the patient must be a resident of the state for 90 days before the operation can be performed, but New York has no residency requirement. For many years, a number of states have permitted abortions if pregnancy is the result of rape or incest, or if a doctor testifies that continued pregnancy will prove fatal to the mother. And more recently many states have passed abortion reform laws that considerably liberalize these rules without making abortions available on demand.

THE OBLIGATIONS OF PARENTHOOD
As soon as a married couple do have children, they become involved in a new area of domestic relations law—their duties and responsibilities as parents. Initially, however, only two simple legal requirements are imposed on a couple who become what the law calls the natural or biological parents of a baby.

All states require a child's arrival to be registered with the records office in the community within a few days. If the baby is born in

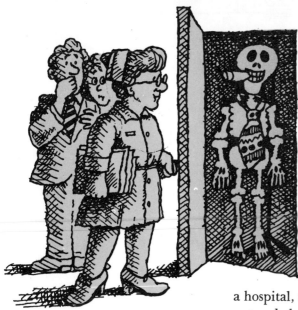

The prospective parents of an adopted child must undergo a careful scrutiny of their manners, morals and home life. If the adoption agency's investigation finds a skeleton in the family closet, it may reject the couple's bid to adopt the child.

a hospital, the hospital usually supplies the form the parents must fill out and also files it with the records office. The parents then get a very official-looking birth certificate from the hospital that suffices in most instances as proof of legal name, age and birthplace. But for some purposes, such as getting a passport, it may not do. In those cases a certified copy of the original file document must be obtained from the county or state records office.

The other legal obligation imposed on parents during the early years of a child's life involves his health. Before he goes to school, the law may require him to have a smallpox vaccination and, in most states, other shots as well.

The complexities of adoption

The law imposes weightier requirements on a couple who decide to adopt a child. The formal adoption proceeding itself is not very complicated: The couple file a petition for adoption with a local court and, if it is approved, they receive a decree of adoption in six to 18 months. They then become the child's parents, and the law views the child as essentially no different from one born to them. But what happens before the petition is filed and what can happen from the filing to the granting of the decree may create legal complexities.

The prospective parents must clear two kinds of legal hurdle before they file a petition for adoption—indeed, even before they have a specific child to adopt. One kind of hurdle is set up by state law; the other, and more difficult, kind takes the form of rulings that the state allows adoption agencies to make and enforce.

Although state laws on adoption differ in detail, they are chiefly concerned with setting a maximum age for each of the would-be parents and with matching the religions of parents and child. Some states —Massachusetts and New York are two—generally restrict the adoption of a child by a couple of a faith different from that of the child's natural mother; other states require preference in adoption to be given to a couple of the same faith as the natural mother's; while still other states—Pennsylvania and Illinois, for example—more liberally interpret the requirement that the religions match.

A couple qualified by state law must still meet the requirements laid down by adoption agencies. Whether these are state-run or private, the fact that they are state-licensed gives them great power. The prospective parents must submit to a searching investigation of their home, habits, manners, income and general stability. If the investigator finds something amiss—anything from too little space to house the adopted child adequately to signs of strain in the marital relationship—the agency will reject a couple's bid for a child. Moreover, agencies are given wide latitude in interpreting state adoption laws. For example, in states that require a matching of religions "when practicable," interpretation of this phrase is usually left up to the agencies. And in New York, where the law is rather vague as to maximum age requirements for would-be parents, the agencies enforce their own view of this matter: Generally, they refuse to entrust an infant to a couple if the wife is over 35, the husband over 40.

Couples who find an agency's rulings too strict or too arbitrary have a legal alternative in most states. They can bypass the agencies and arrange to adopt a child privately. Often such arrangements are sponsored by a doctor or minister—people likely to hear of the existence of an unwanted child. But even if the adoptive parents avoid agency regulations, they must meet the basic qualifications required of them by state law, and they must file an adoption petition with a court, just as they would if the child came via an agency.

Among the papers that must be filed with the petition, the most crucial document is the consent to adoption—also called a surrender or relinquishment—that the natural mother signs when she puts her child up for adoption (if she is or has been married to the child's father, he may have to sign, too). This document is not necessary if the child is a foundling, abandoned by his parents, or if the child has been totally separated from his parents by court order and has thus become a ward of the state. But since about half of all babies eligible for adoption are children given up by unwed mothers, the consent-to-adoption document is of overwhelming importance.

And it is here that many an adoption proceeding begins to founder, for in a number of states the consent to adoption may be legally ruled invalid even if the natural mother has signed it.

Obviously coercion or fraud invalidates a consent. If a natural mother was unduly influenced to give up her baby by, say, a welfare counselor or even by her own family, the court will set aside the consent. A case of fraud might involve a divorcee who finds that she cannot support her small daughter and relinquishes her for adoption without ever trying to contact her ex-husband. The girl is adopted and goes to live with her new parents but a year later the natural father finds out about the matter and objects. He can recover his child on the ground that he was not given notice of the adoption proceeding; his ex-wife's failure to inform him—or to tell the adoption agency that he even existed—constitutes a form of fraud.

In some states, the court may invalidate a consent executed before the baby is born or shortly thereafter—a measure obviously designed to prevent an unwed mother from being pressured at a time of great personal tension. Other states refuse to accept the consent unless a representative of the state department of welfare fully and carefully explained to the mother the seriousness of relinquishing her child. And in a few states the law allows the mother to revoke her consent at any time before the adoptive parents obtain a final decree of adoption from the court. Since at least six months must elapse between the filing of the petition for adoption and the awarding of the final decree, this waiting period gives the mother ample time to reconsider her original decision. It also presents the adoptive parents with the prospect of months of anguished uncertainty. The state laws permitting the revocation of a mother's consent to relinquish her child give rise to the majority of the heart-catching adoption battles that periodically make newspaper headlines.

Although most adoption laws tend to favor the natural mother, all states provide one kind of safeguard for the adoptive parents. Each state assumes responsibility for the normal good health of the children offered for adoption.

The problems of illegitimacy

In past centuries children born out of wedlock could not be legitimized later, nor could they vote or hold office. Now many—though not all—of the social and political disabilities from which the illegitimate person once suffered have been struck down.

Most states provide that a child automatically becomes legitimate if his parents marry after he is born, although some states require that the father publicly acknowledge the child as his. Many states also provide that even if the parents never marry, a child becomes legitimate if the father petitions a court for a judgment of legitimacy. Two states —Arizona and Oregon—have in effect eliminated the entire problem by declaring that all children are automatically legitimate.

Parental obligations toward a child who has not benefited from the legitimizing process have also evolved over the centuries. Today it is the mother who has legal custody of an illegitimate child, and she is bound by law to support him. The father is compelled to contribute if the mother proves in court that he is indeed the father. Occasionally such charges are untrue but difficult to disprove. A man involved in a paternity suit has two defenses aside from simply showing he never knew the mother. One is to convince the jury that she had intercourse with other men at the time the child was conceived. The second is to take a test to compare his blood type with those of the mother and the child—but such tests are rarely definitive. If the child's blood type differs from those of both the mother and the accused man, the man could not have fathered the child. If the child's blood type matches that of either adult, however, the test proves only that the man *might* have fathered the child, not that he did.

One of the rights formerly denied an illegitimate child is the right to sue for damages for the wrongful death of a parent. Nor could a parent sue for damages suffered by the death of an illegitimate child. These restrictions were lifted by two Supreme Court decisions of 1968; in both cases the majority opinion was written by Justice William O. Douglas. In the first case, five illegitimate children had sued a doctor for damages, claiming that his inadequate medical treatment of their mother had led to her "wrongful death." A Louisiana court had denied them the right to recover damages because of their illegitimacy. Justice Douglas held that this decision deprived the five children of the constitutional right of equal protection under the law. In the second case, Douglas asserted the right of a mother to sue for the "wrongful death" of her illegitimate son in an auto accident.

Every state provides one kind of safeguard for adoptive parents—the state assumes responsibility for the normal good health of the children offered for adoption.

One tradition that still holds good, however, concerns the question of inheritance. An illegitimate child has the right to inherit from his mother's estate but not from his father's—unless the father specifically leaves a bequest to the child in his will. If the father dies without having made a will, his illegitimate child—unlike his legitimate children—has no claim on his estate. In part, the law is aimed at discouraging the hordes of people who would pop up every time a rich man died, claim to be his illegitimate offspring and demand their share of his fortune.

Your legal responsibilities to your children

The law's once great concern for the circumstances of a child's birth is now eclipsed by concern for the child's upbringing. Parents' moral obligation to provide basic care and support for underage children is today backed by the full force of the law. What must be provided are the same necessaries a husband must give his wife—food, clothing, housing, medical care when needed, plus one other item, education. If parents willfully fail to provide at least a reasonable minimal level of these things for their children, the state's welfare agencies and courts are empowered to step in and compel them to do so.

Legal action is taken, however, only as a last resort. If an investigator found that parents were failing to provide minimal food, clothing and shelter, either willfully or out of indifference, they would usually be issued a warning. If the neglect continued, the state welfare department could ask a court to remove the child from the parents' care and make him a ward of the state.

The law also considers medical care a necessary. If a parent fails to provide his youngster with even minimal medical attention he might be found guilty of criminal neglect. And if, for religious or any other reasons, a parent refuses to permit needed surgery or blood transfusions, he can be forced to do so by a court order. The parents' legal duty to provide medical care for their children applies even if for some reason they are not present when the need for it arises. If your daughter slips and breaks her ankle while she is alone at home, and a neighbor takes her to the hospital to have the bone set, you are responsible for the medical bills.

This legal principle, in fact, applies to all necessaries. If a neighbor acts *in loco parentis* (literally, in place of the parents) and provides your child with something that you would have provided had you been there, you must shoulder the costs. Suppose that you have gone away on a month's trip, leaving your child with a reliable babysitter. There is a sudden cold snap, the sitter digs your son's warm coat out of the closet and finds that he has outgrown it in the past year. She takes it upon herself to buy the boy a new coat to wear to school. A court might decide that the sitter had the right to do what she did, and that you are responsible for the bill. The same might be true if the sitter had replenished the food supply or made the house more habitable by having the furnace fixed.

As to education, the law requires you to send your children to grade school and high school, at least until the age of 16. If you do not approve of the local public schools, you may send them to a private or parochial school, as long as the school's curriculum is approved by the state's board of education. But what if none of the schools in the community measure up to your own standards? Can you educate your children at home or, as some religious groups have done, set up an independent school? The laws on this subject are mixed. In some states parents who have proved that they are capable teachers and are using approved teaching materials have been allowed to educate their children at home. In other states the courts have ruled that home instruction, however competent, still deprives children of the normal social and intellectual experience of going to a school and mingling with other children.

Some court decisions indicate that a college education is beginning to be considered a legal necessary, if the parents can afford it. One such decision, handed down by a Missouri court in 1959, involved a divorced couple and their daughter. The girl had excelled in painting and art history at high school. She and her mother, with whom she lived, decided that she could better further her art training at Washington University in St. Louis than at the University of Missouri, a state institution where her tuition and fees would have been minimal. And so the mother asked her ex-husband to send the daughter to Washington University, where the considerably higher cost of tuition and other expenses would have led to a sharp rise in the amount of money he was contributing to the girl's support. When he demurred, his ex-wife brought suit. The judge ruled not only that he should send his daughter to college, but that he should send her to the college of her choice. If this case serves as a precedent, it seems probable that, for affluent Americans at least, the money for college will increasingly be assumed to be a child's legal right.

Beyond the necessaries of food, clothing, shelter, medical care and education is a less tangible one that parents are also legally obliged to provide: a household in which the children are safe from physical harm and reasonably free of extreme stresses that can cause psychological damage. The law does not object to spankings, but beating a child severely enough to cause bruises, welts or any other physical injury is a serious criminal offense, punishable by imprisonment. And courts will remove habitually mistreated children from their parents and make the children wards of the state.

The courts can also remove children from parents who are chronic alcoholics or severely disturbed psychologically or given to sexual practices that may impair the morals of a minor. Generally, however, the courts go to great lengths to avoid separating children from their parents except, as one judge put it, for "the gravest reasons." One California court leaned over backward in an action brought by local welfare officials against a couple who had separated to live with new partners without benefit of divorce; each of the women had her own children with her. The welfare authorities sought to have the children removed from the two newly established households on the ground that the adults were living in sin and thus impairing the morals of the youngsters. By the time the case got to court, however, the couple had begun divorce proceedings. Taking this fact into account, the court ruled that both households, no matter how adulterous,

A sporting-goods merchant who sells golf clubs to a juvenile golfer has to refund the money on demand in most states—even if the merchandise has been used by the youngster.

seemed relatively stable, that the mothers were caring properly for the children, and that the youngsters themselves seemed perfectly content despite the unorthodox rearrangement of parental relationships. The children were left with their mothers.

Can you use a child's inheritance?

How is the normal, expense-burdened family going to meet the increasing cost of necessaries the law requires for child care and support? One source of money that sometimes presents itself is an inheritance a child has received from a doting grandfather or maiden aunt. Is it permissible for parents to use this money for college or other expenses?

Usually the law says no, emphatically, and the court generally ties up the funds to prevent unauthorized use. Parents may not use a child's own property (including money they have given him) to help defray the cost of supporting him. Legally, they are only the custodians of their child's money and must turn it over to him intact when he comes of age. There is one exception, however—when the parents cannot pay for the child's necessary expenses. They may then petition the court for permission to dip into the child's inheritance, and the court will probably allow this if the need is shown to be real.

Your legal liabilities for your children

Having children entails not only responsibilities for supporting them, but also certain legal liabilities for their actions. This does not mean you are responsible for everything a child does. When a child gets into one of those accidental scrapes that inevitably attend childhood, it is just that—an accident. For example, if your six-year-old son engaged in a roughhouse with a neighbor's boy and inadvertently knocked out one of the boy's teeth, you would not be obliged to pay for the dental work. The other boy's father must foot the bill; this is one of the responsibilities he incurred by having children. If he was not prepared to pay for such damage, he ought to have kept his son out of the scrimmage. Nor is your son liable for the action, because his conduct is typical of other children of his age.

On the other hand, should a child habitually do something that is potentially dangerous to other children, the parents are legally responsible for supervising him or her. Assume that a 12-year-old girl, a tomboy at heart, makes a practice of fabricating rock-hard snowballs for use in snowball fights. Her father has commented to his friends about this habit but does not stop her. One day one of these frozen missiles connects with a neighbor's daughter, badly injuring an eye. The neighbor has grounds for damages from the father who knowingly allowed his daughter to use such dangerous weapons.

You are also liable for any damage your child does while acting under your instructions. Suppose you have told your son to paint the fence. In his zeal he splatters paint over a neighbor's car parked on the other side of the fence. You are legally obliged to pay for the damage to the car. You, rather than your son, are responsible, since he was acting as your agent *(Chapter 6)*.

A similar point of law is involved if your son decides to make a purchase. If he charges it with your permission, or under your orders, you must pay for it. But let us say your son is a precocious 11-year-old golfer. You and he agree that he needs something better than those women's clubs he has been using. Perhaps on his birthday . . . but then he walks by the local sporting goods store and sees a $75 set of irons in the window. On an impulse he walks in and gets them, assuring the store owner that they can be charged to you. Must you pay for them? The law says no. You can march down to the sporting goods store, compel the merchant to take back the irons and demand that he cancel the charge—even if your son has already used the clubs. However, if he had paid cash for them and then damaged them, in some states the cost of the damages would be deducted from his refund.

The law reads this way to protect minors both from overzealous salesmen and from their own lack of mature judgment. But a minor who can be shown to be capable of exercising mature judgment in a particular situation is not protected from the effects of his actions. Suppose your pint-sized golfer can drive a ball 150 yards; he is so good, in fact, that you do not hesitate to take him out on a Saturday with adult members of your regular foursome. While you are writing down the scores from the last hole your son steps up to the tee of the next hole, a 150-yard par 3, and drives. The ball zooms off and strikes an elderly

A New York court once ruled that a boy who could drive a ball 150 yards was "for all purposes an adult golfer" and liable for the injuries he caused another golfer, even though minors are infrequently held liable for damage claims.

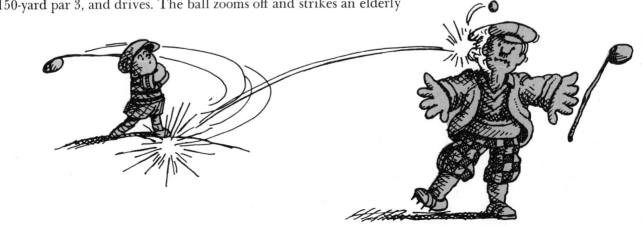

gentleman who is still on the green, trying to sink a putt. The ball your son has whacked strikes this man hard enough to send him to the hospital. Is your son liable for damages? In a case that involved much the same circumstances, a New York court ruled in 1968 that an 11-year-old who could hit the ball 150 yards and play with a grown-up foursome was "for all purposes . . . an adult golfer." In short, he should have had the judgment not to drive when a man was still on the green. The court ordered the boy to pay the damages. If he did not have the money, his father would not have had to pay; the boy would have had to pay the damages as soon as he began earning an income. And the judgment against him would have stood for 20 years.

In this case the judge concluded that—at least as far as golf was concerned—the 11-year-old boy was capable of mature judgment. He would not have been considered capable of it in a situation in which he inadvertently injured another boy while doing something boys ordinarily do, like horsing around in a swimming pool. "The rule," one judge said, "is that a child is only required to exercise that degree of care which the great mass of children of the same age ordinarily exercise under the same circumstances, taking into account the experience, capacity and understanding of the child."

WHAT YOUR CHILD CAN—AND CANNOT—DO LEGALLY

Children, no less than parents, have their rights under the law. They also have what the law calls disabilities—restrictions upon certain actions because of the very fact that they are children. In an era of widespread parental permissiveness and juvenile independence, some of the disabilities may strike parent and child alike as archaic; nevertheless, they are legally enforceable. For example, a child may not choose to live elsewhere than under the parental roof. Neither may he keep his own earnings; these belong to the father, presumably to help ease his legal obligation to support his offspring. All states impose a further injunction upon the young: they cannot undergo medical treatment or surgery without parental consent.

On the other hand, a child has a legal right to own property and to engage in a business enterprise. He or she can also make a contract —but here the party with whom the contract is made must beware and try to evaluate the youngster's sense of responsibility. For in many cases the law gives a child the further right to disavow a contract and back out of even a written agreement.

In recent years, however, the growing economic clout demonstrated by the younger generation has led to curbs on this power of disaffirmance, as it is called. At one time the courts held that in all

instances contracts made by minors for anything other than necessaries were voidable at their whim. Minors can no longer disavow certain types of contracts—for example, those that involve loans for
educational purposes, and those that involve bank accounts. To take
a far-from-rare case, suppose your gadget-mad teen-age daughter drifts
through a department store blithely writing checks for $100 here and
$150 there, all the while aware that her checking account contains
only $68.32. This spending binge is no longer dismissed as a girlish ca-
price; the law now holds her fully liable to the bank for her action.

In considering your child's rights and disabilities under the law,
it is obviously important to know what the law means by childhood.
By classic legal definition the age of childhood ends, and the age of
adulthood begins, on the stroke of midnight of the day before the
21st birthday. But this magic moment is not the deciding point in
every instance. An under-21 child automatically becomes an adult by
the act of entering the armed forces; and in most states he or she
achieves legal maturity by marrying.

In addition, the age of adulthood has been pushed back, by various state laws, for certain specific purposes. The right to marry without parental consent may be granted by some states at the age of 18,
or, if the girl is pregnant, at 16. The right to receive birth-control
counseling or treatment for venereal disease without parental consent is permitted by some states to 18- or 16-year-olds. Some states
have also saddled those under 21 with a serious burden: They have
been made subject to prosecution for adult crimes at 18 or even 16.

The approval in mid-1971 of the 26th Amendment to the U.S.
Constitution, lowering the minimum voting age from 21 to 18, may
have the most far-reaching implications of all. Many lawmakers, having concluded that an 18-year-old is mature enough to vote, believe
that this age, rather than 21, should serve as the basic criterion in the
granting of other adult rights as well.

What if your child leaves home?

A child may become a legal adult much sooner than the law specifies
if he leaves home with his parents' blessing, spoken or implied. He
then has the right to emancipation—that is, elevation to the status of
adulthood—if he meets certain standards of mature conduct.

The concept of legal emancipation for minors is a very old one,
dating back to the Roman Empire, and until modern times a formal
proceeding was required. A father who decided that his 17-year-old
son was man enough to fend for himself would take the youth to
court and make a statement to that effect for the court record. There-

by the son exchanged the rights and disabilities of childhood for the rights and responsibilities of adulthood, while at the same time the father was relieved of the obligation of care and support for the son. Although some states still provide for this procedure, it is no longer much used. Today, a child's claim to legal emancipation is likely to depend on proof of his ability to maintain a residence apart from the parental home, to provide his own economic support, and to do both without hazard to himself or to the surrounding community.

As a practical matter, the need to formally emancipate a child ordinarily arises only when some court action is involved. If, in the course of the proceeding, the judge is persuaded that the child has met the standard criteria, he may then and there pronounce the child legally emancipated. This status, once granted, is permanent.

A child who leaves home without his parents' permission is not emancipated—no matter how well he can fend for himself—but a runaway. And the law will help return the runaway to parental control. The parents may simply report the matter to the police, who will seek the child and return him. If the parents file a runaway complaint in juvenile court, however, the complaint automatically subjects the runaway, once found, to a court hearing. A first offender usually gets off with a reprimand from the judge; a second offender is usually placed on probation. Runaway repeaters may land in a state-operated training school, there to stay until reaching 21 or fulfilling the term imposed by the court.

A child in trouble with the law

A child as young as seven who commits an act that, if committed by an adult, would be a crime can face charges for this act, and all states have set up special juvenile courts to deal with such youngsters. The proceedings are civil rather than criminal, and the objective is to supervise and rehabilitate a child who has gone wrong.

A humanitarian concern was, in fact, the motive force behind the development of separate courts and separate laws for juveniles. This concern arose during the course of the late 19th Century in reaction against a number of horrifying abuses of child offenders—such as the hanging of an eight-year-old boy who had burned some barns —and in an honest desire to promote the welfare of the young. Sometimes the separate system of juvenile justice has worked with humanitarian results—and often it has not.

Take the laws on juvenile delinquency. A typical legal definition of what constitutes delinquency can be very broad indeed. New York state law, for example, defines a delinquent as someone who is so ungovernable that he is beyond parental control, and who also violates a law. Under this definition the habitual truant or runaway can be adjudged delinquent. Many cities, moreover, have ordinances that make it a punishable offense for those under 16, or in some instances under 18, to be on public streets or sidewalks without parental permission after 9 or 10 p.m.

Obviously, it is not difficult for the delinquency laws to be interpreted and enforced capriciously, especially in an era when many American youngsters have turned nomad, restlessly on the move. Often police will pick up a youth whose clothes or long hair they disapprove of and charge him with vagrancy or loitering. Many a juvenile delinquency statute has been resurrected from long disuse in order to keep "undesirables" out of a town.

The juvenile courts, too, have proved capable of error and abuse. When these courts were founded, around the turn of the century, they were meant to spare the youthful offender the rigors of a regular court proceeding. A specially trained judge, backed by a team of social workers and child psychologists, was to sift the facts of the case and determine what would truly be best for the child. There would be no jury, no lawyers, no record kept of the proceedings—which would be conducted more like an informal interview than a trial. But today only a few communities can afford teams of social workers and psychologists, and not all judges have turned out to be kindly, understanding or specially trained. Moreover, in many large cities the juvenile courts are badly overworked; in Washington, D.C., three judges hear an average of 10,000 cases a year—about 14 a day per judge.

What, then, are parents to do when a child gets into trouble with the law? The simple answer: Locate a lawyer as quickly as possible. Even though the juvenile courts often dispense with lawyers, a juvenile suspect has a right to counsel. Further, the parents should make sure that the lawyer is present during what juvenile courts call the "intake" stage, the "fact-finding hearing" and the "dispositional hearing." The child need not admit he did anything. He has the right, guaranteed to all citizens by the Constitution, to remain silent, refusing to give answers that might tend to incriminate him.

The critical importance of obtaining a lawyer for your child in trouble may be illustrated by the now famous case of Gerald Francis Gault. At 15, he was accused by an Arizona neighbor, Mrs. Cook, of having made a lewd telephone call to her. The police picked him up at his home while his parents were out and hustled him before a juvenile court judge. According to Arizona juvenile court custom, there was no jury, no lawyer, no warning against self-incrimination, no transcript of the proceeding. The youth did not even have a chance to face his accuser: Mrs. Cook was not asked to testify. The judge sentenced Gerald on the charge to the Arizona Industrial School until he reached 21—barring parole, a six-year sentence. (Under the Arizona Criminal Code, an adult convicted of having made lewd calls would get no more than two months in jail or a $50 fine.)

Gerald's parents tried to appeal the case but found that Arizona law did not provide for appeals in juvenile cases; with no transcript to study for flaws and errors in the trial, there seemed no basis for an appeal anyway. In time, however, their lawyer obtained a review of the case in the Arizona Supreme Court and ultimately the case reached the U.S. Supreme Court, which passed judgment on it in 1967.

The Court's reaction to the Gault case was strong. The majority opinion was that young Gault had been denied most elements of the basic principle of justice that the law refers to as due process (*Chapter 9*), and that it was intolerable for juvenile suspects not to have some of the safeguards afforded by the law to more mature offenders. Henceforth, the high court ruled, a juvenile tried for an offense that may result in commitment to an institution must have the opportunity to see a lawyer—provided and paid for by the court if the juvenile and his family cannot afford counsel—and he is also entitled to many of the normal legal safeguards of an ordinary trial.

One of these safeguards, however, was not extended in a Supreme Court decision of 1971. It involved a 15-year-old Pennsylvania youth, Joseph McKeiver, one of a group of about 30 boys who were accused of assaulting another boy and taking 25 cents from him. McKeiver and the others were picked up and brought to juvenile court for the usual civil proceeding; had they been adults, they would have had to stand trial in criminal court on charges of robbery and assault. The juvenile court judge placed them all on probation. McKeiver's parents appealed the decision on the ground that the boys had not been given a jury trial. But the Supreme Court denied their appeal, ruling that juvenile courts were originally designed to serve as substitute parents, to advise and counsel rather than pass judgment, and that they therefore did not need to use juries.

Nevertheless, the majority opinion—written by Justice Harry Blackmun—went to some pains to acknowledge that all was not well with the juvenile court system. It recognized that the "fond and idealistic hopes" of those who had founded it three generations ago had not been realized: "Too often," Blackmun noted, "the juvenile court judge falls short of that stalwart protective and communicating figure the system envisaged. . . . The community's unwillingness to provide

people and facilities and to be concerned . . . the scarcity of professional help . . . and our general lack of knowledge all contribute to dis-
satisfaction with the experiment."

THE PROBLEMS OF AGING PARENTS

In stark contrast to the many legal obligations that parents owe children, the legal obligations that grown-up children owe aging parents
are almost nonexistent. In most states so-called family responsibility
laws require over-21 children to assume the support of over-65 parents or grandparents who are indigent. The law also specifies when
and how a child can take charge of a parent's business affairs, assume
legal guardianship of a senile parent and, if necessary, commit him to
the care of an institution.

But by and large the law is mute in this area of family relations.
The necessaries of food, clothing, shelter and medical care, which a
husband must provide his wife and which parents must provide their
minor children, just do not enter into the legal picture as essentials to
be supplied to aged parents by their offspring. A grown son or daughter who chooses not to regard this care and support as a moral obligation cannot be held to legal account either.

The lack of safeguards for the rights of senior members of a family is largely due to a fundamental change in American living and
working habits. Not many decades ago, most Americans earned their
incomes by farming or running modest family businesses. The typical
family lived on a farm or in a small community and included its aged
members as a matter of course. They shared the house with the others, helped out in the fields or barn or shop or kitchen and, when they
grew too old, were tended by their juniors—again, as a matter of
course. No laws seemed needed to govern this arrangement.

Now, however, most Americans live in cities, are salaried employees and reside in apartments or homes not always adequate to
house three generations. At the same time important changes have
come over the oldest generation. Medical advances have made it possible for many more of them to enjoy an extended span of years; the
number of Americans living today who are 65 and over is an unprec-
edented 20 million-plus. Many more of them than in the past pursue
active lives of their own choosing, and many more live alone and like it
—at least until medical or financial disaster strikes.

The law concerning the rights of aged parents—and the elderly
in general—has simply not kept pace with these developments. Of the
laws that do exist, some in fact discriminate against rather than protect people over 65. For example, insurance companies are legally per-

A juvenile in trouble with the law
has the same right to legal
counsel as an adult has. He is
also entitled to many of the
constitutional safeguards of
an adult trial, including the right
to refuse to answer questions.

mitted to deny automobile insurance to older drivers or increase the rates charged. And a federal law that prohibits employers from refusing to hire, or from firing, an employee because of his age, extends this protection only up to age 65. A 64-year-old man who is fired on the sole ground that he is too old is legally allowed to file a complaint with his state's Division of Human Rights or with the U.S. Department of Labor. But an obviously vigorous man of 65, who still has much to contribute to his job, may be let go by a company that sets its retirement age at 65, and there is nothing he can legally do about it.

Help from government

In the early 1930s the U.S. woke up to the growing size of the aged sector of its population and to the need for laws to deal with the special problems of older people, laws that would take into consideration some of the changing patterns of American family life.

In lieu of laws that would have imposed full and sole responsibility for care and support on the children of an aged parent, the early framers of old-age legislation proposed that the federal government guarantee by law to provide lifelong financial help, via monthly checks, to retired Americans of 65 or over. This principle was embodied in the landmark Social Security Act of 1935.

Across the years the act has been repeatedly amended—always in the direction of greater liberalization. The financial benefits themselves have been steadily raised. The age at which women could begin to receive them has been dropped to 62. For both men and women, eligibility requirements have been eased. Initially, benefits were available only to wage earners; later they were extended to people who were self-employed and to all Americans of 72 or over, even if they had never worked. In 1965 the government took another giant step in expressing its evolving concern for the aged. By law it provided for part-payment of their medical bills, setting up the Medicare program as an integral aspect of Social Security.

Neither Medicare nor other Social Security benefits, of course, are reserved for aged parents. Spinsters, bachelors and childless married people are no less entitled to them. But in the case of aged parents, these momentous federal laws tend to safeguard family stability almost as effectively as do state laws that directly govern the relations of husband and wife and of parent and minor child. Whether by making older people less dependent on the whim of a grudging child or by helping relieve the financial burden on an ungrudging one, the federal laws have removed one of the greatest potential—and actual —sources of friction that the modern family faces.

The states, too, have begun to pass laws designed to benefit the aged. Laws that lower bus and subway fares for people over 62 and that roughly halve the cost to them of gas, electricity and telephones now exist in many cities. And many states, aided by the federal government, encourage the construction of public housing for the elderly by pledging to underwrite part of the costs.

Handling the older person's finances

There are several ways in which a younger member of a family can help an aged parent or grandparent cope with one important problem: the handling of day-to-day finances. Any of these arrangements can, in fact, be initiated by the older person.

The first is the granting of power of attorney, authorizing one person to act as another person's agent. A simple document effects the arrangement (*pages 185-187*). It gives the agent the right to manage the older person's funds, write checks to pay for his or her expenses, transfer money from a savings account to a checking account—in short, to take whatever financial moves may be called for.

A second method of helping an older person manage his or her financial affairs is to employ a "representative payee." This is much like the power-of-attorney arrangement. The older person arranges to have all the checks due him sent to the representative payee, who then sets up a special fund for whatever money comes in to the older person—Social Security checks, veterans' benefits, stock dividends —and from the fund pays the older person's bills. A simple agreement drawn up by a lawyer and signed by those concerned is enough to formalize the matter; it does not have to be passed on by a court. Neither the representative payee nor the agent granted power of attorney need be a younger member of the family; many banks are willing to function in this capacity for a moderate fee.

There is, in addition, a third legal way of managing an older person's financial affairs but it is one in which a bank, rather than the children or grandchildren, must serve as manager. This method is the setting up of a trust. Having a lawyer here is essential, for trust law is extremely technical. But the nub of the matter is not complicated. The older person's assets are set aside in a trust, which is normally administered by the trust department of a bank. The bank's trust officers pay the person's expenses from this fund in accordance with the particular provisions embodied in the legal papers that created the trust. Trusts can be irrevocable (that is, unalterable for the person's lifetime) or revocable—the older person may cancel the arrangement any time he wants.

Both the power-of-attorney and representative-payee arrangements are also revocable. In short, these methods offer older persons aid without rendering them financially helpless; they retain ultimate control over whatever money is involved.

A question of capability

Suppose, however, that an older person has become manifestly unable to manage his or her affairs successfully. Then the law generally provides a number of ways for someone else to take hold through an incompetency proceeding, which may lead to one or more of several types of guardianship.

An incompetency proceeding in New York, for example, involves three main steps. Usually a son or daughter files a petition of incompetency with the probate court. It is, as a rule, accompanied by a statement from a doctor that the older person's ability to deal with the day-to-day world has failed. A hearing is then held before a "sheriff's jury"—made up of six people—and a "referee." The petitioner and the doctor offer evidence to support the assertion that the older person is mentally incompetent—incapable of handling at least one significant area of life. After hearing the evidence, the sheriff's jury and the referee submit a report for review by the probate court judge, who may then hand down a decree of incompetency if he is convinced that the older person is unable to cope.

Many lawyers feel that the incompetency proceeding is dubious if not dangerous. It can be employed by members of a greedy family simply as a device for keeping an elderly relative from spending his money (or taking a new young spouse)—so that there will be more of his assets left for them to inherit. Abuses of the incompetency proceeding have been sufficiently widespread to stir a movement for reform among senior citizen groups, mental health associations and lawyers themselves. Two of the reforms they have advocated are that court-appointed watchdog panels be set up to review each incompetency proceeding, and that the proceeding itself be subject to the same guarantees that prevail in all other civil cases.

In any case, declaring a man incompetent may have severe psychological and legal repercussions, for the decree makes him very much a second-class citizen. Depending on how incompetent he is adjudged to be, he may no longer be allowed to spend his own money, dispose of his own property, enter into contracts, marry, change his domicile—in short, he may be almost entirely deprived of his individual freedom. If the older person objects to the petition or feels that members of his family are filing it for selfish reasons, he has a right to be represented by a lawyer. This right to protest often discourages an ill-founded incompetency proceeding, as does the cost —$3,000 to $5,000 in legal fees and court costs.

But an incompetency proceeding does not always take away all of an older person's freedom. It may leave him control over those areas of his life where he can still operate effectively; it only removes from his control the area, or areas, in which he has become shaky.

Types of guardianship

When someone is declared incompetent, he becomes the "ward" of a "guardian" appointed by the court. Depending on the individual circumstances, the guardian may be a son or daughter or grandchild, or the ward's own spouse, or a close friend or lawyer. Legally, there are three types of guardian:

■ Guardian of the person. The guardian becomes, in effect, the ward's custodian, charged with his care, feeding, sheltering, maintenance and preservation from harm. Under this form of guardianship the guardian has no control over the ward's property.

■ Guardian of the estate (conservator). The guardian is empowered to manage, invest and protect the ward's property, real and personal, tangible and intangible. However, the ward retains title to the property, and all uses made of it by the guardian must be cleared and approved by the court.

■ Guardian *ad litem* (in litigation). This is a special guardian appointed for the express purpose of representing the ward, and protecting his best interests, in any lawsuit that may come up. The guardian may not agree to any final settlement of a suit without the court's approval.

How a conservatorship might work may be seen in the hypothetical case of Mr. Jones, now 70. Jones has run a small but profitable business all his life. With advancing age he has become unable to remember the names of his best customers, forgets to send out bills and mixes up deliveries. His business procedures have become so unreliable that his company, which he and his aging wife depend on for their livelihood, seems endangered.

Jones has also developed a couple of other foibles—buying expensive clocks and barometers virtually every time he goes by a favorite ship supplies shop near his office and dispensing $10 bills to needy cronies when he meets them on the street. Nevertheless, Jones still manages his checkbook with reasonable accuracy, and he and Mrs. Jones are clearly able to care for themselves and their house.

Jones's son perceives his father's failings and petitions the pro-

When commitment is necessary
The legal safeguards that surround the commitment of a mentally incompetent person to an institution are indicated in this form required in Minnesota. A hearing is required (paragraph 1), only a court can make the final decision (paragraphs 4 and 5), and the person whose competence is questioned must be notified of the hearing in advance so that he can engage a lawyer if he so wishes (paragraph 8). And this form is only one of many documents that must be signed—by welfare investigators, attorneys for the person being committed, court officials and the petitioner—before the commitment of a Minnesota citizen is settled.

M.S. 253.37 Sub. 1   New Com. Act form No. 9   8-70 1M

STATE OF MINNESOTA   **PROBATE COURT**

COUNTY OF RAMSEY

ACKNOWLEDGMENT OF PETITIONER

CONCERNING IMPLICATIONS OF A

JUDICIAL COMMITMENT PROCEEDINGS

Re:

_____
Mentally Ill—Mentally Deficient—Inebriate

I, _____, desiring to file a petition for the judicial commitment of the above named person hereby acknowledge the following, to-wit:

1. I fully understand the implications of a petition for judicial commitment and that it constitutes an application to the probate court to hold a hearing, at which my presence will be required, to determine if said person is in need of treatment and hospitalization as I intend to allege; and that a judicial commitment of said person can result in said person's loss of freedom and temporary suspension of drivers license.

2. I fully understand the requirement of the law to be that a petitioner must be a reputable person, and that included among the qualifications of a reputable person are sincerity of purpose and freedom from any malice.

3. I fully understand that any hospitalization of said person will be expected to be compensated for.

4. I fully understand that if the court after the duly held hearing determines that said person is in need of treatment and hospitalization, the court will order commitment of said person to the proper hospital for such treatment.

5. I fully understand that if the court after the duly held hearing determines that said person is not in need of treatment, the court will discharge said person and order an immediate release from any further custody.

6. I fully understand that said person, if not already hospitalized, will be taken into custody and ordered held for observation, evaluation and for hearing in the psychiatry section of St. Paul-Ramsey Hospital; or if said person already is hospitalized, that the hospital will be ordered to hold said patient for examination and hearing.

7. I fully understand that if I desire said person to be taken to the psychiatry section of a hospital other than St. Paul-Ramsey Hospital, I first must have engaged a private psychiatrist to make arrangments for the admission of said person into that hospital.

8. I fully understand that at least five days notice of the hearing has to be given to said person personally and to such other persons as the court determines; that said five days notice is given when and immediately after said person is in custody in order that said person cannot contend that he is being unduly deprived of his freedom and right to a timely hearing according to law; and that said person has the right to engage an attorney, and that if an attorney is so engaged, every effort will be made by such attorney to obtain said person's immediate release.

9. I fully understand that said person will be under the custody and control of the superintendent of the hospital in which said person will be ordered held, and that the attending psychiatric staff and said superintendent are qualified to diagnose the condition of said person after observation and will be making a report thereof to the court together with their recommendations.

10. I fully understand that I should give my full cooperation to the attending psychiatric staff and superintendent of the holding hospital and follow their recommendations in due respect to their qualifications and their interest in for what is best for said person.

Dated_____, 19___.   _____
                                                               Petitioner

I acknowledge that I have a copy of the above.

_____
                                                               Petitioner

bate court to be named the conservator of his business, to remove it from his father's control before it goes under. But that is all he asks to remove from his father's control. If the elder Jones wants to go on buying expensive barometers and giving cash to his old friends, that is his privilege. Such behavior may be economically unsound, but it is not incompetent, as is his management of his company. If the court agrees that Jones is, indeed, no longer able to function in his business, it will award a limited conservatorship to his son.

Commitment

For elderly people who become not just incompetent in one area of their lives but utterly incapable of handling even the simplest details of existence—people who seem clearly in danger of being victimized by a society with which they can no longer cope—the law offers another alternative. It arranges for their care by consigning them to an institution where their activities will be supervised. But commitment, the legal term for this arrangement, is a last drastic step.

Removing an aged person from the community—"putting him away," in society's harsh phrase—is a step that any normal family would want to avoid. In recent years the halfway measure of the nursing home has come into increasing use; but such homes are costly, and many will not accept people whose physical condition has deteriorated to a marked degree. Sometimes a family may find itself with no alternative but to commit the older person to an institution.

The legal processes involved in commitment vary in detail from state to state, but in broad outline the procedures follow a pattern. In most states a person may be committed to an institution in two ways: he may commit himself voluntarily, or he may be committed on application to the probate court from his relatives, guardian or physician. However, if the commitment is not voluntary, he must usually be represented by a lawyer and have a court hearing. The guardian or relatives or doctor who applied for the commitment must prove in court that the person is not only incapacitated and of unsound mind but in need of confinement in an institution. The burden of proof is on those seeking the commitment.

This is at least a partial safeguard against wrongful commitment. A further safeguard is the judge himself. The intent of the law is always to avoid infringing on personal freedom without cause. Most judges are loath to deny liberty to a person whose behavior, however erratic, does not make him patently dangerous to himself or society.

By **DAVID S. THOMSON**
MONRAD G. PAULSEN, Consultant

4
The home

Buyers vs. sellers,
landlords vs. tenants

The house of everyone is to him as his castle and fortress, as well for his defence against injury and violence as for his repose.

So wrote Sir Edward Coke, Chief Justice of England, in a decision he handed down in 1605. More than three centuries later, the principle of law he enunciated survives. The concept of your home as your castle—whether it be a house that you own or quarters that you rent—underlies some of your basic legal rights. The laws that entitle you to bar your home to police search without warrant, to restrain a neighbor who poses a hazard to your premises, to pursue your own interests there—such rights are intended to make you master of your castle insofar as it is possible to do so.

The qualification, however, is an important one. In this area of the law, as in all others, an individual may not exercise his rights to the detriment of society as a whole. And so, along with your prerogatives as a homeowner or tenant, you have obligations and restrictions as well. You may not, for example, build an addition to your house that violates a local zoning ordinance; nor may you let music blare forth from your apartment window at dawn if your community has clamped down on noise nuisances after midnight.

The law's concern with your dwelling place begins with the initial question of your right to occupy it. If you buy the property, you must do so by means of a legal instrument known as a deed, which confirms your ownership—your "title" to the property—against all claims. If you rent a place, another legal document, the lease, conveys certain rights to you and allows the landlord to retain others. Acquiring property is, of course, the more complicated procedure.

For most people, buying a house is the largest single investment of a lifetime. And because of the legal complexities involved, it can be as much of a strain on your nerves as on your budget. But it need not be—if you understand some points of the process, and the functions of some of the people you come into contact with along the way. In broad outline, a typical house-buying transaction spans six distinct steps: (1) negotiating the price with the seller; (2) signing the contract of sale; (3) obtaining a mortgage; (4) carrying out the "title search" to be sure the seller has a right to sell; (5) drawing up the deed; and (6) conducting the closing, the legal ceremony at which money changes hands and title passes from seller to buyer.

From the start to the finish of this transaction, one all-important law should be kept in mind: the so-called Statute of Frauds, another of our major legacies from England. The Statute, which has little to do with frauds, was enacted in 1677 to bring order out of the chaos resulting from the practice of transferring property by word of mouth.

Over the years it has been adopted by every one of our states. One of its chief provisions is that all transactions involving real estate must be in writing. Moreover, the written evidence of the sale must be officially recorded and filed in a local public-records office where anyone may examine it. Without the safeguards of written records, there would be little to prevent someone else from claiming ownership to property you have acquired—he could simply say that in a deal sealed by a handshake he had gained title to the property long before you did, and therefore it was his, not yours.

PRELIMINARY NEGOTIATIONS

Negotiating the price of a house is an art that one man may relish and another find tiresome in the extreme—whether he be the buyer or seller. The ritual, almost as elaborate and formalized as a serious game of bridge, begins when you have found the house you want. The seller starts with the announcement that he is "asking," say, $25,000. The word "asking" means, of course, that he wants you to make a bid, just as your bridge partner wants you to do when he bids "one club." So you bid "$20,000," the seller looks outraged but not too outraged, and you leave saying that you have a couple of other houses to look at; he counters with the statement that he has another prospective buyer coming in who is desperate to acquire the house. After assorted backings and fillings and offers and counteroffers, the two of you settle on a price: $22,500.

At this point both you and the seller are considerably relieved. You have looked at 10 other houses and are anxious to get your family settled in before school opens. The seller is sick of strangers trooping through his house and making *sotto voce* comments about his wife's poor taste in carpet colors. The result: Buyer and seller, after shaking hands and sharing a round of celebratory cocktails, decide to draw up a "binder." This is a piece of paper saying that the seller agrees to sell, and the buyer agrees to purchase, at the agreed-upon price. The buyer also puts up a deposit that he will lose if he fails to go through with the deal. This manner of sealing the deal, both men think, is a splendid idea.

It is not, from either of their viewpoints. If the binder does not contain the statements appropriate to a legal contract, it is unenforceable and useless to both buyer and seller. And even worse, it may turn out that it is legally enforceable, if it happens to be worded in a way the courts will recognize—that is, if it names both parties, if it specifies what is to be sold and the price, and if it bears the prospective seller's and buyer's signatures. Thus, something like the following would be enforceable: "This 1st day of April, 1971, George Smith, the seller, agrees to sell, and Henry Brown, the buyer, agrees to buy, the house and lot at No. 12 School Street, for $22,500, and herewith tenders $500 as evidence of his good faith. Such sum may be retained by the seller if the buyer fails to make the purchase. [Signed] George Smith and Henry Brown."

But even this binder, though enforceable, actually protects neither party. Is buyer Brown certain at this point that he can arrange financing for the house? Is he sure that seller Smith has clear title to the property, and so has the right to sell him the house? What if the house is damaged by fire or some other catastrophe before the final sale? Who, then, will pay for the damages?

Or consider the situation from seller Smith's standpoint. During the dickering over the price, he shrewdly did not bother to mention that his company is transferring him halfway across the country within the next few months; that would have given Brown a little extra leverage in the bargaining. Moreover, Smith plans to use the sale money from Brown to buy his next house. But the binder does not protect him against the possibility that Brown may be unable to obtain a mortgage to buy the house. In that case Smith will have only the cold comfort of Brown's $500 deposit and grounds for a lawsuit charging default on a contract. He will also have a house that he must unload even more quickly, at perhaps a lesser price than $22,500.

The binder, in short, is an instrument favored by laymen but not by lawyers. They believe that it is far better to wait until a properly drawn contract of sale is ready, setting forth all its terms of agreement and stating what will happen if either buyer or seller should fail to meet the terms.

If, as a buyer, you feel impelled to tender a deposit, or if the seller insists on one, make sure that your check bears no more notations of what it is for than an identification of the property and a statement that a contract of sale is to be prepared later. If the house is damaged by fire before the sale goes through and you decide not to buy as a result, you may lose your deposit, but you will be sure not to be stuck with a house you do not want since your agreement to buy remains oral and the check alone, so long as it does not specify terms, does not constitute the written contract the Statute of Frauds requires.

The contract of sale

A binder like the one drawn up by Smith and Brown is merely an inadequate and incomplete contract of sale. Under the Statute of Frauds a contract of sale, to be enforceable, need do no more than an en-

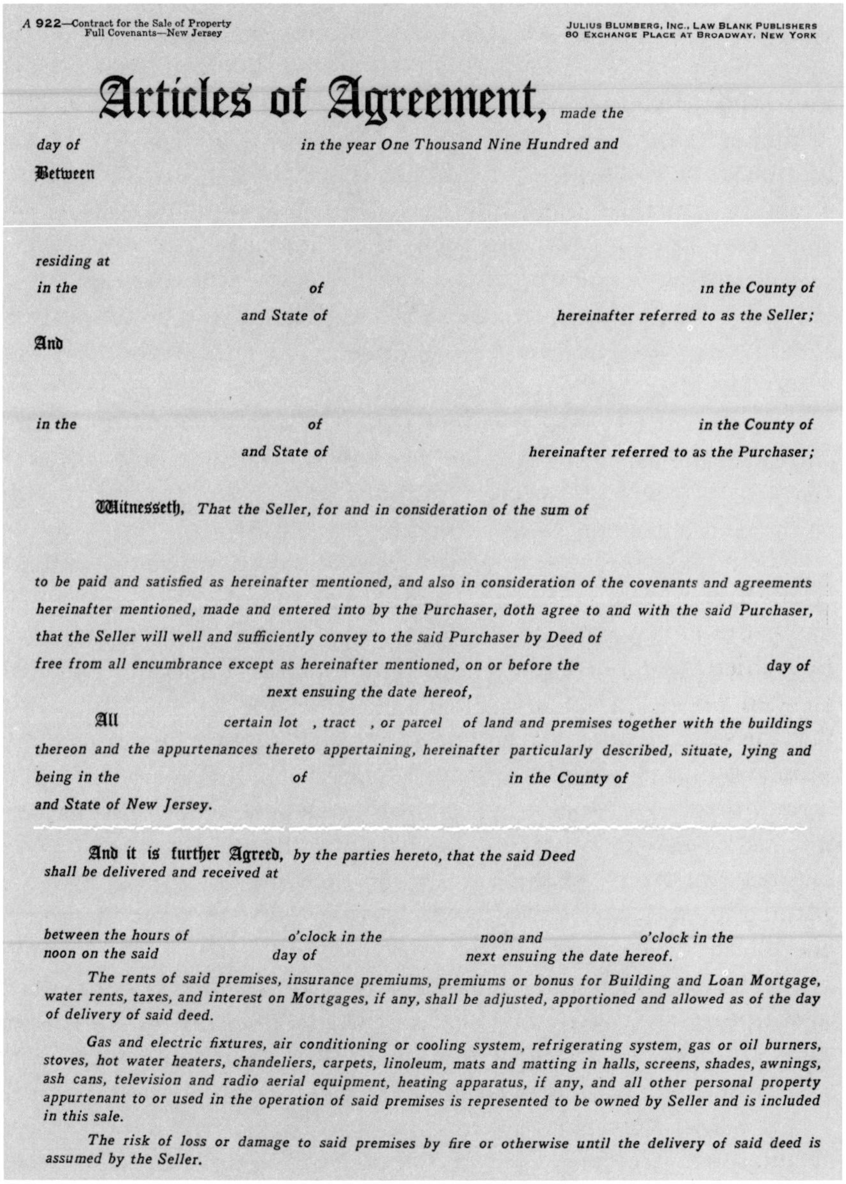

A 922—Contract for the Sale of Property
Full Covenants—New Jersey

JULIUS BLUMBERG, INC., LAW BLANK PUBLISHERS
80 EXCHANGE PLACE AT BROADWAY, NEW YORK

Articles of Agreement, made the

day of   in the year One Thousand Nine Hundred and

Between

residing at
in the   of   in the County of
                              and State of   hereinafter referred to as the Seller;

And

in the   of   in the County of
                              and State of   hereinafter referred to as the Purchaser;

Witnesseth, That the Seller, for and in consideration of the sum of

to be paid and satisfied as hereinafter mentioned, and also in consideration of the covenants and agreements
hereinafter mentioned, made and entered into by the Purchaser, doth agree to and with the said Purchaser,
that the Seller will well and sufficiently convey to the said Purchaser by Deed of
free from all encumbrance except as hereinafter mentioned, on or before the   day of
                              next ensuing the date hereof,

All   certain lot , tract , or parcel of land and premises together with the buildings
thereon and the appurtenances thereto appertaining, hereinafter particularly described, situate, lying and
being in the   of   in the County of
and State of New Jersey.

And it is further Agreed, by the parties hereto, that the said Deed
shall be delivered and received at

between the hours of   o'clock in the   noon and   o'clock in the
noon on the said   day of   next ensuing the date hereof.

The rents of said premises, insurance premiums, premiums or bonus for Building and Loan Mortgage,
water rents, taxes, and interest on Mortgages, if any, shall be adjusted, apportioned and allowed as of the day
of delivery of said deed.

Gas and electric fixtures, air conditioning or cooling system, refrigerating system, gas or oil burners,
stoves, hot water heaters, chandeliers, carpets, linoleum, mats and matting in halls, screens, shades, awnings,
ash cans, television and radio aerial equipment, heating apparatus, if any, and all other personal property
appurtenant to or used in the operation of said premises is represented to be owned by Seller and is included
in this sale.

The risk of loss or damage to said premises by fire or otherwise until the delivery of said deed is
assumed by the Seller.

A contract of sale

Standard forms cover most of the major points that
should be embodied in the contract of sale that
establishes the terms of a deal for a home. Part of one
such contract is shown here. It has space for, among
other things, the price and the date for the closing, and
it lists many of the fixtures that go with the house.

forceable binder does: name both parties, identify what is to be sold and specify the price—all in writing and signed by both seller and buyer. But to protect both parties the contract should say much more, providing for all those contingencies overlooked by Smith and Brown. Allowing for every potential complication may seem a difficult if not impossible task. But in fact there are only so many things that can go wrong between the signing of the contract of sale and the closing. And so drawing up a contract of sale can be a relatively routine matter —if left to the lawyers representing both sides. There are standard forms for this purpose available in most states, and with your lawyer's eye on your particular interests an adequate contract can be drawn with little delay.

At the very least, the contract should cover each of the major points in the check list overleaf. But there are a number of other provisions, and qualifications of the major points, that astute lawyers include in the contracts they prepare for their clients.

One sticky point that frequently comes up is the need to distinguish between a "fixture" and a "furnishing." Ordinarily, fixtures stay with the house, while furnishings may be removed by the seller. But which is which? Generally speaking, a fixture is anything so associated with a fixed location than an average person would assume that the seller intended to leave it there permanently. A furnishing is defined by law as something that can be used or enjoyed anywhere. Fixtures ordinarily include built-in wall cabinets or bookcases and anything attached to brick, stone or plaster. Plumbing and electrical fixtures also come under this category—even if the homeowner has put in an unusual, expensive sink or living-room spotlights to display his collection of paintings. The art collection itself is indisputably a furnishing, removable by the seller unless his tastes have since turned to sculpture and he offers to include the paintings in the sale contract. Outdoor fixtures include the shrubbery and garden plants as well as any sheds or other structures.

It would seem obvious that draperies, rugs and awnings are furnishings, not fixtures, since they are generally usable anywhere. But hold on. Suppose the house has an outsized picture window, and the draperies for it are custom-made. Are they usable elsewhere? Suppose the floor is covered by wall-to-wall carpeting. Is this not "attached" to the house? Are not the awnings attached? Appliances like refrigerators, washing machines and clothes dryers are commonly regarded as movable and fall under the classification of furnishings. But what if they have been built in? Innumerable lawsuits have arisen over such questions, and it is unwise to take the answers for granted. Rather

A CHECK LIST FOR A CONTRACT TO BUY A HOUSE

The paper that commits you to buy a house —the contract of sale—can make sure you get what you thought you were getting, but only if it is carefully drawn up. Some of the key provisions a lawyer puts into a contract to protect both the buyer and the seller are summarized here.

1 A valid contract must, besides naming buyer and seller and stating their intention to complete the sale, describe the property precisely. But is the description correct? There is only one way to be certain that the apple trees behind the barn do indeed lie on your side of the boundary as you were assured by the seller: Commission your own survey.

2 Tugs-of-war over the property need not involve you in complex legal difficulties if the contract makes the seller responsible for prior claims that might cause trouble. You may not learn about all claims that exist until after the title is searched *(page 101)*, but if serious ones turn up, you want to be able to cancel your deal without monetary loss. You will be able to get out of the contract if the sales agreement requires the seller to list all restrictions on the property and all debts for which the property is security, to guarantee that the claims listed are the only ones there are and to attest that there are no claims that could involve you in future litigation.

3 The purchase price must be stated to make the contract legal. But the contract should also specify the amount of the deposit you put down and how much more will be paid when the deed is delivered, as well as how it is to be paid—with cash or a certified check. The deposit is normally left with either the buyer's or the seller's lawyers; this way the seller cannot touch the money until he meets the terms of the contract. If he does not, the buyer can get his deposit back.

4 The date for final transfer of ownership should be stated. This date is not rigidly enforced, however, unless the contract says "time is of the essence"; otherwise transfer may be deferred a reasonable time.

5 Who loses if the house burns down between the time you sign the contract and the time ownership is legally transferred? You or the seller? The courts have sometimes ruled one way, sometimes the other. But it will not be you who loses if the contract says the premises will be turned over "in the same condition as they are now, reasonable wear and tear excepted." To protect both parties, the contract usually specifies the type and amount of insurance to be carried and settles who is to pay the premiums. It is also common practice to ask the insurance company to amend policies so that the separate interests of both seller and buyer are fully protected as soon as the contract has been signed.

6 The contract of sale spells out financing arrangements in some detail. You probably expect to borrow money to pay for the house. You can make the deal contingent on getting a mortgage loan, and you can even specify terms you anticipate. Then if the bank turns down your application or asks stiffer terms than you specified, you can cancel the contract and get your money back. The contract also lists some costs, such as real estate taxes, that you will prorate with the seller.

7 Misunderstandings often arise when the seller takes things he believes are his personal property but you believe go with the house—garden plantings, for instance. To avoid such disputes the contract should stipulate who gets items in question. Without such a listing you must rely on fuzzy distinctions: Anything an average person would assume to be a permanent part of the house or land is a "fixture" and goes to the buyer. Anything else is usually a "furnishing"—rugs or curtains, for example—and belongs to the seller.

A picture to protect the buyer
A picture of a newly purchased home as it looked when the contract of sale was signed may become invaluable evidence in any later dispute—if, for example, the handsome stand of trees the buyer thought he was getting is gone by the time he takes title.

than risk a dispute that may land in court, it is sensible for the buyer to ask for a detailed list of what is being sold with the house, item by item, and to have the list incorporated in the contract of sale.

The condition of the property when the buyer eventually takes possession is also a frequent source of dispute between him and the seller. The contract of sale should state that the premises will be "in the same condition as they are now, reasonable wear and tear excepted." This "damage clause" theoretically protects the buyer from being forced to purchase a house that between the signing of the contract and the final closing turns into a heap of charred ruins or has lost the handsome stand of trees that made it so desirable. But there is something else for the buyer to remember. When the contract does not specifically assign the risk of accidental loss to one party, the courts in different states follow different rules in deciding disputes that arise on this score. In some states judges hold that the buyer should get what he bargained for and not less. In other states judges hold that once the seller has signed the contract he has already given up legal control over his property in most respects, and that therefore it is the buyer who should take the risk of any accidental loss.

Regardless of the judicial interpretation in your own state, it is far better—whether you are buyer or seller—to specify in the contract just who is to assume the cost of accidental loss. The best guarantee of protection for both parties is to arrange for adequate insurance to cover the property from the time of signing the contract of sale until the closing. The contract should specify the types of insurance, the amounts of coverage, and who is to carry it. The policies carried by the seller before he signs a contract of sale may not be valid after he signs—most homeowner policies lapse if there is any change in title to the property, and some courts consider that a change in title has taken place once a contract of sale has been signed. Therefore the most practical course for both seller and buyer is to have all insurance policies endorsed to protect both parties as soon as the contract of sale is signed. Often this arrangement takes only a telephone call.

The damage clause and proper insurance coverage protect a buyer against defects in the property that occur after the contract is signed. But what about defects that were already there? At the least, there should be a clause in the sale contract providing that, at the time of the closing, the premises will not be in violation of building and zoning laws. Still, it should be emphasized, the ancient rule of *caveat emptor*—let the buyer beware—applies with particular force to real estate transactions. There is no legal protection against an aging furnace, leaky roof, damp cellar, crumbling foundation, inadequate insulation or the like. You cannot get your money back later if you find that the house is in poorer condition than you thought. You are presumed to know the condition of what you buy from the moment you sign the contract of sale. The only exception occurs where a defect is so hidden —for example, in a pipe that runs underground—that a buyer could not detect it by reasonable means. Hiring a professional house inspector to look the place over is a good precaution for a buyer to take. (Such specialists are listed in classified telephone directories under "Inspections.") If the seller refuses to hold off showing the house, the buyer must take his chances, either hoping that the house will not be sold to someone else in the meantime or signing the sale contract and accepting whatever defects there may turn out to be.

The remedies available to both seller and buyer, in case one or the other defaults on the terms of the contract, should be clearly set forth in the contract. These default clauses help avoid lawsuits when a sale falls through. The contract usually provides that if the seller cannot, after reasonable efforts, meet all the terms to which he has agreed, the buyer can cancel the contract and recover his deposit in full. Or the buyer can choose to accept the property as is, with whatever defects may exist at the time of closing, by paying the agreed-upon purchase price in full.

Another major point for the buyer to bear in mind is that the seller's spouse should also sign the sale contract, relinquishing all rights in the property. States with community-property laws give property rights to both spouses even though the particular property is owned by only one of them. Moreover, making both spouses sign a contract of sale is also a precaution in the event of the later death of either spouse. Some states that do not have community-property laws grant dower rights to widows, and curtesy rights to widowers, entitling them to a certain share of the value of property owned by their spouses during the marriage *(Chapter 12)*. If the buyer of a house does not secure the signatures of both spouses on the contract, the surviving spouse may later lay claim to part of the property that has been sold.

Obtaining a mortgage

At the same time you are preparing to sign a contract to buy a house, you will probably be making arrangements to borrow a substantial part of the purchase price. The customary form for such borrowing is a mortgage, usually from a bank or other lending institution in the area of the property you want to buy, or from the seller himself. (In California and a few other states, somewhat different loan arrangements called deeds of trust or trust indentures are used instead of mortgages. They place title to the property in trust with a third party, rather than with the lender, until the loan is paid off.)

When the lender agrees to give you the loan, you give him two documents in return: (1) a "promissory note," saying that you will repay the loan on certain terms (over how many years, at what intervals and at what rate of interest), and (2) a "mortgage deed" to your property as security for repayment of the loan. The mortgage deed gives the lender the right to sell your property to recover the loan if you should fail to repay it or fall behind in your payments.

In that unhappy event, the lender is said to "foreclose" the mortgage. This involves a judicial proceeding and, as a consequence, the sale of the property. From the proceeds the lender takes the amount still owed him, and the balance—if any—goes to the ex-owner. If the purchase price obtained from the sale of the property does not pay off the debt in full, the mortgage holder can get a deficiency judgment against you—a court order that allows him to sue you for the remainder of the debt. All this sounds alarming but, while foreclosures do take place, most lenders will go to considerable lengths to avoid making a foreclosure, giving you additional time to make payments. Moreover, you may ask the lender to insert a clause, both in the mortgage agreement and in the promissory note, giving you a grace period in which to catch up on payments before foreclosure action is started.

Throughout the states, most mortgage or deed-of-trust agreements contain certain standard provisions in addition to those detailing the schedule of payments and giving the lender the right to foreclose if the schedule is not met. Most of these provisions protect the lender, for he controls the purse strings: You cannot buy the house without him, and while he may be your friendly banker, he is in a position to dictate terms. His powers are not quite as formidable as they sound. The mortgage agreement will probably, for example, contain a clause stipulating that you keep the house in good repair and see that it does not depreciate in value. Some mortgage agreements may even stipulate how often a house must be painted. But in practice the good-repair and value-depreciation clauses mean simply that you must keep your insurance policies against fire and other losses in force by paying the premiums promptly; that you avoid committing violations of the local building codes; and that you refrain from removing a porch or other major structure on the property—thus, conceivably, causing a depreciation in value. In most instances insurance policies are made payable to the lender rather than to you. And undoubtedly you will have to let the lender know the name of your insurance company and agree to have the company notify the lender if damage policies are no longer in force. You may simply have switched companies, but if the lender does get a notice of cancellation from the original company, you will get a quick letter from the lender reminding you that you must carry insurance (you are unlikely to get a foreclosure notice—even though the mortgage agreement may specify that the lender can start legal action when a policy lapses).

There are also some clauses that benefit you rather than the lender—if you can get them. One is a prepayment provision, permitting you to pay off the mortgage sooner than the agreement requires without being charged a special fee for this privilege. Prepayment is greatly to your advantage if you take out a mortgage at a high rate of interest and interest rates drop later—you can then refinance the house at lower interest charges. Another advantageous clause permits you to let someone else "assume the mortgage" if you later decide to sell your house; the new buyer thereby takes over the balance of the payments on your mortgage, after paying you what you would get in cash. Such a provision may be an asset in selling a house, for it saves the potential buyer much of the trouble of obtaining a new mortgage and may provide him with a mortgage at an economical rate.

When arrangements for your mortgage agreement have been completed, the lending institution will give you a "letter of commitment," stating that it will let you have a mortgage—on the terms, you hope, that you specified you had to get in the contract of sale. First, however, the lender will run a credit check on you *(Chapter 7)* to make certain that you can meet the mortgage payments and will also insist that a title search be made of the property you plan to buy.

The title search

When you own property you are said to have "title" to it—a carryover from the time when the titles of English noblemen were based on their landholdings. Thus, when you institute a "search" of the title to property you want to buy, you are making sure that the seller offering you the property actually owns it—that he has "certainty of title"—and that you will thus have clear and indisputable possession of the property yourself once you have paid for it.

The title search—a check of local records kept in the office of the town or county clerk—is also intended to ascertain whether there are any "encumbrances" on the title. These are legal burdens on the property. They may include zoning restrictions that bar you, say, from running a business in your home; building restrictions that determine whether or not you can add a garage or put on a porch; "easements,"

A search to settle property rights
Before the bank grants a mortgage and before the sale is consummated, the title to the property must be "searched." A lawyer pulls out old records in the "chain of title" as far as 40 or 50 years back, to see if there are unsettled claims to the property. If there are none, the present owner has "certainty of title," and so will you when you make the purchase.

A modern deed to land may still say that the property will be yours "to have and to hold." The phrase comes from medieval days when a king retained title to land in his domain and allotted it to loyal followers, who could only "hold" it for him.

which give someone else the right to use the property (for example, to drive through it to reach the main road); and "liens," which are claims against the property for bills unpaid by the present owner —there may be a "mechanic's lien" filed by a painter or plumber who has done work on the property and has not received his payment.

The bank will have its own attorney conduct a title search (and you will pay for the expenses of that search), but you should have your own search conducted as well. The reason you should not rely on the bank's search is that it protects only the bank. Even though you pay for it, the bank's lawyer is working for the bank, and if a problem about the title comes up, he is accountable only to his client.

Frequently, title searches are conducted not by a bank's lawyer or a potential buyer's lawyer, but by title-insurance companies specializing in such work. Whoever makes the search needs, first, a thorough and perfectly clear description of the property. The method of identifying a piece of property depends not only on the part of the country it is in, but on whether it is in an urban or a rural area. In Midwestern and Western states, identification is commonly made by means of the survey of public lands that was undertaken by the federal government when these areas were first settled. The survey divides the entire region into rectangular tracts, subdivided into ranges, townships, sections, half-sections, quarter-sections and even smaller subdivisions. Within each section, small lots are usually located by local maps or plans. In Eastern states, the "metes and bounds" (meaning measures and boundaries) of a particular piece of property identify it by reference landmarks like houses, roads, brooks or trees. In tracts developed for housing, the developers have a map showing the boundaries of each lot. Many cities identify property by block and lot number.

Once the title searcher is armed with an adequate description of the property, he ordinarily starts by inspecting a copy of the present owner's deed at the town or county clerk's office; then he turns to a so-called grantor-grantee index, in which the deed was recorded when the owner bought the property. This entry indicates from whom he bought it. The searcher then looks up the name of that man and finds the name of the next previous owner, and so on, back through earlier and earlier buyers, or grantees, in the "chain of title." How far back? It depends on local custom or on the value of the property. In most cases, it is safe to limit a title search to the past 40 or 50 years. The statute of limitations may have made older claims invalid.

At whatever point the searcher decides to stop going back into the title record for the names of all the grantees of the property, he then starts with the oldest deed in the chain of title and retraces the record forward to the present, examining the record of every seller, or grantor, of the property. He does so to be sure that one of them did not convey the property or some right to it—say, an easement permitting a neighbor to run a sewer pipe across the land in back of the house—to anyone outside the chain of title, who thus may have some claim on the property. Such a claim would have to be cleared up before your lawyer would advise you to buy the property.

Besides this index and the deeds, the title searcher will also consult several other kinds of documents that are usually kept in the town or county clerk's office. These records show whether there are unsettled claims against the property resulting from debts or unpaid taxes. Such claims may deny the seller the right to sell his property.

A few states have established a simpler system for recording deeds called a "tract index," keyed to the description of the property sold rather than to the names of the various buyers and sellers of former years. The city or county covered by each tract index is divided into blocks of numbered lots, and at the clerk's office there is a volume for each block with a separate page for each lot, listing all the transactions involving any land within the lot. Having all this information on one page obviously helps the title searcher, but even so he must follow through just as he did looking at the grantor-grantee index; that is, he must check all of the references to recorded documents.

When the title searcher informs you that the title record is clear and that you can buy the property you want, he will usually give you an "abstract of title," a paper summarizing what he has discovered. This document gives you reasonable assurance that there will be no claims to involve you in later legal problems.

Drawing up the deed

Once you are assured that the title is clear, your lawyer can proceed to draw up a deed, or indenture. Usually this step is much less complicated than preparing the contract of sale or the title search since the seller and buyer have already agreed to the basic provisions of the deed—they settled these points when they signed the contract of sale. The actual drawing up of the deed is so circumscribed by tradition and the requirements of law that there is ordinarily not much for an attorney to do. In this role he may be, as the courts sometimes call him, merely a "scrivener"—a pen wielder copying ancient phrases. A clause in a modern deed to land may still say that the property will be yours "to have and to hold." The phrase comes from medieval times when a king retained title to all land in his domain and parceled it out to loyal followers, who could merely "hold" it for him.

There are now three basic types of deed; the contract of sale will have stipulated which type you are to get. Any of them can serve to transfer title to a property from one owner to another; the difference lies in the degree of assurance a seller offers that the title has no flaws, and that he has full right to sell the property. If your title search has been conducted properly, it is highly unlikely that you will have to make use of the seller's assurances; nevertheless, they are important to have in the event that a flaw in the title does turn up.

A "general warranty" deed is one in which the seller warrants that the title is free against any valid claims that arose before or during his ownership of the property. This deed is the most secure type, for it makes the seller—and his heirs—personally responsible for the validity of the sale forever. But because a general warranty deed is so all-encompassing, it is not easy to get.

A "special warranty" deed is only slightly less secure. In it the seller simply guarantees that he himself has done nothing that would cause the title to be defective—for example, that no encumbrances placed on the propery during his ownership still remain. But he makes no guarantee about encumbrances that may have existed on the property before he bought it. If there are prior claims that might cause trouble, they should be turned up during the title search. The special warranty deed gives quite general protection to the buyer without seriously burdening the seller, and it is the one that is usually provided in the sale of a house.

A "quitclaim" deed, sometimes also called a "deed without covenants," is one in which the seller conveys what title he has, "if any." He promises you nothing about claims that may exist except that he will not himself contest your ownership of the property. This type of deed is obviously not a desirable one for home ownership, and a buyer's lawyer will generally refuse to accept one. Land records in most of the country are now so complete and clear that questions about claims can usually be turned up during a search and resolved by the seller, permitting issuance of a special warranty deed.

A major question that often confronts the buyer at the time the deed is being drawn is whose name should be on it—the husband's alone, the wife's alone, or both their names. There is no one simple answer to this question, and in making the decision a lawyer's advice is particularly important. How the matter of the form of ownership is resolved may have many kinds of consequences—it may affect the kinds of claims that a creditor may be able to make against the property, and what happens to the property if the couple later separate or are divorced or if one of the couple should die. There are three forms of

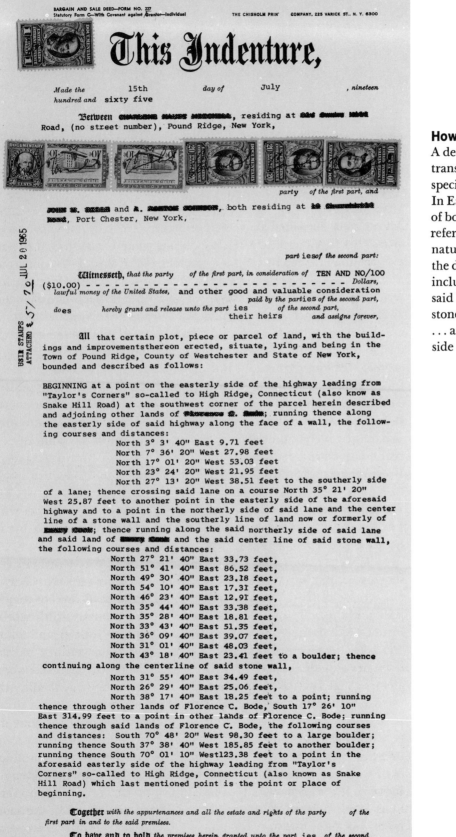

BARGAIN AND SALE DEED—FORM NO. 227
Statutory Form C—With Covenant against Grantor—Individual   THE CHISHOLM PRIN' COMPANY, 225 VARICK ST., N. Y. 6300

This Indenture,

Made the 15th *day of* July *, nineteen*
hundred and sixty five

Between ~~CHARLES MARY MEDOMA~~, residing at ~~224 Snake Hill~~
Road, (no street number), Pound Ridge, New York,

party of the first part, and

~~JOHN M. FERER~~ and ~~A. NEWTON JOHNSON~~, both residing at ~~12 Churchill~~
~~Road~~, Port Chester, New York,

part ies of the second part:

Witnesseth, *that the party of the first part, in consideration of* TEN AND NO/100
($10.00) - *Dollars,*
lawful money of the United States, and other good and valuable consideration
paid by the parties of the second part,
do es *hereby grant and release unto the part* ies *of the second part,*
their heirs *and assigns forever,*

All that certain plot, piece or parcel of land, with the buildings and improvements thereon erected, situate, lying and being in the
Town of Pound Ridge, County of Westchester and State of New York,
bounded and described as follows:

BEGINNING at a point on the easterly side of the highway leading from
"Taylor's Corners" so-called to High Ridge, Connecticut (also know as
Snake Hill Road) at the southwest corner of the parcel herein described
and adjoining other lands of ~~Florence C. Bode~~; running thence along
the easterly side of said highway along the face of a wall, the following courses and distances:
     North 3° 3' 40" East 9.71 feet
     North 7° 36' 20" West 27.98 feet
     North 17° 01' 20" West 53.03 feet
     North 23° 24' 20" West 21.95 feet
     North 27° 13' 20" West 38.51 feet to the southerly side
of a lane; thence crossing said lane on a course North 35° 21' 20"
West 25.87 feet to another point in the easterly side of the aforesaid
highway and to a point in the northerly side of said lane and the center
line of a stone wall and the southerly line of land now or formerly of
~~Emory Cook~~; thence running along the said northerly side of said lane
and said land of ~~Emory Cook~~ and the said center line of said stone wall,
the following courses and distances:
     North 27° 21' 40" East 33.73 feet,
     North 51° 41' 40" East 86.52 feet,
     North 49° 30' 40" East 23.18 feet,
     North 54° 10' 40" East 17.31 feet,
     North 46° 23' 40" East 12.91 feet,
     North 35° 44' 40" East 33.38 feet,
     North 35° 28' 40" East 18.81 feet,
     North 33° 43' 40" East 51.35 feet,
     North 36° 09' 40" East 39.07 feet,
     North 31° 01' 40" East 48.03 feet,
     North 43° 18' 40" East 23.41 feet to a boulder; thence
continuing along the centerline of said stone wall,
     North 31° 55' 40" East 34.49 feet,
     North 26° 29' 40" East 25.06 feet,
     North 38° 17' 40" East 18.25 feet to a point; running
thence through other lands of Florence C. Bode, South 17° 26' 10"
East 314.99 feet to a point in other lands of Florence C. Bode; running
thence through said lands of Florence C. Bode, the following courses
and distances: South 70° 48' 20" West 98.30 feet to a large boulder;
running thence South 37° 38' 40" West 185.85 feet to another boulder;
running thence South 70° 01' 10" West 123.38 feet to a point in the
aforesaid easterly side of the highway leading from "Taylor's
Corners" so-called to High Ridge, Connecticut (also known as Snake
Hill Road) which last mentioned point is the point or place of
beginning.

Together *with the appurtenances and all the estate and rights of the party of the*
first part in and to the said premises.

To have and to hold *the premises herein granted unto the part* ies *of the second*
part, their heirs *and assigns forever.*

USED STAMPS ATTACHED $57.70 JUL 20 1965

How a deed locates land

A deed, or "indenture," that
transfers property must carefully
specify the land being transferred.
In Eastern states identification
of boundaries often depends on
references to man-made and
natural objects. Reference points in
the deed at left, for example,
include "the face of a wall . . . a
said lane . . . a center line of said
stone wall . . . a large boulder
. . . another boulder . . . an easterly
side of the highway."

joint ownership by husband and wife *(Chapter 12),* and the choice among these three is important because it can determine how the property may be disposed of by sale, gift or will.

THE CLOSING

All the steps described above do not make you the owner of the property. That happens only when the deed is actually transferred to you, usually in a lawyer's office. This ceremony—the closing—is sometimes thought of as akin to a mysterious rite of induction into a secret fraternal order. Many a home buyer who has been through one has come away confused, because a lot takes place in a relatively short time.

There are many outstretched hands at a closing because a great deal of the procedure is devoted to settling the costs of the entire property sale—not only your costs but the seller's as well. It is, in fact, helpful to arrive armed with advance knowledge of what these so-called closing costs will be, whether you are the buyer or seller. Your lawyer should be able to give you a close estimate of them. Some are prorated —shared by buyer and seller; if, for example, Smith has paid a year's real estate taxes in advance, but sells the house to Brown on July 1, Brown must give Smith half of the tax money.

The settlement sheet

For the closing process, an exact "settlement sheet" is drawn up. It has three parts:

(1) What the seller gets. This section of the settlement sheet shows what the buyer still owes the seller. From the agreed-upon purchase price of the house are deducted the amount of the buyer's deposit and the seller's prorated share of taxes, water and utilities bills, insurance premiums and any other items specified in the contract of sale as the seller's responsibility. The remaining sum must be paid to the seller either in cash or by certified check. The sum involved is usually very large—several thousands of dollars—and is generally supplied partly from a mortgage loan and partly from the buyer's own funds (his "down payment").

(2) What the seller pays. The second part of the settlement sheet itemizes the seller's costs, which usually include any unpaid back taxes or water or electric bills, a deed-transfer tax, his attorney's fee, his broker's fee if he has used a real estate broker, and the cost of any liens or other claims that must be paid off before the title to the house is entirely clear.

(3) What the buyer pays in addition to the balance he owes the seller. The buyer's cost usually include his attorney's fee, the title-

There are many outstretched hands at a real estate closing. Besides the balance due the seller, the buyer may have to pay his attorney's fee, a bank service charge, a mortgage tax, a mortgage fee, and even the cost of a credit report on himself.

recording fee, and costs related to the mortgage he has obtained. These can include a bank service charge, a state mortgage tax, a fee to the bank attorney for drawing up the mortgage, the fee for recording it, a fee for surveying the property, an appraisal fee (if the buyer has had a professional appraiser go over the house), the cost of a credit report on the buyer made by the mortgage lender, the cost of a title-insurance policy (the one that protects the bank), and the cost of life insurance to cover the mortgage payments in case the buyer should die before they are paid up. A buyer may also pay for his own title-insurance policy at the closing.

Just the business of writing all the checks required at the closing makes it quite an affair. But there is more besides, for a number of papers must be examined and discussed. Spread out on the table may be all of the following: the contract of sale, the deed, the seller's insurance policies, his receipted tax and water bills for the past year or two, his utilities and fuel bills, his mortgage documents, a survey or plan showing the boundaries of the property, the abstract of title, a title-insurance policy, perhaps a bill of sale for personal property, and documents showing that the seller has cleared up any defects that might have existed in the title. If the house being sold is new, there will also be a "certificate of occupancy," a document showing that the house has been checked by a building inspector and that it meets the local building codes.

The cast of characters

Quite a few people are likely to be looking at and discussing all these documents. The parties present ordinarily include the seller and his wife, the buyer and his wife, their respective lawyers, the real estate broker, a bank officer, and perhaps also a representative of the title-insurance company. Other people may attend as well—local workmen, for example, if there are mechanic's liens to be paid off.

Many of the papers at the table are simply there to be passed around and scrutinized by the lawyers. But a number of papers must also be signed by the buyer and seller. At a given moment this is what might be going on when you close on a house:

You hand the seller a certified check for the down payment. Then you and your wife give him the rest of his money by endorsing over to him your mortgage check, which has been made out to you both by your bank in return for the promissory note and mortgage deed you have just signed. The seller usually endorses this check and gives it to his banker to pay off his mortgage. (If the principal still outstanding on his mortgage is less than your mortgage, he gets change—a check from his banker; if not, he hands an additional check of his own to his banker.) Since the seller's mortgage loan is now paid in full, his banker gives him a "Satisfaction of Mortgage" that wipes out that bank's claim to the property. The representative of the title-insurance company hands your lawyer the title-insurance policy for his perusal before you sign it. The seller's lawyer has just passed the seller the deed for him and his wife to sign, after which the lawyer will pass it to your attorney. The real estate broker, just to be helpful, is calculating the exact costs of prorated bills, figures that both lawyers will look at and, hopefully, approve in a few minutes.

Last-minute problems

Problems do arise at, or just before, closing, but they need not force postponement of the sale. Just prior to the closing, your lawyer will visit the local records office to recheck the registry of deeds in order to bring the title search up to the last moment. Often a mechanic's lien will be recorded just a day or two before the closing, when an unpaid workman hears that the house is being sold. This claim can be cleared up at the closing simply by payment of the workman's bill. But suppose the furnace suddenly breaks down and cannot be fixed by the time of closing. In such an event you can withhold a certain amount of the purchase price, depositing it in what is known as an escrow account. The money is turned over to a third party—usually the attorney for either the buyer or the seller—who will hold it "in escrow" until the furnace is fixed. If the furnace is not repaired by a pre-arranged date, you receive the money that is in escrow. An escrow arrangement is often useful at the closing if a new house is being sold and the work on it has not been completed; perhaps the driveway has not yet been blacktopped or the landscaping finished. The use of an escrow account is far simpler than postponing the closing.

Finally, remember that getting the deed does not fully protect your title. This full protection comes only when the deed is recorded. Failure to record the deed may leave you open to fraud. If the seller is a cheat, he might sell the same property to someone else. That buyer's title search will not show your ownership—your deed is still unrecorded, remember—and when the inevitable lawsuit arises, the court may award the property to him rather than to you.

SELLING A HOUSE

When the day comes that you decide to sell your house, all that you have been through as a buyer will guide you as a seller. Besides seeing to it that your interests are protected in the contract of sale, and understanding what you are promising in the deed you will give the buyer, you must think of your mortgage. If the buyer takes it over, you may still be legally liable for payment in case he defaults. To be relieved of such liability, at the time of your sale you will have to get the bank to accept the liability of the new buyer in your stead—or settle up your mortgage and tell the buyer to get one of his own.

As a seller, you are also more likely to be dealing with a real estate broker, who acts as your agent in finding and dealing with prospective buyers. You, not the buyer, pay for his services—the commission is usually 5 or 6 per cent of the sale price but is sometimes a flat fee. Disputes over brokers' commissions in real estate transactions are a common cause of litigation. Most such cases arise when a sale falls through after the broker has legally earned his commission and the homeowner is reluctant to pay it. Ordinarily, a broker is entitled to his fee once he has produced a customer for the house who is willing and able to buy on terms acceptable to the seller —even if no sale then takes place. If you sign an agreement with a broker that says nothing about his commission, this rule is the one that courts apply. There are, of course, many reasons why a sale may fall through despite the initial readiness of both parties to complete it. As a seller, you can protect yourself against paying a broker's fee while your property remains unsold by insisting on a provision in your agreement with him that makes his commission contingent on completion of the sale. Your lawyer will usually add such a provision to the broker's standard form, and a broker may do so himself—if asked.

The broker's fee

The amount of payment due a broker is also, on occasion, a matter of litigation. Ordinarily the amount of the commission, whether it is a percentage of the sale price or a flat fee, is specified in your contract with the broker. However, not all states require that the commission rate be specified, and some states do not even require that the agreement be in writing. Since the seller-realtor contract is preliminary and incidental to the actual transfer of property, the Statute of Frauds does not, at this point, impose its requirement that an agreement be in writing. And therefore, confusion over the amount of the commission often results.

When there is no written agreement between seller and broker, or if the agreement does not specify the commission, the courts tend to settle disputes by holding that a broker is entitled to "reasonable" compensation. What is "reasonable" is not decided by how hard the broker may have worked to sell a house, but by the standard rates set by a local real estate board. Such brokers' organizations exist throughout the country, and if you have any reservations about the amount of commission a broker asks for, you can ascertain the prevailing standard from the local real estate board. If there is no local real estate board, shop around a bit. A broker looking for clients may be delighted to offer you a lower rate than the one charged by a busy colleague down the street.

In most states, brokers are licensed—a fact to the seller's advantage, since a licensed realtor risks his professional position if he does anything unethical. Some states, however, do not license brokers, and there a seller must beware. It is possible for you to engage a broker without realizing you are doing so—and still become liable for his fee. You may find that a friendly neighbor, during a casual conversation on your front lawn, offers to help you find a buyer for your house. If he does find a buyer, and you send a bottle of Scotch as thanks, he may return it—along with a bill for his commission. This has happened, and has resulted in both lawsuits and lost friendships.

If you are selling your house and buying another one to move to, you may find yourself attending two closings within a few days. In this situation, it is logical for you to expect to use the money you get for the house you sell to pay for the house you buy. But if something goes wrong and you do not sell your house, you may still be legally obligated to buy the other house—without the money at hand to pay for it. To protect yourself against this possibility, you can seek to incorporate a clause in the contract of sale for the new house making the purchase contingent on your having sold your present house. Such a clause could, for example, set a date for closing of the second house one week after the sale of the first. Another safeguard would be to ask for an "option to buy" the second house, securing a certain period of time—say three months—beyond the closing date set for the sale of your own house, and giving the owner of the second house a deposit in return for the option. He cannot sell to anyone else during the option period, and if you do buy the place, your option deposit becomes the deposit on the purchase price. If you do not sell your own house and cannot buy the other, you lose the deposit.

THE HOMEOWNER'S RIGHTS AND RESTRICTIONS

The deed to your property says not only that you have acquired the premises but that you are entitled to "the quiet enjoyment" of them. But your neighbors, too, are entitled to the quiet enjoyment of their premises—and that fact necessarily puts limitations on what you may do while you live in your house.

There was a time when your freedom to do whatever you wanted to do on or with your own property was virtually unlimited. But the needs and mores of modern society have tended increasingly to place restrictions on a property owner. Almost nowhere in this country today do you control your holding as completely as your grandfather did his property a few score years ago. Take, for example, the matter of zoning restrictions.

The right of state or local officials to impose such restrictions on your property was first firmly established in a Supreme Court decision of 1926. The Court held that the village of Euclid, Ohio, could enforce a zoning ordinance against a land developer who claimed that the ordinance was a "cloud" on his title—an encumbrance, in effect. The zoning pattern established by Euclid—dividing the area into residential, commercial and industrial zones, and regulating the sizes of lots and the heights of buildings in each zone—has come to be known as Euclidean zoning and is followed today in most parts of the country. The Supreme Court did rule, in later cases, that zoning powers were limited, but defined those limits so broadly—allowing a locality to make zoning restrictions for reasons of "public health, safety, morals or general welfare"—that lower courts since then have upheld restrictions based solely on property values and even on purely esthetic considerations. In 1923 a woman in Cleveland Heights, Ohio, was refused a permit to put up a house of cement and glass because the zoning board decided that it would have violated regulations by contrasting sharply with the traditional wood-and-brick dwellings making up the rest of the neighborhood. She sought relief, but the Ohio Supreme Court upheld the Cleveland Heights zoning board —despite a vigorous dissent by one justice arguing that the woman should not be required "to sacrifice her choice of architectural plan . . . under the official municipal juggernaut of conformity."

Zoning ordinances may also restrict your right to make changes in your house. Whether you can build a second story, a porch or a garage; whether you can add a guest house to your lot; how near to your boundary line a new wing can extend—such matters may be regulated by the zoning rules for your neighborhood. If your house is part of a development, the limits on your right to proceed with what you think of as improvements on your house may even be written into your deed. If some zoning ordinance does loom as a problem for you, you can apply to the local zoning board for an exception, a variance. If you are refused, you can take the matter to an appeals board in most localities, and ultimately to court. But you ought to be aware that courts tend to side with the zoners.

Assuming that you do have the right to make the kind of alteration or improvement you want, you may still be required to get a building permit from local authorities, usually through the office of the town or county clerk. In most places, a building permit is not hard to obtain; its purpose is not to restrict what you can do but to ensure that the work is carried out according to standards set to protect your own safety and that of the neighbors. A local building inspector will come by when the work is done to verify that these standards have been met. As a practical matter, if you are simply paneling a playroom or putting down floor tiles or adding a kitchen cabinet, you probably will not have to obtain a building permit; in certain localities, work costing less than a specified amount can be performed without the formality of a permit.

Plain fences and "spite" fences

Your right to quiet enjoyment of your property ordinarily includes the right to fence it off, so long as the fence meets the local zoning requirements. In most cases you can put up a fence that you feel is necessary to protect or increase your privacy even if it means that by doing so you cut off a neighbor's view of some distant scenery, or reduce the amount of light reaching his house. You generally have this legal right, but you may want to exercise it cautiously and with consideration for your neighbor, for fences can often lead to disputes.

Many a court case has involved a quarrel between two neighbors over the erection by one of them of a "spite fence," one built to cause annoyance or get revenge. The court will order the fence builder to take his fence down, or lower it, only if the complaining neighbor can prove that the fence was put up out of malice—and that it serves no useful purpose to the person who put it up. But malice, or spite, is very hard to prove in court, and if the fence builder can show that there are reasons why a fence would add to his enjoyment of his own property, the courts will usually uphold his right to build his fence and enjoy it as he wishes.

Nuisances and neighbors

In exercising your right to do what you like on your own property, you may sometimes—knowingly or unknowingly—do something that annoys or offends your neighbor—who may go to court to accuse you of creating what the law calls a nuisance. For example, it may annoy a neighbor if you seek to park your car in a spot that obstructs the view from his front porch. He may be able to stop you if he can prove to a court that whatever you are doing impairs his own right to privacy

You may be guilty of committing a nuisance by not repairing something offensive on your property—a chimney that belches smoke onto the wash next door, for instance.

and possibly his health and safety, or interferes substantially and unreasonably with the use and enjoyment of his property. Among the most common situations that lead to legal wrangles between neighbors are loud noises, excessive smoke and fumes, smells, profanity, indecency and unleashed pets.

In nuisance cases an owner's right to use his property as he sees fit must be weighed against the right of other people to the quiet enjoyment of their own property. Generally the courts are loath to interfere with an owner's use of his property if he has created a nuisance merely as the result of pursuing his own interests, even if these are bothersome to his neighbors. The courts generally apply the same standard used in judging a spite fence. They will rule against the offending property owner if he has created the nuisance out of malice. But establishing the intent to annoy is not always easy. If you do want to sue a neighbor over a nuisance, you should be very certain of your ground—you must be prepared to prove serious loss, damage or interference with your own enjoyment of your property, as well as unreasonable conduct on your neighbor's part.

Pets are often a special problem in the nuisance category. There is an old saw that "a dog is entitled to one good bite." The "one-good-bite" rule, however, no longer applies in half the states, which have passed "strict liability" laws making an owner liable for damages caused by a dog's bite, even if it was part of friendly old Fido's first unexpected attack.

You may be guilty of committing a nuisance under the laws of most counties and towns simply by not repairing something dangerous or offensive on your property. A faulty septic tank or a chimney that belches black smoke onto the wash next door, for example, could be ruled a nuisance that endangers the health of adjoining property owners. Allowing one's house to become dilapidated to the point that it constitutes a danger to others also falls in the category of nuisances; letting the house go unpainted generally does not. A run-down house is not legally a nuisance.

There is a special type of obligation in the case of children. This concerns what the law, somewhat misleadingly, calls an "attractive nuisance"—meaning one that might attract children to a place where they could be hurt. Children, happily, are curious; unhappily, they are also careless. The pile of lumber you have amassed in the backyard to use to repair the tool shed will probably prove irresistibly fascinating to the boy next door, but if he breaks his clavicle while exploring it, his father can sue you on his behalf.

Among the most common attractive-nuisance cases are those involving unprotected swimming pools, unsafe playground equipment and backyard tree houses. But anything from an uncovered hole on the front lawn to an unlocked barn with a ladder leading to the hayloft may constitute an attractive nuisance if a child hurts himself while exploring. Technically, this problem is one of your liability for injury to a trespasser. (For more about trespassers' possible claims, see page 120.) Most courts can be counted on to make allowances for a child's innocent adventuring. If he is hurt on your property and the

If a child hurts himself while exploring your property—some common cases involve unprotected swimming pools —you may be liable. You need not make the place child-proof, but you, rather than the child, must exercise reasonable care.

court feels that you could have taken some reasonable precaution that would have prevented the accident, the court will very likely hold you liable for the child's injuries. You, rather than the child, must exercise reasonable care to protect him from mishaps.

Your rights to your neighbor's land

When you buy a house, certain easements may go with it, permitting you to make use of a neighbor's land for some specific purpose. Ordinarily the easement is described in the deed of the owner whose land is affected, and once an easement is granted by a property owner to his neighbor, it is permanent and irrevocable unless both parties agree to terminate it. Often an easement is created when an owner of a large tract of land wants to sell the back lot on his property. He might give a buyer an easement of access through his own property if there is no other easy route between the parcel he is selling and the street. But once an easement is recorded in the local registry of deeds, it need not be mentioned again in any later deed to be effective. It is said to "run with the land," applying to later buyers long after the agreement was made.

In addition to easements on your neighbor's property you may also benefit from certain restrictions—called restrictive covenants—that exist in his deed. Such restrictions, for example, may prevent him from cutting down certain shade trees or from obstructing the view from your back porch. These restrictions may have been placed on your neighbor by the man who sold him the property in order to protect the privacy of land he himself retained. Restrictive covenants were also used in past years to prevent an owner from selling property to Negroes or other non-Caucasians. But the Supreme Court has ruled such covenants unconstitutional.

You may obtain the right to use a neighbor's land for some purpose without getting a permanent right to do so. If he simply agrees to let you use part of his land—his driveway, for example—he is giving you a "license." A license can be oral or in writing, but the agreement should clearly indicate how long the licensee may retain the right that is granted, how the license can be revoked, and whether the license applies only to the licensee personally. Otherwise the granter of the license may discover that he has agreed to a permanent easement that will run with the land, making the property difficult to sell at some future date.

If the nature of the rights you get or grant is left uncertain, disputes easily arise. For example, if Smith asks his neighbor Adams for the right to drive a car across a field behind Adams' house, Adams may say, "Sure, go ahead." He has thus given Smith a license to use his land, a permission he can revoke at any time. Suppose, however, that Smith then bulldozes some bumps and ruts out of Adams' field to make it easier to drive across and spends a fair amount of money doing so. Adams might not be able to revoke the license easily. Even though the agreement was not in writing, a court might rule that a binding contract was reached because Smith had given Adams some "consideration" in return for the license. It is wiser to put the license in writing and make sure the terms are carefully spelled out.

Under some circumstances, you can acquire an easement to use part of a neighbor's land simply by using it long enough. How long depends on local law, varying from as little as five years in some states to 30 in others. The way you use the land must clearly demonstrate that you are claiming a right to use it. Your use of the land must be what is termed "hostile." This term means not that you have to snarl at your neighbor when you meet him but rather that your use of his land does not depend on his consent. You must also use the land continuously and in full public view, so that the neighbor can be expected to (or ought to) know about it. If your use of a neighbor's land meets all these conditions, you may acquire what is known as an easement by "prescription."

The same situation, of course, holds true for you and your land. If people on your street get into the habit of taking a short cut across a corner of your lot, and you do not stop them, their use of the path may in time give them a prescriptive easement. You will no longer have the right to stop them from cutting across the lot, and you will not be able to build anything on that part of your lot or do anything else there that would obstruct their right of way. You would be wise to consult a lawyer if you ascertain that someone is making regular use of part of your property. However, there is a method that is often employed to keep the neighbors from acquiring an easement without being completely unneighborly about it; all you have to do is to put up a barrier once a year, serving notice that you are exercising your right to keep your neighbors off your land to protect it from a prescriptive easement. Such "one-day barriers" are a common device, regarded by the courts as sufficient evidence that people have not had "continuous" use of your land for a period of years.

Your neighbor can acquire not only an easement to but even ownership of your property, or you can acquire ownership of his, if either of you occupies the other's land (rather than merely uses it) under the same open, continuous and hostile conditions. You or he could then claim the ownership by what is called adverse possession. Such rights of ownership extend beyond neighbors to total strangers; anyone who sets up a shack on your property under the stipulated conditions acquires possession.

Government claims

One way in which a property owner may lose not only certain rights to parts of his property but the property itself is by failing to pay his real estate taxes when they are due. You are unlikely to lose your property because of a $75 plumber's bill, even though the plumber files a mechanic's lien, since the plumber is required to notify you that he is taking legal action to seize, and perhaps sell, your property to satisfy the debt. A mortgage-holder must also notify you if he intends to foreclose. But unpaid real estate taxes are considered "automatic" liens; in other words, the tax authorities do not have to inform you that they have a lien against you.

In fact, your property may actually be sold to make up for unpaid taxes even though you did not know that you were behind in your payments. Suppose that by some error in the mail delivery you do not receive your tax bill. That failure to receive the bill is not accepted as an excuse for not paying your taxes when they are supposed to be paid. You are still expected to know when taxes are due, and how much you owe. There is only one means of fending off this calamity: Pay your real estate taxes on time and check regularly at your local city hall to see whether any such taxes relating to your property are on record as being unpaid, either in whole or in part.

Even the most cautious watch over your property rights and obligations may not protect you if the government needs your land, for it has a right to take it away from you if it is needed for certain purposes. As population pressures grow, federal, state and local governments increasingly exercise this power of eminent domain, or condemnation. Using it, any one of them may take over all or part of your property to build a school, highway, airport or hospital. You are, of course, entitled to compensation—"fair market value" for what is taken by condemnation. In practice, you will first be offered an amount in settlement. If you decide to contest it because the sum seems inadequate, you have a right to a condemnation proceeding, with the outcome to be decided by a jury, a judge or a commission. At this proceeding you must bring in a real estate broker or appraiser or any other witnesses who can help you establish the worth of the property. Ordinarily, when a property is taken by condemnation, the owner suffers a variety of inconveniences—the expenses of packing and moving to a new home, for example. For the most part there are no legal

It may be perfectly legal for you to prune the branches off a neighbor's overhanging tree. But beware: The court may rule that you did not have the right to do on your own what the court would have ordered your neighbor to do anyway.

means of redress for such expenses. Some states provide for compensation in these cases; some do not. Generally, the losses incurred by an owner in cases of eminent domain are hard to recover.

Encroachments

Anything you build—or plant—on your property that extends across your boundary line onto your neighbor's property is called an encroachment. The most common kinds are hedges that grow onto a neighbor's property, a tree that spreads its branches over the line, and a fence or wall or driveway that you have situated slightly beyond your own boundary. If your neighbor does not ask you to remove the encroachment, you may get the right to keep it there, by the principle of adverse possession, after a prescribed number of years. Until then, however, your neighbor has a right to insist that you remove the encroachment, and in that case you must do so.

You, of course, enjoy exactly the same right if the neighbor encroaches on your property. You can insist that he cut off the branches of a tree growing onto your side of the boundary even if it means that the tree might die. If a contractor has placed your neighbor's driveway several inches onto your land, you can insist that he have the contractor remove the encroaching pavement and restore your land to its original condition.

If your neighbor refuses to remove an encroachment, you can get a court order forcing him to do so. You also have a remedy known as "self help," the right to remove the encroachment yourself. This right varies from state to state. It may be perfectly legal for you simply to prune the branches off a neighbor's overhanging tree, shear his hedge or tear down his fence. But you should be prudent about exercising such rights. In some cases, the court—remember, the neighbor can also go to court—may rule that you did not have the right to do on your own what the court would have ordered your neighbor to do. If you cut the branches off his tree and the tree dies, your neighbor may be able to win a suit for damages, even though a court might have ordered him to cut the branches off himself.

You are far better off, of course, if you settle such disputes in a neighborly way, out of court. Litigation in these matters often creates wounds that take years to heal, and the issues are seldom worth the trouble that accompanies legal wrangling.

Obligations to visitors

Your right to enjoy your property gives you the right to invite people to come there—and to keep intruders away. You may put up a "no trespassing" sign warning off strangers, and you can hold trespassers —even a crash-landing balloonist—responsible for damages they cause. But when someone does come onto your property—by invitation, by mistake or even against your wishes—you also assume certain obligations toward him simply because you own the property. Bear in mind that even if you, like most homeowners, have an insurance policy to protect you against claims for damages done to people on your property, you may not be covered against all eventualities. For one thing, when you take out the policy you are obliged to disclose all the hazards on your land: If you fail to mention one, you may not be covered if it causes an accident to a visitor. Moreover, a standard clause in such policies provides that you must notify the insurance company about any change in your property that might increase hazards. If you dig a large hole on your land and do not tell the insurance company about it, you may not have protection if someone falls into it and sues you for the injuries he sustains.

Whether you will be held legally responsible for harm that oc-

A trespassing balloonist
Your right to enjoy your property gives you the right to keep intruders away, and you can hold trespassers—even a crash-landing balloonist—responsible for any damages they cause.

curs on your property depends on the reason the injured person was there in the first place. If he is an out-and-out trespasser, you are legally liable for an injury he sustains only if you deliberately or recklessly created the hazard on your property that caused his injury. If he is someone you invited for purely social reasons, you are liable for an injury he sustains if you did not warn him of dangerous conditions he would not discover on his own. If he is someone you invited for business reasons, you may be liable for an injury the visitor incurs even if you warn him of the hazard.

In the case of business guests, therefore, you are responsible for keeping your property in reasonably safe condition. Suppose, for example, that you have hired a babysitter for a Saturday night. Suppose further that you have not only let a loose tread on the cellar stairs go unrepaired, but have also failed to replace a burned-out bulb at the top of the stairs. You might not be liable for injuries to a babysitter if, on her own, she goes exploring and falls down the cellar steps in the dark—since in this situation she has no greater right to this part of the house than a trespasser would have. But you would be liable if you had told her that she had the free run of the entire house.

You are also liable if a workman hurts himself on your property —but only if it is your fault, not his. Say an electrician is rewiring your house. If a rung of your ladder gives way while he is on it so that he falls and breaks an arm, you will have made yourself liable for his injury. But if he had gotten his own ladder and fallen from it, all he could have collected from you was the payment for his work.

A homeowner's liability extends to people who regularly come onto his property uninvited. You may be held accountable for dangerous conditions on the part of your property near the street. If passersby often wander a few steps onto your lawn, and one of them breaks a leg stumbling into a trench you forgot to fill, you may be liable; as a habitual passerby he is not regarded as a trespasser. But suppose a real trespasser appears. You are under no legal obligation to make your grounds or house safe for him.

RENTING A HOME
The practice of leasing land began in the Middle Ages as what amounted to extortion, and there is many a tenant today who regards his lease for his apartment in the same light. In medieval times, however, it was the tenant who turned the profit. He was a money-lender, and when he provided funds to a hard-up landowner he exacted in return a lease on the land—a lease that gave him the right to keep all the income from the land for a long enough time to make a huge profit.

In time, the English courts took measures to protect landowners against unscrupulous acts by such tenants, and as this area of law eventually evolved the landlord-tenant relationship came to favor the landlord. Now courts and legislatures have begun to recognize that the tenant's position is made even more disadvantageous by the tight housing markets in most cities. In many recent cases, particularly those involving the poor, courts have restricted the traditional powers of landlords and have even overruled provisions of leases that were already agreed to and signed.

Provisions of a lease

A lease is, of course, a legally binding arrangement, and either you or the landlord can go to court, if necessary, to have its terms enforced. Before you bind yourself to paying a considerable amount of rent for the duration of the lease, you ought to know what the lease says about the following matters: What services must the landlord provide? Who is responsible for painting and repairs? What restrictions are there on your use of the place? Can you renew the lease? Can you sublet—rent your quarters to someone else? Can you, or the landlord, terminate the lease at any point?

These matters are not only of considerable economic importance to you as a tenant, but are also the most common points of misunderstanding. Ordinarily a landlord, or his agent, will present you with

Hazardous is the home

A home can be a booby trap for others and even an insurance policy may not cover all eventualities. Your dog may bite the mailman, your boy may belt a ball through a neighbor's window and a caller may trip over a loose step—and you assume some obligation because these misadventures occurred on your property.

a printed lease—a standard form—to sign. (For samples of clauses in printed lease forms, see page 18.) You can ask him to delete provisions that you find objectionable or to add provisions that meet your particular needs. A standard-form lease usually provides a blank space at the end for just such "additional articles." Whether the landlord will agree to changes will depend largely on your bargaining power. But even his refusal to grant you a reasonable clause may not deprive you of all the rights you want: Local ordinances give you some rights and protection.

One major right you have, and one major right the landlord has, need not be written into a lease and yet both are legally enforceable as "implied covenants." You have the right to privacy in your apartment. Your landlord has the right to get the premises back in good condition. But what if you move in and discover shortly thereafter that the condition of the premises is not what you expected it to be? It is not unusual for a new occupant of a luxury apartment to discover that the walls are so thin the quarrelsome couple next door are always within piercing earshot. In such a case you are out of luck. Local laws generally require little more of a landlord than that he rent his property free of health hazards and safety dangers. If a condition is merely unpleasant, the law holds, you should have noticed it before signing the lease. Unless your lease contains a provision in which the landlord specifically promises to keep the premises habitable, tenantable, in good repair, or otherwise "fit," you ordinarily have no legal remedy. You may have to put up not only with paper-thin walls but with faulty plumbing, windows that will not open, crumbling plaster and cooking odors. You cannot as a rule use such conditions as a reason for breaking your lease.

There are, however, a few exceptions. You may break the lease, for example, if the landlord intentionally concealed a defect or if, under certain circumstances, you were unable to inspect the premises before signing the lease. In housing-short cities, tenants often sign leases for apartments that have not yet been completed. If you do so and later discover unfit conditions, you may have grounds for breaking your lease; but you would have to show that an inspection of the part of the building that was completed when you signed the lease could not have disclosed the defect you later found.

Some courts also hold a landlord responsible for renting a place in fit condition if the premises are furnished and leased on a short-term basis. This rule was laid down in an English common law case in 1843 in which a man who rented a furnished house at "a watering place" was allowed to break his lease because the house "was greatly infested with bugs." You may benefit from the precedent set at that English watering place when you sign a lease, sight unseen, on a house at the beach for next summer.

Who makes repairs?

Most tenants assume that it is the landlord's obligation to make all repairs on the premises, and most landlords do in fact see to major repairs as a matter of course. However, some repairs are the tenant's responsibility. Under English common law, a tenant was required to keep his premises "wind and water tight," and, in general, do what he could to prevent deterioration. This rule is still the law in most states. Normally a tenant must repair—or pay for the repair of—broken windows; make certain that water is not pouring in through a broken damper in the chimney; tighten shutters to keep the wind from blowing them off; and check the guying on the TV antenna to prevent the wind from knocking it over and gouging a hole in the roof.

There are some repairs that you may not be legally required to make, but that the landlord may not have to make either. If, for example, you rent a house and the furnace breaks down, you may not have to fix it, but if you do not you may have to live without heat. In such a case you may be required to shut off the water to keep the pipes from freezing. In an apartment house, on the other hand, the landlord must maintain and repair all basic fixtures—such as plumbing, heating and electrical systems—that serve the entire building. He must also keep "common" property, such as the halls, the exterior and the roof, in safe and usable condition. He does not have to make repairs within the apartment. You can ask the landlord for a clause in the lease specifically putting the burden of repairs on him, but you probably will not find such a clause in any standard lease he hands you to sign. More likely, you will find a clause that not only puts it on you to make repairs, but states that the landlord is not responsible for his failure to make them, that if he does make repairs he can charge you for them, and that if you are inconvenienced while he is making them, it is not his fault.

If a landlord does choose to make repairs, he is responsible for faulty work. When the plaster ceiling over the bed of a Los Angeles couple fell on them, they sued the landlord and were awarded damages. Even though their lease did not require him to repair a crack that had appeared in the ceiling, he had had it fixed, and the court made him pay damages for the accident that followed. Had he let the ceiling alone, he would not have had to pay a cent in damages.

The matter of repairs can be costly in other ways. If a guest is hurt by a dangerous condition on the premises you are renting (and are responsible for repairing), you may be liable. A renter, like a homeowner, should carry liability insurance.

If a tenant holds a lease requiring him to make general repairs, and no exceptions are detailed, the prevailing rule is that he must repair everything; if he has leased a house rather than an apartment, he must even replace the building if it burns down. The California Supreme Court once ruled against a tenant as follows: "If the injury proceeds from the act of a stranger, from storms, floods, lightning, accidental fire, or public enemies, he is as much bound to repair as if it came from his own voluntary act." Many landlords do carry fire- and extended-coverage insurance policies at their own expense, and promise to do so in the lease. A tenant should make sure this is the case, or else carry such insurance himself. There have been instances in which a tenant has had to rebuild his rented house after it burned down, incur the costs of finding another place in the meantime and continue paying the rent of the original place as well. The law no longer gives a landlord such drastic advantage over a tenant. In many states a tenant has no further obligation to pay rent when there is no longer any place to occupy.

But even if the landlord undertakes to make substantial repairs and to carry insurance against total loss, a tenant may be liable if he detects a sign of danger to the property and either does nothing to correct the condition himself or fails to let the landlord know about it.

A warning against waste

As a tenant, you are obliged by law to return the premises to the landlord in the condition they were in when you took possession, except for ordinary wear and tear. This rule is what lawyers call the doctrine of waste. It means that you may not cause the property to deteriorate —and that if you do, the landlord can sue you to recover damages for his loss. It also means that you may not do anything to alter the character of the premises, even if you think the alterations improve the property. If you cover the crumbling wooden flooring with handsome tiles, remove plaster to expose the fine old bricks of a 19th Century fireplace, or otherwise turn the house or apartment into a better place, the landlord could sue you for damages—and then charge the next tenant a higher rent because of your improvements.

More commonly, disputes over waste involve a landlord's claim that you have caused some small damage that he must repair before re-renting the apartment—left holes in the walls where you hung pictures, for instance. Since you are not ordinarily responsible for "reasonable wear and tear," you cannot be charged for broken door-knobs, scuffed flooring or the like. But if you attach a bookshelf to the wall and, after removing it, leave the wall in need of complete re-plastering, you have probably committed waste, and a court may hold you liable for it. If your lease says so, you may have to repaint after a stated period of occupancy or when you vacate the premises—or pay the landlord for repainting. But if there is no such provision in the lease, painting is the landlord's obligation. In some localities, the law specifies how often he must paint.

Usually a landlord takes a deposit from you as "security" or "liq-uidated damages," and when you leave he deducts his repair costs from this deposit before returning the balance to you. If you find that he has deducted charges for what you consider simply reasonable wear and tear, your only remedy is to sue him—if the amount is worth it. It usually is not.

What services must a landlord provide?

Traditionally, a landlord had little obligation to provide a tenant with anything more than the place itself. Unless he specifically agreed in the lease to provide some service—grass-cutting or garbage remov-al, for instance—the law did not require any services of him. Even now, if you rent a vacation cottage or a house in the suburbs, your land-lord may not have to provide any services. However, if you rent a city apartment, local laws ordinarily entitle you to certain basic services whether or not your lease spells them out. Generally, a landlord must provide heat and hot water; in some communities the law fixes ex-actly how much heat a landlord must provide his tenants, and the hours of the day and days of the year when he must provide it to them. In some localities apartment houses of a certain size must be pro-vided with a janitor or superintendent. An apartment-house landlord in a large city may also be required to provide garbage disposal, ex-termination and elevator service.

If your lease does not mention the landlord's responsibilities for services you think he should supply, ask him about the matter before signing. Even if he says he does not have to provide some basic ser-vice, you can check with local housing authorities. He may have to pro-vide the service after all, by law.

Protection against crime is one "service" that the courts have only recently begun to regard as a landlord's obligation. A decision by the District Court of Appeals in Washington, D.C., in 1970 held that "when a landlord has notice of repeated criminal assaults and robberies . . . [he has] a duty to take those steps which are within his powers to minimize the predictable risk of his tenants." The court did not specify the steps a landlord should take. It simply noted: "The landlord is no insurer of his tenant's safety, but he is certainly no bystander." Although this is only one opinion of one court, it suggests that in the future a tenant may be able to insist on more safeguards than landlords have usually been required to provide.

YOUR RIGHTS IN YOUR RENTED HOME

As a renter of property you are ordinarily entitled to many of the owner's basic property rights: the right to "quiet enjoyment" of the premises, to invite anyone you please—and within the limits of your neighbors' equal right to quiet enjoyment—to do anything you like within the confines of your home. Moreover, as a renter you have the right to live there, as one court has put it, "unmolested in any way by the landlord." However, you may have to accept limitations on these rights when you sign a lease. Many standard leases prohibit anyone except members of your family from occupying the premises without the landlord's written consent, and require you to provide written notice to the landlord if anyone else moves in. Some leases even give the landlord the right to approve of visitors and guests, allowing him to evict you if he finds them offensive. Under such a provision, you may not even be able to install a friend as caretaker in your apartment while you go on vacation.

Ordinarily, you have the right to keep a pet in your apartment unless the lease specifies otherwise. When it does permit you to keep a pet, however, you may not be entirely in the clear: If enough neighbors complain that George, the dog, is too noisy, the landlord may insist that you get rid of him—no matter how much a member of the family you consider him.

Normally you have the right to keep a pet in your apartment, unless the lease says otherwise. But if enough neighbors complain that George the dog is too noisy, the landlord may insist that you get rid of him—even though you may consider him a member of the family.

The difficulty of reconciling conflicting rights to rented property was demonstrated in the borough of Queens in New York City in 1966, when the courts there became something of a battleground between noisy and complaining neighbors. In a civil court in Queens a middle-aged couple contended that their neighbors upstairs were destroying their peace and quiet with heavy walking and the raucous sounds of children at play. The judge said sympathetically of the complaining downstairs neighbors: "At the end of the toilsome day, like tired fish, they are only too happy to seek out these quiet backwaters of the metropolis to recuperate for the next day's bout with the task of earning a living." But when the upstairs neighbor made the point that his home was his castle and no one could tell him what to do in it, the judge was also understanding. "The difficulty of the situation here," he noted, "is that one man's castle is directly above the castle of the other." The judge decided for the upper castle; since the family upstairs was already in residence when the people moved in downstairs, he ruled in favor of the noisemakers.

At about the same time, another judge in the same borough of New York was deciding a suit brought against a couple whose two young daughters were aspiring musicians, practicing on violin and flute for more than three hours a day. As the learned judge noted, the neighboring tenants might agree with Keats that "heard melodies are sweet but those unheard are sweeter," but the defendants seemed to feel with Nietzsche that "without music life would be a mistake." The decision was in favor of the young musicians. To limit their practicing hours would mean, in effect, that no serious musician could live in an apartment, and the judge declined to impose such a restriction. He did add, however: "The court expresses the hope that the defendants will not so avail themselves of the rights here accorded them as to conclude with Longfellow that 'the night shall be filled with music.'"

At the very least, these cases suggest that your right to "quiet enjoyment" of your premises may be less a right than you expect.

Your right to renew or break your lease
A landlord has no obligation to let you stay on in your apartment after your lease has run out—except in certain areas of the country, notably New York City, which retain, in whatever modified form, the rent-control regulations dating back to the housing shortage of post-World War II days. You may, however, ask for an option to renew when you sign your original lease. If the landlord agrees to this provision, the clause should specify how long the new lease will be for, and what the rent will be. Bear in mind that in some localities the law

sets specific limits on how much of a rent increase a landlord is entitled to obtain when he renews a lease with the same tenant.

Suppose, on the other hand, that you want to move out before your lease is up. Since a lease is a legally binding agreement, you will normally be liable for paying the rent due for the entire term of the lease whether you stay or not.

You will not have this liability if you have been fortunate enough to obtain certain provisions in your lease. One typical clause allows you to terminate the lease on a month's notice if you forfeit an extra month's rent. Another might allow you to leave if your landlord breaks any of the provisions of the lease at any time. Even in the absence of such provisions you may have the right to move out without further obligation if the landlord fails to keep the premises safe for human occupancy. In such a case, the law considers that you have been, in effect, "evicted."

The tactic of the rent strike

Suppose, however, that the landlord fails to keep the property safe for human occupancy and you do not want to move. Some people faced with this problem have decided to stop paying rent—they staged "rent strikes." Check with your lawyer before you become involved in such a tactic. Only certain states, among them California, New York and Pennsylvania, hold rent strikes legal. And the laws in those states vary as to the manner of withholding rent. Some allow you simply to keep the rent money; others permit you to use it to repair the defective conditions; while others require you to place the money in an escrow account and give the landlord a specified amount of time, perhaps six months, to clear up the problem. It is also more prudent to act in conjunction with other tenants.

Bear in mind that the courts as of today have permitted rent strikes only in cases where a landlord's failure to clear up a defect endangers the health of the tenant—a leaky roof, for example, or a malfunctioning elevator in a skyscraper apartment house.

Subletting?

Your right to sublet the premises you have rented is ordinarily defined by the terms of your lease. You may be granted the right to sublet at will, or only with the landlord's permission, or not at all. Commonly, if a landlord grants any subletting rights, it is conditioned on his approval of the subtenant. But if you are getting such a provision in your lease, you ought to ask for more—a clause providing that such approval will not be "unreasonably withheld." Thus, for example, if your landlord withheld approval simply because the sub-tenant dresses like a hippie, you could probably get a court order overruling him.

If you sublet, the law as a rule holds you—not the subtenant—liable for the rent. If he fails to pay the rent, or damages the premises, or violates the terms of the lease in any other way, the landlord can hold you responsible.

When can the landlord evict you?

If you break any important provisions of your lease—damage the premises, create a nuisance or fail to pay the rent—the landlord can do one of two things. One, he can seek a court order directing you to perform your obligation under the lease, to repair what you have damaged, or cease making noise or to pay the rent due. Or he may get an eviction order from a court, directing you to move out forthwith—and thereby terminate the lease.

Local law prescribes the steps that he must take to get you out of your apartment. Generally, he must first serve notice that he is taking legal action against you—often all that he needs to do is post a "dispossess" notice on your door. After a fixed time, often three days, he can get an eviction order in another court proceeding, at which time you can appear in court to argue your side of the case. If you do not show up in court or if the judge rules against you, the landlord gets the right to put you off the premises. If you do not move out yourself, he can ask the sheriff to come and put you and your belongings out on the street. It may sound like something out of the 19th Century, but it still happens.

There are many disputes that may arise between you and your landlord. Virtually all can be settled without legal action. This course is always wisest, since even if you win a case in court you may have to pay some of the court costs as well as your own legal expenses in bringing the suit. The caution applies not only to renters but to property owners as well. In many real estate transactions strict insistence on legal rights and on adherence to proper legal forms would prove an obstacle to a sensible and simple agreement. In some parts of the country you may not be able to buy a house at all if you insist that every single legally important provision of a contract of sale be included in your contract. Local customs and traditions may be a sufficient safeguard of your interests in such circumstances. And there are times when it is best simply to trust the people you are dealing with.

By **JAY BRENNAN,**
A. JAMES CASNER, Consultant

5
The automobile

Rights on the highway
—and liability
for accidents

One sure and quick way to arrive at legal problems in America is by automobile. Each year no fewer than 40 million U.S. drivers are ticketed or arrested for crimes involving their cars. Some 25 million vehicles are damaged annually in accidents that must, by law, be reported to the authorities and at least that many roll away with minor, unreported damage. More than 50,000 Americans are killed by automobiles each year, and two million more are injured. According to Daniel Patrick Moynihan, one of the first prominent sociologists to concern themselves with traffic safety, "about one out of every four cars manufactured in this country winds up with blood on it." The American who does not face at least one accident claim and one traffic summons during his driving lifetime is as rare as the policeman who never makes an arrest. It is not surprising that the automobile is the subject of more statutes and cases in United States law libraries than any other mechanical object—including the gun.

The law does not wait for damage or death to keep its eye on you and your automobile. Wherever you live, local and state regulations govern the ownership and use of automobiles, their licensing and registration, insurance requirements and the offenses that lead to traffic tickets. Many of these statutes may affect you whether you drive or not, applying as they do to passengers, owners and pedestrians. And the law's interest goes well beyond the questions of public safety and order, guaranteeing you peaceful enjoyment of one of modern society's most useful machines.

YOUR LEGAL RIGHT TO OWN A CAR

Everyone has the same right to own an automobile that he has to own a lawn mower or a refrigerator. Even a person who cannot possibly drive a car—such as a blind man—may legally possess one. There is one important stipulation, however: the ownership must be a matter of record, just as ownership of a house is. This record is usually a certificate of title, comparable to the deed to a house, stipulating that the person named on the certificate is the legal owner of the car and listing anyone who has a financial interest in that ownership, e.g., a finance company or bank. In states that do not require a title certificate, the record of ownership is a bill of sale, listing the two parties to the transaction when the car last changed hands and indicating any financial encumbrances.

When you buy a car, new or used, the dealer usually arranges for you to receive a certificate of title from the motor vehicles department. If you buy on time, the name of the bank or finance company is indicated on the certificate along with yours—and the lender usually

takes physical possession of this key document, keeping it until you pay off the debt or sell the car.

At some time you may want to buy a used car that still has payments due on it. Such a deal can become a bit complicated, since the seller has no legal right to dispose of property encumbered by debt. You can ask the seller to pay off his debt first, then give you a clear, unencumbered title—but he seldom has the cash required for this arrangement. Or you can ask the finance company to let you assume the remaining payments; if the company agrees, it should give you a written statement authorizing the transfer of ownership. More likely, you will engage in a three-cornered transaction in the finance company office: You pay the seller, he uses some of this money to pay off the finance company and the finance company turns the title over to you.

Because the moneylender generally holds onto the title certificate for a mortgaged car, there is little danger you can unwittingly buy a car encumbered by an unpaid debt. But if you do, the creditor can repossess the car, repaying you a fair price minus the cost of repossession and the debt still owed. To recover such a loss, your only recourse is to sue the fraudulent seller for damages. The sure way to avoid this kind of problem when buying a car from an individual is to check with your state's motor vehicles agency and make sure the seller owns the car free of debt.

You must, of course, keep the record of ownership so that you can sell the car later on—or prove your right to recover the car in the event it is stolen. If you have such a record, you can use it to regain possession of a stolen automobile even though it is in the hands of another person who innocently purchased it from the thief. That second buyer is legally out of luck.

Proof of ownership is the first step toward getting a car on the road —but only the first step. With that proof, you can apply for registration and license plates, which are required of any powered vehicle operating on a public road. They are granted only if the vehicle meets certain mechanical standards, and some states demand an inspection of the car to make sure. All cars sold by dealers—whether Detroit-made or imported—are equipped to fulfill the requirements of all states, but if your mechanically minded teen-age son decides to assemble his own Gran Turismo, he must provide it with four-wheel dual-system brakes, windshield wipers, windshield washers and all the other legally required niceties before he can use it anywhere except on a private track. While foreign cars sold in the United States meet American registration standards, most cars made abroad for use abroad do not, because standards for such things as windshield glass and headlights vary from country to country. These cars, occasionally bought by unwary tourists, cannot be registered in this country without costly modification. If you plan to bring home a car you buy on a trip overseas, make sure it is built to American standards.

Two other stipulations govern the issuance of automobile registration. In many states the car must be covered by liability insurance or the owner must in some other way guarantee payment of damages in the event of an accident. Finally, the car must be registered in the state where it is ordinarily used. All 50 states honor out-of-state registrations as long as the vehicles make only temporary use of the local highways. If you intend to remain in a state other than your own for more than a few months, you must generally apply for an additional registration in that state, usually within a 60- to 90-day grace period. Driving an out-of-state car after the grace period has expired is considered a misdemeanor, tantamount to driving an unregistered car. Some states even require you to take out a local license and registration if you intend to reside there 30 days or more. If your family spends the whole summer in another state, check the local law to see if you must register the car in that state. Exceptions to these rules are often made for certain categories of people. In many states, members of the armed forces who are stationed there are allowed to keep their home-state plates on their cars.

YOUR RIGHT TO DRIVE A CAR

While anyone may own an automobile, complete with plates, not everyone is allowed to drive one—at least, not on public streets and highways. Most states refuse to license anyone who is a habitual drunkard or addicted to the use of narcotics that make him incapable of driving. Physical or mental disabilities can also be grounds for refusing a driver's license. In addition, nearly all states require an eye examination, a driving test on the road and some proof of understanding of highway regulations before granting a license.

To determine an applicant's qualifications for a license, nearly all states demand rather personal information of applicants—arrest records, health histories and so on. It is sometimes tempting to bend the truth, but remember that misrepresentation could be considered falsification of an official document and a misdemeanor. There is one exception. The courts permit a lady to conceal her age, so long as she proves she is over 21, a gallant doctrine first pronounced by a New York judge who ruled that the only reason for including the birth date on a license was to show that the driver was not a minor. If a woman admits her majority, he ruled, the law is satisfied.

A model traffic ticket

Concerned about the confusing traffic procedures used throughout the United States, the American Bar Association has endorsed a uniform ticket that has been adopted by many localities. It is made out in quadruplicate. The officer retains one copy; the offending driver gets one; and two go into local police department and state automobile licensing files, thus assuring that the ticket cannot be fixed.

Jurisdiction
The top lines of the ticket record the legal jurisdiction in which the offense occurred and give it a file number.

Identification
This section records the exact time of the offense, the name, address and vital statistics of the driver, and a description of his automobile.

Degrees of offense
Next to a list of the most common violations (in left column, inside box), the ticket displays three columns of other offenses, each of which aggravates the original one. The degree of aggravation increases column by column. Making an improper left turn from the wrong lane, for example, is more serious than failing to signal a left turn. By checking one of the boxes, the officer gives the violation a precise classification that will be used in court.

Prevailing conditions
Additional factors such as weather and traffic conditions at the time of the violation provide the court still further evidence—speeding past pedestrians near a school during a fog, for example—on which to judge the case.

Cop and court
The bottom of the ticket has room for the signature of the complaining officer. The driver also signs, thus acknowledging receipt of this summons and promising to appear in court.

UNIFORM TRAFFIC TICKET AND COMPLAINT

1

CASE No._____ DOCKET No._____ PAGE No._____

STATE OF _____
COUNTY OF _____ SS. **No.** [ ]
☐ CITY ☐ VILLAGE ☐ TOWNSHIP OF ____ **SUMMONS**

IN THE _____ COURT OF _____

You are hereby Summoned to appear personally before this court to answer for the following offense:

ON_____ THE_____ DAY OF_____ 19____, AT_____ A.M. P.M.

2

NAME _____
LAST   (PLEASE PRINT)   FIRST   MIDDLE
STREET _____
CITY - STATE _____
AGE_____ BIRTH DATE_____ RACE_____ SEX_____ HT._____ WT._____
DRIV. LIC. No. _____
VEH. LIC. No._____ KIND_____ NUMBER_____ STATE_____ YR._____
MAKE_____ STYLE_____ COLOR_____

UPON A PUBLIC HIGHWAY, NAMELY AT (LOCATION) _____

DID UNLAWFULLY (DRIVE) (PARK) (OPERATE) IN THE CITY, VILLAGE, TOWNSHIP, COUNTY AND STATE AFORESAID AND DID THEN AND THERE COMMIT THE FOLLOWING OFFENSE:

3

Leading Causes of Accidents

SPEEDING (over limit) (____ m.p.h. in ____ m.p.h. zone)	☐ 5-10 m.p.h.	☐ 11-15 m.p.h.	☐ over 15 m.p.h.
Improper LEFT TURN	☐ No signal	☐ Cut corner	☐ From wrong lane
Improper RIGHT TURN	☐ No signal	☐ Into wrong lane	☐ From wrong lane
Disobeyed TRAFFIC SIGNAL (When light turned red)	☐ Past middle intersection	☐ Middle of intersection	☐ Not reached intersection
Disobeyed STOP SIGN	☐ Wrong place	☐ Walk speed	☐ Faster
Improper PASSING AND LANE USAGE	☐ At intersection ☐ Between Traffic ☐ Lane Straddling	☐ Cut-in ☐ On right ☐ Wrong lane	☐ Wrong side of pavement ☐ On hill ☐ On curve
	☐ Following too closely	☐ Failure to yield	

Other Violations:
In Violation of Section: _____

☐ State Statute   ☐ Local Ordinance in such case made and provided.

NAME / Last / First

PARKING:
Meter No. _____ ☐ Overtime   Prohibited ☐ Area   Double ☐ Parking   Expired ☐ Meter
(Describe) Other ____ parking violation

4

Conditions that Increased Seriousness of Violation

SLIPPERY PAVEMENT	☐ Rain ☐ Snow ☐ Ice	CAUSED PERSON TO DODGE		PD PI FATAL
DARKNESS	☐ Night ☐ Fog ☐ Snow	☐ Pedestrian ☐ Driver ☐ JUST MISSED ACCIDENT		☐ Ped. ☐ Vehicle ☐ Hit Fixed Object ☐ Right Angle ☐ Head on ☐ Sideswipe ☐ Rear end ☐ Ran off Roadway ☐ Intersection
OTHER TRAFFIC PRESENT	☐ Cross ☐ Oncoming ☐ Pedestrian ☐ Same Direction			

TYPE ACCIDENT

AREA: ☐ Business ☐ Industrial ☐ School ☐ Residential ☐ Rural
HIGHWAY TYPE: ☐ 2 lane ☐ 3 lane ☐ 4 lane ☐ 4 lane divided

Middle

YOU ARE NOTIFIED THAT THE OFFICER WHOSE SIGNATURE APPEARS BELOW WILL FILE A SWORN COMPLAINT IN THIS COURT CHARGING YOU WITH THE OFFENSE SET FORTH ABOVE.

_____
(Signature and Identification of Officer)

5

NOTICE TO VIOLATOR: READ BACK OF THIS SUMMONS CAREFULLY, BRING SUMMONS WITH YOU.

COURT APPEARANCE:_____ DAY OF_____ 19____, AT_____ M.,

ADDRESS OF COURT _____
I PROMISE TO APPEAR IN SAID COURT OR BUREAU AT SAID TIME AND PLACE.
SIGNATURE _____

In any state, a driver's license is a privilege, not a right, and is issued on the condition that the state may suspend or revoke it if you abuse it. A serious violation of traffic regulations—or repeated infractions of minor rules—may cause a license to be suspended for a short period of time, after which it is automatically restored. For more significant lawbreaking—drunken driving, for example—a license may be revoked; a new license application cannot be submitted until a year or more has elapsed.

YOUR RIGHTS AND OBLIGATIONS ON THE ROAD

To paraphrase an old saw, your car is almost your castle—that is, your constitutional liberties, including the right to privacy, are almost as protected when you are in your car as they are when you are at home. However, since an automotive castle hurtles about with such devastating force and some people use cars to commit crimes or to flee from the law, all state and federal jurisdictions give the police broad powers to stop a vehicle and, if necessary, arrest the driver and search and seize the vehicle. But for each of these rights the police must have "reasonable cause" to act.

The requirement of reasonable cause was established during Prohibition. One day in 1927 a Mississippian named Chrestman, who was driving a car without a muffler, was stopped by an officer and asked to appear in court to explain the violation. Before Chrestman could drive away, the officer became suspicious of his behavior and decided to search the car. He found a quantity of "unlawful, intoxicating liquor"—bootleg booze—and promptly arrested Chrestman for transporting it. The county court convicted Chrestman on the bootlegging charge, but an appeals court later reversed the decision, on the ground that the officer had no right to search Chrestman's car without first making a legal arrest. The search was unlawful, and without it, the liquor could not have been found. Therefore, said the court, Chrestman and his car could both go free.

The Chrestman case and others like it largely put an end to the routine police practice of following the car of a suspected wrongdoer, watching for some minor traffic violation for which the driver could be stopped, and then searching the vehicle on contrived grounds. Today, in most cities and states, a car can be searched only to obtain evidence pertaining to the actual offense for which it was stopped. Suppose a man returning from a hunting trip gets a ticket for an illegal U-turn and in searching the car the police discover in the trunk a deer that has been shot out of season; they cannot sustain charges against the driver for poaching, since discovery of the deer is unre-

A point system at work

One of the states that use a point system in recording a driver's violation is California. Under that state's law, each conviction for a moving traffic violation is placed on the driver's record, kept by the state department of motor vehicles. A specific number of points is assigned to each violation. For example:

■ Any accident in which the department decides the driver is responsible—1 point.

■ Any conviction involving unsafe operation of a vehicle—1 point.

■ Driving while license is suspended or revoked—2 points.

■ Causing property damage by hit-and-run—2 points.

■ Drunken driving without injury or property damage—2 points.

■ Reckless driving, whether or not it causes injury or property damage—2 points.

The department can revoke or suspend the license of any driver who accumulates four points or more in a 12-month period, six points or more in a 24-month period, or eight points or more in 36 months. The driver is given a hearing before any action is taken.

lated to the offense for which the car was originally stopped. Only if they had stopped the car on definite suspicion that it contained illegal cargo—if a game warden had earlier seen a suspicious object being placed in the trunk, for instance—would the court be likely to rule they had grounds for the search.

When the police seize an automobile that has been used to transport contraband, there is a rather strange legal quirk affecting the car (but not the driver). The car itself is in effect arrested. Under the provisions of various laws relating to smuggling, the vehicle can become the property of the state, and the owner can be made to forfeit his ownership. In one such case, a California mother had given her son permission to drive her car, unaware that he was using it to transport narcotics. After he was picked up, the state confiscated her car and sold it at auction.

Not only does the Constitution protect your car against unjustified searches; it also protects you against vague charges of wrongdoing. Whether you are stopped for a serious offense or a simple traffic violation, you have a right to be clearly informed of the charge. A traffic policeman, for example, who pulls you over for running a red light must make this fact clear on the ticket. He cannot simply jot down a cryptic notation "Violated City Ordinance Number 314.11(2)." Because you cannot be expected to understand such a charge, you could have the ticket thrown out of court on constitutional grounds.

Understanding the charge is generally scant comfort in traffic court, however. The weight of evidence almost always favors the policeman filing the complaint, and a plea of guilty is usually expedient. Often such a plea can be entered and the stipulated fine paid by mail, eliminating the bother of a court appearance; even when this convenience is denied local residents, it may be extended to drivers who live far from the court.

There are times, however, when pleading guilty to take the easy way out of a traffic offense may lead to deep trouble. Payment of the fine is equivalent to a conviction. If the ticket was issued immediately after an accident, for example, this conviction may prejudice a damage suit. More commonly, conviction for a relatively minor violation of traffic laws may result in suspension of a license, a severe hardship to anyone who uses his car in his job.

License suspension for a minor offense is particularly likely in those states using a point system to penalize habitual violators of traffic rules. A certain number of points is assigned for each violation of the more important rules, and the driver who accumulates more points

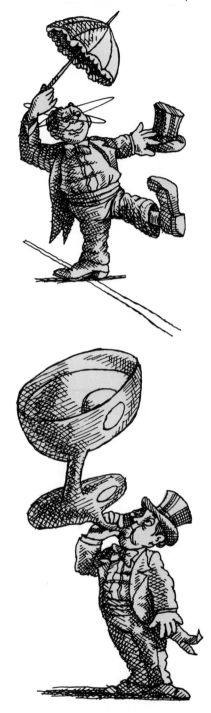

than the permitted total within a specified period automatically loses his license. If your state operates on the point system and you have several points on your record, do not plead guilty to a minor violation without thinking about it carefully. The points attached to the latest violation may be enough to push the total over the top and deprive you of your license. When this is possible, the judge, who has your entire record before him, is in some states required to warn you of the consequences of a guilty plea.

If you decide to fight a traffic ticket, get a lawyer—preferably one who handles such cases frequently. His expertise and familiarity with the court will speed things up considerably. If you decide to represent yourself, then try to get someone else who was present at the time of the alleged offense to testify in your behalf so that it is not simply your word against the word of the traffic policeman. It is normally desirable to demand a jury, whose members may be sympathetic because most are probably motorists themselves. Finally, if you lose your case in traffic court, you still have a clear right, in most jurisdictions, to appeal your conviction to a higher court.

AUTOMOTIVE CRIMES

Peccadilloes like running a stop sign carry real hazards, physical as well as legal, but they belong to the lesser class of lawbreaking called violations or petty offenses. Far more serious are misdemeanors and felonies. They are most often punished by imprisonment as well as fines and revocation of the driver's license. Three common crimes that involve the most severe penalties are driving while intoxicated, leaving the scene of an accident and vehicular homicide.

Drunken driving

In most states even a first offense for drunken driving is a misdemeanor, punishable by a fine, a short jail term or revocation of the driver's license—or all three. In determining drunkenness the law takes into account the medical fact that some people can consume greater quantities of alcohol than others without showing any obvious effects. It is not necessary to show the effects. That is, a suspect does not have to act drunk in order to be charged with driving while intoxicated; the police need only prove that he is legally under the influence of alcohol. Various tests are used to determine this. Although a driver once could refuse such tests, nearly all states now assume that any driver using a public highway has automatically consented to any tests of his fitness to drive there. Refusal violates the conditions under which he was issued a license, and the license can be revoked.

Tests for drunken driving
Some courts accept such simple tests as requiring a driver to walk a straight line or recite "Peter Piper picked a peck of pickled peppers." But the most common method uses devices to trap the driver's breath for an analysis of the amount of alcohol in his system.

The law is so strict about drunken driving that in many states an intoxicated driver who turns over the wheel of his car to a companion who is not entirely sober is just as susceptible to a criminal charge as if he had continued to drive the car himself. There have even been instances when pulling off the road to sleep it off did not prevent prosecution for drunken driving. In one such case, a tipsy Arizona truck driver parked at the side of the road but neglected to turn off his engine. The police, relying on a legal technicality that the truck was still operating and that operating a vehicle is tantamount to driving it, charged him with driving under the influence; he was held guilty.

Alcohol is not the only substance that can cause legal problems for a driver. Most courts interpret the laws against driving while intoxicated to apply to driving under the influence of any substance that you know to be incapacitating—including narcotics, tranquilizers and many medicines. Even insulin has been considered intoxicating in a few instances. In some states, the law simply requires the driver to be in a condition fit to operate his car safely, and a driver who is unfit from any cause—even illness—can be penalized.

Hit-and-run accidents

Leaving the scene of an accident is one of the most serious automotive crimes on the books. All states require that a driver who has struck —or even scraped—another object, whether it be another vehicle, a fence, a stray dog or a person, must stop immediately to investigate the damage and leave his name, address and registration number. The offense is so serious that in·some jurisdictions a hit-and-run driver's passengers are often convicted along with him, as accessories—even when their involvement is passive. In one case, a Virginia man who said nothing when the woman he was riding with struck and injured a man, then sped on, was also convicted for leaving the scene of an accident. Some lawyers have argued that the hit-and-run statutes violate the constitutional protection against self-incrimination, but in 1971 a divided U.S. Supreme Court ruled against them.

All states expect a driver to give assistance to anyone who has been injured by his action. California law goes further and demands that a driver not only assist the injured but also carry out their personal requests to the letter—such as informing their relatives of the accident, summoning a doctor or taking them to a hospital. A driver who fails to carry out any of these requests can be prosecuted for violating a section of the hit-and-run law.

The most common plea that a hit-and-run driver makes is that he did not know an accident had occurred. If the facts support his claim, the courts are usually lenient. But if the blow struck by the car was hard enough for the driver to have heard it or at least felt it, the court will probably rule against him.

Vehicular homicide

The accidental killing of a person is not a crime, unless the cause of the death was more than simple carelessness. Criminal charges are seldom filed against the driver after a fatal accident. Instead, civil actions are instituted, to fix legal responsibility for the death and set monetary damages to be paid to the heirs. On the other hand, a criminal charge of involuntary manslaughter is sustainable in some states if the driver's actions leading up to the accident broke the law. Suppose that just before the accident occurred he had run through a stop sign. This violation, though minor in itself, could be enough to convict him of the manslaughter charge and send him to prison.

Because it is often difficult for investigators to reconstruct details of a fatal accident when at least one of the key witnesses is dead, the state will sometimes press for a criminal indictment and trial simply to sort out all the conflicting evidence. Consequently any driver who has been involved in an accidental death—no matter how innocent of wrongdoing he may be—should be prepared for such a charge and consult an attorney immediately.

When a death is due to wanton recklessness, the law labels the offense voluntary manslaughter, for which the penalty in some states may be 15 years in prison. Normally a charge of voluntary manslaughter is lodged only against those drivers who display such complete disregard for the lives of others that the resulting death seems almost a conscious act on their part.

In some states, Wisconsin among them, any driver who had been drinking prior to a fatal accident is automatically assumed to have displayed this degree of recklessness and is charged with voluntary manslaughter, regardless of whether or not he is legally intoxicated. This distinction made all the difference in the case of a Wisconsin man named Victor Peckham. Peckham was driving carefully along a country road one night in July 1941. As another car approached, both Peckham and the other driver dimmed their lights, momentarily obscuring a stretch of the road between them. Suddenly Peckham saw two children at his side of the road and swerved sharply. But he swerved too late: one child lay dead, the other was injured. The oncoming driver later testified that the accident appeared unavoidable, that Peckham had done everything possible to prevent it from happening. Normally, under such circumstances, Peckham would not have been charged

with any crime; but when it was disclosed that he had been drinking, he was automatically charged with the serious crime of voluntary manslaughter. He was convicted and sent to prison.

DAMAGE SUITS

An automotive crime, whether it involves a relatively harmless case of illegal parking or a serious one of drunken driving, falls under the same kinds of restraints that apply to other crimes. Conviction may be punished by fine or imprisonment or both. Most often, however, the automobile brings you into contact with the law in a different way, by damaging property or injuring people—wrongs that are not necessarily committed against society as a whole but against individuals and that involve the torts of civil law. Trials for such wrongs are separate and different from criminal proceedings, and the wrongs are redressed not by fines or jail sentences meted out by the state but by monetary damages awarded to the injured plaintiff.

Some automobile accidents, of course, involve both crimes and torts. If a drunken driver speeds into another car, he will usually be tried first by the state for his crimes. Then the owner and occupants of the other car may, on their own initiative, institute civil proceedings to force him to pay for the harm he caused. The criminal trial generally precedes the civil one, and the first may influence the outcome of the second. Who—if anyone—collects how much in damages depends partly on who bears how much blame for the accident, and that issue may be influenced by a conviction on criminal charges arising from the accident. However, the final assessment of blame remains for a civil damage suit, whether or not a crime has been committed.

The civil trial must decide a number of questions before granting damage awards, but the first of these is the matter of blame: Who among the parties involved failed to exercise the required care for the

rights and safety of others? The question seldom has a simple answer.

The absence of care and caution is called in legal terminology negligence. It means what you would expect: the failure of a "reasonable man" to exercise "ordinary care" to avoid injuries to himself or to others. But this elementary definition is insufficient. So much is at stake, especially when a serious accident has occurred and extensive damages are being asked, that the definition of negligence must be amplified and refined in order to enable judges and juries to decide each case fairly. For this reason the law recognizes two distinct degrees of negligence, "ordinary" and "gross." In addition, there are two separate systems of dividing up the blame for negligent behavior, "contributory" and "comparative."

Negligence—ordinary or gross?

Ordinary negligence, the lesser of the two degrees, normally involves an accident that is caused by nothing more than simple carelessness —failing to see an approaching car, for example. The careless driver could be wholly at fault and entirely responsible for the consequences. And the consequences could be serious. Yet even if the accident results in the death of another person, the court would hold the careless driver guilty of ordinary negligence. He probably would not face criminal charges, but he probably would be held entirely at fault for the victim's death and would have to pay damages to the victim's heirs —with certain crucial exceptions noted later.

At the other extreme are examples of such reckless negligence, like uncontrolled speeding or total drunkenness, that the law categorizes them as gross, willful or wanton, and throws the book at any driver who displays such complete disregard for the safety of others. Criminal charges are usually brought in these cases, and a driver who is found guilty of gross negligence may be required to pay his victims

Acts of God are a law unto themselves. Suppose a bolt of lightning knocks down a tree that hits your car—which then collides, in succession, with a pedestrian, another car and a house. Even after all that, you would not be held liable.

not only heavy personal damages, but "punitive" damages as well. These damages constitute extra punishment that avenges the harmed individual rather than the state.

Sharing the blame

Categorizing negligence by degree is one way the law maintains control over the amount of litigation that can arise as the result of accidents. Many people believe that anyone who is injured in an accident can always collect damages from someone. Not so. In many cases, no damages are awarded unless gross negligence is proved. In other cases, damage awards may be reduced or eliminated, depending on how blame for the accident is apportioned among those involved. And acts of God are a law unto themselves. Suppose a bolt of lightning knocks down a tree, and the falling tree hits your car, which then collides with a pedestrian, another car and a house. Even after all that, with no evidence of human fault, you would not be held liable.

The blame for most accidents can be laid to the drivers of the cars involved and even their passengers. To apportion blame, most states use a system of law known as contributory negligence. The term refers to action that was not the ultimate cause of an accident, but that contributed to the cause. It was this kind of carelessness that cost a Mr. White of Tulsa his right to collect when a wild motorist slammed into his car with such force that repairs came to $500. White was not even inside the car at the time. It was double-parked. The court ruled that White's own act in blocking the way was a factor contributing to

Mr. White was not inside his double-parked car when a motorist slammed into it. But the court ruled that White's own act in blocking the way was a factor contributing to the collision.

the collision. Under contributory negligence laws, neither party involved in an accident is allowed to collect damages if it turns out that both contributed in any way to the cause of the accident. White lost his suit for damages and paid the repair bill himself.

The reasoning behind such laws is that no person should be permitted to benefit from his own carelessness. Most lawyers would hesitate to accept an accident case if there was a chance that the opposing side could prove contributory negligence. And often, if such an accident case does reach court, the judge or jury will find contributory negligence and the plaintiff will get nothing.

The principle of contributory negligence has proved so unfair in many instances that several states have replaced it with a system known as comparative negligence. Under this method, the negligence of each party in an accident is carefully apportioned by a jury, and the party who can be shown to have been the most negligent is required to pay damages to the others. But the amount of damages awarded is determined by each party's share of the negligence involved. If White had lived not in Oklahoma but in Wisconsin, which applies rules of comparative rather than contributory negligence, he might have fared better in court. The jury might have assigned major blame—perhaps 80 per cent—to the other driver. Then White could have collected $400 of the $500 it cost to fix his car.

Some examples of negligence

Any erratic or careless act behind the steering wheel of an automobile can be considered negligence, but there are several examples that crop up frequently in court cases.

■ Falling asleep at the wheel or blacking out. The courts almost always place the whole burden of negligence on a driver who has fallen asleep at the wheel, for sleep rarely occurs unexpectedly and without warning. A driver who ignores the usual signs of drowsiness or fatigue and continues to drive until he loses consciousness has failed to exercise normal care and can, under some circumstances, be charged with gross negligence. The drowsy driver who refuses to turn over the wheel to a passenger after narrowly escaping a collision is practically certain to be held grossly negligent. The only possible excuse for losing consciousness at the wheel is a sudden blackout caused by a fainting spell, a heart attack or a stroke. Even so, drivers with known heart trouble or a record of previous strokes have been held negligent in accident cases on the grounds that they should have anticipated a recurrence and refrained from driving.

■ Failing to keep a sharp lookout. Another frequent ground for a negligence charge is simple inattention: The driver turns to speak to a passenger, leans over to pick something off the floor or fishes for a map in the glove compartment. One case that is quoted in legal textbooks involves a cab driver of rather small stature who ran down and killed a child who had run out in front of his vehicle. The driver insisted that he was not negligent because he could not have seen the child. The court noted that "because of his stature, the hood of his own automobile prevented him from seeing objects in front and close to him." However, this fact did not deter the court from deciding that the accident involved negligence. "It is true that persons of small stature may and do lawfully operate automobiles," said the judge, "but . . . that condition imposes upon them the duty of exercising greater watchfulness to avoid injuring others."

■ Failing to maintain control. A third common category of negligence cases arises from two types of collision: ramming into the car ahead and sideswiping another vehicle while trying to pass it. Either type of accident indicates an inability on the driver's part to maintain control of his vehicle—and loss of control is grounds for a charge of negligence. Many rear-end collisions are caused by tailgating—following the car ahead too closely. A driver who can be proved to have tailgated bears the burden of negligence in any damage claim.

■ Operating an unsafe vehicle. If a sudden blowout causes a driver to veer into the path of an oncoming car, he will be absolved of negligence—if he can prove that the defects in the tire were unknown to him. But if the tire had obviously worn thin before the blowout, he will be held negligent for not maintaining a safe vehicle.

■ Failing to dim headlights. In the case of a collision caused by one driver's momentary blindness in the glare of oncoming headlights, both drivers could be found negligent, one for not dimming his lights, the other for failing to react to the emergency and take precautions. The law expects a driver in such a situation to slow down until the oncoming car has passed or pull off the road altogether. He may be found guilty of contributory negligence if he fails to do so.

The last clear chance

The attempt to lay blame for negligence where it belongs is so persistent that sometimes the law makes interesting exceptions to its own rules. Under the doctrine of contributory negligence, for instance, most states bar the collection of damages when both parties are at fault. But under certain unusual circumstances, the concepts of "the last clear chance" and "discovered peril" apply, and contributory negligence can be set aside. A classic example involves a woman who was waving goodbye while backing her car out of a friend's driveway. A man driving along the road saw her in time but failed to slow down because he had the right of way and assumed she would stop. She did not. He ran into her and killed her. Clearly the woman had been guilty of negligence, but the court allowed the woman's heirs to sue the man, and they won. Commenting on the case, a legal textbook explains, "The defendant is liable not because he was more negligent or because his negligence was later in time, but on the ground that the decedent was ignorant of her danger and the defendant continued driving after being aware of her ignorance." In other words, he had a last clear chance to avoid the tragedy and failed to heed it.

THE LAW OF LIABILITY

Closely related to the law of negligence is the question of legal liability. The law draws a fine distinction between these two kinds of responsibility for protecting the rights of others. In many circumstances you may be held negligent—guilty of an act that caused the accident —but not liable, that is, not answerable for the damage caused. In other circumstances you may be innocent of any negligence but still liable for damages. Liability depends on the relationships between the person at fault and the people or property harmed. But it can also extend to a blameless person—the owner of a car driven by someone else, for instance—and even to the manufacturer of the car.

The driver is clearly responsible for people and property outside the car. If he runs into another car and his negligence is established, he must pay for its repair and for injuries inflicted on its occupants. Liability for pedestrians is even more stringent. The automobile is potentially so dangerous that the courts often give pedestrians the benefit of the doubt. Nevertheless, they have an obligation as well. Some judges have ruled, for example, that pedestrians who were hit after they had shielded their vision with umbrellas in rainy weather were guilty of contributory negligence and could not recover damages.

When it comes to the people who are riding with the driver, his liability is much more limited. If the passengers are members of his immediate family—his spouse, children or parents—he may have no liability in most states. These states continue to subscribe to the doctrine of family immunity, which prohibits such suits on the grounds that they would promote discord between close relatives. But this doctrine is increasingly being ignored—and it no longer applies in many

The pedestrian's rights
Laws protecting pedestrians are especially strict in California, where a judge once ruled against a driver who had merely come too close. "A pedestrian," he said, "is not entitled to just as much space as his body, clothes and buttons require. His heart must be free from attack."

states—because of the unfair way it works out in the majority of cases: It prevents recovery of monetary damages that will be paid not by the driver himself, but by his insurance company.

A similar limitation on liability applies to unrelated passengers who are considered what the law calls gratuitous guests. That is, they have simply been offered a ride. They are denied damages from the driver of the car in which they are riding unless it can be proved that he was guilty of gross negligence. One reason for these limitations, which apply in most states, is to discourage collusion between a driver and a passenger who might try to fake an accident in order to collect damages from an insurance company and then split the proceeds. Staging an accident that seems to involve gross negligence is fairly difficult; in some jurisdictions the jury must believe that the driver was "consciously indifferent" to his passenger's safety, and convincing the jury that this state of mind existed is a task no lawyer accepts lightly. Since most attorneys handling accident cases base their fees on a share of whatever damages they can hope to win, few are willing even to accept cases in which a guest statute is likely to rule out damages.

The guest statutes apply to people who are receiving a ride as an accommodation, a friendly gesture. If your neighbor offers you a lift into town or your friend says "Let's use my car" when you go out for dinner, you are riding as a guest, and his liability toward you is limited in most states. Such is not the case with many other drivers who might give you a ride. If you are a member of a car pool with two of your neighbors, for example, each of you is, in effect, a paying passenger, since the car pool is a business arrangement in which each member swaps services with the others in turn. As a business passenger, you escape the limitation of the guest statutes; your driver is liable for harm that befalls you even if his negligence is ordinary—proof of gross negligence is not necessary. You are considered a business passenger, rather than a guest, whenever you ride with a real estate man in his car while looking for a house or with an automobile salesman when he demonstrates a new model. You would also qualify as a business passenger if you were reimbursing the driver of a car for his gas and oil on a trip between, say, New York and San Francisco. (But if you share the expenses and the driving with your host, your legal status could be that of co-agent, and you share liability equally.)

The responsibilities of the passenger

A driver's liability for harm that may come to his passengers depends not only on the relationships between them but also on the passengers' actions. A passenger may lose his rights to damages if he condones negligent behavior and willingly takes his chances with the driver. As one judge commented in ruling against an unsuccessful plaintiff, "He permits himself to be driven carelessly to his injury" —and therefore assumes an equal share of the responsibility for it.

A classic instance of an injured guest's shared responsibility for an accident concerns a young man named James Renfro, who was being driven along a Tennessee road one foggy night by a man named Dinkins. Dinkins was driving too fast for such weather, and Renfro told him to slow down. Testifying later in court, he said that he warned Dinkins, "You'd better hold this thing," but that Dinkins had replied, "Hell, boy, you ain't scared, are you?" Renfro admitted he was, but Dinkins still refused to slow down. Finally he lost control of the car on a sharp curve and drove over an embankment, seriously injuring Renfro, who then sued for damages. The judge ruled against him on the grounds that he should have demanded that Dinkins stop the car and let him out.

The responsibilities of the owner

The chain of responsibility in automobile accidents can go far beyond driver and passengers. The owner—even if he is not present when the accident takes place, let alone at the wheel—may be held liable in certain circumstances. He could be found negligent, for example, if he lent his car to a person whom he knew to be a heavy drinker, and the evidence showed that drinking contributed to the accident. Since the owner placed the car in dangerous hands, he might be liable for the harm that resulted. More often, though, the owner's liability for his vehicle comes about because of his relationship to the

In some states, you cannot collect damages if you are injured while riding as a guest in someone else's car unless you can prove that the driver was guilty of wanton negligence.

driver. Suppose, for example, you ask a neighbor to use your car to run an errand for you, and in the course of doing so his own negligence causes an accident. Because he may be considered your agent, you are as liable as he is. The only way you could escape liability would be to prove that your neighbor ignored or recklessly exceeded your instructions. If he took a detour to run an errand of his own, for instance, and the accident occurred while he was engaged in doing something you had not asked him to do, he was no longer acting as your agent, and liability for damages would probably be his alone.

You would also probably escape liability if someone used your car without your knowledge or consent, but not if that person was a member of your family. The family purpose doctrine followed in many states holds that part of your responsibility to your household is to provide transportation for all its members. Any member who drives your car is thus acting automatically as your agent, on family business, and if he has an accident, you are liable for damages done.

The responsibilities of the manufacturer

The liability for the harm a car causes can extend to almost anyone —or any agency—that had anything to do with the vehicle: manufacturer, used-car dealer, rental company, repairman. Increasingly, the law recognizes that a mechanical flaw may contribute to an accident, and it attempts to place liability on the source of the flaw.

The manufacturer's liability was first established more than half a century ago, in 1916, the year a gravestone dealer named Donald MacPherson took his new Buick out along a country road in upstate New York. MacPherson was tooling along at eight miles an hour when one of the wheel spokes suddenly crumbled, causing his car to flip over. MacPherson was injured. With commendable foresight, he called in an expert carriage maker to examine the car, and the expert testified that the hickory wood used in the spokes was defective. MacPherson sued Buick for damages.

Buick based its defense on a traditional legal doctrine known as privity, according to which a company is liable for its products only to those it directly sells them to—in this case, the automobile dealer. But MacPherson hired an experienced lawyer, a man named Edgar T. Brackett, who proceeded to build his case on three cogent arguments. One was that the manufacturer had been negligent in failing to inspect the wheel after purchasing it from a subcontractor. The second was that the automobile was inherently a dangerous machine—a novel idea at the time. The third was that the time-honored doctrine of privity ought to be set aside, since MacPherson had every right to seek redress from the very people whose carelessness had led to his accident. In finding for MacPherson, Judge Benjamin Cardozo, the distinguished jurist who later became a U.S. Supreme Court Justice, wrote: "Precedents drawn from the days of travel by stagecoach do not fit the conditions of travel today. If the nature of a thing is such that it is reasonably certain to place life and limb in peril when negligently made, it is then a thing of danger."

Many later motorists attempted to match MacPherson's success in suing a manufacturer but failed because the law continued to demand proof (as it had from MacPherson) that the manufacturer had indeed made a defective, accident-prone machine due to negligence —proof often difficult to produce. But in 1955, the law took a far more liberal tack after Mrs. Helen Henningsen of New Jersey, driving her 10-day-old Plymouth at 22 miles an hour along a smooth four-lane highway, suddenly heard a loud noise that she later said "came from the bottom, by the hood. It felt as if something cracked." Something had, all right, for the new car's steering wheel spun uselessly in Mrs. Henningsen's hands. Veering wildly off the road, she crashed into a brick wall, injuring herself and totally demolishing her car. So smashed was its front end that it was virtually impossible for the Henningsens' lawyer to determine the precise nature of the defect, much less to prove negligence on the part of Chrysler. Normally, Mr. and Mrs. Henningsen's suit for damages would have ended right there. But the judge permitted their lawyer to present a novel argument to the jury: the manufacturer was liable for an obvious defect in its product solely on the basis of its warranty. The manufacturer argued that under its standard 90-day 4,000-mile warranty on parts and service, it could not be held liable for defects. The jury, however, agreed with the judge's instructions that the purpose of a warranty *(Chapter 6)* is not to limit the manufacturer's liability but to safeguard the buyer, and it awarded damages to the Henningsens for her injuries and the loss of her car. Chrysler appealed, but a higher court upheld the verdict on grounds that such a warranty "gave little and withdrew much" and could not be used by the manufacturer to avoid liability.

Although the Henningsen case and similar ones since have made manufacturers liable for defects in their products whether negligence can be proved or not, this liability applies only if a flaw is the cause of the harm and if it existed at the time the car left the manufacturer's hands. These qualifications are important. If you have an accident and suspect that it may have been caused by a defect in the car, the defect should be pinpointed by an expert as quickly as possible, before repairs are made—preferably even before the wreckage is hauled away. The detective work in such damage suits must be extremely precise, for establishing proof of defective workmanship is difficult.

In theory an automobile manufacturer's liability for defects extends throughout the life of the car, but in practice it virtually disappears after the first owner sells the car. By the time an automobile has become a used car, it will probably have been repaired so often that a court would have difficulty fixing responsibility for a defect on the manufacturer. Even so, you are not without legal protection. Repairmen are held to the same accountability as manufacturers, and the seller of a used car is required to inform you of any known defect and advise you to have it repaired. Rental agencies are subject to even stricter rules. Because they are engaged in the public transportation business, they are obliged to keep their cars in top-notch mechanical condition and to meet stringent safety requirements.

MEASURING THE COSTS

The law not only establishes blame, sorts out the liabilities of the parties to an accident and punishes the wrongdoers, but also guides the victims as they add up their losses and assign them a monetary value. If the accident is serious, the costs will include not only the damage done to the car, but medical and hospital bills for injuries as well as monetary compensation for time lost from employment; and if someone has been killed, a price must be placed on death.

The easiest figure to compute when calculating losses in an accident is the damage done to the car; a couple of estimates from repairmen provide clear evidence. Beyond that, if you need a car for personal or business reasons while your own is being repaired, the law will usually allow you to add the cost of a rental car to your total bill for repairs. If your car is demolished in the accident, however, the court would probably disallow an extended use of a rental car on the assumption that you would have to replace your own car anyway.

It is a good deal more difficult to estimate the dollars-and-cents cost of injuries done to a person. The law takes three factors into account: (1) the total medical expenses, as seen in the doctor and hospital bills; (2) the economic losses suffered as a result of being laid up or deprived of future income because of permanent disabilities; (3) the "pain and suffering" endured as a direct result of the injuries.

The medical bills are generally no problem, even when, as sometimes happens, injuries are not entirely cured at the time of settlement; the costs to date are often doubled or tripled to take care of future medical expenses. The claim filed is based on the total hospital and doctor bills whether or not they were covered by medical in-

HOW TO GET RID OF A LEMON

In spite of efforts by manufacturers, new cars are sometimes sold with defects. How can you return such a car before it causes you serious trouble? There is no sure way, but it can be done if you follow certain legal procedures. The following steps are based on the experiences of a lawyer who got his money back on a defective automobile. You should get your own lawyer's advice before trying to use the full range of recommendations.

Test-drive the car before you buy it and get assurances from the dealer that he will repair any defects that might show up. If you take the car in for repairs, present the service manager with a list of defects you have found; keep a copy of this list. Keep an accurate log noting the dates on which you return the car for repairs and the results. It is important to give the dealer as many opportunities as he needs to make the vehicle safe.

If you decide it is too dangerous to continue driving the car and the dealer refuses to reimburse you, leave it in the dealer's lot with a list of complaints posted on the windshield—including each defect that is still unrepaired. These defects must be serious, affecting the safety of the car and its passengers. Before you leave the dealer's lot, remove your license plates from the car and take them with you to indicate that the vehicle no longer belongs to you. Make a note of the mileage, for future reference. To further strengthen your legal case, send the dealer a notarized letter containing your final complaints. Inform him—and here a lawyer can help you choose the correct phraseology—that you have turned over ownership and possession of the car to him. Make it clear that you have revoked your earlier acceptance of the car and demand a refund of your purchase price.

To make your return of the car final and more legally binding, cancel your official registration and the insurance policy you hold on the car and notify the dealer by registered mail that you have taken these additional steps to revoke ownership. Stop by the dealer's, if possible, and take a look at the odometer of your former car. If the dealer has run up any mileage whatever on it since you left the vehicle in his possession, this fact can be presented in court as evidence that he has accepted your automobile as his property and no longer considers it to be yours.

The lawyer who used this procedure got his money back before the lawsuit he filed against the dealer ever reached court, so it set no actual precedent for other lawyers to follow. If you are still making payments on a troublesome car —the lawyer in question had paid by check—you and your attorney will have to send copies of your communications with the dealer to your bank or finance company (the lender actually holds title to the car) and include the lender in any lawsuit that you file.

surance. Neither is it normally a problem to arrive at a figure for loss of income for a certain period; missed paychecks are simply added up. But if injuries should cause permanent disability, the computations are not so simple. Take, for example, the considerations put forth by the lawyer for a promising bank officer whose legs were crippled in an accident. Although the banker earned only $8,000 a year at the time of the accident, he was slated for a promotion that would have raised his salary to $15,000 a year. The new job, however, would have required him to be physically active in the field, inspecting properties in which the bank had an interest—a job for which he was now disqualified by his injuries. His lawyer, calculating that the man's income could not now exceed $10,000 a year, estimated that his total loss of income for the rest of his life amounted to $100,000. The jury agreed.

Far more difficult to calculate in monetary terms are those subjective consequences of accidents that the law refers to as pain and suffering. It is impossible to put an accurate price tag on feelings. When dealing in this area lawyers usually try to guess the attitude and generosity of the jury hearing the case and ask for an amount that they think the jurors will find reasonable. One lawyer, for example, may set a price to one jury of $5,000 on the pain caused by a displaced vertebra. The same lawyer, arguing before a different jury, might put the cost of the same affliction at $50,000.

The bulk of these cases are handled by lawyers specializing in negligence. According to some estimates auto-negligence cases account for about 80 per cent of the civil court actions in the United States; most lawyers engaged in general practice therefore have some degree of competence in negligence law. But if the case is a major one, the man in general practice will probably refer you to a specialist in negligence—and you will find such a man well worth his fee. He will ask you to deliver a complete account of the accident, including names of witnesses. He will also insist that you make a full disclosure of the truth. Nothing so angers a negligence specialist as the discovery in court that his client, claiming to suffer a back injury as a result of the accident, has in fact a long history of back pain.

The specialist will probe every angle of your case, examining photographs, police reports and witnesses and obtaining information on weather and road conditions. You will discover that he will be knowledgeable in some areas of medicine, particularly those involving neurological and back injuries. He will evaluate your chances of financial recompense, institute the legal action and arrange a settlement—or, if necessary, proceed to trial. The lawyer who specializes in negligence cases is of necessity a trial lawyer, prepared to go into court to press the other side toward a satisfactory settlement when the occasion demands it.

His fee is usually "contingent"—meaning that he gets a percentage of whatever award is won, or nothing beyond expenses if the case is lost. The lawyers' percentages vary from state to state, but generally they are about one third of the total award.

While the amount granted the complainant for pain and suffering is almost always determined by the persuasiveness of the specialist and the state of mind of the jury, the jury does not have the last word. If the judge feels the jury was motivated by passion or prejudice, he can reduce the award or require that the case be reassessed by means of another trial. Many of the large awards that make newspaper headlines are whittled down to a fraction of their original size before they are finally paid.

Computing the cost of death

The most difficult and tragic task of all is placing an economic value on life itself. In general, the law recognizes two different categories of damages when trying to assess the cost of death. One category permits the estate of the deceased to recover for harm he himself had suffered. In this category are recompense for the pain the deceased had endured, even though he is no longer present to describe it, and hospital and medical expenses. In general, funeral costs are also permissible, although a few states disallow them since these are costs that everyone must incur eventually.

The second category includes damages due not to the deceased but to his heirs. In many states the widow and children of a breadwinner, for example, can expect a sum equal to the income he would have earned and contributed to their support through the remainder of his life. A widower can recover the costs of hiring a housekeeper to care for his home and children. Occasionally the elderly parents of a young victim may win a sum equivalent to the support their child would have provided them in their old age. But the parents of a young child may seldom make such a claim, on the hard but practical ground that the death of the child actually saved them money—the money they would have spent raising and educating him.

In some states there is no limit to the damages that may be awarded heirs for "wrongful death." One of the highest awards ever granted went to a New York widow, Alice B. Dalio, in 1970, after her husband, a shipping assembler, was killed in a four-car collision caused by two tailgating motorists; the jury found the two tailgaters responsible and ordered them to pay Mrs. Dalio the equivalent of her hus-

TEXT CONTINUES ON PAGE 158

Automobile accidents often involve such confusion that the drivers involved may fail to take the proper steps to protect their legal rights. This illustrated check list tells you what to do immediately after the accident. The check list on the following pages details further steps.

1 Your first priority, after stopping your car, is to care for anyone who has been hurt. To avoid further injuries, you should not try to move a victim unless failure to do so—when the vehicle is on fire—could endanger his life. Send for a doctor or an ambulance—or both, if necessary—as soon as possible. (There are legal as well as humanitarian reasons for these precautions.)

2 Take steps to protect the scene of the accident and prevent further collisions by stationing someone to warn approaching traffic. If it is night, see that any flares, reflectors or flashlights that are available are placed as warning signs.

3 Notify the nearest policemen or the highway patrolmen, and inform them of the nature of the accident so that additional emergency measures can be taken, if necessary.

4 Jot down the name, badge and precinct number of the officer who investigates the accident. His official report may be useful to you later if the other parties involved file a claim for damages.

5 Keep your ears open for remarks that may be made by others involved in the accident or by witnesses, but do not make statements of your own that might be used against you in court.

6 Write down the names and addresses of as many witnesses as possible. If they don't wish to become involved, remind them that they may need similar assistance some day and that they have a legal obligation to testify to what they saw. Try to get each witness to sign a short statement describing what he saw, if only a few words long. ("I saw the black Chevrolet run the red light and hit the green Ford.") Such statements are often admissible evidence even when the witnesses are no longer available to testify.

7 Telephone your insurance adjuster from the scene, if possible. If not, notify your insurance company within 24 hours, even if you have suffered no injuries or damages. The company may have to defend you later against damage suits.

8 Make a sketch of the accident, including such things as the distances involved, the direction in which the vehicles were moving and the position of skid marks. This can be used for reference later.

9 Accept no payments at the scene of the accident, not even a token sum offered to cover your out-of-pocket expenses. If you do so, you may be releasing the other party from further financial liability.

10 If considerable damage has been done to the vehicles involved and the police are not pressing to remove the wreckage, try to summon a professional photographer (often listed in the Yellow Pages under "Photographers, Legal") and have him photograph the scene —including the wreckage—from all sides. He should also take pictures of physical evidence that might provide a better record of the accident than the sketch you have made.

11 Do not leave the scene of the accident until you are certain you have exchanged and collected all the information necessary to file a complete report.

12 If you are injured, do not refuse any offer of medical assistance. If you are taken to a hospital or treated by a doctor, note down the doctor's name and his diagnosis.

The check list on the preceding pages explained the steps to take immediately after an automobile accident to protect your rights. Here are further steps to be taken before you make a settlement.

1 See your own physician if you suspect you have even a minor injury and ask him to write down in his records your explanation of what happened. These notes will be useful later if he is called to testify concerning your injuries.

2 As soon as possible, file any necessary reports of your accident with the state motor vehicles bureau or whatever other agency may be stipulated in the state in which the accident occurs. Some states require that a written report be submitted within 24 hours concerning any accident in which a person has been injured or killed, or in which damage has been done in excess of $50 or $100. Other states allow as long as 10 days for such reports, but some insist that if the driver himself is unable to make the report within the required time, some other person must do it for him. Failure to comply with these laws is usually considered a misdemeanor and grounds for suspension or revocation of the driver's license or registration.

3 If the accident was serious, give both your lawyer and your insurance agent a full description of what took place while the facts are still fresh. Bring up anything that might help them protect your interests. If the police at the scene seemed sympathetic to your version of what happened, for example, mention this to your lawyer. He might then interview the officers as possible witnesses.

4 Be circumspect if you are contacted by the other party or by his lawyer or insurance representative. Make no statement, sign no document unless your own lawyer is present to advise you.

5 If you have not already done so, have all four sides of your automobile photographed, and record the time and date the pictures were taken on the back of each. These will serve as proof that none of the damages you may claim occurred after the accident.

6 Do not be surprised if your lawyer or insurance representative asks to see your medical or other records in order to check into your background. He must try to anticipate any weak points in your case that the opposition may bring up if the case comes to trial.

7 If you are claiming damages for injuries, the other party has a right to have you examined by his own physician to verify your medical claims. But discuss only your injuries with him, not your accident. If he seems too curious for comfort, refer him to your lawyer—but note down exactly what questions the doctor has asked you and the time and place of the examination. Your lawyer may be able to use this information later as evidence of the other side's desperate tactics, and it may give him some bargaining power in dealing with the other side's attorney.

8 Get estimates of the cost of repairing your car from at least two qualified repairmen. In the event of a damage suit, the court may average these figures to reach a reasonable sum for settlement. Also make an inventory of any other damaged property —including the clothing you were wearing at the time of the accident. This could be added to your total claim for damages.

9 If you suspect that an original defect in your car, or one that could have resulted from a repairman's inferior workmanship, may have been responsible for the accident, do not allow any further repairs to be made until all of the parts in question have been carefully inspected by an engineering expert engaged by your lawyer. Otherwise, the defects may be repaired and covered over before you have a chance to prove that they existed prior to the accident. If you are able to prove the existence of a defect, you may have a case against the repairman or manufacturer responsible.

band's expected earnings, a total of $334,500. A number of states, however, discourage such huge settlements by putting a ceiling on damage settlements that can be paid to heirs; usually it runs between $50,000 and $75,000. Because there are no such restrictions on damage claims for injuries, lawyers sometimes say, in a macabre comment on the law's inequities, that it may cost a driver less to kill his victim than merely to maim him.

The insurance company

If you visit a courtroom during an accident trial, you will never hear a mention of insurance. The trial is always between individuals (or between individuals and an organization, such as the company that owns one of the cars involved). The suits often involve several people: If two cars collide, the drivers generally sue each other, and their passengers sue them both (simply to make sure not to miss a chance to collect from someone). This requirement of claims against individuals is rigidly maintained on the theory that evidence of insurance has no bearing on the fault of any individual (it also discourages jury members from being as liberal with damage awards as they might be if they knew the defendant did not have to pay everything out of his own pocket). But everybody understands that in most cases the suit is really against the defendant's insurance company: It is the insurance company that probably provided the lawyer and that will pay at least some of the damage award.

The insurance that stands behind the defendant in an accident trial is liability insurance—it pays for the harm he or his car did to others, but not for harm done to him. Normally the insurance company assumes this responsibility from the moment it agrees to issue insurance, even if the agreement is made only over the telephone and the company has still to receive the first premium. The extent of its responsibility is the face value of the policy. If the damages awarded come to more than the face value, the policyholder must pay the difference —with one exception. If an insurance company refuses to settle out of court on a claim that falls within the limits of the policy and a jury eventually grants a damage claim higher than this limit, the company may be liable for the difference. In one such case, the claim against a California woman who was insured up to $10,000 could have been settled out of court for $9,000. The woman's insurance company, however, refused to agree to this amount and let the suit go to trial, and the jury subsequently awarded the plaintiff $100,000. Although the insurance company claimed legal liability for only $10,000 of this sum, the woman sued the company and forced it to pay not only the total

$100,000 awarded to the plaintiff, but also an additional $25,000 to her in personal damages for the mental anguish she had suffered as a result of the insurer's stubbornness.

Your insurance policy generally provides protection for you whenever you drive any ordinary car, no matter whose it is, and it also covers claims against you for damages caused by your car, no matter who drives it. These terms are spelled out in a number of clauses, some of which can be tricky. If your policy, for example, insures both the family car and the one your teen-age son drives, the protection afforded your son may be limited in ways that do not apply to you, as the person who owns both cars.

Many of the important clauses depend on information you supply the insurance company—how the car is used, who uses it, where it is garaged—and the company has a legal right to the truth. Many people fudge, however, for the facts enable the company to evaluate the risks involved and decide how much to charge for a policy—even whether to issue one at all. It is very tempting to say that a car is used only occasionally on business when it is actually driven 10 miles to work five days a week or that a young son's car is garaged safely at home in the quiet suburbs when actually he keeps it near his apartment in the city where he has a job. Such misstatements are dangerous. In the event of an accident the insurance company could refuse to honor its commitment to protect the policyholder on the ground that misrepresentations on his part invalidated its contract. More likely the company would cancel the policy outright or refuse to renew it when it expired.

The loss of insurance—or the inability to get it in the first place —is a growing problem for which the law offers only uncertain remedies. An insurance company is privately owned, and like any private business, it can serve you or not, as it chooses. If you live in what is known as a high-risk area, for example, where accidents are frequent and the costs of paying off damages are high, your insurance company may arbitrarily put you into a high-risk category, limiting its coverage and charging a high premium. It may even cancel your policy or refuse to renew it. But a company that intends to take such action must notify you of its intention from five days to two months in advance, depending on the state. Some states do not require the insurer to explain its refusal to renew. But in every state it must be prepared to explain its reasons for canceling.

What you can do to hold or get insurance also depends on where you live. In a few states you have a right to some sort of insurance protection. Those states require you to have liability insurance for your car; if you do not, the car registration is refused or canceled. If you cannot get a policy on your own, you can ask an insurance agent to apply to the state, which will put you in its high-risk pool and order a company to issue you a policy (the protection is limited, and the rates are very high). In every state you can also write a letter of protest to your state insurance commission or to the state attorney general if you think you have been denied insurance for reasons that are frivolous or mistaken—particularly if the reason may be based on incorrect information from an investigator *(Chapter 7)*. But if obtaining liability insurance becomes difficult, your best help may come not from the law but from a friendly insurance broker who values your business and can look for a company that will insure you.

Making sure you have liability insurance of your own is only part of the problem. What happens if you try to collect damages from someone else who is insolvent and uninsured? In several states, all automobile liability policies are required to provide for payment of the policyholder's medical costs in the event he is the victim of a hit-and-run driver or an uninsured driver. In most other states, insurance companies provide similar coverage on their standard liability policies for a small extra charge. In these cases you make your claim for damages to your own insurance company. Some states have established special funds from which injured motorists and passengers can claim compensation. In those states you must first win your suit against the negligent uninsured driver and then apply to the court for an order directing the fund to pay up.

At one time people had a difficult time collecting for damages caused by government-owned vehicles. Local, state and federal governmental agencies were immune from civil damage suits on the ground that the liability of the government for the torts of its employees would place an excessive burden on the taxpayers. Under the Federal Tort Claims Act of 1945, however, civil damage claims can now be filed against the U.S. government for harm suffered in accidents involving federally employed drivers. Most state and municipal governments have followed suit. California, for instance, was required to pay damages to a motorist hit by a motorcycle patrolman pursuing two speeders. Normally emergency vehicles such as police cars, fire trucks and ambulances are exempted from liability in case of an accident because they automatically have the right of way. But one of the conditions of their exemption is the use of sirens or flashing lights to alert motorists to the emergency. And this the California patrolman had forgotten to do.

If you are harmed by a government vehicle, be sure to see your lawyer immediately. Claims must be made very soon after the accident or the right to sue is lost, and if you delay in filing the required forms you may forfeit any chance of recovering damages.

A new development in insurance

In an effort to cut through some of the red tape involved in settling damage claims arising from automobile accidents, two leading authorities on automotive law, Robert Keeton of Harvard and Jeffrey O'Connell of the University of Illinois, have worked out a "no fault" system of insurance. Modified versions of this new plan were adopted in 1970 in Puerto Rico and Massachusetts. In its original form, as the title of the plan indicates, no blame would be assigned for accidents. The entire concept of damages based on negligence would be eliminated. Instead of trying to collect from someone else for harm done to you, you would turn to your own insurance company, which would reimburse you for your out-of-pocket costs. Since no party to an accident would be required to prove negligence in order to secure redress, the tangled web of claims and counterclaims would be done away with —along with trials, emotional scenes before juries, huge damage settlements and, hopefully, much of the cost of insurance.

The system actually adopted in Massachusetts stops far short of the original proposal. It requires the owner of every car to carry insurance that will pay the medical bills of anyone injured while riding in the car—up to a maximum of $2,000. But if any person suffers harm that comes to more than $2,000, he must go back to the old system and claim damages from the person whose negligence caused the harm. Similar plans have been proposed to the legislatures of other states, but they have been slow to catch on, and only action by the U.S. Congress seems likely to remove the automobile from its position as one of the chief problems of the law for many years to come.

By **DON A. SCHANCHE**
PAGE KEETON, Consultant

6 Business

The legal safeguards
of contracts
and warranties

"The business of America is business," said Calvin Coolidge, and in at least one sense he was right. Business transactions of one kind or another make up an important part of most people's lives. You recognize your business involvement when you buy shares of stock or support a friend in a commercial venture. But even when you check your car in a parking lot, buy a newspaper, make a dentist's appointment, order flowers for your wife, hire a one-day-a-week cleaning woman or engage a plumber to fix a leaky pipe, you are entering into a business transaction—and every one of these transactions involves the law.

Licensing regulations, the Social Security Act, various fraud statutes and many other laws regulate business activities. But for most dealings between a businessman and his customers, legal questions involve mainly the law of contracts. One party, in return for a certain consideration, agrees to supply the other party with certain goods or services. Even the corner news dealer who sells you a paper every morning is a party to a business contract. In exchange for your consideration —a dime or so—he agrees to provide you with a current, readable paper. If the paper he hands you turns out to be torn or two days old, he has broken his contract. You have a right to get your money back, and a court would, in theory at least, enforce that right.

The law of business contracts is immensely complex. It covers every transaction like an invisible web, defining the rights and responsibilities of both parties, providing guidelines for enforcing every conceivable kind of agreement. Hundreds of years of accumulated statutes, decisions, precedents and exceptions have gone into the making of it, and commentaries on the field of commercial law fill entire libraries. If you are thinking of entering into any sort of major business deal—investing in an oil-prospecting firm, for instance, or patenting an invention or opening a gift shop—you should not do so without seeing a lawyer. On the other hand, the law as it applies to most everyday transactions that you and your family are likely to encounter generally follows certain easily understood principles. These principles are spelled out in a compilation of business law called the Uniform Commercial Code, which was drafted in the 1950s to modernize and standardize rules on various aspects of business law. It applies to bank checks and sales of goods, including warranties, the drawing up of contracts, rules of business performance and remedies for nonperformance. The U.C.C. is the model for the business laws of every state in the Union except Louisiana. And even Louisiana, whose laws are based in part on the French code inherited from Napoleon in 1803, has adapted its law wherever possible to conform to the precepts

If you slip on a banana peel that a merchant has carelessly left in the aisle, he can be held responsible for your injuries.

But if you wander through a door marked "Employees Only," you have only yourself to blame if you knock something over and break your neck.

EMPLOYEES ONLY

of the U.C.C. As a result of this standardization, the rights and responsibilities of buyers and sellers are similar throughout the country, although specific laws vary somewhat from state to state.

THE BUYER'S RIGHTS

The commonest kind of commercial transaction is a direct sale. You go into a store, choose something you want—a package of razor blades, a book, a set of dining-room furniture—pay for it and carry it off or arrange to have it delivered. Your responsibilities to the merchant are few in number, and they amount to little more than behaving like a respectable citizen while on his premises. The law will not permit you to disrupt his business by starting a fist fight in his aisles or delivering a political harangue from his mezzanine. It will not force him to sell you goods, and neither, obviously, will it permit you to pay him with counterfeit money or a bad check.

On the other hand, you have many rights in your relationship with the merchant, and they begin the moment he opens his doors and invites you to walk into his store. First of all, you have the legal right to expect that he will take reasonable precautions to see that you come to no harm on his premises. It does not matter why you came in—to buy, to browse or simply to meet a friend—you are still there at the merchant's invitation. If you trip over a mop or slip on a banana peel that he has carelessly left in the aisle, he can be held responsible for the resulting injuries. He is not, however, responsible for injuries you suffer as a result of venturing into areas customarily closed to the public. If you wander through a door marked "Employees Only," you have only yourself to blame if you knock something over and break your neck.

Such legal concern for your right to physical safety in a store is long established and now almost taken for granted. What is new is the law's concern for your right to satisfactory goods when you make a purchase. For thousands of years the ancient Roman warning that the buyer must beware loaded the dice against the consumer. If you got the wine home and found it was vinegar, that was your tough luck; the time to complain was before you handed over your money. But now the law has become much more considerate of buyers. It recognizes the great discrepancy between the power of the consumer, who is an individual, and the power of the maker or seller, which is generally a large organization. To compensate for this imbalance, it forces manufacturers and merchants to stand behind their goods. If what you buy is not as represented, you have legal recourse: You have a right to return it and get a repair, replacement or refund, or, if the product's deficiencies have caused you harm, to be compensated with monetary damages.

This right to satisfactory goods has been greatly strengthened as the courts have repudiated old doctrines that had limited the responsibilities of manufacturers. Now the makers of products, as well as the stores that actually sell products to consumers, are accountable for quality. And their accountability is much broader today. It is seldom necessary to prove that a product failed because the maker was careless; it is usually sufficient simply to show that it failed.

Express and implied warranties

The most important legal protections that safeguard your purchases take the form of a series of guarantees, technically known as warranties. They are more numerous and precise than many people realize. They may be either express, meaning put into words, or they may be implied, meaning that the law considers them present whether they are mentioned or not. In either form they are your principal protection against unfair treatment in the marketplace.

An express warranty is a promise made by the merchant or manufacturer as part of his effort to induce a sale. The most familiar example is the warranty notice that comes along with major appliances like refrigerators, lawn mowers and television sets. It usually specifies a length of time—six months, three years or whatever—during which the manufacturer promises that his product will be free of defects caused by poor workmanship, and it states that should such a defect turn up, the manufacturer will repair or replace the defective part.

One form of express warranty that increasingly carries weight is the sales pitch. The law has moved fast in this field. Until the early 1960s, advertisements were regarded by the courts as mere come-ons, designed to get the consumer interested in a product and kindly disposed toward it when he saw it in a store. But the influence of modern advertising on people's buying habits is so overwhelming that the courts now tend to treat factual statements in ads as express warranties. If the ad for a food blender says it will purée carrots and celery, but it stalls every time you put a carrot in, you are entitled to ask for your money back. Equally enforceable warranties are the representations made to you by salesmen. The fact that these representations are made to you alone, not flashed to the entire nation across a tele-

Even the news dealer who sells you a paper is a party to a business contract. In exchange for your payment, he agrees to provide you with a current, readable paper.

vision screen or printed in four colors in a magazine, does not make them any the less binding.

In reading an ad or listening to a salesman, however, pay close attention. The law will protect you from any misstatement of fact, but its interpretation of what is fact may be much stricter than your own. A statement such as "This $100 suit is really worth $200" may sound factual to you, but in the eyes of the law it is a mere statement of opinion. To the salesman the suit may seem worth $200, to another authority it may be worth only $75, but the salesman has a right to express his opinion even if he is wrong. On the other hand, if the salesman says, "This suit cost $105 wholesale and we're selling it at a loss," or if he says, "This suit is 100 per cent Australian wool," these are statements of fact. He has to stand behind them.

Salesmen and advertisers often exaggerate. The law expects them to. And it expects you to be able to discriminate between facts and puffs. When the salesman says that a suit will wear like iron, he does not mean that it will literally last as long as a 15th Century coat of mail. And if you believe an advertisement's claim that a particular hair tonic assures a man of getting his girl, do not expect to hold the manufacturer responsible when your girl runs off with a rival who uses greasy kid stuff.

The liberties a seller can take in phrasing his advertisements are denied him when he writes labels for his products. The label is a much more formal—and more strictly interpreted—kind of express warranty. If the tag on a sweater says machine-washable and -dryable, it must mean what it says; and it must generally give you specific warning if special care must be taken. If the label on a packaged cake mix promises a cake that tastes of butter, it must state whether the mix contains real butter or merely flavoring. And the hair tonic label says nothing about enhancing sex appeal.

The very name of the product may be a form of express warranty. When you buy something that the seller calls a lawn mower or a can opener, he is in effect promising you that it will cut grass or open cans. The law will hold him to this promise. The law may waver, however, when the name of the product is ambiguous. In all 50 states you are guaranteed that a carton marked "eggs" contains objects that are edible, ovoid and produced by fowl. But what about a product marked eggnog mix? In some states, the law holds that the name carries an express warranty that the mixture contains genuine eggs; in others, the law is satisfied if the mixture merely has an eggy taste (so long as the label does not claim otherwise).

In addition to any express warranties given by a seller to a buyer,

Automatic Clothes Dryer Warranty

Westinghouse promises to the original purchaser, to repair or, at Westinghouse's option to replace any part of this automatic clothes dryer which proves to be defective in workmanship or material under normal family use, in the U.S.A., for a period of one year from the date of purchase. During this one year, Westinghouse will provide, all labor and parts necessary to correct such defects, free of charge, if the appliance has been installed and operated in accordance with Westinghouse written instructions furnished with the appliance.

This warranty does not cover damages resulting from external causes such as abuse, misuse or acts of God.

Westinghouse Electric Corporation, Mansfield, Ohio

SINGER
GUARANTEE

WE GUARANTEE that each SINGER* sewing machine has been carefully manufactured and is in perfect operating condition on delivery. When subject to normal family use and care, any parts requiring replacement at any time owing to defects in material or workmanship will be replaced without charge.

THIS GUARANTEE does not apply to parts requiring replacement owing to natural wear or to abuse or negligence of the user or in the event the machine is serviced by other than a SINGER representative or Approved Dealer or with parts other than those supplied by The Singer Company.

IN ADDITION to the above guarantee of parts, each machine will be inspected and adjusted whenever necessary without charge for labor for a period of one year from date of purchase.

THIS GUARANTEE is effective only with respect to the person making the purchase from The Singer Company or one of its Approved Dealers. The original Sales Agreement, or Cash Receipt, must be presented to obtain the benefits of the guarantee.

AGREEMENTS inconsistent with the foregoing shall be void and of no effect.

THE SINGER COMPANY

Warranty

GENERAL ELECTRIC RANGE

IF YOUR NEW GENERAL ELECTRIC RANGE (INCLUDES FREE-STANDING AND BUILT-IN OVENS, BUILT-IN COOKTOPS, AND HOODS) FAILS BECAUSE OF A MANUFACTURING DEFECT WITHIN ONE YEAR FROM THE DATE OF THE ORIGINAL PURCHASE, GENERAL ELECTRIC WILL REPAIR THE PRODUCT AT NO CHARGE TO YOU. BOTH PARTS AND SERVICE LABOR ARE INCLUDED.

THIS WARRANTY IS YOURS AS THE PURCHASER FOR YOUR HOME USE AND IS FOR PRODUCTS PURCHASED AND RE-TAINED WITHIN THE FIFTY STATES OF THE U.S.A. AND THE DISTRICT OF COLUMBIA, REGARDLESS OF WHETHER OR NOT YOU MOVE. OF COURSE, IT DOES NOT COVER DAMAGE BY ACCIDENT OR MISUSE. SERVICE WILL BE PROVIDED BY OUR FACTORY ORGANIZATION OR OUR AUTHORIZED SERVICE OR-GANIZATION IN YOUR AREA. ALL YOU NEED DO IS LOOK US UP IN THE YELLOW PAGES, WE ARE NEARBY.

GENERAL ⓖⓔ ELECTRIC

RANGE DEPARTMENT   APPLIANCE PARK
LOUISVILLE, KY. 40225

Concise guarantees of performance

The warranties that state a manufacturer's willingness to stand behind his products are now usually simple and straightforward statements, free of the bewildering fine-print clauses that once sharply restricted the buyer's rights. In concise fashion the warranties shown here promise repairs and replacement of parts when necessary but contain conditions—for example, the warranty is, of course, void if the purchaser has misused the appliance.

there are also guarantees that are neither written nor spoken but are nonetheless assumed to be in full legal force. These promises are known as implied warranties, and if they did not exist, the world of commerce would be a no man's land.

The first of these implied warranties is the warranty of salability, which guarantees that the seller owns the item and has a legal right to sell it. If it turns out that an item you purchased was either stolen goods or legally belonged to the seller's creditors and not to him—and you have to give it up to the actual owner—the seller is required under this warranty to refund the money you paid him.

The second—and increasingly useful—implied warranty is the one that attaches to a product's merchantability. A warranty of merchantability assures you of the right to assume that the product is fit for the use to which such products are normally put—provided you purchase it from a merchant who regularly deals in that particular kind of goods. An umbrella should not be full of holes, a razor blade should not have a saw-toothed edge, a suitcase handle should not pull out the first time you lift the suitcase. When a product does not meet the normal conditions of use, the retailer or manufacturer can be held responsible. He can also be held liable for any damage done or injuries suffered as a result of the product's nonmerchantability.

The courts now hold manufacturers and sellers so strictly to this implied warranty that almost any defect in a product may be considered a violation of the warranty. But the defect must exist within the product, not be a result of your improper use of it. For instance, the law will not hold your liquor dealer or a distiller responsible because you got sick from drinking a whole bottle of his Old Snakebite. But it would probably fix the blame on him if one drink alone had made you violently ill, and a chemical analysis of the remainder of the bottle proved that it contained a dangerous proportion of fusel oil. It might order him not only to return your money but also to pay for damages—including the cost of the chemical analysis.

Warranties of merchantability apply not only to products themselves but to the containers or wrappers in which they are packaged. If a bottle of soda water blows up because the bottling was defective, that, too, is a breach of warranty.

There is a further implied warranty—that the product will not only be fit for ordinary purposes but will also perform the specific task you required of it when you bought it. But this so-called warranty of suitability applies only when you must depend on the seller for advice. If you ask a nurseryman for a low-growing plant to use as a green border around a rock garden, and he sells you something that sprouts bright red leaves and grows four feet tall, he has broken his warranty of suitability.

While the protection granted consumers by warranties of suitability and merchantability is steadily being broadened, it still has a number of loopholes. You cannot claim that a seller violated his warranty of suitability, for example, when you do not need to depend on his advice. You might have no case against an erring nurseryman if you were yourself president of the local garden club. The law would assume you were well enough informed on horticultural matters to evaluate for yourself whether or not the plants you were buying would be suitable for use as a border.

Warranties of merchantability are also void if, before you make your purchase, the dealer suggests that you examine the merchandise but you fail to do so and thus miss an opportunity to discover an obvious defect. Suppose a dealer asks you to try on a raincoat before you buy it but you are in a hurry and discover only later that one sleeve is slightly ripped. You have waived your warranty and are out of luck. Suppose, on the other hand, that you do try it on and look it over thoroughly. Four days later you bring it back, claiming that one sleeve is three inches shorter than the other. Again you are out of luck. For although such a coat would normally be nonmerchantable, the dealer could legally say, "Sir, you tried it on; I assumed you wanted a coat with one sleeve longer than the other." If the defect was hidden, however, and could not have been ascertained by your inspection at the time of purchase—the coat was not sufficiently waterproofed and soaked up rain like a sponge the first time you wore it—the warranty would be there to protect you. It would also be there if the dealer simply showed you a sample of the coat for your inspection, and the coat he actually shipped you turned out to be defective.

A warranty of merchantability can also be canceled by the seller —but only if he announces that cancellation in advance and in a conspicuous manner, either by advising you at the time of purchase or by printing a disclaimer in bold type. "As is" and "with all faults" are two phrases commonly used for this purpose. If you have received such a warning, you cannot hold a shopkeeper accountable for any flaws in the merchandise that turn up when you get your purchase home. A shotgun that does not shoot straight is tough luck for you if it was marked "as is."

But some warranties are binding no matter what the circumstances of sale. If the "as is" shotgun blows up in your face, the merchant is absolutely responsible. He has no right to sell you a defective product whose defects make it dangerous. He is also bound at all times by the

A law for the consumer

A warranty is a guarantee. So says one of the many federal laws that have been proposed to protect consumers. Part of one bill is reproduced here, showing sections intended to pin down sellers' responsibilities for the merchandise they offer. The bill, in addition to insisting on the specific kinds of guarantees that the warranties must include, requires that all written warranties be expressed in "simple and readily understood language." It also provides the Federal Trade Commission with new powers of enforcement in the field of consumer protection.

92D CONGRESS
1ST SESSION

S. 986

IN THE SENATE OF THE UNITED STATES

FEBRUARY 25, (legislative day, FEBRUARY 17), 1971

Mr. MAGNUSON (for himself, Mr. MOSS, Mr. HART, Mr. INOUYE, Mr. KENNEDY, Mr. MCINTYRE, Mr. PASTORE, and Mr. PEARSON) introduced the following bill; which was read twice and referred to the Committee on Commerce

---

A BILL

To provide minimum disclosure standards for written consumer product warranties against defect or malfunction; to define minimum Federal content standards for such warranties; to amend the Federal Trade Commission Act in order to improve its consumer protection activities; and for other purposes.

15   (4) "Reasonable and necessary maintenance" consists
16 of those operations which the person guaranteed reasonably
17 can be expected to perform or have performed which are
18 necessary to keep any consumer product operating in a pre-
19 determined manner and performing its intended function.

20   (5) The term "repair" may at the option of the war-
21 rantor include replacement with a new, identical, or equiva-
22 lent consumer product.

23   (6) The term "replacement" shall include the refund-
24 ing of the actual purchase price of the consumer product less

1 reasonable depreciation based upon actual use if the war-
2 rantor is unable to effect replacement and repair is not pos-
3 sible or cannot be timely made, or if the person guaranteed
4 is willing to accept such refund in lieu of repair or replace-
5 ment.

13   (9) The term "warranty" includes guaranty, and to
14 warrant is to guarantee.

express warranty that the product is what he said it was: a shotgun so badly damaged that it will not shoot at all is legally not a gun. " 'As is,' " one judge has noted, "does not mean 'as isn't.' "

Settling disputes

All the warranties in the world will not prevent you from occasionally getting into a dispute over a purchase. You open a pack of razor blades and they turn out to be rusty; the new set of dining-room furniture arrives and the chairs are wobbly. Most stores will take back merchandise for refund or replacement even when they are not legally required to, simply because keeping customers satisfied is good business. But sometimes a seemingly justified claim for refund or replacement is refused. And sometimes defective merchandise causes harm that calls for recompense. If a friendly settlement cannot be reached, you have several legal remedies available. Most states now have consumer protection agencies that can help you get fair treatment. The best way to seek assistance is to explain your problem in a letter to the state attorney general's office, which can either take action itself or refer your complaint to another agency that can. If such steps fail, then you must ask a court to help you get what is due you. The simple filing of legal papers may bring action after your letter and telephone remonstrations have failed.

If the sum at stake is substantial, you will almost certainly want to engage a lawyer. But you need not write off a smaller claim simply because it does not justify a lawyer's fee. In many cities you can take your case to a Small Claims Court, in which you make the arguments yourself in informal surroundings; even where no Small Claims Court exists, there are courts of lower jurisdiction that permit you to serve as your own counsel. (The procedures involved in pursuing a claim in court are described in Chapter 10.)

When a dispute over merchandise reaches court, it usually takes the form of a suit for monetary damages. The loss or injury caused by unsatisfactory purchases must be measurable in terms of money. The damages that are involved may be of two kinds: general and special. General damages refer to the merchandise, and usually represent the difference between what you paid for and what you actually got. If you order $200 worth of lumber, for example, and half the lumber turns out to be warped, you have a claim against the lumber dealer for $100 in general damages. Special damages compensate you for further loss you may have suffered as a result of the defective merchandise. But special damages are awarded only if there is a direct, causal relationship between defect and loss—what the law calls proximate or foreseeable as opposed to remote and speculative. This is a nice point in law that in effect sets limits on what a consumer can reasonably hold a seller accountable for.

Suppose you buy a suitcase from a luggage store and use it to ship some clothing across the country. Among the items in the suitcase is your wife's new mink coat, valued at $1,500. Because of faulty workmanship the suitcase bursts open in transit, the fur coat is ruined and your wife is so upset she needs tranquilizers for a month. You have a claim in general damages against the luggage dealer for the total cost of the suitcase—since it broke in normal use, it was nonmerchantable and therefore worth nothing. You also have a claim in special damages against him for the cost of your wife's coat, on the grounds that the luggage dealer should have known that his suitcase might be used to carry valuable articles of clothing—in other words, the damage to the coat was "proximate" to the suitcase's faulty workmanship. On the other hand, you would be unlikely to sustain a claim of special damages for your wife's nervous collapse—because, the law would say, the luggage dealer could not possibly have foreseen such consequences of his action. The link between the damaged suitcase and the damaged coat was obvious and foreseeable, but the link between the damaged suitcase and your wife's nerves was not.

There could be a direct connection, however, between the faulty suitcase and an accident that caused your wife several broken bones. Suppose, for the sake of argument, that the handle of the new suitcase was not firmly attached, and that in lifting it you pulled off the handle, causing the suitcase to drop on your wife's foot. In that case you could claim special damages for your wife's injuries—and also for the pain and suffering those injuries cost her.

An action for damages against a dealer or manufacturer should be pursued, as the law says, seasonably. This means within a reason-

Suppose you buy a suitcase and pack your wife's new fur coat in it. The suitcase bursts in transit and the coat is ruined. If this happens because of faulty workmanship, you can collect damages to pay for the luggage and the coat—but not to compensate for your wife's emotional travail.

able length of time after the sale or after you have discovered the defect. Actually, the law states that you must bring action for a breach of warranty on a sale of goods no later than four years after the date of purchase or your discovery of the defect, depending on local statutes. This is an outside limit. The law is usually sensible about the interval within that period. But if you wait too long, it may assume you have made your peace with your purchase. It may be unreasonable, for example, to let several months go by between the time you complain to a merchant about a suit that does not fit and the time you sue the merchant for damages. How is the court to know that you are not simply trying to get your money back because you gained weight?

Your right to satisfactory service

The legal rules change to some extent when, instead of buying goods, you contract for a service—for your car to be parked, your teeth pulled, your roof repaired, your hair cut. Unlike a contract for the sale of goods, which remains valid even when the ownership of a business changes hands, a contract for services is nontransferable. If you contract to buy a refrigerator from Jones, and Jones sells his business to Smith, Smith has to deliver on the original contract, and you have to take the refrigerator, paying Smith the money you formerly owed Jones. But if you contract with Brown to paint your house, and Brown calls up on the appointed day to say that he is sending his brother to do the job, you do not have to accept his brother.

In the area of service contracts most states grant implied warranties that are not so different from the warranties of merchantability and suitability that apply in the sale of goods. A housepainter, for example, is expected to do his job in a careful and workmanlike manner. A doctor, while performing his services, must meet the accepted standards of his profession. But these kinds of implied warranties have

proved difficult to define. A "self-defrosting" refrigerator that requires a blow torch to melt the ice is clearly not self-defrosting. But only human judgment can decide whether the housepainter has botched the job or a doctor's failure to identify a minuscule blob on an X-ray is actually an example of malpractice. Or whether a dry cleaner has damaged a suit to the point that it might be described as unwearable. Or whether you were justified in sending home a butler hired for a six-hour party after one hour with one hour's wages because he broke too many glasses. How many glasses must a butler break to be adjudged to have failed to buttle?

In only one area of service does the law apply the same warranties that pertain to the sale of goods—and that is in the serving of food or drinks. When a restaurant serves you, its food must meet the same standards of merchantability as the items you buy in a grocery store. If the hollandaise sauce on the broccoli gives you food poisoning, the restaurant is guilty of breach of warranty. The warranty would not apply, however, to the gastronomic standards of the chef. You might think his *saltimbocca alla romana* was inedible and therefore nonmerchantable. But in fact he could say, "That's my way of making *saltimbocca alla romana,* and you owe $6.25." Legally he would be within his rights.

Sometimes, too, it is hard to tell whether you are paying for goods or a service. A dramatic example, still unresolved by the law, involves the blood used in transfusions: Is the patient buying the blood from the hospital as a commodity or is he paying for the transfusion itself as a service? Millions of dollars in damage suits stand or fall on this technicality. Some courts have ruled that the blood is a commodity and comes, like any other commodity, with an implied warranty of merchantability. Consequently anyone catching infectious hepatitis from tainted blood is entitled to damages from the hospital on that ground. Other courts have held that the transfusion of blood is a service, and therefore no warranty of merchantability is involved. No claim could be sustained against a hospital unless the blood became tainted through actual negligence, in which case you would be covered by the implied warranty of reasonable care.

No matter what kind of warranty is involved in a service, you are further protected by the special licenses that are normally required of those who dispense the service. Anyone can open a clothing store, sell any style and charge what he likes. Not everyone can dispense medical care, repair plumbing, cut your hair or drive a cab. If the service affects health or safety, its practitioners are generally required to be licensed and to pass tests of fitness for their tasks. And if the service is a public utility—a necessity and generally also a monopoly—the rates charged are regulated.

The law also insists that many services be universally available. A cab driver cannot refuse to take you where you want to go if it is in his normal area of operation. Hotels, restaurants, trains and planes must accommodate you without regard to race, color or sex. No law, however, prohibits a restaurant from refusing to serve men without ties or women in pants. The practice of stipulating certain dress may be snobbish but it is not illegal.

These restrictions aside, most business transactions involving a service are considered to be private contracts between two free agents, subject to very little outside control. If the service is unsatisfactory, the buyer has no recourse unless he can prove that the service was performed without reasonable care and also that he suffered a definite monetary loss as a result. In most instances the word "reasonable" gains an extra meaning in this area of law because of the special qualifications presumed to be possessed by those who set themselves up to supply services. In the case of blood transfusions, for example, a hospital is not free of responsibility simply because a warranty of merchantability may not exist. The hospital is required to take all precautions generally deemed necessary in the medical profession to prevent the use of tainted blood; if it does not, the injured patient can be awarded damages for the institution's lack of care.

It is not always easy to prove that a service has been carelessly per-

A label on a product must mean what it says. A "self-defrosting" refrigerator that needs a blow torch to melt accumulated ice is clearly not self-defrosting—and you can get your money back.

formed. Doctors are increasingly being sued for malpractice by patients. But the standard question "Has the service been performed with reasonable care?" may have different answers, depending on the circumstances. If you undergo a routine operation in a fully equipped hospital but arrive home with a ragged scar and continuing abdominal pains, your complaint of negligence may be justified. You certainly have a case against the surgeon if it turns out your postoperative pains were caused by a surgical instrument that had been left inside the abdomen. But if the operation is an emergency, performed with a penknife in a sailboat on the high seas, the doctor's performance would obviously be judged differently.

Circumstances so influence the outcome of a service that total failure does not necessarily mean the service was unsatisfactory. The cleaner who cannot remove the spots from your suit is entitled to full payment provided he used standard techniques. Similarly, a doctor cannot be held responsible for the failure of his treatment so long as he has followed recognized medical procedures. If you are rushed to the hospital with a severe pain in your right abdomen and the attending physician performs an emergency appendectomy for what turns out to be indigestion, the physician could probably claim legitimately that he was acting with reasonable care. But if he examines you cursorily, sends you home with a physic and the next day your appendix ruptures, he might be liable for the harm that befell you.

Because the results of a service can seldom be guaranteed, you are entitled to advance warning if the outcome is known to be especially uncertain. Many malpractice cases have been decided on the basis of whether or not the patient knew what the medical treatment entailed. The courts have ruled that, except in emergencies, a doctor must explain the potential dangers in such a way that the patient understands the risks before giving his permission for the treatment.

The requirement for reasonable care extends to more than the technical aspects of a service. An electrician who comes to your house to repair the wiring may be expected to leave the place more or less in the condition in which he found it. If he sets fire to your furniture, he has plainly failed to exercise reasonable care. Similarly, if you leave a blue suit with the dry cleaner for cleaning, you have a right to expect that he will not dip it in a solution that turns it bright orange.

Bailors and bailees

Leaving clothes at a dry cleaner's for cleaning is one common example of a branch of contract law often encountered in service transactions. It is called bailment. One party, the bailor, leaves personal possessions in the care of another party, the bailee, for a limited period of time and for a specific purpose. Most bailments are mutually beneficial —you get your clothes cleaned, the dry cleaner gets your money—and during the period of bailment the bailee is expected to exercise reasonable care in the storage and handling of the bailor's property. Frequently, however, bailees try to limit that responsibility; two notable examples are parking lots and checkrooms in restaurants.

Parking lots often display large signs saying, "This is a contract. It limits our liability. Read it." In somewhat small print the sign explains that the management is not responsible for damage to your car or its contents, or that it is responsible for only a limited amount, usually a small sum. In some states, such warnings on signs and receipts can indeed limit your chances to collect if the item you leave in the bailee's charge is lost or damaged. The matter often hinges on how prominently the disclaimer is displayed. In many states, however, you are often under no legal obligation whatever to read the disclaimer or even to pay any attention to it. For there are certain responsibilities in bailment that the bailee cannot avoid simply by putting up signs. A parking lot, in accepting your car, is responsible for taking normal care of it. If an attendant bangs up the fender or ruins the transmission, the owner of the lot is fully responsible for the damage, no matter what the sign says. He is equally responsible for the safety of anything that normally belongs in a car, like a spare tire or a jack. If a stranger rolls a spare tire out of the lot, the attendant can reasonably be expected to notice and to check on where it came from and where it is going. But if your wife left her fur coat in the car, he is not responsible for stopping a man walking out of the lot with a fur coat over his arm—not unless you had told him about the coat and he had specifically agreed to watch out for it. Similarly—depending on state laws—a restaurant checkroom may be responsible for your coat, but not for the wallet you leave in its pocket.

You have a case against the surgeon if your pains following a routine operation were caused by a sharp surgical instrument left inside the abdomen.

The principles of bailment also apply when you take temporary possession of something by renting it. If you rent a floor sander, you have a legal right to expect that it will indeed sand floors, will not zoom out of control and rip up the boards, and will not set fire to the sanding dust. The merchant who rented you the machine can in return insist that you take proper care of it while it is in your possession; you must not leave it sitting out in the rain.

But if, instead of renting, you borrow an item or agree to take care of it for someone else, the rules of bailment may change. If your neighbor is going on vacation, for example, and asks you as a favor to him to keep his car while he is away, you (as the bailee) are required to exercise no more care than you would for your own automobile. That is to say, nothing special. If you leave it out overnight and a tree falls on it or an unknown third party sideswipes it, you cannot be held responsible. On the other hand, if you proposed the bailment and asked your neighbor to let you use his car while he was gone, you would be required to use more than ordinary care to protect his property. If he returns and finds it badly dented—even if the harm occurred through no fault of yours—you are obligated to pay for the repairs—unless you can somehow produce a third party who is really responsible for the damage to the car.

The broken contract

When you have arranged for any kind of service, and the service is not performed in a legally acceptable manner, the other party has broken his contract with you, and you have several options, depending on the nature of the contract. You can either refuse payment altogether or pay only for what his performance is really worth, a factor that a court will have to establish. Suppose, for example, that a painter agrees to paint your house by June 1. He does not complete the job until June 5. If his failure to finish on time causes you to lose money, you are legally entitled to deduct that loss from his total bill. If he walks off the job on June 1, promising to return on June 15, you can discharge him and refuse to pay even for the part he has done. And if your daughter is being married on June 6, and you need the painting job finished in a hurry, you can hire another painter and demand that the first painter reimburse you for the financial loss you incur by hiring the second painter.

Mere inconvenience does not usually entitle you to damages for unsatisfactory service. If you do not like the way a barber cut your hair, your vanity may be wounded but you do not necessarily have grounds for a lawsuit. If you happen to be a professional model, however, and your agent can testify that you lost a job because of the way the barber altered your appearance, the circumstances change: You could now prove monetary loss. But you would still have to show that the loss of the job was a direct result of the barber's incompetence. If, say, you were so upset about the haircut that you went out and got drunk and came home with a black eye, your unsuitable appearance would be only indirectly the result of the barber's workmanship, and no damages would be warranted.

An award of monetary damages is generally as far as a court will go in making up for a broken contract. Only if you can show that you have suffered "irreparable harm"—damage for which money is not fair compensation—will the court consider ordering the party who broke his promise to make good on it and perform what he said he would perform. If such an order is issued, he must obey it or go to jail for contempt of court until he does.

This drastic action may sometimes be taken when the broken contract involves the sale of land, for every piece of land is considered unique: the plot next door is not exactly the same as the one you were promised, therefore a court will hold a seller of land in contempt until he turns over to you the plot he said he would. But a court will never require the performance of a service, no matter how unique that service may be. Forcing a ballplayer, for example, to live up to his contract and play center field every day would be the equivalent of involuntary servitude, forbidden by the Constitution. Furthermore, the judge would have to visit the stadium each day to evaluate the center fielder's performance and decide whether he was giving his all as required by the court order. (A court will, however, issue a negative order, preventing a unique player from serving a competitive team —and thus forcing him to live up to his original contract if he wishes to earn a living at his trade.)

Disagreements over service arise not only from unsatisfactory performance but also from plain misunderstanding. The contract you have entered into may not say what you think it does. In an ideal legal world, every commercial transaction, no matter how small or seemingly insignificant, would be preceded by the drawing up of a document to be signed by both parties, specifying in detail what is involved in the way of work to be done; and at what price; and when; and where; and which parties, if any, would be liable in case of delay; and how the parties would arrange to change the terms; and what precise legal definitions would apply to the words in the document.

In the real world, however, things happen far differently. People make agreements every day, sometimes in hasty and slipshod ways. They use ambiguous language, forget essential details and create fertile seedbeds for future dispute. One often unexpected result is that they end up with what is not legally a contract at all.

No matter how careful you are in spelling out the details of the service you expect to get, you have no legal right to the service at all unless you make an arrangement that is a contract. To be enforceable it must meet several requirements. It must specify the service; it must stipulate a return for that service; its terms must be clearly accepted by both sides; and it must be entered into freely, without pressure or resort to fraud. Neglecting one or more of these essentials is easier than you might think.

Be specific about prices even in an oral contract. If, for example, you tell a workman to fix up your house as long as it doesn't cost too much, his idea of what you mean might amount to an arm and a leg.

Let us say you wake up one rainy morning with water flowing through the ceiling onto your bed. You call up Olsen the roofing contractor and frantically ask, "Can you fix my roof, and how soon?" "Sure I can fix it," he says, "sometime this week." If you leave the conversation at that, you may have a promise from Olsen, but you do not have a contract. To be binding, a contract must involve "mutuality of obligation"—some quid must be exchanged in return for some quo —and you have not offered to pay Olsen any specific amount in return for his services.

Perhaps Olsen has been specific but you have not. He may say, "You need new gutters or your roof will start leaking again. If I don't hear from you to the contrary, I will put them up next Monday for $200." "Let me think about it," you answer, and go away for a week. When you come back, you find the gutters in place, the job finished. When Olsen bills you for $200, you do not necessarily have to pay him. The court would probably rule that there was no contract between the two of you because there had been no definite agreement on terms. In effect, Olsen would have done the job as a volunteer. By the same token, he could then voluntarily remove the gutters—and be within his rights.

Neither is there a contract if Olsen says, "I can fix the roof in a week, but I can't do it for less than $400." In this case Olsen has committed himself to a specific length of time but not to a specific price. If you and Olsen then bargain over the price, the only amount that figures in the contract is the last offer made. Suppose, for instance, you turn down Olsen's original offer of $400 and make him a counteroffer of $300. If Olsen accepts that figure, a contract is made—you and he are in business and neither of you can alter the terms of the agreement without breaking the contract. If he remains silent to your counteroffer, however, and finally you say, "Okay, I'll pay you $400," Olsen is at perfect liberty to reply, "Sorry, my figure is now $450." Olsen is not contractually bound to do the work for the original estimated figure he had mentioned because an estimate does not constitute a definite offer.

Mistaking an estimate for a definite offer is a common cause of disputes over services. Suppose Olsen says, "I'll fix your roof this week, and it looks like the job will come to maybe $400." He has committed himself to do the work, but he has not committed himself to a price.

If you then say, "Okay, go ahead," you have a contract—Olsen has clearly offered to provide a service and you have clearly offered to pay him. But you have committed yourself to pay him what he asks after the job is done; his estimate is only an estimate. You have no legal way to force him to stipulate a firm price in advance, and you must generally depend on a craftsman's reliability as protection against being overcharged. However, if a court feels that you have been outrageously overcharged, it will probably not force you to pay the full amount Olsen has billed you.

Sometimes a contract that is truly a contract becomes void simply because of the conditions under which it was executed. Suppose Olsen and you have agreed on a price of $400 for your roof, and the contract is firm. Halfway through the job, in the midst of a pouring rainstorm, he comes to you and says, "Look, I need an extra $200." Looking up at the gaping holes in your roof and the water gushing in, you agree to the new terms. But when the job is finished, you can demand the return of the extra $200. There are legal reasons why you would probably win. The first is that the new agreement had been made under duress—which the court would not allow. The second reason is that in most states no agreement for additional money for a service is binding if it does not also entail more work—and Olsen was offering you nothing extra for the additional $200.

You may have received the impression from all this that a binding contract is hard to make. Not at all. So long as both parties are in agreement, a legal contract is a very easy thing to execute. In fact, some contracts need not even be written down but can be made orally. (There are some specific exceptions to this. The most important ones are that agreements must always be in writing when they deal with the purchase of land, the sale of goods worth $500 or more, or the performance of any service that cannot be completed within a year.) Be careful how you word an oral contract. If you tell a workman to fix up your house as long as it does not cost you an arm and a leg, his idea of what you mean may be different from yours. For this reason, it is a good idea to follow up an oral agreement with a written confirmation of the actual terms so that there will be visible evidence in the event of a dispute. The law will investigate whether the written document includes all the basic points on which the parties have agreed; any separate oral understanding that contradicts or substantially modifies this agreement will not stand up. Suppose, however, that you sign a contract to have your home carpeted. The contract says nothing about the completion date but the dealer promises you orally that he will finish the job before the cocktail party you are planning to give over the holidays. This kind of oral understanding will be accepted because it merely supplements the original contract and does not contradict it.

Those kinds of contracts that must be put in writing need not be full-fledged legal documents but can be in the form of an order blank, a letter, a notation on the back of an envelope—provided it contains some salient facts indicating that an agreement has been made and that it has been signed, initialed, or even rubber-stamped with the name of the other party to the agreement.

BUSINESS DEALS WITH INDIVIDUALS

Transactions involving established merchants, licensed craftsmen and professionals are the heart of commerce, and the primary aim of business law is to keep that heart beating as smoothly as possible. But there are also many transactions in which you deal with another private person like yourself. You may answer a classified ad and arrange to buy furniture from its owner, for example. Or you may make a deal with your neighbor to build a fence between your properties and split the costs. These are business contracts too, and they are just as legal and binding as the ones you enter into in a store or a doctor's office. But the law does not regard them as matters of great public concern, and so it is correspondingly less insistent on your right to a fair return for your money.

When you buy something from an individual, you lose some warranty rights and you keep some. In general, you often take what you get and must be satisfied with it—unless the seller has deliberately concealed some dangerous defect from you. The warranty of suitability —fitness for a particular purpose—still applies in such sales. If you buy one of neighbor Brown's bicycles, for example, after explaining to him that you need one that will get you up the big hill at the end of the block, neighbor Brown is obligated to sell you a bike that will meet the requirements. And if the bike will not make the hill, you can get your money back. But if the seat suddenly falls apart, you are probably out of luck. A disintegrating seat would be a breach of the warranty of merchantability—a guarantee that the product is fit for ordinary use. However, no such broad warranty comes with goods sold by an individual like neighbor Brown, because he is not an established dealer and therefore cannot be expected to know about the durability of every seat.

Even the warranty of salability, which ensures that the seller really owns the goods and has a clear legal right to dispose of them, is uncertain when the seller is an individual. Though the seller may assure you that the goods actually belong to him, he may, innocently or not, be misleading you. And if some creditor has a prior lien on the goods or has accepted them as security for a loan, he may be able to take the goods away from you as certainly as if they had been stolen. Your only recourse is to sue the seller to get your money back. It is a good idea, therefore, to make sure that no such liens exist before buying anything from a private party. Perhaps the most prudent course of all is to make no substantial purchase from a private person unless you know something about him. It has sometimes happened that people have bought secondhand bedroom sets, only to discover a few days or a week later a book of unpaid coupons from a finance company hidden away at the back of a bureau drawer. In most such cases, the new buyer is obliged to make the payments on those coupons if he wants to retain the merchandise.

Dealing with minors

Among the other problems you may run into in dealing with private individuals are those involving business deals with minors. If the person with whom you do business is legally under age (21 in many states, 18 in others), you may find yourself bound by a contract that is not binding on him. For the law assumes that a minor does not know enough about life to enter into a formal business agreement *(Chap-*

A prudent course for the buyer is to make no substantial purchase from a private individual unless you know something about him.

ter 3). Suppose, for example, that you agree to pay a 16-year-old $100 for a motorbike that he subsequently decides is worth $200; he could legally refuse to go through with the deal and you could do nothing about it. If you are the seller of the motorbike and the 16-year-old is the buyer, he could drive the bike around town for a year, have an accident and wreck it, even sell it, then bring it back to you and claim that he had never wanted the bike in the first place. In some states you would have to give him back the money he had paid you for the bike; in other states you could subtract the cost of the damages he had done from this payment.

Minors are not the only bad risks in a business transaction. You may also get into trouble if the person with whom you made a deal turns out to have been drunk, senile, insane or otherwise mentally incapacitated. He may be able to claim that he did not know what kind of deal he was getting into and therefore cannot be required to go through with it. The courts, however, take a very hard look at such claims. If you buy a watch from Smith for $100, and Smith later claims that he was intoxicated when he sold it to you and wants the watch back, the court may suspect that Smith has simply found a better deal elsewhere. It will insist that Smith produce proof of his intoxication and prove, too, that he was so thoroughly, hopelessly drunk that his reason was impaired.

Being the boss

The law of sales contracts is one of the most varied and continually changing of all the domains of business law. Running it a close second is the law dealing with relations between employers and employees. But if your role as an employer is limited to hiring a once-a-week cleaning woman, an occasional babysitter and a neighbor's son to mow the lawn, your interest in the laws regulating minimum wages, collective bargaining and workmen's compensation is probably peripheral, for such laws do not apply to domestic labor, except in a few states. The one exception occurs when you hire a foreign domestic worker. The law says that you must pay an alien the prevailing wage that nonalien workers receive for the same job. But when you hire an American citizen, both of you are free agents as far as the terms of employment are concerned, and the only law you would seem to have to worry about is the law of supply and demand.

Not quite, however. In the first place, the wages of a domestic who receives $50 or more per quarter-year must be reported to the Internal Revenue Service, and you and the domestic must each pay Social Security taxes amounting to 5.2 per cent of the wages. You can pay the domestic's share of the taxes if you wish, but both shares must be paid. This is one of the most frequently ignored of all U.S. laws. But if you do ignore it, you do so at your peril. Suppose the maid who has been serving you for 10 years dies suddenly, leaving several young children. In studying her case to determine why her survivors' benefits are so low, the authorities may discover that no one has paid Social Security taxes for her. You would therefore be stuck for 10 years' back taxes, plus fines and interest.

Another aspect of the law to keep in mind when you hire a cleaning woman or babysitter is that each is an invitee in your home—just as you are the storekeeper's invitee when you enter his place of business. You must exercise due care to see that neither comes to harm *(Chapter 4)*. If either trips on a loose stair tread and falls, or is injured by a faulty dishwasher or an inadequately insulated vacuum cleaner, you are responsible for the damage and will be required to pay the medical bills. In most states the "homeowner's" type of fire insurance may cover your legal liability, but this protection is not provided in every state; check your policy carefully.

Principals and agents

Besides being responsible for your servant's safety while he is on your property, you are also responsible for damage he causes in the performance of his duties. This obligation is part of an area of law dealing with what are known as principals and agents. When you ask the neighbor's son to burn off dried grass in your yard, and the fire spreads to your neighbor's yard, the law considers that you have set the fire because the boy was acting as your agent. Even if you did not specifically ask him to burn the grass but simply said, "Take care of the yard," the fire might still be legally your fault—if the court is convinced that burning off dead grass was a routine part of lawn care and that you had not expressly forbidden your agent to do it.

You can orally authorize someone to act as your agent, or you may do so in writing. In either case you, as the principal, authorize another, as your agent, to carry out some transaction for you. If the authorization is in writing, it is called a power of attorney. This may be informally executed—in a personal letter or a brief memorandum —or it may be formally drawn up on a special legal form *(box, next page)*. A principal-agent relationship, or agency, is normally created for a limited period of time, ranging from a few days to a few years, and it usually implies that the principal is unable to appear in person and act for himself, either because he is ill or because he is too far away. If you break both legs and are confined to a hospital bed for several weeks, for example, you can give someone else power of attorney to do your banking for you and pay your bills. Or if you live in Connecticut and have agreed to purchase a piece of land in Arizona, you can authorize a friend in Arizona to take title to the property in your name by assigning him power of attorney. All states require a written agreement when the agency is created to acquire or dispose of land and whenever the period of time covered by the appointment exceeds a year. And every state requires a power-of-attorney form to be no-

A principal-agent contract

One way to empower another person to look after your business interests is to give him a written power of attorney, usually made out on a printed form like the one at right. It has spaces for your name and your agent's name, followed by a list of transactions the agent is authorized to handle for you. His actions are then as legally binding as if you had taken them personally. You can limit the agent's powers by crossing out certain transactions. This form is signed and witnessed on the back.

Power of Attorney
Statutory Short Form

T 44 JULIUS BLUMBERG, INC., LAW BLANK PUBLISHERS
80 EXCHANGE PLACE AT BROADWAY, NEW YORK

NOTICE: THE POWERS GRANTED BY THIS DOCUMENT ARE BROAD AND SWEEPING. THEY ARE DEFINED IN NEW YORK GENERAL OBLIGATIONS LAW, ARTICLE 5, TITLE 15, SECTIONS 5-1502A THROUGH 5-1503, WHICH EXPRESSLY PERMITS THE USE OF ANY OTHER OR DIFFERENT FORM OF POWER OF ATTORNEY DESIRED BY THE PARTIES CONCERNED.

Know All Men by These Presents, *which are intended to constitute a GENERAL POWER OF ATTORNEY pursuant to Article 5, Title 15 of the New York General Obligations Law:*

That I
(insert name and address of the principal)

do hereby appoint
(insert name and address of the agent, or each agent, if more than one is designated)

my attorney(s)-in-fact TO ACT
(a) If more than one agent is designated and the principal wishes each agent alone to be able to exercise the power conferred, insert in this blank the word "severally". Failure to make any insertion or the insertion of the word "jointly" will require the agents to act jointly.

First: in my name, place and stead in any way which I myself could do, if I were personally present, with respect to the following matters as each of them is defined in Title 15 of Article 5 of the New York General Obligations Law to the extent that I am permitted by law to act through an agent:

[Strike out and initial in the opposite box any one or more of the subdivisions as to which the principal does NOT desire to give the agent authority. Such elimination of any one or more of subdivisions (A) to (K), inclusive, shall automatically constitute an elimination also of subdivision (L).]

To strike out any subdivision the principal must draw a line through the text of that subdivision AND write his initials in the box opposite.

(A) real estate transactions;	[ ]
(B) chattel and goods transactions;	[ ]
(C) bond, share and commodity transactions;	[ ]
(D) banking transactions;	[ ]
(E) business operating transactions;	[ ]
(F) insurance transactions;	[ ]
(G) estate transactions;	[ ]
(H) claims and litigation;	[ ]
(I) personal relationships and affairs;	[ ]
(J) benefits from military service;	[ ]
(K) records, reports and statements;	[ ]
(L) all other matters;	[ ]

tarized whenever the empowered agent is going to be dealing with what the law calls sealed instruments—documents issued under an official seal, such as a deed or a will.

GOING INTO BUSINESS

Another area of business law that may occasionally concern you has to do with your actual participation in a business. Suppose, for example, that you want to help out a deserving nephew who is about to set himself up in a supermarket. The easiest and most informal way of underwriting his venture is simply to give or lend him some money, in which case you would have no legal connection with his activities. Or perhaps you want to go into partnership with him. If so, you should be careful about the kind of partnership you set up. Do you want to be actively involved in the management of the business, which means assuming a share of the risks? Or do you simply want to sit on the sidelines and collect a return on your investment? The first of these two kinds of arrangement is called a general partnership. The other is known as a limited partnership.

In a general partnership, each partner—and there can of course be more than two—makes some sort of contribution in cash or property or skill, and all share equally in any business commitments made in their joint name, as well as in the profits. If your nephew signs an order for two hundred cases of salad oil to be delivered to your joint place of business and cannot pay for the order, you, as his partner, will have to foot the bill—even if you disapprove of the deal, the terms or your nephew's method of operating. Obviously a general partnership is a serious undertaking; you should not even think of forming one without getting professional legal advice.

You can avoid many of the problems and responsibilities that arise in such a situation by joining your nephew in a limited partnership. Here, as a limited partner, you can put up money but leave the actual running of the business to your active partner, or partners. You are not responsible for any debts or commitments made by your active partners on behalf of the partnership, and if the business goes broke all you can lose is your original investment. A lawyer's advice is again essential, for you must be sure to behave like a limited partner —which means having nothing to do with the running of the business. If you begin spending a lot of time at your nephew's place of business, giving advice, correcting the bookkeeping, making business calls and sending out letters on your nephew's business stationery, you will be acting as a general partner in the eyes of the law, and you could be held liable for your nephew's debts. You must also be sure to register yourself as a limited partner in each state in which you and your nephew do business. If you register only in New York, and your nephew also does business in Connecticut, you will be considered a general partner in Connecticut unless you have filed the limited partnership papers there as well.

The easiest way to avoid all these legal difficulties and responsibilities is to have your nephew incorporate his business and then to buy shares of common stock in the corporation. As a stockholder in any company you cannot be held legally accountable for anything the management does, and you need not show any personal interest in the way it runs things. Indeed, many of the people who buy stock in a company do not even know exactly what products it makes or where its factories are.

While ownership of common stock burdens you with no responsibilities, it gives you a number of legal rights. These vary from state to state, but in all states they include a voice in the election of the directors of the company, the men chosen to help run it. The laws generally stipulate that these elections take place at regular meetings, which you as a stockholder have a right to attend. You also have a right to ask questions at such meetings and to receive regular reports on the company's financial situation.

When there is to be an election at a stockholders' meeting that you cannot attend in person, the directors may send you a proxy statement to sign, a document permitting them to cast your vote as they please. You are not required to sign such a statement because it is not obligatory that you vote—and you can always revoke your proxy if you want to, as long as you do so before the vote is taken.

Stockholders ordinarily take no part in the setting of a company's policy or in its day-to-day operations, and directors are ordinarily not required to get stockholder approval for their actions. But if the majority of a company's stockholders disapprove of the decisions of its directors, they have a right to band together and vote the directors out of office. And if the directors propose to change the fundamental nature of a company or its form of management, they are required by law to submit these changes to the stockholders for approval. Radical changes in the operation of a company are obviously more important to the stockholders of a small company than a large one. After all, if you do not like the way the directors of General Motors run the business, you can sell your stock. But if you own stock in a small, closely held business you may not be able to sell it so easily.

Suppose you have invested in Aztec Plastics, a small locally owned concern whose shares are not traded on the local or national security markets. The directors of Aztec announce that they are going to acquire Olmec Wafers and merge with Toltec Resins and use the cash from all three concerns to start a new business, a car-rental service. They cannot go ahead with this plan unless a majority of the stockholders approve.

While stockholders have no voice in the day-to-day management of a company, they can exact damages from the directors if they can prove that the directors are managing the firm improperly. Courts are extremely reluctant to second-guess boards of directors, however. It is most unlikely that you would get anywhere by suing the management of Aztec Plastics because they happened to lose money; there is no law against bad business judgment. But if you could prove that Aztec had willfully and deliberately deprived you of money that should have come to you as dividends, the courts might rule in your favor. In several spectacular cases the courts have done just that. In 1919 a Michigan court ordered Henry Ford Sr. to pay out $19 million in delayed dividends when stockholders in the Ford Motor Company complained that they were getting an unfair share of the Ford profits. And in 1941 George Washington Hill, the president of American Tobacco Company, was ordered, along with four vice presidents, to pay back $1.5 million in bonuses for similar reasons.

PAYING WITH CHECKS

In all the business transactions discussed in this chapter, it has been assumed that payment would be made in cash, but a more common way of making such payments is by check. The use of checks has become so widespread that most people tend to think of them as being identical to cash. Even if, through an oversight on your part, the check bounced, the merchandise would still be legally yours—although, of course, you would owe the store the money.

According to law, when you sign a check, the bank must obey the instructions contained on it. That is, the bank must pay out of your account whatever sum you have specified to the person you have designated, the payee, or to any other person to whom the payee has duly made over his rights. If the check is a forgery, passed in your name, the bank is required to reimburse your account for the full sum. Not even the cleverness of the forgery releases the bank from this obligation. Banks used to spot forgeries by examining the signature on a check, and technically they are still supposed to do so. But in practice most banks now rely on the computer's ability to detect, and reject, any falsification of the magnetic-tape account number printed on the check. Of course if the check is a real one, and only the signature is forged, the computer offers little protection. If a number of your blank checks disappear, you must inform the bank immediately, since any negligence on your part that makes forgery possible might relieve the bank of liability and place it back on you. It might also be wise if you are involved in such a situation to close your current account and open a new one. In this way you will help the bank to prevent the illegal passing of a check drawn to your account.

If a bank refuses to honor one of your checks, claiming by mistake that you have insufficient funds, you sometimes have a right to demand more than an apology. There is a case of a lady who wrote a check to pay off part of a debt to a finance company. Although her bank balance covered the check, the bank mistakenly refused to honor it. As a result, the finance company preferred charges against her. These were eventually dropped when she explained the situation; and she sued the bank, claiming "grievous mental anguish." The court awarded her damages and the bank was obliged to pay them.

A bank is also obliged to honor a stop-payment order canceling a check you have made out. The order may be issued orally or in writing; if you phone in such an order, however, it must usually be followed by a confirming letter. If the bank fails to honor the order, either deliberately or through negligence, it must credit your account with whatever sum it allows to be paid out on the check you tried to stop. But there is an interesting twist to this law. If the check slips through and the bank would have to discriminate against another honest party in order to honor its obligation to you, it need not recredit your account. Let's assume, for example, that you have purchased a TV set from a man down the street who is moving away, and you pay by check. You discover after you get the set home—and after the man has left town—that the set does not work. You contact your bank and request it to stop payment on the check. Normally, the bank would be required to comply. But another party has entered the scene. The man who sold you the TV set has already endorsed your check and passed it on to the local grocer in payment for his grocery bills. The grocer in turn has deposited the check to his account. Since the grocer has parted with something of value—his groceries—in return for your check, the money cannot be legally denied him. A court will have to decide which of two innocent parties—you or the grocer—is to be the loser, and in this case it may very well be you. If creditors like the grocer could not accept checks in lieu of cash and deposit them as cash in their own accounts, the entire commercial system would be undermined; the court, therefore, would probably decide in the grocer's favor and approve payment of the check.

While the bank has responsibilities to you, you in turn have responsibilities to the bank. First and foremost, you must have enough money in your account to cover the check when it reaches the bank. If you do not, you have committed a crime and could be hauled into court. Merchants seldom press such charges, however, unless they suspect deliberate fraud.

You must also take care to write your checks so they cannot be easily altered. Suppose you make out a check to someone for five dollars, but leave so much blank space after the five in both places that the receiver of the check—or someone through whose hands it passes—can easily add a couple of digits and the word "hundred" in the appropriate places to convert it into a check for $500. The bank, seeing a perfectly valid check drawn to your account, will pay out the $500 in good faith, and you cannot hold the bank responsible for your carelessness in handwriting. You are out $495.

You are expected to examine the regular statements from the bank in order to spot any errors, overpayments or possible forgeries that may have slipped through. A bank is always responsible for arithmetical errors it may have made, but it is not indefinitely responsible for restitution for forgeries. In most states, if you wait longer than a year to report that your signature has been forged on a check —or longer than three years to report a forged endorsement—the bank will no longer have to make up the loss.

In fact it is never a good idea to delay any action dealing with a check, no matter what the circumstances. Checks, by their very nature, are short-term commercial instruments, meant to speed up the exchange of money, and they may become stale. Stories are common of people who absent-mindedly stash away checks and forget about them, only to discover when they present the checks for payment that they are holding worthless pieces of paper. No bank, says the law, is required to honor a check that is presented more than six months after the date written on it. If what you are interested in is delayed payments, a whole new realm of law becomes operative: the law of credit. For business transactions based on credit, see the next chapter.

By **ROBERT WERNICK**
LAWRENCE P. KING, Consultant

7 Credit

Charge accounts, loans,
installments—
and the bills

It was an unremarkable day for John Gibbon and his wife, Helen. In the morning John drove to a gas station near their suburban home, had the car's tank filled and headed for his office in the city. On the way he stopped at a florist's and ordered roses to be delivered to Helen the next day, their 12th wedding anniversary. Around noon he and two colleagues from the office lunched together at a restaurant; feeling expansive, he picked up the tab for all three. Before leaving the office for home, he took time to write out checks covering a few personal bills, among them one from the Diners' Club, another from Master Charge for a new camera he had recently bought, and a bill for the final installment on Helen's car.

For Helen Gibbon, housewife, the day was filled mostly with routine. First, the baker delivered the bread and took her order for the next day's anniversary cake. Then the laundryman arrived, and as she was putting away the clean linen, a salesman rang the bell, wanting to sell her a vacuum cleaner. Her old cleaner was wearing out and the one offered seemed a good buy, so she signed up for it. Later she drove to the dentist's for her appointment, had a quick lunch downtown and spent a couple of hours at the hairdresser's. On the way home she picked up a box of detergent and a six-pack of her husband's favorite beer at a market where she had a charge account.

That evening, just as John, Helen and their 10-year-old son Steve were about to sit down to dinner, the boy who delivered the daily paper called to collect $3.60 for the monthly billing. John reached into his pocket, but his hand came out with only a couple of quarters and some nickels. "It's astonishing," he said to his wife. "Today I bought gas, a surprise for you, took two friends to lunch, paid four or five bills—and I haven't got a dollar in my pocket and haven't had all day!" Helen searched her purse with no better luck. "Same here," she confessed. Finally young Steve came to their rescue with money he had earned mowing the neighbor's lawn.

The Gibbons had neglected to carry cash with them because they have grown accustomed, like millions of other Americans, to buying almost all of their necessities, luxuries and services on credit. They can charge anything from dental work to a wash-and-set on the credit extended by their community's professional men and tradespeople. The Gibbons also have a wallet-fattening stack of credit cards—"plastic money"—that are good for a tankful of gas or a fly-now-pay-later European vacation. They know that when their house requires repairs, they can arrange a loan with a bank, credit union or finance company to cover the cost.

Consumer credit—the kind you and the Gibbons use—has be-

Measuring a credit line

Stores that offer charge accounts frequently assign customers a credit line, or maximum credit limit. A customer with a hefty savings account and a paid-up home might be allowed to charge up to $1,000 at any one time. The store might feel that an apartment-dweller, say, with a smaller bank balance—was a poorer credit risk and snip off his (or her) credit line at $250.

come a vital part of the U.S. economy. More than $127 billion worth of such bills were outstanding at the end of the year 1970. That $127 billion represented approximately 13 per cent of the nation's gross national product. In the past Americans prided themselves on paying "cash on the barrelhead." Today they eat, drink, drive, travel, clothe themselves and purchase their houses with a minimum of cash and a maximum of credit.

Credit has become such an essential part of modern American life that it is governed by a large body of state law, which has been strengthened and broadened by two federal laws, the 1969 Consumer Credit Protection Act (the "Truth in Lending" act) and the 1971 Fair Credit Reporting Act. Together all these statutes regulate the fees that may be charged you for credit, stipulate how the charges are to be stated, give you the right to examine—and if necessary, correct —reports on your credit, protect you against shady business practices peculiar to credit transactions, prohibit any organization from mailing you credit cards you did not ask for, limit your liability in case your credit cards are lost or stolen, and in the event of financial disaster, spell out what happens if bills cannot be paid.

Knowing how these and other laws governing credit operate —and being able to recognize situations in which you as yet have no clear legal protection—will help you to make credit work for you and not against you.

APPLYING FOR CREDIT

None of the laws on credit grant you an automatic right to credit. In fact, the potential lender has every right to refuse to give you credit if he feels that you might not be able to fulfill your single responsibility: to pay your bills. Consequently, whenever you apply for credit you will be asked a number of standard questions designed to reveal your "creditworthiness." You will probably be requested to fill out a form, including answers to such questions as where you work, how long you have worked there, what your salary is, what bank accounts you have, whether you own or rent the place in which you live, and what other credit or charge accounts you have.

The answers to such questionnaires are used to determine not only if you are a good credit risk, but also how much credit you can be expected to handle. Department stores, banks, finance companies and credit card companies often set up a "credit line," or maximum credit limit, for applicants. In establishing a credit line, such firms frequently assign a certain number of points to each of the applicant's answers, add them up and then compare the total with a predetermined scale. For example, one large store allows an applicant five points if he owns his own home; someone who rents his living quarters is considered a poorer credit risk and is assigned only three points. If he has a checking account, he gets two points; if he has a savings account, he gets three; if he has both, he gets six points. Various occupations are rated according to their relative stability and pay scale. An applicant who totals 30 points is considered such a good risk that the store lets him charge as much merchandise as he likes; if his total score falls below 12 points, he is denied credit altogether. Those whose scores are somewhere in between are granted credit, but a limitation is placed on it. Customers with a medium credit rating might be allowed to owe only, say, $250 or $500 at any one time.

Does a store have a right to ask you so many personal questions? It does indeed; there are no legal restrictions on the information a store—or bank—may elicit from a person asking for credit. Further, there is a tendency among courts to expect lenders to investigate thoroughly those to whom they extend credit. If a merchant fails to check the credit rating of his customers, a judge may assume that he was all too eager to unload shoddy goods—or to collect the interest charged on the time-payment contract. In one case an appliance dealer had sold a freezer to a couple without investigating their credit rating. The freezer turned out to be faulty, but the dealer refused to take it back, insisting that the husband and wife were legally obliged to continue paying for it. When the dealer sued, the judge ruled against him, citing as one reason his failure to check the credit rating.

You are not, it should be added, legally bound to answer all the questions asked when you apply for credit. In many cases, your application will be accepted even if you do not answer them all. But it is unwise to omit—or misrepresent—an important fact, such as the existence of a large unpaid debt. If you did, and your financial affairs became the subject of a court case, you could be accused of fraud. In any event, important omissions will probably be discovered when your application for credit is processed. Large stores, major banks and credit card companies do not rely on your word alone. They check you out through one of the nation's many credit bureaus—companies whose primary business is to keep records on Americans who use credit. The credit bureau's data will tell whether you have a history of paying your bills promptly, or slowly, or not at all. If the bureau says you are a good credit risk, your application is likely to be approved. If you have large outstanding debts, your credit rating will have plummeted toward zero—with predictable results for your application.

Credit bureaus have become omnipresent in the United States in recent decades. The largest trade association of credit bureaus, Associated Credit Bureaus Inc., has 2,200 member bureaus across the U.S. and Canada that give credit information to some 400,000 stores and other grantors of credit. Among them, the member bureaus churn out 110 million reports on the credit reliability of would-be borrowers each year. These and similar organizations constitute a storehouse of detailed financial and personal data on virtually every American who has ever had a charge account or borrowed money anywhere in the country. They are legally free to gather information about you provided they disclose it only to persons with a legitimate interest in your affairs. A store that contemplates granting you credit is considered to have such an interest; an inquisitive neighbor who simply wonders how you can afford two cars is not.

Most medium-sized cities have only one major credit bureau, which keeps records on all the local citizens who have ever applied for credit with any of the local banks, merchants, hospitals, professional men and so forth that the bureau serves. A typical file on an applicant will list his current and past charge accounts, show any overdue debts and indicate how promptly he pays his bills. If he has been mentioned in the local newspapers—for winning a lottery or marrying someone's wealthy daughter—there may be clippings about him. If he has ever been sued in court for nonpayment of a bill, a record of this suit will undoubtedly be in his file. And if he moves to another town, this information is supplied to the bureau in that town as soon as he applies for credit there, for nearly all bureaus cooperate by routinely exchanging data.

PROBLEMS WITH CREDIT BUREAUS

Although a credit bureau's information about a morally and financially responsible individual may seem harmless, it does not always prove to be so. The files may contain incomplete, misleading, out-of-date or even erroneous information. This problem is compounded by the use of computers, which many of the bureaus as well as the stores they serve rely on to file and provide data. A bookkeeper in a store, for example, might find a note in his records that you did not pay the

bill for your new suit because it was unsatisfactory and was returned. Most computers are not smart enough to allow for such contingencies, however; unless a clerk feeds in new information, they
just note a payment missed. This incomplete information may then
be transferred to the credit bureau's computer, and you are on record
as being a slow payer. Further, it often proves difficult to argue with a
computer. A Virginia housewife refused to pay $13 to a department
store because she had never received the bedsheets they kept billing
her for. With mounting annoyance, she repeatedly wrote to the store,
explaining that the sheets had never arrived. But the clerks never
told the computer, and it, unable to appreciate her dilemma, just
kept grinding out bills—and notations that month after month the
housewife was failing to pay. This information automatically went to
the file in the local credit bureau. When the luckless Virginia woman
tried to open a charge account at another store in the community, she
was turned down.

How dangerous such faulty credit data can be—how it can stick
to your record wherever you go and jeopardize not only your reputation but also your livelihood—is illustrated by the troubles that pursued a radio reporter named Leon Sanders. While living and working
in Shreveport, Louisiana, in 1964, Sanders bought an automobile that
proved to be a lemon—one so bad that the dealer agreed to take it
back. Somehow, the credit bureau in Shreveport misinterpreted this
affair and entered in Sanders' record a report that the car had been repossessed for Sanders' failure to pay.

Sanders became unhappily aware of this error when he moved to
Waco, Texas, in 1966, and applied for a mortgage so he could buy a
house. His application was turned down because the Waco credit bureau, having been informed by the Shreveport bureau that Sanders
had had his car repossessed, listed him as a bad credit risk. Sanders
did everything he could to have this erroneous report corrected, even
persuading the automobile company to write letters to both credit bureaus denying that it had ever repossessed Sanders' car. The Waco bureau still refused to make the correction—on the grounds that it never
corrected information coming from another bureau. Sanders sued the
bureau and won a $500 damage award.

But this was not the end of Sanders' troubles. In 1968 he moved
to another radio reporting job in San Antonio and bought a new car.
He had hardly driven it out of the dealer's showroom before the report came in from Waco about the alleged repossession. The San Antonio car dealer panicked and even before the first payment was due
hauled the car right out of Sanders' driveway. Thoroughly annoyed

by this time, Sanders sued the car dealer and won $800 in damages. But the lawsuit had made Sanders' professional situation in San Antonio so uncomfortable that he felt it best to move on to another radio reporting job in still another city.

Your rights with the credit bureau

Sanders' successful suits against the Waco credit bureau and the San Antonio car dealer were unusual in the 1960s. But his difficulties, and those of many people like him, came to the attention of Congressional investigating committees. The result was the passage of the federal Fair Credit Reporting Act, which became effective in 1971 and helps to prevent such nightmarish entanglements.

This law protects you from false or misleading credit bureau reports in a number of ways. First, if your application for credit is turned down because a lender has received an unfavorable report, the firm that rejected you is required to supply you with the name and address of the credit bureau issuing the report. You are entitled to similar notification if a credit bureau's report causes you to be turned down by an insurance company to which you have applied for a new policy or by a prospective employer to whom you have applied for a job.

Armed with the credit bureau's name and address, you can then demand to know the "nature and substance" of the material in your file. You can do this in person or by telephone. If you go to the credit bureau's office, all you have to do is establish your identity. The requirement that you show some credentials—a birth certificate, draft card, driver's license or credit cards—is needed to ensure that no prying outsider can gain access to your file. If you are too busy to go to the bureau's office, you can find out what your file contains by first writing a letter. The credit bureau will then send you a form requesting identifying information; if your reply checks with the information already in the credit bureau's files, they will suggest a telephone interview, at which time identification is considered complete if the number you are calling from is listed in your name. (If you call from your office, the bureau will verify that you are employed at that number before revealing any information.) In either case, you now have a right to make the credit bureau reveal everything, good and bad, that your credit record contains, except medical data.

You can, for that matter, check on your credit status even before you have undergone the unpleasant experience of being rejected. Even if you have only a suspicion that a negative credit report may be circulating—one that might result in a denial of credit, insurance or employment—you are entitled to ask the bureau to recheck and if necessary, correct its information. You may encounter one problem, however. A merchant who has already rejected you as a credit risk must identify the particular bureau on whose report he based his rejection; but when you try to trace a negative report before it causes difficulties, you may have some hunting to do. If you live in a community large enough to have several bureaus, you might have to contact a number of them before locating the one that has your file.

If your file contains material that you consider false, incomplete or obsolete, you have a right to challenge its accuracy. The bureau must then recheck its data. The Fair Credit Reporting Act requires that this rechecking be done "within a reasonable period of time" —which the bureaus interpret as meaning within 10 days. At the end of the reinvestigation, the bureau must delete from your record any challenged material it has found to be faulty, uncheckable or more than seven years old.

There are two exceptions to this last rule. First, a credit bureau may continue to include bankruptcy information in its reports for 14 years rather than seven. Second, the bureau is not required actually to destroy out-of-date adverse information. It may include this old information in a report requested by a prospective employer if the job involved pays $20,000 or more a year. Evidently the Congressmen who wrote the Fair Credit Reporting Act thought that an employer filling such a responsible position had a right to all information about an applicant, even if its validity was questionable. For similar reasons, the bureau may also include such old information if its report is to be used in connection with a life insurance policy with a face value of $50,000 or more, or a request for credit of $50,000 or more.

In some cases you may not be able to prove that derogatory information is incorrect: Was the lamp you refused to pay for damaged before you got it home or after? When there is a dispute, you can enter your version in your record, inserting a statement up to 100 words long giving your side of the story. The bureau must include this statement in all future reports about you. If you so request, the bureau is also obligated to send copies of your statement to anyone who has had access to the credit bureau's information during the previous six months (if the material was used in connection with employment, it must be sent to anyone who has had access to it during the preceding two years). The bureau must give you the names of all these people who have received an erroneous report about you, giving you the opportunity to correct their misimpressions of you.

Not only must the people at the bureau tell you the nature and substance of all data in your file—except for medical information they may have acquired—but they are also required by law to disclose their sources of information, with one exception: They need not reveal the source—only the substance—of what is known as "soft data." This consists of information gathered by a bureau through a private investigation intended to shed light on your character, general reputation, personal characteristics, mode of living and the like. Such information may be derived from conversations with a member of your family, friends, neighbors or business associates. Before the Fair Credit Reporting Act, the bureaus argued that if they were forced to inform consumers of the source of soft data, the sources would soon dry up, and Congress allowed them to maintain secrecy on this point. The only way you can discover who supplied hearsay information about you is by bringing a court action against the credit bureau. Despite these restrictions on your access to soft data, you have a right to know when someone asks for such information, at which point you can demand to know the nature and scope of the bureau's investigation into your character and way of living.

To help you keep your record straight, the law specifies that credit bureaus must have qualified personnel on hand during normal business hours. They will assist you to understand the reports in your credit file. Such help is free if you get in touch with the credit bureau within 30 days of being informed that an unfavorable report about you is circulating; otherwise the bureau can charge you a modest fee —usually about four dollars.

There are penalties for credit bureaus that do not live up to the requirements of the law. If you feel that your complaints have not been attended to, check with the nearest office of the Federal Trade Commission or the consumer protection agency or attorney general in your state. You might even have grounds for a damage suit if violations of the law result in economic loss.

PROTECTING YOUR CREDIT CARDS

Much of your use of credit probably involves credit cards—the handy, wallet-size plastic rectangles issued by stores, banks and oil companies as well as by such credit card companies as Diners' Club and American Express. There were more than 300 million credit cards in circulation in 1971 and they were proliferating at the rate of 100 million a year. While a credit card is a great convenience, until recently it could be a mixed blessing. If a card were lost or stolen it could be used to run up huge bills, and even after the lawful cardholder reported his loss to the issuer, there were no laws clearly defining who was liable for the illicit purchases—the cardholder or the issuer.

In 1970 Congress grappled with this problem of lost cards and liability. One result was an amendment to the Truth in Lending Act providing that you may no longer be mailed an unsolicited credit card, which could easily fall into the wrong hands before it reached you. The law also sets limits on your responsibility for unauthorized use of your cards. Once you notify the issuing company that a card is missing, you owe nothing for purchases made with it after that time. And you cannot be held responsible for more than $50 for charges run up before you were able to sound the alarm. The burden of setting up a rapid and efficient notification system, Congress said, is on the issuer. Banks and other credit card companies must now provide you, at the time a card is issued, with notice of your $50 liability as well as a stamped, self-addressed notification form to be used should your card be lost or stolen.

It is well to remember that time is crucial, especially if you are missing a number of cards. The $50 maximum applies to *each* card, and a thief might be using all of them. To avoid such dangers, keep a careful record of all your cards—their account numbers and the names of the issuing companies. The moment you become aware of having lost a card, report the loss by telephone to the company involved, and in order to be able to confirm your call, record the name of the person you speak with. This is considered valid notice until you can mail the notification form. Also, it is well to destroy your old card if a credit card company sends you a new one—some credit cards are automatically renewed periodically.

YOUR RIGHT TO TRUTH FROM LENDERS

These rules on credit card responsibilities are only part of the broad credit protection afforded by the Truth in Lending Act. The essential purpose of this law is just what its name implies—it requires merchants, banks and all other organizations offering credit to tell you plainly the terms of the agreement you sign. The charge for credit must be stated in dollars and must also be translated into an annual percentage rate of interest. If this rate seems to you to be exorbitant, you can then shop around for more reasonable terms. Both the finance charge in dollars and the annual percentage rate must be printed on the installment agreement in bolder type than that used for other entries and must also appear on all monthly statements.

The law forbids lenders to conceal finance charges. It was once fairly common, for example, for a merchant to quietly add several dollars to the cash price of an item if you decided to buy it on time. A television set that would have cost $200 had you offered to pay cash for it, suddenly cost $225 when you came to sign the installment contract. Now, unless you are told what these price differences are and how much they come to, they are illegal. So is the padding of finance charges with extras—for a credit bureau fee or for insurance—again, unless you are told what they are. In addition, a lender must now tell you if you will save on interest charges—and how much you will save —if you find yourself able to pay off all the remaining installments ahead of time. Some merchants cancel the interest charges on the balance if you pay it off in a lump, and some do not. Either way is legal. But the lender has to inform you so that you know where you stand.

Stores and other sources of credit must also tell you how they plan to bill—whether the billing will be based on your previous balance or an adjusted balance. A finance charge based on your previous balance is computed on the sum you owed at the beginning of the billing period—it does not take into account payments you may have made since the last billing and does not include credit you may have received for merchandise returned. In other words, if your previous balance at a store was $100 and you paid off $50, the finance charge would be figured on the $100 rather than the $50 you actually owed at the time the statement was made out. But if the finance charge is based on your adjusted balance, it will be computed on precisely the amount you owe at the closing date of your statement. Obviously it is to your benefit to deal with credit sources using the adjusted balance system. Most states, however, consider both methods of computation legal, on the theory that once credit lenders have informed you of what their system is, you are free to accept it or to march out and take your business elsewhere.

Part of the billing information the lender must disclose is the rules for late payments. You must be told the date after which an extra charge will be made. If there is a late charge, each bill must have printed on it "Pay this amount before (date) to avoid any additional finance charge." Most stores and credit card companies allow 20 days. Some retailers, however, have been known to mail out their bills several days or even weeks after the date given on the statement, thus shrinking the period during which you are expected to send in your payment. Check the dates on your statements.

Although credit protection legislation has corrected some major abuses in billing practices, it has not yet come to the defense of a consumer faced with an erroneous bill. Such errors have become increasingly common since computers began to take over record-keeping,

and the burden of righting these mistakes rests on you rather than on those responsible for the error. Demand that corrections be made as rapidly as possible and be wary of a credit source that repeatedly makes mistakes in its own behalf.

BORROWING MONEY

Another area in which the consumer must still be watchful is the borrowing of money. You may be taking out such loans more often than you think. When you go to a bank or a finance company and arrange a personal loan, you know you are borrowing money. But you are also borrowing money, in effect, when you buy a TV set on the installment plan or buy a car on time. You get the merchandise now, probably for a small down payment. For all practical purposes, you have borrowed the money for the rest of the purchase price.

One special problem of borrowing money, as money, arises when you agree to be "co-maker" of a loan for a friend. A co-maker guarantees the loan and is legally just as liable for paying it back as the man who applied for and got the money. If a friend for whom you serve as co-maker falls ill and cannot pay his indebtedness—or proves to be a false friend and simply disappears, leaving his debts behind —you will have to pay up. At the very least you should read what the note says with extreme care (and be pretty sure of your friend).

Many agreements for borrowing money, including some offered by large banks and well-known dealers in installment-plan purchases, contain catches that can bring the unwary borrower to grief. One provision that often turns up is a so-called acceleration clause. It states that your failure to pay even one installment gives the lender the option to "declare this note immediately due and payable, without notice or demand." In other words, you must then pay off the entire loan—and right away. Not every lender applies this clause rigidly. Most will not demand full payment when you miss a single installment, particularly if you notify them of your reason for missing it. Some will not demand full payment even if you skip two installments.

Those sneaky balloon payments

"Balloons" are generally inflated final payments on bank loans or installment purchases—payments that clean up the debt but demand twice (or more than twice) the amount of money you have been paying in the previous regular monthly installments. They can suddenly fish-hook a large chunk of money out of your pocket. If you cannot pay off the balloon, you may have to refinance the balance of your loan—and sometimes on more costly terms. Credit contracts must now warn you in bold type if they call for a balloon payment and must specify refinancing terms.

But by the time more than three are skipped, the lender usually demands the total amount still owing. If the lender sues for his money, another clause in most contracts lets him recover not only the amount of the loan still due, but also the court costs and attorney's costs he incurred in reclaiming his money. (Some states, however, forbid the creditor from tacking on the lawyer's fee.)

You should also be wary of a loan contract clause calling for a "balloon payment"—generally a final payment more than twice as large as the regular, equal payments that have preceded it. Say you have been paying $40 a month for 11 months toward a total of $600; for the 12th and last payment you may be expected to pay all the rest in one lump—$160. Borrowers sometimes request such a system of payment, anticipating a change for the better in their financial circumstances that will enable them to pay off a loan more quickly with such a whopping final installment. But some loan contracts include a balloon payment whether you request it or not. In either case, the Truth in Lending law provides that it must be called to your attention by the use of the term "BALLOON PAYMENT" printed in large type, with a clause added that states whether that payment may be refinanced and how. Before this warning went into effect, unsuspecting borrowers would suddenly discover that a balloon payment was expected of them. Unable to assemble the money, they would arrange for the lender to refinance the loan to enable them to pay off the balloon. But they would find to their grief that the refinancing, more often than not, was at higher terms than the original loan.

Installment contracts

Installment credit sale contracts generally have the same clauses as bank and finance company contracts—and several more besides. Many are what is known as conditional sales agreements, which means that the lender retains a "security interest" in the merchandise until the purchaser completes all of the payments. Until then, in effect, the lender still owns it. If the purchaser stops paying, the lender can repossess it. He can take the merchandise back even if the purchaser has completed as many as 10 of a dozen payments.

In some states the purchaser's indebtedness is not erased by simply giving up the merchandise, which the lender can then resell. The purchaser is still bound by a "deficiency judgment," which may or may not be spelled out in the installment contract. A typical deficiency clause reads: "In the event of repossession of said property the seller shall have the right to apply the proceeds of disposition to the reasonable expenses of retaking, holding, preparing for sale, selling and the like, reasonable attorney's fees, legal expenses incurred and satisfaction of indebtedness. Any surplus shall be paid to the buyer or as otherwise required by law. The buyer shall be liable for any deficiency." In other words, a merchant not only can repossess and resell the goods, but also can force the buyer to pay the difference between the resale price and the sum he still owes on his installment contract. For example, a woman bought a vacuum cleaner and still owed $60 in installments when it broke down. She asked the store to repair it. The store refused, pointing out that her installment contract did not provide for servicing. Since the vacuum cleaner was useless in its current condition, the woman let her payments lapse. The store repossessed the appliance, resold it for $20, then obtained a court judgment against the woman for $40—the resale price deducted from what she still owed—plus $43 for fees, interest and court costs.

In a few states a deficiency judgment can be issued without the purchaser ever being summoned to court. This can happen if the installment contract includes another subclause, a so-called "confession of judgment," by which the purchaser confesses in advance to being guilty if he misses his payments and waives his right to defend himself in court. Confession of judgment clauses have been outlawed in some states and in others they are often ignored by judges because there is a growing school of thought that considers them unconstitutional, denying a person the 14th Amendment's guarantee of due process.

Many courts also feel that deficiency judgments themselves —while legal—are, in the words of one judge, "oppressive, confiscatory and unconscionable." The judge used these harsh words to describe a 1963 deficiency judgment involving a man who had bought a battery for his 1955 Oldsmobile from an automobile supply dealer. The car owner had not paid outright for the battery, which cost $29.30, but had signed a credit agreement pledging not only the battery but the car itself as security. When the man missed a payment at a point at which he still owed $11.75, the dealer repossessed the car, which was sold at public auction. This sale did not decrease the defendant's debt, however, but increased it, since he was charged $45 for the repossession process, $35 in auctioneer's fees, $70 for garaging the car until the auction—and 25 cents for being late with his payment. The defendant was given credit for the $50 his car had brought at auction, but his debt that had begun with $29.30 for the battery now amounted to $128.80, including a $16.80 fee for the dealer's attorney. The judge hearing the case was shocked. It reminded him, he said, of the old observation, "For want of a nail, a shoe was lost; for want of a shoe, a horse was lost; for want of a horse, a kingdom was lost." The judge continued: "For want of $11.75, the defendant lost the battery, lost his 1955 Oldsmobile and was being sued for $128.80." He ruled against the dealer.

Such cases have led a few states to pass laws restricting deficiency judgments. In Utah, Oklahoma, Indiana and Idaho a full-scale deficiency judgment cannot be obtained against a buyer unless the merchandise cost more than $1,000. If it cost less, the seller can reclaim it and resell it or he can let the buyer keep the goods and sue for the remaining payments—but he cannot do both. Wyoming and Colorado have similar laws, differing mainly in the limitation on cost.

The holder in due course

Perhaps the most persistent cause of disputes over installment contracts lies in the ultimate source of the money you borrow to finance the purchase. While the agreement covers a merchant's extension of credit to you, the merchant himself seldom actually lends money. Except for the largest department stores, few merchants are financially able to tie up large sums in extending credit to their customers. They must turn to a third party whose business is lending money. When a merchant says, "I will finance your purchase for you," he usually means that he will arrange to have it financed by selling the contract he has signed with you to a bank or finance company, which will give him cash in exchange. The bank or finance company then proceeds to collect your payments. This procedure is perfectly legal; it is the standard method of financing consumer purchases. Virtually all installment contracts contain somewhere in their forest of clauses one something like this: "In the event of the transfer and assignment of

The installment contract

The contract shown in part at right has clauses and warnings that are required on the paper you sign when buying on time. It specifies a "default charge in the event of late payment," for example, and tells the buyer that he gets a "prepayment rebate" on the finance charge if he pays early. The box *(upper right)* has space where the merchant must list all credit costs added to the cash price.

S 146—Retail Installment Contract: Goods and Services:
Federal Reserve Regulation Z: All Jurisdictions.

COPYRIGHT 1969 BY JULIUS BLUMBERG, INC., LAW BLANK PUBLISHERS
80 EXCHANGE PLACE AT BROADWAY, NEW YORK

RETAIL INSTALLMENT CONTRACT (SECURITY AGREEMENT)

Dated..19......

Buyer...

Seller...

street address (residence)

street address

city & state .... zip .... telephone

city & state .... zip .... telephone

BUYER HEREBY PURCHASES the following articles of personal property and accessories thereto (hereinafter referred to as the "chattels") and grants a security interest in the chattels and proceeds therefrom to Seller subject to the terms and conditions on the face and reverse sides of this contract:...

Cash Price $........................

Sales Tax, if any   _____

Cash Price plus Sales Tax $........................

THIS CONTRACT IS NOT PAYABLE IN INSTALLMENTS OF EQUAL AMOUNTS. BUYER HEREBY AGREES

TO pay Seller the Total of Payments in...equal monthly installments of

$............................. each, the first installment to be due and payable one month from the date hereof and all subsequent equal monthly installments on even date in each successive month thereafter, and

AN INSTALLMENT OF $................... **WILL BE DUE AND PAYABLE ON**...............................19......

which payment ☐ is / ☐ is not a BALLOON PAYMENT (a final payment is a balloon payment if it is more than twice the amount of the equal monthly installment).

(1) Cash Price (include taxes if they are to be financed)		$_____
(2) Total Downpayment		
Cash	$_____	
Trade in	$_____	
(Items Traded:		_____
..............................)		
(3) Unpaid Balance of Cash Price (1) minus (2)		$_____
(4) Other Charges:		
physical damage insurance		$_____
creditor insurance		$_____
....		$_____
....		$_____
....		$_____
official fees		$_____
(5) Amount Financed (3) + (4)		$_____
Accrues from ....19......		
(6) **FINANCE CHARGE**		$_____
(7) Total of Payments (5) + (6)		$_____
(8) Deferred Payment Price (2) + (7)		$_____
(9) **ANNUAL PERCENTAGE RATE**		_____%

INSURANCE AGREEMENT

(a) Cost of required physical damage insurance $............................... BUYER MAY CHOOSE PERSON THROUGH WHICH THIS INSURANCE IS TO BE OBTAINED.

(b) Cost of creditor insurance: ☐ Life $............ ☐ Disability $............ CREDITOR INSURANCE IS NOT REQUIRED BY SELLER
☐ I desire creditor insurance checked above ☐ I do not desire creditor insurance

.......................19...... ....19...... ....
date   Buyer's signature   date   Buyer's signature

SECURITY INTEREST Seller retains title to, and shall have a security interest and lien in and upon the chattels, the proceeds therefrom, all equipment at any time added thereto and returned or unearned premiums from insurance policies on the chattels, to secure payment and performance of Buyer's obligations in this contract. Any additional indebtedness representing amounts which may be expended by Seller (1) in release or discharge of taxes, liens and incumbrances and (2) to procure required physical damage insurance on the chattels shall also be secured by this contract.

DEFAULT CHARGE IN THE EVENT OF LATE PAYMENT If any installment is not paid within 10 days after it is due, a charge will be payable by Buyer as follows: 5% of the unpaid installment or $5 whichever is less.

ATTORNEY'S FEES CHARGE IN THE EVENT OF DEFAULT In the event of any default reasonable attorney's fees and costs of collection will be charged where permitted by law and as more fully set forth on the reverse side of this contract.

TIME IS OF THE ESSENCE OF THIS CONTRACT.

PREPAYMENT REBATE Upon prepayment in full Buyer is entitled to a rebate of the **FINANCE CHARGE** in accordance with the rule of 78. No rebate less than $1 will be paid.

Disclosure statements pursuant to state law that are inconsistent with the Federal Truth In Lending Act:...

NOTICE TO BUYER (1) Do not sign this contract before you read it, or if it contains any blank spaces. (2) You are entitled to a completely filled in copy of this agreement. (3) Under the law, you have the right to pay off in advance the full amount due and under certain conditions to obtain a partial refund of the credit service charge.

IN WITNESS WHEREOF, each Buyer signing below executes this contract and acknowledges receipt of a completely filled in Buyer's copy of this contract executed by Seller on the date and in the year first above written.

RETAIL INSTALLMENT CONTRACT

....
Buyer's signature   signature of Seller's agent or officer

....
Buyer's signature   title

GUARANTEE

The undersigned (if more than one, jointly and severally) guarantees prompt and full performance and payment according to the tenor of the within agreement, to every holder hereof, and, in the event of default, authorizes any holder hereof to proceed against the undersigned, for the full amount due including reasonable attorneys' fees and costs and expenses of collections, and hereby waives presentment, demand, protest, notice of protest, notice of dishonor and any and all other notices or demand of what ever character to which the undersigned might otherwise be entitled. The undersigned consents to any extension of time of payment granted by any holder and waives notice thereof.

THE UNDERSIGNED ACKNOWLEDGE(S) RECEIPT OF A COPY OF THIS GUARANTEE. Dated.............................19......

....
Guarantor signature and address   Guarantor signature and address

TRIPLICATE: BUYER'S COPY

the seller's rights hereunder, the word 'seller' shall be understood as referring to the subsequent holder of this contract." This "holder in due course" has taken over your promise to pay, and now you owe him the money.

In the past, if the merchandise for which he lent money proved worthless, he could point out that he did not manufacture the article or sell it to you. That fact, until recently, relieved the holder in due course of responsibility for the merchandise. No matter how bad it was, he could collect the full amount due under the contract.

Suppose, for example, that a man named Jones bought a color TV set and a costly new antenna from a local dealer and agreed to his installment payment plan. But soon Jones found that the TV set did not operate properly with the antenna he had been sold. When he threatened to withhold payments unless the TV set was adjusted, the dealer shrugged. He no longer felt responsible for Jones's purchase since he had sold the installment contract to a finance company. Jones then called the finance company, but the people there informed him that they knew nothing about adjusting TV sets—their business was lending money. Frustrated, Jones stopped making payments. The finance company sued him and won. Jones not only had to continue making payments, but also had to pay attorney's fees as part of the collection costs incurred by the finance company.

This sort of separation of responsibilities between merchant and lender has a long history in credit law. Less than a decade ago most states considered that a holder in due course was "an innocent purchaser for value in good faith." Such a philosophy encouraged the easy negotiability of promissory notes by relieving the purchaser of the note of the need for interfering in the business of his merchant clients. It encouraged the flow of money and credit and stimulated business. But it brought a lot of heartache to consumers who got stuck with faulty goods and found nobody willing to take responsibility for them. And it also stimulated collusion between dishonest merchants and dishonest finance companies. A merchant could knowingly sell a bum appliance and then sell the installment contract to an equally unprincipled friend who ran a finance outfit. Both could then deny any responsibility for the worthless appliance—and the finance company could also legally demand payment in full. In one case a used car dealer sold a woman a car that was about to break down—and had been stolen as well. He then sold her installment contract to a finance company, which compelled the woman to continue her payments on the car even after it was found to be a stolen vehicle.

Indignation over such abuses led consumer groups, in the mid-

1960s, to put pressure on courts and legislatures to re-examine the philosophy that viewed purchasers of promissory notes as totally innocent parties. And in 1967 the New Jersey Supreme Court ruled in favor of a couple named Owens, who had been sued by a finance company for discontinuing payments on merchandise they had not received. The Owenses had signed an installment contract with a record company that promised them 140 stereo albums, 12 to be delivered with the down payment and the rest over a period of five years. Shortly after the contract was signed, the stereo company sold it to the finance company. The first 12 record albums arrived as promised, but although the Owenses paid their installments for a year, they never received another record. The stereo company had gone out of business. The finance company, however, was still very much in business. When the Owenses stopped payments on their contract, the company claimed its traditional legal right to payment as an innocent holder in due course and took the Owenses to court.

In nearly every other case of this kind, the plaintiff had automatically won the suit. But this time it turned out that the finance company was not an innocent purchaser of the contract. In fact, it had worked so closely with the now-defunct stereo company that, in effect, it had controlled the stereo firm. The court rejected the finance company's claim to payment and pointed out that in the field of negotiable instruments good faith was an all-important consideration. How could the finance company be an innocent purchaser in good faith when it had every reason to know that the record company, which it all but controlled, was in extremely shaky condition and might go under at any moment?

Around the same time, legislators in other states began drafting laws to restrict the presumption of innocence that had always been granted holders in due course. A number of states have enacted statutes stipulating that the consumer must be notified when his installment contract has been sold to a subsequent holder and must be given a period of time—generally 10 to 90 days—in which to inform the new party to the contract of any defects in the merchandise. If the purchaser thereafter stops payments because of these defects, he has provided himself with legal grounds for a defense in court in case the holder in due course brings suit. Four states—Massachusetts, Washington, Alaska and Hawaii—have gone further. Those states simply make the holder in due course responsible for the merchandise. Mas-

The elusive holder in due course
When a customer (a) buys a television set on time from a merchant (b), he signs an installment contract promising to pay. Often as not the merchant (b) turns right around sells the contract to someone else (c) —a bank or finance company. So the customer no longer owes the merchant; now he (a) must pay the financier (c), who has become the holder in due course of the contract. The merchant is out of the picture, and in many states the customer has to continue paying the holder in due course even if the TV set proves faulty.

sachusetts and New York add another safeguard in the form of a so-called Specious Cash Sale law. Suppose a store in either state routinely sends its credit customers to a particular bank or finance company to take out a loan in order to pay for a piece of merchandise in cash. There is no installment contract and no holder in due course—but under the law the lender is still responsible for the merchandise.

Your best protection against difficulties in installment buying is to heed the warning that the laws of most states insist must appear prominently on the face of a contract: "NOTICE TO THE BUYER: Do not sign this agreement before you read it or if it contains any blank spaces." Better yet, read it at least twice before you add your signature. Do not skip a paragraph because it seems innocuous or is difficult to understand. Draw a line through any blank space so that nobody can add clauses after you have signed. If something in the contract is not clear to you, ask for an explanation (if a large sum is involved, consult a lawyer). In addition, do not rely on oral promises. If a merchant makes you an oral promise, ask him to put it in writing; merchants who are reputable will not object to doing so.

However, if you do have the misfortune to sign an agreement that you later suspect is unfair, do not despair. Even though all the clauses seem to indicate that you have to meet your payments, a court may sometimes decide that the agreement was so drastically one-sided and unfair that it cannot be enforced by law—and you may be able to obtain a release from it.

This remedy cannot always be counted on. Many installment schemes that have tricked purchasers are upheld by the courts despite the harm they cause. One deal that, when used by unscrupulous sellers, causes losses to the unwary is the "referral plan." Usually it promises bonuses to the buyer who refers friends to the selling company so that they in turn will make purchases. Many states consider referral plans to be lotteries and declare them in violation of state lottery laws, but some states permit them. Some such plans work out profitably for everyone involved. But many are hoaxes designed to entrap gullible buyers. For example, a Midwestern couple signed up for an expensive home movie camera—at a price exceeding its normal retail value. The salesman explained that for every friend the couple turned up as a potential customer, his company would pay the couple a handsome cash bonus that would more than offset the cost of each payment on their own camera. The camera soon arrived, and the couple submitted the names of a dozen friends who might also be interested. But several weeks later the couple received a payment book from a bank that had taken over their agreement as the holder in due course. They discovered that instead of a business arrangement guaranteeing them bonuses, they had signed an installment contract totaling nearly $600. When the couple objected to making payments for a camera that they had been assured would be theirs for nothing, the bank coldly informed them that unless they paid, the husband's wages as well as their home could be attached.

A uniform code for credit abuses

Although a number of the abuses that long plagued consumers using credit have been either outlawed or restricted in at least some areas, plenty still remain. Most states have different laws concerning credit, and in some states they are less protective of the consumer's rights than they are in others.

In an effort to provide all Americans with uniform legal safeguards, a national commission proposed in 1969 a Uniform Consumer Credit Code with provisions for correcting some of the worst abuses suffered by credit shoppers. The code has been voted into law, with various modifications, in some Western and Midwestern states, and it is being considered in the legislatures of most of the other states. Among other things, its provisions forbid referral plans and confessions of judgment, restrict balloon payments and deficiency judgments, and limit the rights of holders in due course. Some groups dedicated to protecting consumer rights contend that the Uniform Consumer Credit Code does not go far enough and have opposed its passage. Others, however, view it as the best attainable improvement to existing statutes, for it does offer a purchaser some protection.

THE BILL COLLECTORS

The law, of course, protects the lenders who extend credit as well as consumers who use it. Anyone who fails to meet his credit payments can face a number of unpleasant consequences. His salary can be attached—garnished—and he can even be taken into court and deprived of his personal property. The courts in some states have the power to seize his home and order it sold to meet the demands of his creditors. Fortunately, matters seldom reach this extreme stage. Most merchants and moneylenders go through a number of gentler procedures designed to help a debtor pay up.

The beginning of the debt collection process is often a tactful reminder to the delinquent customer, slipped in with his monthly statement. "Perhaps you were away," it may read, "but you seem to have overlooked our bill." When the reminder does not produce results, the creditor resorts to a letter—but the point at which this step is taken may vary from customer to customer, depending on the size of the bill and the customer's past payment record. Some merchants begin to send dunning letters 15 days after the first notice of delinquency; others wait as long as three months—and even then, the language of their letters may be exceedingly polite. "Dear Customer," runs the credit letter of one fashionable New York City specialty shop, "We know that you are as concerned with Good Taste in credit as you are in clothes."

The purpose of these letters is, of course, to collect money; but failing that, they also have a secondary goal: communication. Credit managers are often quite sympathetic to customers who will take the trouble to write or telephone, explaining the reason for delinquency. Sometimes they will allow the customer to skip a payment or two and make up the deficit later, when he is in better shape financially; sometimes they will agree to accept token payments for several months. Banks and finance companies are usually willing to refinance a burdensome loan, reducing the size of payments while extending the period over which they are paid. Owners of smaller neighborhood stores frequently offer to take back merchandise and cancel the rest of the bill. Every creditor's aim is to get his money back, not to get his customers into trouble with the law.

When dunning letters produce neither payment nor explanation, the creditor moves into the next phase: He uses the telephone. The manner, however, is still polite. "Good morning, Mrs. James," a pleasant voice will say, "we were just wondering if there was some problem about the amount of our bill. Or perhaps about the merchandise itself." This courteous approach is standard practice among department stores—so much so that many of them enroll their credit department employees in special classes to learn the "art of short friendly persuasive telephone conversations." When telephoning fails, department stores often employ another weapon: They can close down the customer's charge account. Though this often jolts the customer into paying his bill, occasionally the response the store gets is unexpected. One husband, when informed that his wife's charge account was being terminated, wrote the store: "Dear Sirs, May I express my heartfelt gratitude."

Collection agencies

Only when letters, phone calls and credit cut-offs fail do stores and banks turn over their debt collection chores to professionals—and their hesitancy to do so is partly a matter of economics. Professional collection agencies and lawyers who specialize in debt collecting are well paid for their work. Their fees range from one third of the amount collected on large debts to one half the amount on small ones. But at this point the fee is usually worth it, for the dunning process, from here on in, becomes increasingly unpleasant. Collection agencies and collection lawyers also start with letters but the letters they send are decidedly severe: "Dear Sir, We write with reference to the past-due obligation of $100 owed to our above-named client. Unless we receive payment of this amount in full within five (5) days of the date of this letter, we are instructed by our client to take such steps as we deem advisable to protect its interests."

If such letters generally contain a veiled threat rather than an open one, it is only because the federal government has begun to look into debt collection practices. In the past, the Federal Trade Commission found, dunning letters have contained threats and abusive phrases that have amounted to unlawful invasions of privacy. "With surprising frequency," the Commission observed, dunning notices "cross the line of wisdom and even of legality." Consequently, it issued a series of guidelines to correct some of the worst of these practices. Under pain of possible fine and investigation by the FTC, collection agencies may no longer send out letters threatening debtors with legal action when no such resort to the courts is actually contemplated. Nor may they threaten debtors with disclosure of their indebtedness in ways that might jeopardize their jobs or their standing in the community.

Similar guidelines, issued by the Federal Communications Commission, warn collection agencies that their telephone tactics may be in violation of laws governing the use of telephones and other means of communication. According to federal rules, telephone companies may not permit their instruments to be used "for a call or calls, anonymous or otherwise, in a manner reasonably expected to frighten, abuse, torment or harass another." This outlaws such practices as middle-of-the-night phone calls, nuisance calls to the debtor's friends, employer, neighbors or relatives, and calls falsely threatening the debtor with legal action.

Most of these FTC and FCC regulations were influenced by court rulings that a certain amount of reasonable pressure is justified to get debts paid, but that it should stop short of physical, social or extreme mental harassment. Thus a Georgia court ruled that a finance company had a perfect right to send a debtor an urgent telegram, demanding immediate payment, on the grounds that "there are some shocks, inconveniences and annoyances which members of society in the nature of things must absorb." On the other hand, a Texas court held that it was unlawful for a creditor to summon a debtor to a neighbor's phone in the middle of the night to receive an "emergency message" that turned out to be a blunt request: "Hello. Please bear up. Why don't you pay your bill?"

The courts tend to frown on the use of social pressure against debtors because in some cases it becomes an unlawful invasion of privacy. Where once a collection agency might have gotten away with such crude tactics as parking a brightly colored truck labeled "We collect bad debts" in front of a debtor's home, the legal profession now warns collection lawyers to refrain from anything that smacks of intrusion on the debtor's private life. The New York City Bar Association, for instance, forbids collection lawyers in that city to communicate with a debtor's employer about his indebtedness. And Massachusetts has passed a law prohibiting a creditor from telling or threatening to tell any person other than the debtor about the debt.

The use of physical force to collect debts is of course illegal. Indeed, such practices have led to lawsuits that cost creditors more in damages than the money they were trying to collect. In Utah, a dentist got into an argument with a woman patient over the size of her dental bill, which she claimed was twice as large as it should have been. The dentist, in a temper, locked the door of the room in which they were arguing and announced that the woman could stay right there until she had written a check for every penny she owed him. After a 30-minute battle of wills, the woman succumbed and paid. But she was pregnant at the time and shortly afterward had a miscarriage, which

Once a bill collector might have gotten away with such tactics as parking a truck labeled "We collect bad debts" in front of a debtor's home, but the courts now frown on the use of social pressure because it may become an unlawful invasion of privacy.

she claimed was caused by the fear and tension engendered during her encounter with the dentist. The court agreed and ordered the dentist to pay the woman damages.

Repossession and garnishment

When a merchant takes a customer to court for failing to pay his bill, he generally tries to repossess his merchandise—and normally the court upholds his right to do so. But the courts draw the line at strong-arm methods of repossession. A Pennsylvania court held a merchant guilty of trespass when he broke a customer's window in order to gain access to her home and remove a piano that she had failed to pay for. In the state of Washington an automobile dealer wanted to repossess a car that had not been paid for and sent a crew of employees to get it. The woman who had purchased the car sought to foil them by sitting behind the wheel and refusing to budge. After much fruitless argument, the dealer's employees unceremoniously dragged the woman from the front seat. The woman sued and the court awarded her damages—because the dealer's agents had used force.

Many creditors, when they take debtors to court, ask the court to assure them of their money by ordering the debtor's salary to be garnished; that is, part of his salary to be withheld every payday by his employer and turned over directly to the creditor. The court may also order a "levy of execution" against the debtor's property, transferring some of it to the creditor. But there are limits to such actions. The court will frequently "attach," or freeze, a debtor's bank account at the start of legal proceedings, for instance, preventing him from using the account until his case has been heard. But nowadays courts in most states generally refuse to grant a levy of execution that would leave a man destitute, partly on the ground that there is no point in turning a debtor into a ward of the state. Also, certain kinds of personal property are classed as necessities and cannot be seized to meet bad debts under any circumstances. Wearing apparel is a necessity in most states, and so is the debtor's wristwatch—but not two wristwatches. Similarly, household furnishings are generally exempt, but not the television set. A man also has the right to keep the tools of his trade; a Georgia court once ruled that while a barber whom a creditor had successfully sued might keep his comb and clippers, he could not hang on to the barbershop's chewing-gum machine.

Similarly, there are legal limits on how much can be garnished from a debtor's salary. This limitation is relatively recent, the result of the passage of the Truth in Lending Act. Before then, the amount of garnishment was left up to the individual states, and it varied widely from state to state. Alaska, for instance, ruled that a debtor, if single, could not be left with less than $200 a month. In North Dakota, the figure for an unmarried man was $35 a week. Under the federal law, however, no debtor's salary can be garnished of more than 25 per cent of his earnings (after taxes and similar deductions) each week. This law also forbids the practice, once common among some employers, of firing garnished employees to relieve their bookkeeping departments of the extra trouble the garnishment caused.

WIPING THE SLATE CLEAN—BANKRUPTCY

When a debtor becomes so deeply entangled in debt that neither garnishment nor a levy of execution against his property is likely to satisfy his creditors, he can in effect wipe the slate clean and start life anew by filing a petition in bankruptcy. Bankruptcy is technically available to anyone unable to pay his debts. It involves turning over virtually all of his assets for distribution among his creditors. This action cancels most of the debts. Although creditors sometimes threaten debtors with bankruptcy proceedings, in fact most bankruptcy petitions are voluntary. In recent years some 99 per cent of ordinary bankruptcies have been initiated by the debtors themselves.

Once upon a time going bankrupt was considered to be a wicked way of skipping out on one's obligations; the bankrupt was a social outcast. Undoubtedly some of this stigma lingers on, but these days —whether as a result of changing mores or changing economic patterns—bankruptcy is a good deal more common than it used to be. In 1948 only 18,510 people filed bankruptcy petitions in U.S. courts; in 1970 there were 250,000. Furthermore, the average petitioner is neither a ne'er-do-well nor a psychopathic cheat—though money mismanagement is likely to be part of his problem. Usually he is an ordinary citizen, living on credit like all his neighbors and paying his bills in small monthly installments. Suddenly he becomes ill or loses his job, or his wife or child is hospitalized and he is hit with staggering medical bills. Instead of leaving town or robbing a bank, he chooses to seek relief by declaring bankruptcy—and the law, while recognizing the validity of the creditors' claims, also recognizes that bankruptcy may be the most humane solution to the problem.

Usually a decision to declare bankruptcy begins with a visit to a lawyer. Though legal aid is not essential—the forms required to file for bankruptcy are available at many business stationery stores—most people feel more secure if they have a lawyer to guide them through the bankruptcy procedure. For one thing, a lawyer can tell them if they have a right to petition for bankruptcy—and some people do not. A person who has previously declared bankruptcy, for instance, may not undertake the process again until after six years have passed. Nor may a person be discharged from certain types of debts through bankruptcy—for example, nonpayment of taxes, alimony or child support, or debts incurred through fraud, such as the issuance of a false financial statement.

Under certain circumstances, bankruptcy is distinctly ill-advised. No one who expects shortly to inherit money or property should apply for bankruptcy, for instance. If he receives his inheritance while undergoing bankruptcy, his creditors immediately get the right to split these new assets among themselves in payment of his debts. Not only does he stand to lose the money that may be due him, he may also lose family heirlooms—paintings, jewelry, rare books, antiques —that he values for personal reasons. Nor should anyone whose business is licensed rush into bankruptcy without considering the consequences; often his license will be revoked. And finally, the process of bankruptcy is so painful for some people, so damaging to their pride, that almost anything—even long-term economic servitude to creditors—may seem a preferable alternative.

Other ways out

Actually, there are some measures short of outright bankruptcy that a lawyer may suggest if he thinks it advisable. One is called debt counseling or debt pooling, and it is in effect an income-planning service. A debt counselor will make up a list of the debtor's financial obligations, including his living expenses; then he will collect the debtor's income, disbursing some of it among his creditors and advising him how best to allocate the rest. Not all states permit debt counseling —too often it has been practiced by dishonest operators who have charged clients exhorbitant fees or even stolen their money.

A second alternative to bankruptcy is called an "assignment for the benefit of creditors." In this kind of action the debtor temporarily transfers management of a piece of property to a third party, who uses the income from the property to pay off the debt. This arrangement, however, presupposes that the debtor owns property sizable enough to bring in a certain amount of money—and few debtors have such assets. The debtor's lawyer may also suggest a third course, in which he himself acts as a go-between to arrange a "composition agreement" with the creditors: In return for an immediately forthcoming payment, somewhat less than the full debt, each creditor agrees to cancel all future payments. Most creditors are naturally reluctant to enter into such an agreement, and lawyers who try to arrange such compromises are advised by law texts to approach the creditors at a time of day when they are likely to be most amiable—over drinks and lunch, for instance.

The legal process of bankruptcy

Of course, if bankruptcy turns out to be the best solution, the lawyer stands ready to advise on this procedure too—although for all its finality, a bankruptcy proceeding is not particularly complicated, nor does it take much time. Usually the whole thing is over in less than two months. To begin with, there is the filing of the petition, literally a plea to the court, asking to be heard: "Your petitioner owes debts and is willing to surrender all his property for the benefit of creditors. . . . He prays that he may be adjudged by the court to be a bankrupt." This petition is filed with the clerk of the nearest U.S. District Court and with it go two additional documents. One is a complete list of the debtor's assets and liabilities, mentioning everything from life insurance, securities, bank accounts and the mortgage payments on his house right down to the grocery bill and the money in his pockets. The other necessary document is a form called a "statement of affairs," which supplies information on such matters as the debtor's income, occupation and tax returns.

As soon as these three documents are filed, the court grants the debtor release from garnishment and other debt collection practices; in one case a debtor even got his cut-off gas and electric service restored. At the same time the court also notifies all of the creditors named in the petition of the debtor's action and informs them that they may file their own individual claims against him. The court then proceeds to schedule a meeting that must be attended by the debtor,

A man petitioning for bankruptcy must provide a list of his liabilities and assets, mentioning everything from life insurance, securities, bank accounts and mortgage payments right down to the grocery bill and the money in his pockets.

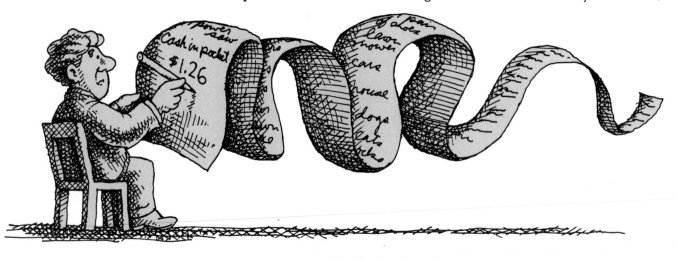

and may or may not be attended by the creditors—depending upon their interest in the case and the extent of their financial involvement with the debtor in question.

Although this examination takes place in a courthouse, it is not a trial and the presiding officer is not a judge. The meeting room is sometimes a judicial antechamber, in effect a conference room (although actual courtrooms are sometimes used), and the examiner is a judicial officer called a referee. The debtor is examined under oath and is entitled to be accompanied by a lawyer, whose counsel he may seek during the course of the questioning. He may refuse to answer a question when he feels that the answer might be likely to incriminate him, but he is subject to charges of contempt of court if he perjures himself or gives evasive answers.

When the referee has completed his questioning of the debtor, he may turn to any creditors who are present and ask them a few questions too. After that, he will decide which of the debtor's assets will be used to appease his creditors, and in what order of priority the creditors will be paid. All of this is normally done in one meeting, and sometimes, when very little money is involved, the procedure lasts only a few minutes. If the debtor's assets are substantial, however, a further step is involved. The creditors will jointly appoint a trustee —usually a lawyer who specializes in bankruptcy law—to convert the assets into cash, which will then be distributed according to the schedule laid down by the federal Bankruptcy Act. The costs involved in administering the bankruptcy procedure have first priority, and then all federal, state and city taxes that are owed. After these are paid, the remainder is divided among the creditors.

The same legal principles that protect a debtor from destitution when creditors garnish his salary or get a levy of execution against his property also protect him in a bankruptcy proceeding. The same kinds of property that are exempt from forfeiture under a levy of execution are generally also exempt from bankruptcy proceedings. These exemptions vary widely from state to state, however, and some are rather bizarre—an indication of how long many of these state exemption lists have been in existence. In Idaho, for example, the law forbids a bankruptcy judgment to take away "the cabin of a miner." Mississippi allows the petitioner to retain "two head of cows and calves, ten head of hogs, twenty sheep and goats each, all poultry and all colts under three years raised in the state." And in some states the law stipulates that a bankrupt is entitled to keep his "seat or pew in a place of public worship." Many states, while allowing a bankrupt's home to be sold to satisfy his debts, specify that the bankrupt may keep a cer-

Alaska allows a person who has declared himself bankrupt to retain "one yoke of oxen, or a span of horses or mules, or two reindeer or six dogs."

tain amount of the proceeds of such a sale. Practical Maine allows a bankrupt's wife to hang on to her sewing machine, her washing machine and her refrigerator. California refuses to strip a bankrupt of his sources of home entertainment—his radio and television set—and also allows him to set aside enough fuel to warm his home for three months, along with $1,000 worth of any stock he may own in a savings and loan association. Most states not only allow bankrupt tradesmen to keep the tools of their trade but also permit bankrupt professional men to keep their professional libraries. California again stretches this concept and is especially lenient. With so many actors and actresses in residence, the state considers an entertainer's wardrobe to be a tool of the trade and over the years has permitted many a bankrupt actress to retain her mink coat. Alaska allows a person who has declared himself bankrupt to retain "one yoke of oxen, or a span of horses or mules, or two reindeer or six dogs."

A special kind of bankruptcy

The bankruptcy regulations were based on the notion that the man undergoing bankruptcy owned property. This assumption was accurate enough back in 1898 when Congress passed the Bankruptcy Act, which, with a number of added "Chapters," or amendments, is still in force. In those days if a man did not own property, he was not a person of substance in his community and could not get credit. Without credit, he would have had a hard time getting seriously into debt —and thus becoming a bankrupt. Today the situation has been reversed. Among the biggest users of credit are wage earners with quite modest incomes and very little tangible property. They live in rented homes, drive cars that actually belong to the finance company and have furniture that is still being paid off. Thus when the average wage earner goes bankrupt, there is usually very little property for his creditors to seize and turn into cash.

During the Depression, when the need to declare bankruptcy befell many people who had always paid their bills, Congress added an amendment, known as Chapter XIII, to the federal Bankruptcy Act. Under its provisions a wage earner, instead of having his debts immediately discharged, pays them off in installments out of his salary. The arrangement is rather like garnishment but has several advantages over it. Since the repayment schedule is set by the court, no single creditor can hound the debtor for a lion's share of whatever assets are available. Also, the schedule is usually arranged so that the debtor retains some 75 per cent of his salary, and the repayment period is usually over within a period of three years. One disadvantage of this process is that a court cannot put a wage earner plan into effect without the approval of a majority of the petitioner's creditors. But there is a compensating advantage. Although a wager earner who uses Chapter XIII to settle his debts is technically bankrupt, he may not be officially labeled as such so long as he meets his payments. He thus avoids the stigma of being listed in credit bureau files and other places as a man who once went bankrupt.

Some lawyers look upon this form of bankruptcy as discriminatory. Rich men, they say, are released from their debts, whereas poor men continue to be saddled with theirs. Other lawyers claim that the arrangement is equitable because rich men have property to offer their creditors, whereas poor men have nothing but their future salaries. Furthermore, these same lawyers argue, if poor men could periodically wipe out their debts by going bankrupt and paying nothing, many of them might carelessly pile up debt on debt, trusting in the courts to bail them out. Whatever the merits of these arguments, bankruptcy is still associated with disgrace and few people are likely to enter into it casually. Indeed there are good reasons not to, for a bankruptcy can lead to subsequent difficulties. Anyone with a record of bankruptcy, for instance, may find that he has a good deal of trouble getting a mortgage on a home.

Curiously, however, other kinds of credit may come to the bankrupt quite easily. He is, after all, a man without debts who cannot use bankruptcy to escape future debts for at least six years. Consequently for certain kinds of purchases—those in which the merchandise itself is security, such as cars, furniture and appliances—a bankrupt is considered by some businessmen to be a very good credit risk. Indeed, some merchants actively seek him out. One furniture dealer in St. Louis routinely sends bankruptcy petitioners a letter saying that he will "personally see to it that credit is extended to you," and one enterprising Chicago storekeeper not only offers bankruptcy petitioners credit cards but also sends each bankrupt a $10 gift certificate. Though a few people are lured by such tactics into sliding thoughtlessly into the easy credit route once again, the majority are not. Having received a second chance, most people are apparently far better able to handle credit sensibly, and to enjoy its benefits without once again falling prey to its dangers.

By **LINDA WOLFE**
LAWRENCE P. KING, Consultant

8
Income tax

The citizen and
the Internal
Revenue Service

As you drive south on U.S. 81 through the broad and lovely Shenandoah Valley, your view is spoiled—more than you know—by a huge, undistinguished brick building on the outskirts of Martinsburg, West Virginia. Recite your favorite incantation and make a hex sign when you go by. The building is the National Computer Center of the Internal Revenue Service, and its giant master computer is fondly referred to by IRS personnel as The Martinsburg Monster.

What the IRS knows about you is all there, part of the 1,000 miles of magnetic tape that contain the income and tax records of the nation's 81 million individual and corporate taxpayers. The Monster provides the last and toughest of several computerized examinations that subject tax returns to two challenges. Your figures are matched against the information that has come from other sources—banks, employer, corporations that pay you dividends, every kind of financial institution. Then your return undergoes a formularized test for honesty in which specific items are compared to the norm for your particular income group. If the computer reacts with either curiosity or outright hostility to a figure in your return, the result could be human scrutiny of your tax return: an IRS audit. And, depending on how both you and the IRS feel about it, the audit could involve you and the U.S. government in a lively legal hassle.

What are the odds that a polite, businesslike phone call or letter will announce that you are being audited? Each year, the Monster selects two and a half to three million tax returns for extra scrutiny. Some are returned to storage with no action taken, but others are sent to a local IRS district office for possible audit. Only one taxpayer in 35, says the IRS, is actually audited. But the higher the income, the shorter the odds. For those with incomes of $30,000 and over, the chances of being audited are one in five.

The income tax audit is just one of the circumstances in which you may find yourself needing help as you thread your way through the complex tangle of tax law. Your choice of a community to live in may be influenced by taxes; so, too, may decisions on investing savings, taking out insurance or making plans for the future. You can scarcely make a move today that is not affected by some aspect of the revenue-raising powers of government. There are more than 81,000 agencies empowered to levy taxes in the United States. You may be taxed not only by township, city, county and state but also by a host of special agencies operating schools, parks, sewer networks—even mosquito-control programs. But the one tax law that regularly affects everyone is the income tax law of the Internal Revenue Code. Understanding some of its more important provisions may help you save money, keep the IRS auditors off your back and give you an idea of what happens if you should be audited. The Code itself is a formidable document. Congress has amended it frequently—sometimes with tax relief for special groups like working housewives, the aged and the blind. Sometimes, too, it has passed "reform" laws, making broad changes that affect nearly everyone.

THE INTERNAL REVENUE CODE

The body of law that results from such a succession of laws and amendments is aptly named a code, for it often seems an undecipherable jumble of discrepancies, contradictions and obscurities. Even the government officials responsible for administering it have trouble understanding all its clauses. After passage of the Tax Reform Act of 1969, a senior official of the IRS found it necessary to write to the Congressional authors of one section, plaintively requesting them to explain what they meant. Clearly, a layman who read and even memorized the Code would still not be sure he understood what "the law" is. (Such an exercise is not recommended in any case, since it would almost certainly produce eyestrain; the Code fills approximately 1,700 pages, and there are no pictures.) It is probably safe to say, in fact, that no one knows what the law is. It is constantly being interpreted, clarified, tested and reinterpreted. Even the seemingly simple matter of a filing deadline has been constantly redefined. The Code straightforwardly requires ordinary citizens to deliver their returns to the IRS no later than April 15. But what about returns mailed in plenty of time but delivered late? The Code provides that "the date of the United States postmark stamped on the cover in which the item is mailed will be deemed to be the date of delivery." But then what about envelopes that have been run through office postage meters and do not bear a stamped postmark of the required type? That question requires further clarification, spelled out for those who care in Regulation 301.7502-(1)(c)(1)(iii)(b).

This complex of tax laws, amplified by regulations, rulings and court decisions, is a morass that can trap even the best-intentioned taxpayer. But it is also the rule book of a game in which the player making the right moves can win prizes known as tax savings. Many people, ignorant of the profitable moves, pay more taxes than they need to. The courts have pointed out that the taxpayer has no obligation—not even a patriotic duty—to arrange his affairs in a way that will benefit the U.S. Treasury. He does have the right to arrange them—within the rules—so that his taxes will be as low as possible. That is, he may be able to avoid a tax if he can find one rule that serves his interests better than another.

Tax avoidance vs. tax evasion

No one, of course, may evade taxes, and it is important here to understand the distinction between tax avoidance and tax evasion. To evade, the dictionary tells us, is "to escape or elude by cleverness or deceit." When a person should have paid a tax but did not, either by falsifying figures or by concealing information, he has evaded the tax and is in for trouble. Evasion is the kind of thing the Martinsburg Monster is good at spotting. On the other hand, there are many ways of arranging financial affairs so that much—or even all—of a person's income is not subject to tax. This is avoiding, not evading. Some methods of avoidance, employed by the rich for the sole purpose of paying little or no taxes, are called loopholes. The Tax Reform Act of 1969 made an effort to close many of these loopholes; some it merely narrowed. But they are of little value to the average citizen anyway, for he generally lacks the capital required to protect his income with oil ventures, real estate syndicates, cattle breeding and similar tax shelters. Still, there are a few basic tactics for avoiding taxes that are available to a family of modest means.

Tax savings are often possible if taxes can be deferred. Obviously you get to keep more of your income if you can put off paying

A pizzeria's taxes
When the IRS suspected a pizzeria proprietor of evading taxes by understating his income, an investigator resorted to an ingenious formula. By dividing the total purchases of mozzarella cheese for the year by the amount of cheese in each pie, he arrived at the number of pizzas sold. Multiplying this by the price per pie gave him a good estimate of the operation's annual income—good enough to get the IRS an additional slice of the profits.

tax on some of it until a year when you are in a lower tax bracket. The law provides several ways for you to postpone some of the tax on certain funds you might put aside for retirement, when your tax rate is likely to be lower than it is during the years when you are working. You might put money in U.S. Savings Bonds, for example. The tax on the interest they return need not be paid until the bonds mature or you cash them in; if you wait to cash them in, you can save on the tax paid on that interest. Many retirement funds and profit-sharing plans set up by employers work in a similar fashion; the money such a plan makes for you each year is not counted as taxable income until you begin to collect it. If you are self-employed, you may be able to set up such a tax-saving retirement plan of your own under special rules established by Congress—it often involves little more than opening a special account with a bank or mutual fund.

One of the most effective ways of avoiding unnecessary payment of tax is to segment income, splitting it into a number of "piles" and creating a new taxpayer for each segment, each one qualified for a lower tax bracket. A favored method, for example, is the outright gift of securities to children, under the Uniform Gifts to Minors Act, with the securities held in a custodian account which brokerage firms will establish on request. You have then given the securities away and each minor child can thus own assets producing tax-free income up to $1,750 a year. The same tax saving can be effected with bank trust accounts, which generally can be established simply by signing trust forms provided by the bank. You should be cautioned, however, to make certain that a formal trust is being established; if it is not a formal trust (Chapter 12), but only a trustee account that enables you to control your child's money, the interest will still be reported as income to the parent. When a trust is created it is treated by the law as a "person"—another new taxpayer, owning the assets of the trust and paying the tax (if any) on the interest earned. There may be disadvantages in certain types of trusts, such as the mandatory distribution of assets to the child at age 21. Trust laws (as distinct from tax laws) must be taken into account. Make sure to have your lawyer explain the conditions and restrictions before you decide to establish even a "simple" trust.

The average taxpayer will limit his taxes not through trust accounts but on the standard forms provided by the IRS itself—in deductions and exemptions, the sums the law allows you to subtract from your income before figuring the tax. These sums provide a fertile field for mistaken assumptions and errors, however, and they account for much skepticism on the part of IRS and its monster computers. Any dubious item is automatically earmarked for audit, so avoiding unpleasant entanglements with the tax laws actually begins from the moment you start to make out your return.

Exemptions

Exemptions are allowed for you and your dependents—wife, children, sometimes others. Each dependent you list takes a large sum off the income on which your tax is calculated, and exemptions are therefore potent tax-reducers. The rules governing dependency and support are extensive, and by a careful reading of them a taxpayer can frequently arrange methods of payment so that relatives, or others he may be helping to support, will qualify as dependents.

Support for a dependent, as defined in the law, is not necessarily provided through payments of money; it can be provided in kind. Among the allowable items of support, for example, is entertainment, and providing spirituous beverages is one way of entertaining a dependent. If Uncle Fred—who is on Social Security and lives in your household—likes a nip or two before dinner, the cost of the nips is includable in your support of him.

But the IRS people who examine returns are well aware that the form of tax cheating requiring the least imagination is the invention of an extra dependent. With depressing frequency, "Gus" turns out to be a beagle with soft brown eyes but no claim to dependency status. ("Why, all of us just think of Gus as a member of the family!") More imaginative was the California bachelor who persuaded his girl friend to move into his apartment, where she tidied up and performed other wifely duties. She lived in his household; certainly he provided

If Uncle Fred, who lives in your household, likes a nip or two before dinner, the cost of the nips is part of the support you provide him—and may lead to an income-tax exemption.

A strict ℞ for tax deductions
The modern drugstore can
contribute an entire catalogue of
health, hygiene and beauty
products to the family medicine
cabinet, but the IRS allows tax
deductions only for those that treat
real ills. Even some doctors'
prescriptions are subject to strict
interpretation. The birth control
pill, for example, is deductible
if required to prevent a dangerous
pregnancy, but not if taken
simply from personal choice.

more than the 50 per cent of her support required by IRS rules; therefore he claimed her as a dependent. But the IRS nipped in the bud
what might have proved a widely popular arrangement by ruling that
support must be provided "without thought of receiving in return a
quid pro quo." It is possible, however, for a nonrelated person living
with you as a member of the household to qualify as a dependent. An
exchange student might qualify, for example.

Deductions
When you list "other dependents," you can usually tell whether the exemption is likely to be challenged. Not so when you use the other
main source of potential tax limitation, deductions. They are the cause
of much confusion over what is and is not permissible; they often induce taxpayers to take an inflated view of their expenses; and they
awaken skepticism among the IRS' electronic and human monitors.

Anyone who chooses to itemize deductions—instead of taking
the standard deduction otherwise employed—is aware that there is a
complex formula governing the sums deducted for medical expenses.
What you may not realize is that the tax laws and rulings defining
these expenses sometimes challenge everyday, garden-variety logic.

The cost of drugs is partially deductible—but when is a drug not
a drug? It has been established that drugs are not necessarily limited
to items that have been prescribed by a doctor. The cost of aspirin,
for example, is deductible. Yet the cost of vitamins is not, unless prescribed by a doctor. How do you make sense of that? The explanation
is found in the general rule defining allowable medical deductions:
the cost of "diagnosis, cure, mitigation, treatment or prevention of disease, or any treatment that affects a part or function of the body." In
other words, anything that treats or prevents a specific problem qualifies, but anything that simply serves to preserve one's general health
does not. Thus the distinction between aspirin and vitamins makes
sense. The IRS is willing to concede that most people do not take aspirin unless something hurts somewhere; under the definition, it presumably mitigates a condition not characteristic of good health. Unless
vitamins are actually prescribed for you, however, you customarily
take them in the hope of maintaining your present robust health.
This mere hope does not rate a deduction. Nor do the advertising
claims of toothpaste manufacturers. Under the rules, toothpaste is out
—argue as you will with the IRS that it prevents tooth decay.

A more complex example of the way this rule works involves
birth control pills. The Pill is available, of course, only on a doctor's
prescription, but is it, in the tax sense, drug or nondrug? Since it does

not treat a disorder, the IRS ruled that the Pill is not a drug. A woman takes it for her own convenience. But one taxpayer decided to contest this rule on the ground that the Pill had been prescribed for his wife by her doctor after a pregnancy had left her seriously ill. As a result, the flat ruling was modified, to the extent of allowing "the cost of oral contraceptives prescribed to prevent childbirth . . . when, in the opinion of the physician, the possibility of childbirth is a serious threat to the life of the wife."

Viewed in the light of the basic rule, the cost of whiskey prescribed by a doctor for a patient with angina becomes deductible. And so are therapeutic baths for patients suffering from arthritis—provided their doctors have ordered the treatment. And you probably would guess that the cost of special-diet foods ordered by a doctor for an ulcer patient also qualify. But you would be wrong. Why? Because the food merely replaces other food that the patient would ordinarily eat; it is not a necessary, additional expense.

There is no logical rule of law that you can apply to determine which of the state and local taxes are legitimate deductions on your federal return. In years past, almost anything labeled a tax by the local taxing authority was deductible. State excise taxes—those on specific items such as cigarettes, liquor, jewelry, theater admissions—formerly were deductible; now they are not. The cost of auto licenses used to be; now it is not. These changes result from amendments to the Code by Congress, and the only rule you can go by is: Taxes that are deductible are the ones that Congress says are deductible. At present they are property taxes, state and local income taxes, a general sales tax, state and local (not federal) gasoline taxes. "The tendency of Congress is to keep chipping away at deductible taxes," said a former Commissioner of Internal Revenue recently, "and there is strong sentiment in some quarters for eliminating them entirely, as a trade-off for a lower overall tax rate."

Although auto license fees are generally not deductible, part of them may be, depending on which state issues the license. If the fee is partially determined by the value of the car, that part of the fee is an ad valorem tax in legal jargon, and it can be deducted as a tax on personal property. This ruling is not information that the IRS likes to publicize. To find out whether you can deduct part of the fee, write the motor vehicles office in your state and ask if your automobile registration fee includes an ad valorem tax, and if so, how much.

Many people forget that interest you pay on borrowed money, and interest charged on credit purchases and installment payments, is deductible. The general rule is that it must be identified as a charge for interest and that you actually paid, during the year, the amount shown in your deduction. That is, you cannot deduct an amount you have been charged but have not yet paid. A bank loan of $2,000 for two years, for example, might be "discounted"—have the interest deducted in advance from the total lent you—so that you receive only $1,760 in cash in hand. To the IRS, however, the interest charge is spread over the two-year life of the loan. Your interest charge is $240 over 24 months. If you make eight payments on the loan during the tax year, you have paid off one third (eight twenty-fourths) of the loan, and your deduction for that year is one third of $240, or $80.

The most common kind of substantial interest charge deducted by taxpayers is that on a mortgage loan. Another deduction available to many taxpayers is some of the cost of department store and credit card accounts. These charges are labeled finance charges, not interest, but you are allowed to deduct 6 per cent of the average unpaid balance for the year—just as if that percentage were interest.

The government encourages you to be charitable by offering you a tax break on what you give away—but only if you give it away to the right organizations in the right way. Two questions about deductions for contributions are uppermost in the IRS auditors' minds: First, is the recipient of your "charitable contribution" an eligible organization? (There are probably more such groups than you suspect.) And second, how much is your gift actually worth? Rules for determining valuation, for tax purposes, sometimes have the appearance of being arbitrary.

The United States government itself, you may be surprised to learn, is a charitable organization. Any contribution you may wish to make to it, or to any of its territories or possessions, qualifies as a charitable contribution. The same is true of state and local governments or any agencies they have created. Deductible contributions can be made to local fire departments and harbor patrols, or agencies involved in noise abatement, urban renewal, dam building and highway safety. State universities, public schools and libraries all qualify. A gift must be made "exclusively for public purposes." As a matter of fact, it is difficult to think of an agency or activity of government that would not qualify.

Among private charities, almost any organization operated for charitable, religious, educational, scientific or literary purposes, or for the prevention of cruelty to children or animals, is eligible for a deductible contribution. But you must be wary. Certain organizations you might think were certainly qualified for deduction are not. A few promoting the laudable cause of conservation, for example, have been ruled ineligible because their principal purpose is held to be the influencing of legislation, and such a purpose disqualifies them. If you have any question about whether a particular organization is listed with the IRS as qualified for deductible contributions, ask your Internal Revenue office.

Rules governing the value of gifts, and the tax liability involved, are lengthy, technical and generally of interest only to individuals in relatively high tax brackets. One tax-saving device, however, has been fairly commonly used at lower economic levels—the gift of property that has gained in value. For example, Brown wants to make a $500 donation to his church parish. He owns 20 shares of Amalgamated Cam and Flange, bought for $5 a share. The current price is $25. If Brown sells the stock in the market for $500, he makes a profit—a "capital gain"—of $400 and he would have to pay capital gains tax on that amount. But suppose instead he donates the stock to his church. He can claim its full market value of $500 as a donation, reducing his taxable income by that amount instead of paying the capital gains tax. A 1969 change in the tax law limits such gifts to "public" charities such as churches; for gifts to "private" charities—foundations, for example —the rules for the deductions are less advantageous to the taxpayer.

There are also special rules for the treatment of "tangible personal property" that has appreciated in value. Suppose Brown owns a painting that he bought for $200. Its present value is $900. He can claim a deduction of the whole $900 only if the organization that gets the painting uses it as part of its "charitable" function—as would a museum of fine arts, for example. If he donates the painting to his church, the painting is not related to the church's charitable function —religion—and Brown must reduce his deduction by half the increase in the painting's value—his deductible gift becomes only $550.

The taxpayer gets even less of a break if he donates "ordinary income property"—things he ordinarily sells as part of his business. Publishers often give books to charitable organizations. As a deduction they are allowed only the cost of the books—not their market value. A painter might be holding, as "ordinary income property," a painting he executed several years ago. Now he is an established artist and could sell the painting for $1,500—but if he donates it to a charity, his allowable deduction is only the cost of the canvas and paint.

A nation of bookkeepers

These deductions and exemptions—and there are many more—will not stand up under law unless they can be substantiated. The tax laws and IRS regulations have turned Americans into a nation of bookkeepers. Well-kept records are the taxpayer's best, and sometimes his only, defense if questions are raised about his tax return. Arming yourself with them can be a time-consuming nuisance—many businessmen keep detailed diaries and mileage logs to account for every mile driven, every nickel of automobile expense, every hotel room slept in during a business trip and every meal consumed while talking shop. Almost as great a problem for some is the matter of storing all these records; perhaps we must also become a nation of warehousemen. For the laws not only stipulate that you keep certain records in order to justify your returns (and even provide a penalty if you fail to keep adequate records), but they also set requirements that govern how long you must keep your records. How long may be very long indeed, depending on the kind of record.

There is one set of records you may have to keep until you die —the papers relating to your house (or more often, houses). The reason relates to the profit you often make when you sell it—to move into a new house, transfer to another town, or give up house-owning altogether for a rented apartment. That profit is a capital gain, and like all capital gains it is taxable. But profits on house sales come under special rules, ones that do not apply to the gain you make, for example, when you sell stock shares for more than you paid for them.

For one thing, the difference between the purchase price of a house and its selling price is not all profit. You must take into account your outlays for improvements (but not for maintenance). Suppose you bought your home for $20,000 and 10 years later sold it for $30,000. But during those 10 years you spent $1,000 to make the basement into a playroom, $300 to build a patio and $250 to landscape the barren backyard. Those expenditures added to the basic value of the house and are part of its cost (money that went to re-shingle the roof or replace moribund rosebushes does not count; it represents maintenance). So the true cost of your house at the time you sell it is not $20,000 but $21,550, and your capital gain is $8,450, not $10,000. Obviously you are going to need receipts from contractors in order to prove, 10 years later, that you rather than the previous owner provided those improvements. Otherwise you may end up paying tax on profit you never made.

Such records may have to be kept even beyond the sale of a house because the tax on the capital gain may not come due until much later. Many people sell one house only to turn around and buy another; their capital gains are paper profits instead of cash in the bank. If you buy a new house within a limited period of time for as much as the selling price of the old one, you must report the capital gain but you need not pay the tax until you sell the new house—or the final house in a chain of increasingly more expensive houses. Each one adds its bit to the total of the capital gains tax that is accumulating. Many people tend to regard this tax as forgiven, but it is only deferred until you break the chain—and you cannot break it without paying a tax unless you move from your last house inside a hearse. At death all liability for capital gains taxes is wiped out. But if you sell a house and do not buy again at an equal or higher price, all capital gains tax that you may have accumulated over many years falls due. At that point, you may need detailed records of your purchase costs, selling prices and any home improvements you may have made dating back to the first house in the chain. (For homeowners aged 65 and over, the law provides a certain measure of tax relief when the last house is sold.)

Some taxpayers discover how important it is to maintain full and well-kept records at the worst time—when they are being challenged in an audit. The IRS has strict rules about what kinds of documentary evidence it will accept at the auditing stage. Do not be surprised, for example, if the IRS refuses to accept a canceled check as adequate evidence of an expenditure. One taxpayer who had been asked to substantiate large medical expenses brought in his canceled checks. He was told he would have to produce the doctors' bills. The request seemed arbitrary to him. To convince him of its reasonableness, the examiner told him this story.

There once was a churchgoer who made a considerate offer to

Well-kept records are the best—or only—defense if questions are raised about tax deductions. Many businessmen keep detailed diaries to account for every nickel of automobile expense and every hotel room slept in during a business trip.

the ushers who handled the collection plates. "I can always use small change in my business," he said, "so after you've counted the money each week we can bag it up and I'll write you a check for the amount of the collection. I can haul it home in my car, and it will save you the trouble of taking all those coins to the bank." The church officials appreciated his thoughtfulness. But after a few years the IRS became curious about the large amounts that the kindly parishioner claimed as charitable contributions on his tax return. It asked him to substantiate these contributions to the church and received in return a stack of canceled checks in odd amounts. Upon investigation, an IRS agent discovered the weekly exchange of collection money, the deductions were disallowed, and the parishioner was penalized for his subterfuge. So, you see, you can never really prove what a check was for.

The law, as well as the auditors who carry it out, is especially rigorous on records of expenses deducted as business travel and entertainment. Until 1962 the IRS followed the "Cohan rule," named for George M. and the tax case he fought through the courts. Cohan's life style in the worlds of Broadway and Hollywood involved lavish expenditures for which receipts were inconvenient to get. He argued successfully that these costs were proper in his line of business and that in the absence of detailed records, a taxpayer should be allowed to estimate expenses. Subsequently, expense account high life became a scandal, with yachts and country club bills and even such exotic "business activities" as safaris being written off as business expenses. Congress finally cracked down. As a result, the IRS is now specific on this point: An agent may disallow any claim not supported by records —and you cannot even take a plausible-sounding claim to court with any chance of winning, for the courts have no authority to allow a deduction on testimony unsupported by records.

You need not only a record but an actual receipt for any single expense over $25, and if you have numerous smaller ones it is advisable to collect as many receipts as possible. Also essential is a diary in which you keep a record of business lunches and entertainment—date, place, who was present, what business subjects were discussed and the amount of the bill, since all these data may not appear on receipts. IRS examiners insist that a business lunch be a "quiet business lunch." They take the attitude that it is very difficult to discuss business when there is a band playing, tables jammed together nightclub-style, and go-go girls distracting your attention.

Records such as business expense receipts need not be kept forever—but do not hurry to clean out your files. Basically the IRS has three years from the April 15 filing deadline for any given year to ex-

Mixing pleasure with business
Even if he contrives to mix a bit of big business with his big game hunting, a vacationing executive will have a hard time convincing the IRS that the expense of taking his secretary on safari should be deductible.

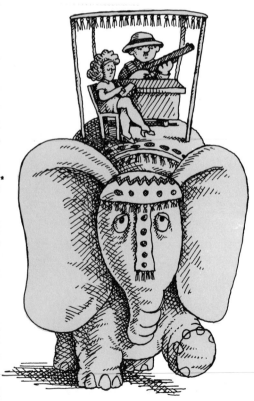

amine your records and assess additional taxes for that year. However, if you failed to report 25 per cent or more of your actual gross income, the IRS has six years to catch up with you and adjust your tax. There is no time limit at all if fraud is involved; civil penalties and fines can be imposed at any time. However, criminal prosecution on tax-evasion charges is barred by a statute of limitations after six years from the filing date.

These are the rule book's outer limits. In actual practice, if the IRS has not contacted you within 26 months after you file a return, it probably never will. Returns for the 1971 tax year, filed April 15, 1972, would probably not be questioned until January 1973, since until then agents are occupied with audits of the previous year's returns. The pulled-out list of returns facing possible audit will be worked over for another 12 months, during 1973, and discrepancies will be investigated. By January 1974 a brand-new list of candidates for auditing has arrived. Any older ones on which an audit has not yet started then normally go back into the file. Moral: You needn't hold your breath forever—but don't be too quick to put your records in dead storage, where they may be hard to find if you need them.

"Under penalties of perjury, I declare"

Even a diligent taxpayer, with a passion for record-keeping and an accurate way with figures, may find that the ever-multiplying complexity of the tax laws, and the forms themselves, are too much for him. Millions of people each year seek professional help in filing their returns. In the weeks before April 15, the professionals blossom wherever there is vacant desk space. Their competence varies greatly and cannot be judged by external appearances. Behind the crudely lettered sign in the window of a neighborhood storefront there may be a highly qualified accountant who, from 9 to 5, works on taxes in some corporate office, then moonlights the rest of the week on the returns of whatever strangers walk in the door. Conversely a chrome-and-glass office advertising a "computerized tax-preparation service" may house someone whose expertise ends at filling in the blank spaces on tax forms and turning the figures over to a data-processing machine. But there is one way you can check on the expert's confidence in his own ability. Ask him if he will sign your return after he helps prepare it.

The line of fine print just above the blanks for signatures on the return—yours, and that of any person who prepares it—begins: "Under penalties of perjury, I declare that . . ." The maximum penalty for perjury in a federal matter is a fine of $5,000 and three years' imprisonment. Although prosecutions on perjury charges are rarely in-

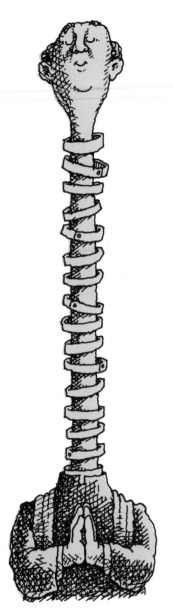

Clerical error

When the IRS doubted a minister's $200 deduction for his clerical collars, he said he meant to claim only $20. But his past returns showed that he had repeatedly made the same "arithmetical error." Moral: The IRS will double-check your figuring, and you should do likewise.

stituted against taxpayers (charges of fraud and evasion carry stiffer penalties), the declaration serves several purposes. First, when a taxpayer signs his name to a falsified return, the declaration has some weight in establishing criminal intent. Second, a tax adviser or accountant who prepares your return has no financial stake—if the IRS finds a tax deficiency, that's your problem, not his—but if he signs the return, he also declares, under penalty of perjury, that it is accurate to the best of his knowledge. If someone who has prepared your return is not willing to sign it, it may be because he is not entirely confident that it will stand up under sharp scrutiny.

The requirement that both husband and wife sign a joint return is also an incentive for the wife to take a careful interest in the family's financial affairs. If there is a tax deficiency, the wife is held equally responsible for the debt. Wives have been held liable for added assessments even though they had no knowledge of their husbands' tax evasions. Legislation passed in 1971, known in tax circles as the innocent spouse change, relieves a wife (or husband) of liability for the tax debt if he or she can prove innocence of any complicity—but only when the concealed amount is more than 25 per cent of the income reported. It applies, that is, only when there is a substantial scheme for evasion. In the case of small, family-return fudging, the spouse can still be held liable, whether innocent or not.

HOW THE MONSTER GRADES YOUR RETURN

The perjury clause can make cheating very hazardous; the computer has made it very difficult as well. In the days when returns still had to be painstakingly checked with eyeball and pencil, there was greater chance for an evasion (or an honest mistake) to slip by. It was impossible to check every return. And it was a matter of odds whether you got caught or not. With today's computerized processing, the chance of going unchecked is approaching zero for the great majority of taxpayers—those whose earnings are subject to withholding.

The almost limitless memories of the IRS computers—the Martinsburg Monster is backed up by other computers at the IRS' seven regional centers—swallow up the amount of your income, from your W-2 form; the amount of interest and dividends you received during the year, from reports required of banks and financial institutions; the amounts paid for any contract work or moonlighting, from forms that are required when payments are not part of a regular payroll; even abnormally large bank deposits you may have made, which all banks are required by law to report to the IRS. Any discrepancy between all this information and what you actually report as income immediately tags your return for possible examination by an IRS auditor.

The computer also compares you to your past self by constructing a profile of the returns in your storage file. If one year you report that 10 per cent of your income goes to charity, for example, when you had previously exhibited no particular commitment to charitable giving, this sudden philanthropy would make the computer curious. It also catches simple mistakes in arithmetic and general carelessness. After processing the early returns one year, the IRS reported that one of every 50 returns contained arithmetical errors or had been prepared from the wrong tax tables. Even big corporations were fallible: The IRS found 95,000 mistakes in 5.8 million corporate returns. Clearly, one way to avoid having an eagle-eyed examiner go over your return is to check and double-check the arithmetic.

The ability of the computer to compare millions of figures and automatically detect discrepancies has increased tax revenues substantially—by $295 million in 1970—merely by catching what the IRS calls math errors. But the Martinsburg Monster goes far beyond matching up figures and checking arithmetic. It puts your return through a quick but elaborate test called discriminant function, or DIF for short. DIF is like a secret military weapon—its effects are clear enough, but its components are closely guarded knowledge. From what has been said and can be safely assumed, it works something like this:

About a dozen so-called "line items" make up the basis of the DIF formula. One such line item that is almost certainly among them is Line 22, Schedule A—"total itemized deductions." When you file, the computer first will note your taxable income—say, $17,000—and then determine what percentage of that income you have claimed for total itemized deductions. It then compares your percentage with the average claimed by other taxpayers in your income group. Suppose the average claim for itemized deductions among taxpayers with a $17,000 taxable income is 16.6 per cent of income. Your percentage claim is rated against that average. On a scale from A to E, for example, you get an A or B if your deductions are a lower-than-average 15.3 per cent, and E if you claim a far-above-average 23 per cent.

You are similarly graded on all the other line items in the formula. A lone worrisome E, as in the hypothetical example, will not automatically flag your return for examination. You might have gotten that E because of large medical expenses, and the IRS recognizes that some individuals are going to have an occasional year with abnormally high medical expenses. If the rest of your grades are A's, B's and C's, the computer will probably blink and flip your return back

The ability of computers like the IRS' "Martinsburg Monster" to compare millions of figures and automatically detect discrepancies has increased tax revenues substantially.

into storage. Allowances are also made for variations in the cost of living from one area to another; the computer knows from statistics fed into it that doctors' fees are higher in New York City than in Horseshoe Bend, Idaho, and will make allowances for these variations when it scans your return. When the Monster is through dealing with your return, it gives you an overall grade—a statistical judgment that indicates how your return compares, as a whole, with those of other taxpayers in your income group.

If it is a failing grade, you will eventually get the attention of a human being in the IRS classification section, where questionable returns are sent for further scrutiny. At this point a carefully prepared and documented return can head off trouble. If you have attached itemized lists of expenses or brief notes of explanation covering apparent discrepancies or information gaps that the computer was unable to read, the human accountants will take these into consideration and the extra effort may resolve the question in your favor.

In 1969, the Monster flunked 2,543,931 taxpayers on the DIF exam, but when the returns were later examined in the classification section, only about half the singled-out taxpayers were found to owe the government money (some three billion dollars). In 40.2 per cent of the questioned returns, the unusual characteristics that had jogged the computer were justified or adequately explained, and no further tax was called for. And 6.6 per cent of the taxpayers whose returns were flagged had overpaid.

Returns are divided for DIF scrutiny into three income levels —under $10,000, between $10,000 and $30,000, and above $30,000. The IRS is more interested in the higher incomes for the same reason given by bank robber Willie Sutton when police asked him why he kept trying to knock off banks. Sutton said: "Because that's where the money is." Since the IRS' limited staff cannot audit all suspect returns, the auditors proceed on the principle that they will collect more unpaid taxes by going after the more affluent taxpayers. If your income is $10,000 or more, your return routinely goes to the classification section; the Monster's opinion is not even solicited. But if you are in the middle income level, if all your income is from wages or salary and if you use the standard deduction, there is little chance of your being audited—far less than one in a hundred, according to one authoritative source.

THE AUDIT BEGINS

But assume the worst: Your return has worked its way through the Monster, the classification section, and back to the local district, where an agent says, "Let's take this one on." What happens now? Generally a taxpayer first learns he is about to be audited when he gets a letter from the district director: "Your return has been selected for examination to determine the correct amount of your tax liability, based on your income and the deductions provided by law." This wording indicates that yours will be an "office audit."

An office audit may be carried on entirely by mail. A letter will ask you to supply by mail evidence supporting certain figures in your return or to furnish additional information about one or more items. If the material supports your figures to the satisfaction of the examining officer, he will inform you of that result in a "no change" letter —no additional payment is required. If your explanations do not satisfy him, the letter you get will tell you that the claim in question has been disallowed, your tax has been recomputed, and your bill for additional tax is enclosed. The entire audit can thus be conducted and closed out by correspondence, and this procedure is increasingly followed in order to save time for both agents and taxpayers.

The office audit conducted through the mail can deal adequately with uncomplicated questions. However, if you feel you can explain everything better across a desk than by letter, you are entitled to an interview. And if the questions raised by your return are not simple enough to be handled by letter, the Internal Revenue Service itself will summon you to its local office. Normally, you will be asked to bring your records, bills, receipts and other supporting material for the return being audited, or covering certain items in the return. Such relatively simple audits, including those conducted by mail, account for about 80 per cent of the returns audited.

An unlucky few first learn they are being audited when an IRS agent rings the doorbell and says he would like to ask some questions. Obviously, an audit of a business, when voluminous records will be involved, will normally—for convenience—be conducted on the taxpayer's premises. But if an agent appears on the doorstep of your home, it is bad news. Take a close look at his identification to see whether he is simply a revenue agent or a special agent of the IRS Intelligence Division. If he is with Intelligence, he is there to conduct a criminal investigation *(page 247)*. Fortunately, unannounced or criminal investigations are rare; the only checkup the ordinary taxpayer is ever likely to face is the routine office audit.

A chat with the auditor

Taxpayers who have gone through office audits often report that the proceedings were businesslike, their examiners courteous and all of it much less traumatic than they had anticipated. It is IRS policy to wipe out the tough-guy image it acquired in past years. A commissioner of Internal Revenue, when issuing guidelines to his audit personnel, warned them, "Never adopt a superior attitude; nor should we take advantage of the taxpayer's technical ignorance."

If you are audited, the chances are that your experience will not be far different from that of a Mr. Green, a stockbroker who lives in Cleveland, Ohio. In a year when he had an income of $30,000, he made what he considered proper deductions to get his taxable income down to $20,000, and on the joint return he filed with his wife he calculated his tax at $4,380. Since all but $200 had been withheld from his paycheck, Green paid the $200 and assumed that was that.

It was not, and Green was notified that his return was being audited. He reported to his local IRS office at the appointed time with a briefcase containing his return, worksheets, records and canceled checks. After waiting in an anteroom with several other nervous taxpayers, Green was called in. He was ushered to a desk, where he was greeted by the revenue agent assigned to his return.

The agent introduced himself, shook hands and made a deliberately noncommittal remark about the weather. Green agreed it was a nice day—although he mentally noted that exactly how nice it was would depend on the outcome of the audit. The agent's opening remark was deliberately banal; IRS has learned the hard way that comments on almost any subject other than the weather can convince a nervous taxpayer that the revenue agent has it in for him. For example, if the agent had noted that the stock market was down again today, Green might easily have concluded that the agent had lost money on the market and was out to make trouble for all stockbrokers. The IRS has a hard enough job to do without letting the taxpayers get thoughts like that.

Having established that the weather was fine, the agent then turned to business. First he asked to see the notification from Green's savings bank showing the interest he had received during the year.

Green produced it, and the amount on it tallied exactly with the amount he had reported on his return, $519. The agent seemed satisfied. "May I see the records supporting your medical deductions?" he asked politely. Green pulled the appropriate folder from his briefcase. His documentation showed that his medical expenses for the year totaled $2,000. "I have three young children," he volunteered, "and you know how that makes the doctor's bills pile up." The agent nodded, again noncommittally.

"Your receipts for prescription and nonprescription drugs come to $400," said the agent.

"Yes," said Green, lighting a cigar and feeling more confident.

"But I notice that you have included the total amounts shown on all the drugstore cash-register receipts in this folder."

"Naturally," said Green. "Those receipts represent drug purchases. And drugs can be included in the computation that gives the total medical expenses deduction."

"True," said the agent. "But tell me something, Mr. Green —where do you buy your cigars? Your toothpaste? The candy for the children? Magazines?"

"Well, I . . ." said Green, "here and there."

"And don't you ever buy hair tonic, lighter fluid, toys or light-bulbs at the drugstore? The agent paused. "I can allow only as much as you can prove represents expenses for deductible drugs."

The agent also challenged other deductions. He disallowed $20 that Green had deducted in local liquor taxes (alcohol taxes are not deductible). He thought Green had been too generous in his allowance for depreciation on the car he used for business, and he disallowed a major deduction that Green had taken for "office in home." An hour and a half after the interview had begun, Green found that $600 in deductions had been disallowed. "You owe us another $192 plus interest," the agent announced.

At this point Green did some fast figuring. He knew he could refuse to accept the agent's decision and could appeal it either through the IRS or in the courts. But he also knew that the agent's figures were probably right—and in any case he would be out far more than $192 in business lost during the time it would take him to appeal the decision. "Okay, you win," Green said. He then signed an IRS Form 870, in which he agreed to pay the additional tax due. Green gathered up his folders, shook hands with the agent and left, feeling not entirely happy but no worse than after a day at his brokerage office when the Dow Jones average dropped 3 points.

Although Green's case was typical, an IRS audit interview does not have to begin or end as his did. The options are many. If you feel the examiner handling your case is hostile, for example, you can request his superior to assign another agent. The need to make such a request rarely arises. In general, IRS examiners are, like Green's, thoroughly correct and polite in a businesslike way. And the taxpayer serves his own interests best by behaving the same way. Adopt a cooperative attitude; answer questions openly, not grudgingly; provide any records that are requested, if you have them—but do not get loquacious and, above all, do not volunteer information. The agent knows what he wants and why, and he will not be shy about asking.

One thing to bear in mind is that an audit is not a judicial proceeding. The normal rule of law, that you are innocent until proven guilty, does not operate here. You have made certain statements in your return—e.g., "My business-entertainment expenses were $1,759 last year"—and the IRS is now asking you to substantiate this figure. The burden of proof is on you. It is not an assumption of your guilt, merely the normal procedure followed when you make any kind of assertion. If you claim, "That is my car," and a policeman comes back with "How do I know that?", you show him your registration.

And if you don't like the decision

Most audits, like Green's, are conducted briskly, and you will know the outcome at once: "You don't have the records to support the deduction for business travel in your car, and I'll have to disallow 50 per cent of the mileage you claim." You can agree to pay the added tax by signing a waiver form and then make payment when the IRS sends you a bill, as Green did—or after signing the waiver you can make payment on the spot to avoid paying future interest that is charged on deficiencies. But should you choose to contest the decision, there is a step-by-step escalation you can follow through administrative hearings and the court system.

If the issue is simple and you feel you received something less than just treatment merely because of an unsympathetic ear, an informal first step may be open to you. Ask for a review of the agent's decision by his group supervisor. In some of the smaller, more neighborly IRS districts, the request may be honored, though there is no provision for it in the rules and regulations, and the IRS does not encourage the procedure.

Your first official appeal is to the IRS district conference. You take this step by stating that you do not accept the examiner's findings. You then receive from the district office a copy of the examining officer's report and the "30-day letter." It states the position of the

IRS in your case and its intent to adjust the tax, and it notifies you that you have 30 days in which to do one of two things: (1) If the deficiency claimed by the IRS is less than $2,500, state in a letter to the IRS your disagreement with the agent's findings; (2) If the deficiency is $2,500 or more, you must explain your objections according to a prescribed formula, as spelled out in instructions from the IRS office.

Each IRS local district has a conference staff that is independent of the audit staff. At one time this separation was not the practice, and there was some reason to feel that the district conference was a case of agents sitting in judgment on themselves, with a strong tendency to reaffirm what they had already decided. In 1964, however, the conference staff was made independent in order to provide for an impartial consideration of the taxpayer's appeal. The result has been that a great many more cases are resolved by mutual agreement. Disputes are heard by an IRS "conferee"—who acts not as a judge sitting in an adversary proceeding, but as a referee responsive to the interests and rights of both government and taxpayer. Most disputes are resolved quickly in the district conference, generally at the first meeting. If the decision upholds the auditing agent's claim, and you accept it, you can sign the same waiver you were offered earlier by the agent, and the case is closed.

If you do not accept the conferee's finding, you can request a hearing at the next administrative level of appeal, the appellate conference. It is similar to the district conference, though more formal. The conferees are not members of the staff of your local IRS office but belong to the Appellate Division, which is attached directly to the Office of the Regional Commissioner of Internal Revenue. A man with long experience in the administrative machinery of the IRS says that "this is where most of the top tax technicians are"—meaning that the men of the Appellate Division have the training and experience to use their own initiative at certain points and make decisions of their own.

You can, if you think the circumstances call for it, waive the district conference entirely and take your case directly from the local examiner to the appellate conference. Such a step may be advisable if a serious legal issue is being raised, since in the appellate conference you can argue legal issues and possibly settle for a reasonable compromise. Such compromises are not generally possible in a district conference, which has only very limited powers of "settlement." The Appellate Division is not so limited. Take, for example, a dispute concerning a Mr. Johnson's savings account in a Los Angeles bank. The IRS has asserted that the money he put in those accounts was taxable income and taxes should have been paid on it. Johnson points out that the deposits came from the distribution of assets held in a trust —a source that previous court decisions had indicated was not ordinary taxable income. If he advances this argument in a district conference, the conferee might say, "Yes, it appears that you are right," and abandon the government's claim for additional tax. Or he could say, "I can't see any merit in that argument," and rule that the entire amount of disputed tax was due. He has to make an either/or decision; the taxpayer or the government must be fully sustained. The Appellate Division, however, has the authority to settle the case somewhere in between, especially if the appellate conferee believes the government is less than certain to win the case should it go to court.

Settling, in this instance, is not at all similar to the compromise that is frequent in court actions for damages, when the opposing parties settle out of court rather than go through the bother of a suit. The appellate conferee is not influenced by considerations of how much it would cost the government to prosecute its demand for additional taxes. He might, however, consider that the government might lose the case because key witnesses are now dead or unavailable, or because the taxpayer has a fairly strong argument on the legal issue at stake. So perhaps he offers to settle for half the disputed tax deficiency. This compromise is known in tax law circles as "settling on the hazards of litigation."

If you and the appellate conferee do come to terms, the added tax will be determined and you will receive an agreement to be signed and returned to the IRS. Technically, this form is only an offer. It has to be reviewed and approved by a supervisor—it usually is approved —and the taxpayer then receives a "closing letter" ending the case. If you reject the decision at the appellate level, however, you receive a notice of deficiency, a "90-day letter." This mean that you have exhausted the IRS administrative machinery and now have 90 days in which to take your case to court.

There is, however, a relatively informal legal step available in lieu of formal proceedings. You can present your case to one of the special small claims courts set up in the 1969 Tax Reform Act. These are tax courts, not to be confused with the local small claims courts to which you might take your case against a dry cleaner for damage to your clothing *(Chapter 10)*. When the amount of the tax deficiency is not more than $1,000, a taxpayer can have his case heard in an informal atmosphere, without the need for a lawyer's counsel. The judges are given discretion to relax the usual rules of evidence and other formal procedures, making it possible for the taxpayer to argue his own case. Most cases are heard and settled in an hour.

The Small Claims Court operates as a division of the U.S. Tax Court, a special part of the federal court system that handles only tax cases. Sessions are held in all major cities at least once a year, and more often in larger cities. There is a $10 fee for filing the petition for a hearing. The petition is an easy-to-cope-with form that is mailed to the U.S. Tax Court, Box 70, Washington, D.C. 20044. As in the case of a petition to the regular Tax Court, it must be filed within 90 days of the notice of deficiency from the Appellate Division. Cases are generally heard within four or five months in the larger cities, or within a year elsewhere. Proceedings in the formal Tax Court take a considerably longer time.

If the size of your claimed deficiency precludes recourse to the Small Claims Court, the only steps left to you in your escalating battle with the IRS are in the federal court system. You can get there in one of two ways after receiving your 90-day letter: (1) Within the allotted time, file a petition for a hearing in the Tax Court; (2) Pay the additional tax, file with the IRS for a refund and, when it is denied, bring suit in either the U.S. District Court or the U.S. Court of Claims. Once your case has reached any of these federal courts, two questions that have been lingering in the background—those of expert help and the cost of your contest with the government—become too pressing to be pushed aside.

In the original audit, anyone who prepared and signed your return may represent you, but he is limited to discussion of the tax liability in the year covered by the return he prepared. At any of the administrative conferences above the audit level, you have the option of being represented by a lawyer, a certified public accountant or an "enrolled agent," a tax adviser who has demonstrated his competence by passing an examination given by the IRS.

The enrolled agent's diploma is a card, known in the trade as a Treasury card. If you are looking for a tax accountant to handle your return and want to ensure professional competence in the event of possible legal problems later on, it is a good idea to ask, "Do you have a Treasury card?" But you can forget the question if your return is being prepared by a lawyer or a certified public accountant. They need no cards because they are automatically qualified to practice before the IRS without examination. So are former IRS agents, who can get on the roster of enrollees merely by making application. All others still have to qualify by examination. At any IRS proceeding, a qualified representative can appear for you, in your absence, but you must sign an IRS form giving him authority to examine your records and make arguments on your behalf. If there is any arguing to be done, it is better to let your representative do it, for he will not be emotionally involved. Moreover, you will frequently find that the result is a better settlement of your case.

When is it worth the cost of being represented? If the IRS simply wants proof of the validity of a certain deduction, and you know you have the necessary records, it goes without saying that you do not need help. But when your right to make a certain claim is questioned, the technical knowledge possessed by a good representative is likely to pay off. And if you carry your case into the court system, you obviously need a lawyer. The cost of administrative appeal is not great, except in terms of your time, but when you reach the courts and need legal representation the fees can become high. And you must add to your cost the 6 per cent interest you are charged from the time the tax deficiency is first assessed until the case is finished—unless you succeed in upsetting the decision. Most taxpayers are understandably inclined to close the case at the audit level unless a considerable sum stands to be won or lost.

CRIME AND PUNISHMENT

Whatever the circumstances of your involvement with the IRS, your course of action should be governed by an understanding of the distinctions the Code makes between different violations of tax laws. The gravity of the violations vary and so do the penalties. At the bottom of the scale is the simple tax deficiency: You had a difference of opinion with the IRS and you lost, but there was neither intent to defraud nor negligence. The penalty for being deficient is 6 per cent interest a year on the additional amount of tax, from the time due until paid. Some enterprising entrepreneurs once used the deficiency penalty as a cheap way, in times of very high interest rates, to borrow money from the government. They would file a return accurately calculating their tax payments at, say, $5,000 and attach a check for $1,000, thereby borrowing $4,000 from Uncle Sam at 6 per cent, much less than the going bank rates. Uncle Sam neatly took care of this ploy in the 1969 Reform Act: For failure to pay tax when due, the charge is a gradually increasing penalty (not interest) up to a maximum of 25 per cent of the deficiency—with 6 per cent interest accumulating all the while on the entire amount.

Next in seriousness on the violation scale comes negligence. Perhaps the taxpayer was aware that he should keep certain records but nevertheless failed to do so and as a result understated his income or overstated his deductions. There was, however, no deliberate scheme to cook the books. The penalty for this sort of negligence is 5 per cent of the net amount due, in addition to the 6 per cent interest on the delayed payments.

For failure to file a return at all, the taxpayer is subject to a penalty of 5 per cent of the tax due, increased by 5 per cent for each month the return is delinquent, to a maximum of 25 per cent.

Beyond the simple tax deficiency or negligence, a violation becomes a matter of fraud. Fraudulent understatement of income, or "civil fraud," is punished by a monetary penalty, but a severe one: 50 per cent of the additional tax assessed. On top of this, there is the usual 6 per cent interest on the tax deficiency and another 6 per cent on the amount of the penalty itself. At times, all this adds up to a penalty almost double the amount of deficient tax.

The definition of civil fraud in tax matters is not a clear one. Decisions have held that it is "not mere negligence or ignorance"; rather, there must be proof of "fraudulent intent." One case that was found to fit that criterion involved a taxpayer whose real income, it was discovered, had been double the income he had reported for three successive years.

A taxpayer has committed a federal crime if his evasion of taxes is "willful." The Internal Revenue Code says that any person who "willfully attempts . . . to evade or defeat any tax" is guilty of a felony. The maximum penalty is a $10,000 fine and imprisonment for up to five years. Paradoxically, to the lay mind, the willful failure to file any return at all is a misdemeanor, a lesser crime. The reason appears to turn on the affirmative act that is involved in the felony—the deliberate filing of the fraudulent return—in contrast to the passive act of failing to file any return. However, anyone who fails to file could conceivably be prosecuted not only for that failure but also for tax evasion. Only a minuscule percentage of taxpayers ever face criminal charges. In 1970, for example, the Intelligence Division investigated 8,000 taxpayers for fraud and recommended only 1,067 cases for prosecution. About half such cases generally end in pleas of guilty or in convictions.

A taxpayer who has deliberately or accidentally committed what the IRS considers to be a crime will quickly become aware of it. Regulations require an agent who, in the course of an audit, encounters indications of fraud to discontinue his audit and refer the case to the Intelligence Division. A special agent, whose function is to conduct criminal investigations, takes over the case. In some circumstances, the special agent may be the one to make the first contact with the taxpayer. Such circumstances may arise when the IRS has turned up suggestions of fraud in its initial examination of the records—or,

A neighbor may notice a fur coat
and a yacht and pass the word
to the IRS that the Joneses have
struck it rich. The T-men rely
on tipsters to catch tax evaders,
and most of the informing
comes from jealous lovers,
spiteful neighbors and the like.

frequently, when there has been a tip from an informer. But whenever or however a special agent comes into the case, he is required to identify himself, to explain that he is conducting a criminal investigation and to give the taxpayer a warning advising him of his constitutional rights.

It is a warning that should be taken seriously. The taxpayer who learns that he is being investigated for fraud should immediately put himself in the hands of an attorney well versed in tax law. He may, if he chooses, invoke his Fifth Amendment right and refuse to allow examination of his records on the ground that such scrutiny might incriminate him. The government cannot obtain his records by subpoena if he uses this right, and information obtained by surreptitious examination is not admissible as evidence. Even if he has been cooperatively allowing an agent access to his records, the taxpayer can, at any time, claim his right under the Fifth Amendment, refuse further access and decline to answer questions. In fact, he can assert that right even during a civil audit if he believes that his records may become evidence in a subsequent criminal action against him (but not if the records may simply serve to prove that he owes more taxes without incriminating him).

SPITEFUL TIPSTERS

The well-trained special agents of the Intelligence Division have other means of building cases—and of getting convictions. Like all law enforcement officers, the T-men rely heavily for leads on tipsters and informers. Every year they run down some 100,000 tips on unreported income. The law encourages this kind of stool-pigeonry by providing for a reward of unspecified amount. (The amount is up to the discretion of the district director, and it depends on the extent, accuracy and value of the information.) But most of the informing is not motivated by venal hope of gain; it comes from the heart. Jealous lovers, ex-spouses, disgruntled secretaries, envious relatives, vengeful competitors, spiteful neighbors and the like provide most of the information on which the IRS agents base their investigations. A green-eyed neighbor, for example, may notice a new fur coat and a yacht and pass the word along to the IRS that the Joneses seem to have struck it rich. Only about 5 per cent of such informers actually apply for the reward. (The IRS then proceeds to watch them closely, by the way, to make certain the tipsters report the amount of their reward as income on their next tax returns.)

Agents use other sources of information to spot the sudden and mysterious appearance of affluence on the part of a heretofore modest taxpayer. They are careful newspaper readers, for example, especially of society columns. When a man claims that he earns only a simple living but throws a lavish coming-out party at the country club for his daughter, the IRS becomes interested. It is also curious about the man who notifies the police that $50,000 in jewelry is missing after his home is ransacked by a burglar. Where did the money come from to buy all those jewels?

The main effort of the IRS, including its special agents, is not to jail people but to collect tax money from them, and prisoners do not make the most productive taxpayers. In one case, the IRS took an uncharacteristic gamble on Uncle Sam's behalf. Seeking to collect about $100,000 in back taxes from a well-known actor, a revenue agent followed the actor to the racetrack at Santa Anita, California, where the actor's horse was favored to win a $20,000 purse. When the horse won, the revenue agent appeared in the winner's circle and announced that he was confiscating both the horse and prize money. The actor's attorney, however, smooth-talked the agent into permitting the horse to be entered in one more race at a New York track, where, he asserted, it was certain to win a purse of well over $100,000. With visions of getting the whole amount due, the agent agreed and even allowed the actor to use his $20,000 Santa Anita winnings to fly the horse East. The horse came in sixth, and IRS got neither win, place nor show on its gamble.

More often the government's tax collectors employ a psychological sure thing. In the weeks just before April 15—every April 15 —newspaper headlines begin telling of tax-evasion indictments, usually involving prominent people whose names are likely to attract attention and to send a ripple of apprehension through the minds of millions of other citizens. Ask IRS officials if they deliberately save up some of their choice cases to break just when a lot of people are beginning to think about marginal ways of saving money on their returns, and the tax collectors just smile quietly.

By **CARLTON SMITH,**
MORTIMER M. CAPLIN, Consultant

9
Crime

What to do—
if you are
the victim
or the accused

The Joneses, a newlywed couple who live in a suburb of Chicago, return home one Saturday night after a movie and discover the house ransacked. The heirloom silver Mrs. Jones's mother had given them as a wedding present is gone; so is the small color TV set they had been buying on time; so is Jones's expensive camera. In fact, virtually everything in the place that is valuable and portable has vanished.

Jones calls the police. On investigation they find that a casement window in the rear of the house has been forced open, permitting someone to enter and remove the Joneses' possessions. It is a classic example of the crime of burglary—"breaking and entering with intent to commit a crime"—an act the law classes as a felony.

The fact that the crime committed was a felony would have taken on added importance had the circumstances been slightly different. Suppose that the Joneses had returned home in time to interrupt the burglar at work. Jones would have then been entitled, at least theoretically, to try to take the man into custody—to make what is known as a "citizen's arrest." Moreover, if the burglar had threatened him so that he thought his life was endangered, Jones would have been entitled to pull out the shotgun he keeps in the coat closet and to shoot the man, foolish though such a move is except as a last resort.

But suppose the Joneses had returned home still earlier and had found the man prowling in the shrubbery—that is, trespassing on their property. Trespassing is a misdemeanor, a less serious offense than a felony. Jones still could have tried to make a citizen's arrest, for in Illinois a citizen may, theoretically at least, make an arrest for a misdemeanor. But he would have had to be absolutely certain the prowler was a trespasser. And had he fired his shotgun to drive the trespasser off, he might himself have been found guilty of a misdemeanor —firing a gun within the city limits. Had he killed the intruder, he might have been accused of murder—the most serious felony of all. And, even if acquitted by a jury, he might still have been the target of a civil suit for damages by the slain man's family.

As even the most casual newspaper reader is aware, situations like those in the fictionalized account above are by no means uncommon in the United States today. Crime has been on the increase for more than a decade. The number of residential burglaries alone rose by 197 per cent between 1960 and 1969; during that same period almost five million crimes of all types were reported each year, with perhaps as many as five million more unreported.

It is entirely possible, then, that the average citizen may sooner or later find himself involved with crime and the criminal law, as victim, witness—or even as lawbreaker. For like the fictional Mr. Jones, who was unaware that he had no legal right to fire at a trespasser, many an American who acts thinking to defend himself, his family, his home or his property may land in the toils of the law, perhaps charged with a major crime.

Of equal concern to most people, the law frequently appears to protect the malefactor rather than the decent citizen. Too often, it seems, a guilty person is let go for what the layman views as a trivial legal technicality. Stolen goods are found in a garage next door to a burglary suspect's house; yet he is released because a court rules that the warrant secured by the police did not give them permission to search the neighbor's garage. A confessed rapist is let off because a court rules that his confession was improperly extracted from him and so is not admissible as evidence.

Moreover, criminals sometimes get off on technicalities and commit other crimes. But statistics belie the widespread belief that law enforcement is lax and the courts soft on criminals. The penalties for lawbreakers are harsher in the U.S. than in other democracies. In a one-year period in England not long ago, only 4 per cent of all offenders who received sentences of a year or more were required to serve five years. The comparable figure in the U.S. was 52 per cent.

The main reason some apprehended criminals go unpunished is that the founders of the nation felt it important to balance the threat of tyranny against the need to control crime. As Benjamin Franklin put it, "Those who would give up essential liberty to purchase a little temporary safety deserve neither liberty nor safety." And so the Constitution, its first 10 amendments—known as the Bill of Rights—and later amendments have provided a number of bulwarks against a potentially oppressive government. Of these protections, few are more precious than the guarantee of "due process of law." This phrase in the Fifth and 14th Amendments assures that no one can be accused of a crime, arrested, tried and imprisoned unless an established judicial procedure is followed. This procedure, based on an automatic presumption of a man's innocence, protects him against coercion by police or prosecutors and ends with a trial before an impartial judge or jury. If these requirements seem to coddle the criminal, bear in mind that they are the honest citizen's safeguards against the imperfect workings of justice.

WHAT IS A CRIME?

There is more crime reported in the United States than in any other country. More than one million local, state and federal laws define criminal offenses—acts considered injurious to the public welfare and therefore prosecuted by the government in the name of society as a whole. Most crimes against people or property are prosecuted under state law. Federal law steps in only when such a crime involves federal property, is directed against the federal government or involves transportation across state lines.

In ascending order of seriousness there are three main categories of criminal offenses: petty offenses, misdemeanors and felonies. The categories vary from state to state. But the fundamental line that divides one category from another is the kind of punishment that may be imposed on a person found guilty of an offense in that category. In the case of a petty offense the punishment is a mild one—usually no more than 15 days in jail and/or a small fine. A misdemeanor is punishable by a larger fine or a longer jail term, usually less than a year in duration. A felony is punishable in some instances by death, but ordinarily by a prison sentence of more than a year; moreover, in the case of some major crimes, the convicted felon may be deprived of certain civil rights, such as the rights to vote, to hold a government job or to serve as an officer in the armed forces.

Petty offenses, which are defined in the main by local ordinances, are essentially minor breaches of the law—but breaches that are nevertheless considered dangerous to public safety. If you jaywalk in Los Angeles, smoke on a Chicago bus or put flowerpots on an apartment window sill in New York City, you have committed a petty offense. In some localities you may also have done so if you fail to observe local building codes when building or repairing your house, or if you fail to clear your sidewalk after a snowstorm. In many states your neighborhood supermarket owner may be guilty of a petty offense if he sells you spoiled milk; the same may be true of the liquor-store owner who makes a sale to a minor.

Misdemeanors, in society's scale of values, are both more harmful and more dangerous than petty offenses. Trespassing, as noted in the case of the prowler on the Joneses' property, is a misdemeanor in Illinois, and the culprit, if caught, could have paid a fine as high as $500 for his act. Had he rushed Mr. Jones and threatened him with a fist, he could have been found guilty of a charge of simple assault, another misdemeanor. And if it turned out that he was also drunk at the time, he could have been accused of yet another misdemeanor—disorderly conduct.

Often a misdemeanor is a petty offense that is made more serious by circumstances or consequences. To park too close to a fire hydrant is usually only a petty offense, but if a fire breaks out and the firemen cannot reach the hydrant because of the parked car, the driver may be guilty of the misdemeanor of interfering with fire-fighting equipment. The driver who ignores a stop sign commits a petty offense that may cost him a fine of $25; but if, while passing the stop sign, he knocks down a pedestrian, he may land in jail. Sometimes a petty offense is raised to the category of a misdemeanor in an effort to rid society of the offense in question; the act of prostitution was so transformed by New York's state legislature in 1969, with the penalty increased from 15 days to a maximum of three months in jail.

Felonies, the gravest crimes of all, include arson, aggravated assault, burglary, grand larceny, rape, robbery and murder. The felony category would seem to be relatively clear-cut, yet often there is a narrow line between a felony and a misdemeanor. The difference between the misdemeanor of simple assault and the felony of aggravated assault may be the difference between punching your neighbor in the nose and losing control so badly you beat him almost to death. Larceny is another example; in most states what makes it the felony of grand larceny or the misdemeanor of petty larceny is the monetary value of the stolen goods. In New York stealing $250.50 is a felony, while stealing $250.00 is a misdemeanor. And some laws are categorized by tradition; in California the felony of grand theft may be charged when a thief makes off with a horse or a cow.

Some of these acts may be considered crimes even if the law was broken innocently. The mislabeling of drugs is a misdemeanor whether done accidentally or not. Bigamy is no less a felony when both parties are ignorant of their unlawful relationship. But most infractions of the law are not judged crimes unless they were accompanied by a "criminal state of mind." This question of mental inclination is not so important in the case of routine petty offenses. But when the charge is a misdemeanor or a felony, the accused must generally be proved to have had a criminal state of mind to be found guilty.

The law, in short, does not wish to administer severe punishment for a harmful act that was accidental or that could not be helped. A man who writes a few bad checks and is charged with a misdemeanor cannot be found guilty if he shows that he made an honest mistake. A climber who stumbles over a rock on a narrow mountain path and accidentally pushes a companion over the side, causing his death, cannot be held guilty of murder.

Criminal states of mind

In assessing the state of mind that accompanied a crime, the law generally considers four questions: Was the act committed purposefully? Knowingly? Recklessly? Negligently? If the answers to all four are in the negative, no one is culpable; if the answer to only one is "Yes," the perpetrator is generally adjudged guilty. Consider, for example, how these four "states of mind" might apply in an act that resulted in someone's death.

■ The purposeful act. If your irascible Uncle Walter has a violent argument with his neighbor down the street, goes back home, gets out his rifle, carefully cleans it, loads it, and returns with it and shoots the neighbor dead, he has acted with purpose and "in cold blood." He is almost certain to be charged with—and found guilty of—the highest crime on the statute books, except for treason: Murder in the first degree is the term used for it in most states, but it is more informally known among lawyers as murder one. It is punishable by a sentence of life imprisonment or death. Suppose, however, that Uncle Walter has been quarreling with the neighbor and suddenly, in a rage, slams him with a shovel and kills him. While he acted with purpose, he did not act with premeditation, and so he is guilty not of murder one, but of murder in the second degree, often called murder two, which carries lesser penalties than murder one. (Killing a person "in the heat of passion" carries even lesser penalties and still another designation: voluntary manslaughter. The classic example of voluntary manslaughter is the slaying by a wife or husband of a spouse who was found in bed with someone else.)

■ The knowing act. It is possible to commit murder by perpetrating another sort of harmful act in the knowledge that it could cause a death. A man who sets fire to his store to collect insurance and causes the death of the family living in the apartment above the store is guilty of murder as well as arson. He may not have wished to kill the people in the apartment, but he knew that they lived there and that he was likely to bring about their deaths.

■ The reckless act. A man who recklessly throws a bomb into a crowd and causes a death can be found guilty of homicide. So can a person

Laws in many a state are rooted deep in the past; in California, for example, the felony of grand theft may be charged when a thief makes off with an automobile, a horse—or a cow.

who fires a gun in jest to frighten someone—but hits him. Regardless of his actual purpose, he knows his action is dangerous, and he shows such an indifference to the value of human life that he may be considered a murderer.

■ The negligent act. A landlord who fails to maintain proper safeguards against fire and whose tenants die when his house goes up in flames can also be found guilty of criminal homicide. A court will not accept his defense that he should not be held responsible because he was unaware of the local ordinances about fire hazards; the law holds that a landlord should know about such regulations and that he disregards them at his own peril.

CRIMES WITHOUT VICTIMS

While criminal law is primarily concerned with safeguarding individuals from outrages perpetrated upon them by others, it also deals with a number of acts that over the years have been regarded as criminal but that have no victims—at least, the people involved do not ordinarily consider themselves victims.

Such transgressions include gambling (most forms of which are illegal except in Nevada), the illegal use or possession of narcotics, and crimes of vice, which encompass not only many types of sexual misbehavior but also the distribution to adults of pornographic material. Brown may not consider himself a victim of a crime if he drops $20 to Smith at the Thursday-night poker game; in fact, he thirsts to win it back next week. It is because such offenses are committed primarily by consenting parties that there is increasing agitation to remove them from the field of crime altogether.

In practice, the law—in the person of prosecutors and police officers—seldom treats these infractions as criminal offenses. The police, in short, exercise discretion. If they hear that strangers have moved in on a local poker game, they might raid it. If they have evidence that money is changing hands at the weekly bridge party at Aunt Jane's, they could obtain authority to arrest Jane and the other ladies—even if the ladies are playing for only a hundredth of a cent per point—but it is unlikely that they will. It is also highly improbable that they will arrest participants in the office pool on the World Series—even though the pool violates the gambling laws—or raid the local church bingo game, which is illegal in many states. But the police and prosecutors do not always look the other way. In San Antonio in 1971 more than 500 people were taken into custody on the misdemeanor charge of "frequenting a gambling house"—after the irate wife of one heavy loser at the craps table made a complaint.

Acts of fornication or homosexuality are not likely to draw the attention of police unless a complaint is received or the conduct is flagrant. Laws against prostitution are better enforced, although it is very rare that the patron of a prostitute is charged with a crime. And while there is a federal statute—the famous Mann Act of 1910—that makes it illegal to transport a woman across state lines for immoral purposes, the law was primarily intended to combat commercialized vice, and it is no longer enforced against private, consenting citizens.

Narcotics laws

In general, laws against the possession of narcotics are rigidly enforced, although the punishments for breaking the laws vary almost absurdly among the states. Texas imposes a maximum of a life sentence for the possession of marijuana (which is legally a narcotic although it is not considered one by all medical experts). In New Jersey, however, a first offender who is charged with possession of less than 25 grams of marijuana—enough to make about 50 "joints"—faces only a period

If the police have evidence that money is changing hands at the weekly bridge party at Aunt Jane's, they could arrest Jane and her guests—even if the ladies are playing for only a hundredth of a cent per point —but it is unlikely that they will.

of probation, and the charge may even be dismissed entirely at the discretion of the judge.

Nowhere is such a lenient attitude expressed toward the truly narcotic or "hard" drugs—cocaine, and opium and its derivatives heroin, morphine and codeine. Illegal possession of non-narcotic but dangerous drugs—habit-forming barbiturates or certain hallucinogens such as LSD—can under federal law lead to a penalty for a first offender of a year in prison and a fine of as much as $1,000.

Even if a person is not using drugs himself, he may be in legal peril if he associates with those who do—a fact that has had serious consequences for a number of innocent young people. If narcotics are found during the search of a car, for example, all persons in the car are often judged to have had possession. Chasing a speeding car in 1956, a patrolman saw one of two occupants of the rear seat throw out what proved to be a packet of narcotics. The driver and the front-seat passenger claimed that they should not be charged because only the pair sitting in the back had had the drugs. No good. The court held that the police had reasonable grounds to believe that each occupant of the car was in possession of the drugs.

THE CITIZEN AS VICTIM

A responsible citizen is not likely to find himself on the receiving end of a charge of possessing drugs, frequenting a gambling house, or any other criminal offense. But what do you do when you yourself become the victim of a crime? Or when you fear that you may become a victim—suspecting, say, that an employee of your company is embezzling funds? And what do you do if you see or hear of a crime committed against someone else—when you notice a group of toughs, for example, taking a schoolboy's bus fare from him?

In most cases you do the obvious: You call the authorities. If a violation of a federal statute involves a felony, the law requires you to report it, but no such requirement applies generally to state laws. In 1964, in a pleasant residential neighborhood in the New York City borough of Queens, a woman was murdered in the street outside an apartment house, and while more than a score of residents heard her cries for help, no one sounded the alarm and no one was later charged with failure to do so. If it is callous not to report a crime to the proper authorities, it is also foolish. You may be assaulted next, or your house burgled or your car stolen.

But which proper authorities? If you have just been robbed at gunpoint, you call the police. If you suspect that you have been the victim of an embezzler, you may take your complaint to the local district attorney's office, where your statement will be taken down in writing. If a crime does appear to have been committed, an investigation will follow.

The citizen's arrest

Only with utmost care should you try to deal directly with a crime by making a citizen's arrest. Private citizens do have many of the same legal powers of arrest as police officers—but these powers are subject to many restrictions, and the laws on this score vary from place to place. Generally speaking, however, a private citizen may arrest anyone he is sure has just committed a felony. If, for example, you see someone running out of a store followed by angry shouts of "Stop, thief!", you have a right to arrest the thief, using a reasonable amount of force to restrain him. But since a fleeing felon is unlikely to take kindly to your attempt to arrest him, and since it is the duty of the citizen making the arrest to take his captive immediately to a police officer or a magistrate, the citizen might literally have his hands full. And if the presumed robber turns out to be merely a frightened citizen running out of the store in an attempt to get away from the real criminal, you may be in serious trouble. Criminal charges of unlawful arrest or even assault can be brought against you, and your innocent fellow citizen may also have grounds for claiming damages in a civil suit against you.

Moreover, in some states the law requires you to be certain that the crime for which you are making a citizen's arrest is a felony; in

A private citizen generally may arrest anyone he sees committing a serious crime. But he should be very sure of his grounds; the man he apprehends may be an innocent fellow-citizen fleeing in fright while the real criminal slips off.

some places such an arrest cannot be made for misdemeanors like trespassing. Beware of rushing to grab someone you spot shoplifting in a jewelry store; if the charge against him turns out to be not a felony but a misdemeanor, you may be liable for false arrest. Remember, too, that in trying to corral and arrest a miscreant, you cannot use a weapon "of deadly force" to do so unless he is physically endangering you or someone else.

Limits on weapon use

The restrictions on the use of a weapon may apply even if a citizen's arrest is furthest from your thoughts—if you are simply trying to protect yourself or your property against a criminal. Legally you may keep a handgun, shotgun or rifle in your house, provided that you have obtained any permits required by local or state law. You may also, in some states and under certain conditions, carry a firearm with you for self-defense when you go out. But before you use the weapon on another person or even point it in his direction, loaded or unloaded, you must be very certain indeed that your life is in danger or that you are faced with the "grave bodily harm" the law specifies. Anyone, criminal or not, who has a gun pointed at him is generally entitled to assume that it is loaded and to take appropriate countermeasures. These restrictions apply whether or not the gun is legally in your possession and whether you use it on your own property or elsewhere.

A 1969 Iowa case illustrates the limits placed on citizens' use of firearms to protect their property. The owner of an unoccupied farmhouse that had been forcibly entered a number of times grew tired of the damage the intruders were causing and rigged a booby trap—a wire attached to a bedroom door and to the trigger of a shotgun. A prowler opened the door, the wire triggered the shotgun and the shotgun blew off part of the intruder's shin. He spent 40 days in the hospital; his leg was saved, but it was badly scarred and two inches shorter than the other one was.

Originally charged with breaking and entering, the maimed prowler pleaded guilty to a lesser charge, "larceny in the nighttime." He was convicted and he paid a fine. Then he filed a civil suit against the farmhouse owner, accusing him of using excessive force to protect his property; he won damages of $20,000 for his injury and $10,000 for malice on the owner's part. The principle that underlay this court decision is summed up in Prosser's well-known text, *The Law of Torts:* "The law has always placed a higher value upon human safety than upon mere rights in property. . . . There is no privilege to use any force calculated to cause death or serious bodily injury . . . unless there is also such a threat to the defendant's personal safety as to justify self-defense."

Protecting yourself legally

But assume that an average citizen does have good reason to fear for his personal safety. Say he happens to be a city dweller, living in a neighborhood where there has been a sharp rise in muggings. Is he —or his wife—permitted to carry a handgun for self-defense? Not if the gun is concealed on his person. Almost every state holds such concealment of a weapon illegal, and many states have extended the prohibition to the concealment of firearms in automobiles. In some states, however, a weapon may be concealed in an automobile as long as it is not "immediately accessible." Under such a statute a man who keeps a loaded handgun locked in the glove compartment of his car is not subject to arrest, but if he has it under his hat on the seat beside him he can be charged.

Weapons less lethal than guns may also cause trouble with the law. With street crimes on the increase women in particular have taken to carrying patented gas guns and spray cans of irritants to use against muggers and molesters. These gadgets are not hard to obtain, but they can cause great harm, and a woman who uses one of them against an attacker may find herself charged with using more force

An illegal booby trap

Tired of prowlers breaking into his unoccupied farmhouse, an owner in Iowa rigged a Rube Goldberg contraption like this one —and when the prowler (a) entered the door (b), a system of pulleys (c) caused a shotgun (d) to fire, wounding the unwary prowler (a). But it is illegal to use a deadly weapon solely to protect property. The injured prowler sued the farmer for damages—and won.

A loud screech for help is a legal —and effective—defense against a molester. One singer, followed by a man in a large car, unlimbered her coloratura and hit "Poh-LEE-EEEce" on C above high C. Her would-be attacker sped away.

than the law permits in a given situation. In New York, for example, the mere possession of spray cans of noxious chemicals, which not only can stun people but also may cause lasting damage to the eyes, skin and respiratory system, is a misdemeanor punishable by a $50 fine or 30 days in jail, or both. This law, while seeming unnecessarily restrictive to some, is designed to keep angry people from spraying dangerous chemicals at each other on the street for frivolous reasons. The law can also be harsh with the jittery citizen who, when approached by an unshaven man on a dimly lit street, raps him across the face with an umbrella; if it turns out that the man was about to ask directions to the bus stop, the umbrella-wielder may be charged with the crime of assault.

What, then, is left within the law to discourage the unwanted attentions of a stranger on the street? The element of surprise is still effective. There is one defense mechanism most women have that is more powerful than that possessed by most men. A girl who had had professional voice training found herself being followed by a man in a large car as she was on her way home one night to her Boston apartment. When the driver pulled alongside and invited her for a ride, she unlimbered her coloratura and hit "Poh-LEE-EEEce!"—reaching, as she recalls, C above high C. Her would-be friend was through a red light at the other end of the block "while I was still holding the note." Not all women are trained coloratura sopranos, but they would do well to remember that even though a scream may not instantly attract help, it may frighten the wits out of a molester—and as a weapon it is perfectly legal.

Should you, despite your best efforts to safeguard yourself and your property, fall victim to a crime and the perpetrator be caught, you may be able to win damages from him through a civil suit. In addition to paying you for the losses you incurred—whether to your person or your property—the award may also include an extra sum as punitive damages. Such damage awards are often made even when the accused is not convicted of his crime, since criminal procedures differ from civil ones. In a criminal trial, the evidence must prove the defendant guilty beyond a reasonable doubt; in a civil trial the defendant can be forced to pay damages simply if the weight of the evidence is preponderantly against him.

THE CITIZEN AS WITNESS

Suppose you have not yourself been the victim of a crime, but have seen one committed. You notify the police or the district attorney. Then what happens? If you have witnessed a murder and the police catch a suspect, you will be asked to identify him at the police station and to swear out a complaint before a judge accusing the suspect of the crime. Later you may be asked to tell your story at a preliminary hearing held by a judge, and then again at a grand jury session. If the grand jury indicts the suspect, and he pleads not guilty, you will be asked to testify at the subsequent court trial.

Some people are reluctant to step forward as witnesses because of the protracted nature of the proceedings; each of the stages—preliminary hearing, grand jury session, trial—is usually subject to delays and repeated adjournments. But despite such drawbacks, the role of witness is an integral part of criminal justice, and most responsible people recognize a civic obligation to testify voluntarily.

The subpoena

If you are reluctant to volunteer or prefer the formality of an official request, a judge, on the petition of either the defense or the prosecution, may issue a subpoena to you. It is an official order to appear in a court, and you ignore the order at your peril. Failure to appear on the required date can lead to a charge of contempt of court. Refusal to testify when ordered to do so by a judge is equally serious. A reluctant witness can be kept in jail until he agrees to talk.

Generally, a subpoena is not "legally served" unless it is personally delivered into your hands; in some states a subpoena may be sent through the mail if an individual appears to be avoiding it. If you ignore a subpoena sent through the mail, the court will accommodate you by sending someone in person, probably armed with a warrant for your arrest. While you may not refuse a subpoena, you will probably be able, if you are ill or expect to be out of town on an important trip, to obtain a postponement of your appearance by explaining the circumstances to the judge who has issued the subpoena.

Not all subpoenas are aimed solely at gaining the spoken testimony of witnesses to a crime. If you have advised the district attorney about a suspected embezzler in your company, you may be served with a *Subpoena Duces Tecum* (you will bring with you). This order requires you to appear with the records to support your allegations. At this stage you should have your lawyer—or the company's —in on the proceedings. He is permitted to be present when you give testimony in any hearing except one before a grand jury, and even there he can remain nearby, and you can consult him before giving an answer to a question a juror asks you.

Should a prosecutor have reason to believe that a subpoena will not guarantee a witness's appearance in court, a judge may issue an order for the arrest of the person and have him placed in custody as a material witness, that is, one whose testimony is deemed essential to the case. Such treatment is unlikely for a cooperative citizen who has filed a complaint. People do, however, spend time in jail as material witnesses. A drifter was not only the victim of but sole witness to an aggravated assault committed by a gambler with a police record. The gambler was able to post bail and was freed pending his trial. The drifter was held in custody as a material witness—after his release from the hospital where he had been treated for injuries sustained in the assault. When the case came to trial some seven months later, the gambler pleaded guilty to a lesser charge, the misdemeanor of simple assault. He was sentenced to six months in jail, a month less than his victim had already spent behind bars waiting to testify. Because of such built-in unfairness, material witnesses are usually jailed only in major cases and under special circumstances—sometimes to protect them from the accused or his associates.

THE CITIZEN AS SUSPECT

The average citizen—conditioned in part by television courtroom dramas—may fear that he will become an innocent victim of the law. Such legal trouble is improbable but by no means impossible, as a sampling of cases on record will show:

■ A Philadelphia man and his landlady, chatting on the street one evening, were identified as a couple who had passed a forged check. They were arrested and—after 10 merchants had corroborated the charge —were indicted, convicted and sentenced to nine months in jail. In time the sleuthing of a private detective agency turned up the real forger. By incredibly long odds the man and his landlady had been the victims of mistaken identity.

■ The head of a pharmaceutical firm in Buffalo, New York, was convicted of a federal misdemeanor when incorrect labels were found to have been pasted on drugs shipped out of state by his firm. He had had no knowledge of the error; nevertheless, he was held to be an "unwitting accomplice" to his employee's criminal neglect.

■ In Beverly Hills an actor with an outstanding record of bravery in World War II emerged from a restaurant and noticed an American flag that had fallen to the sidewalk. As he picked up the flag, two women coming out of a nearby office leaped to the conclusion that he had torn the flag down. Taken aback, he walked to his car and drove off, but the women jotted down his license number, and he was arrested for "desecrating the American flag." After weeks during which his reputation was severely jeopardized, a judge dismissed the charge, saying he could not believe that anyone with the defendant's war record could have been engaged in desecration of the flag. "You never know," says a lawyer who recounts this case to his clients, "when lightning will strike."

It is on the rare occasions when lightning does strike that the full value of constitutional safeguards becomes plain. For then the accused —innocent or guilty—finds a full panoply of safeguards designed to guarantee him his rights. These protections extend from the moment he becomes a suspect, to the search of his person or his property, to procedures at the station house or the district attorney's office, to his plea of guilty or not guilty, to his trial if there is one, and even beyond.

The search of the home
One of the most explicit of your protections in the event of any brush you might have with the law is stated in the Fourth Amendment to the Constitution. It says that authorities cannot search your home for evidence of a crime unless they have given good reasons to a judge and have obtained from him a written order specifying where they may search and what they may seize. These constitutional restrictions originally applied only in federal cases, although many state constitutions had similar provisions. Then, in a landmark case in 1961, the Supreme Court extended the protection of the Fourth Amendment to guard citizens against unwarranted searches by the police in all states. Cleveland police, claiming falsely that they had a search warrant and ostensibly on the trail of a fugitive, had forced their way into the home of Dollree Mapp, a local landlady. They found no fugitive but came upon some allegedly obscene books and papers. Miss Mapp was tried and convicted on a charge of possession of pornography. When the case reached the Supreme Court, the Justices agreed with the contention of Miss Mapp's lawyer that the material had been illegally seized and ruled that evidence obtained in this fashion could not be used to convict.

Before a policeman can get the search warrant that gives him permission to invade your house, he must appear before a judge and swear that he has "probable cause" to believe that certain evidence of a crime will be found in the search. The term "probable cause" has been defined as meaning that his reasons are such as would lead a cautious man to take action. He cannot simply be guessing—for example, playing a hunch that you have a stolen painting in your basement because he saw you buy an art book relating to the stolen canvas. The warrant must, in addition, specify whatever it is that the police are looking for and must also describe the premises to be searched.

Once armed with a search warrant to inspect your premises a policeman must still follow carefully determined procedures. He must knock, identify himself as an officer, show his warrant if requested and give you time to read it. Exceptions exempt policemen from these rules. Many state legislatures have passed "no-knock" laws similar to one approved by Congress in 1968. Under these laws police may obtain a warrant to break into a house without warning when the items being sought, such as drugs or gambling slips, might be quickly and easily destroyed. The no-knock rule may also be applied when an officer believes that his life would be endangered if he identified himself as an officer and announced his intention of conducting a search.

Even if you know your home to be free of evidence of crime —and no matter how indignant you are at the suggestion of criminal involvement—you may not refuse entry to or resist an officer with a warrant. If you refuse entry he is legally entitled to proceed with the search, and if you resist you may be subject to a charge of obstructing an officer in the performance of his duty. If you feel that he may be violating your constitutional rights, you should tell the officer that you are not consenting to the search, and you may later seek damages from the police in a civil suit or bring charges against the officer in criminal court. Such suits are rarely won.

Anyone who wishes to may waive the Fourth Amendment's protection and invite the police to conduct a search without a warrant. Some police naturally welcome this means of avoiding the process of obtaining a warrant, and they try whenever possible to talk a householder into allowing them to search without one. However, once consent is given to police entry into the house, whatever is turned up may be used as legal evidence; the consenter forfeits his right to challenge evidence as illegally obtained. A Massachusetts businessman who regularly rented his Cape Cod house for the summer returned one September day to close the place for the winter. That evening an old high-school chum, now a sergeant on the local police force, appeared at the door asking permission to "look around." Permission was granted, and in a closet the sergeant discovered a hypodermic needle and a scorched tablespoon with traces of heroin on it. No charge came out of this discovery; the tenants—who might or might not have been the culprits—had left the state, and the district attorney, believing the businessman's story of ignorance, did not move to prosecute him on the charge of possession of a narcotic. But one cannot always rely upon the presence of a kindly district attorney.

If you do choose to consent to a police search without warrant, remember that the consent may be given only by an adult resident of the house *(Chapter 11)*. The law's interpretation of your "home" is a broad one indeed. Not merely your house or apartment is included; if you happen to be in a hotel room, or—in some circumstances—in your car or on your boat, you are entitled to the protections that apply in your home. However, the Supreme Court has held that an officer may search a car or boat without a warrant—if he has reasonable ground to believe he may find evidence of a specific crime. Such searches are allowed on the assumption that since boats and cars are mobile, they may be out of reach before the officer can obtain a warrant.

The search of the person

The Fourth Amendment protects you against unreasonable search not only at home but on the street and in other public places. The police do have the right to "stop and frisk" a person on the street if they sus-

Limits on police search

Armed with a warrant to search for one thing, police officers may not hunt for another thing that may be illegally in someone's possession. If officers seeking stolen jewelry find a small arsenal, the weapons may not be evidence in the jewel case—unless they were used in the theft. But this suspect smiles prematurely. Such weapons as bazookas or submachine guns are contraband—if found during a search, they can be seized and the possessor charged with a crime.

pect he is about to commit a crime—but only if they stay within limits set forth in a Supreme Court decision of 1968. The "stop" means that the officer may ask the suspicious character to identify himself and account for his presence in the area. The "frisk" is strictly limited to a "patting down" of clothing in a search for weapons—and for nothing else. As Chief Justice Earl Warren summed it up: "The sole justification of the search . . . is the protection of the police officer and others nearby, and it must therefore be confined in scope to an intrusion reasonably designed to discover guns, knives, clubs, or other hidden instruments for the assault of the police officer." The Court later applied this guideline in overturning the conviction of a man found guilty of narcotics possession. It did so because the evidence had been obtained when an officer went beyond "patting down" and found drugs by thrusting his hand into the suspect's pocket.

The restrictions against search of the person are loosened when someone is actually arrested, whether on the street or at home. Anything found on a suspect that bears some relationship to the crime for which he is being arrested may be seized for use as evidence, and so may objects like weapons that may not relate to the crime but may be illegal. This power, called search incident to arrest, also has its limitations. It does not give the police the power to follow up a man's arrest by going through his whole house unless they have a warrant

A policeman has the right to "stop and frisk" a suspect in the street—but only if he follows procedures set forth by the Supreme Court. The officer may pat down clothing for a weapon; he may not reach into a pocket for narcotics.

permitting the broad search. They have the right to search in the immediate vicinity of the arrest, to prevent the suspect from obtaining a weapon or destroying evidence immediately accessible to him. But they can go no further. If, for example, the police arrest a man sitting at a kitchen table, they may search any drawers in the table but not the kitchen cabinets.

THE ARREST

An arrest takes place when a policeman—or a private citizen—takes someone into custody. (Thus, you are not arrested when you get a speeding ticket since you are not taken into custody and your freedom of movement is not impeded; such a summons is known as an alternative to arrest.) Some arrests are made under the power of an arrest warrant. To obtain such a warrant the police officer must go through procedures identical to those required when he obtains a search warrant: He must provide careful identification of the individual, specify the crime and describe the reasons for believing the individual is guilty—citing, as in the case of a search warrant, probable cause and not mere suspicion. With an arrest warrant police can break into your house, despite your protests, just as they can when they have a search warrant.

But most arrests are made without a warrant. The officer must simply have probable cause to believe that the person arrested has committed a crime. The officer does not need to have absolute proof that wrongdoing has occurred, and he need not have seen the crime committed; he must only know facts and circumstances that would lead a reasonable person to believe that the man he is arresting has committed a crime. If the officer hears on his car radio that a suspect of such-and-such a description has fled the scene of a bank robbery in an automobile of a certain model, and he encounters you a few blocks away, fitting the description of the suspect and the car, he has probable cause to arrest you. But he cannot do so on mere suspicion. Suppose that you are one of a group of men who get together in the evening to watch baseball games on television in a neighborhood where there have been a number of burglaries. One night the host's set breaks down, and you walk over to your own home to pick up your portable so that the boys can continue watching the game. Returning to join them, you are arrested by a policeman on a charge of burglary. This arrest is invalid—a man carrying a TV set in a burglary-ridden neighborhood may be a suspicious sight but not one that constitutes probable cause for arrest.

An improper arrest can have several consequences. No physical evidence found as a result of it may be used in court. More important to an innocent citizen—and sometimes to police officers—it may give an innocent citizen the right to file a charge of false arrest in a state criminal court, a suit for damages in a state civil court and an action against the officer in a federal court under the Civil Rights Act of 1964. In the first case cited above, in which the officer arrested you because you fitted the description of a fleeing felon, you would not win a suit for false arrest; the officer had probable cause to believe that you were the culprit. In the second case you would have a better chance of winning such a suit, since the officer acted on mere suspicion. But a lawyer would undoubtedly advise you not to sue in either event unless great harm has been done to you or your family. Such a suit takes time and considerable money in legal fees; moreover, the burden of proof would be upon you, the plaintiff, to prove that you were indeed illegally arrested.

Whether you think the arrest is valid or invalid, it is unwise to offer resistance, although you are legally entitled to in most states when you are being illegally arrested. (But in at least one state, New Hampshire, resistance to illegal arrest is itself illegal.) An officer is entitled to use as much force as he feels necessary to take you into custody —including deadly force if he believes his life is in danger. In any event, quibbling with the officer about the legality of arrest is impractical; go quietly and let your lawyer argue about it later.

At the station house

Suppose the unthinkable comes to pass: You find yourself under arrest, in the station house being interrogated. What do you do?

First, stop talking and call a lawyer. You are required to do no more than identify yourself to police officers, and you may stop answering questions at any time, even though you may already have volunteered quite a bit of information. Moreover, you are protected against being pressed to answer police questions at this stage by a Supreme Court decision of 1966, *Miranda* v. *Arizona*. A police officer is now required, when arresting a suspect, to caution him about his protections against self-incrimination. The policeman must inform the suspect of his right to remain silent, warn him that if he does answer questions the answers can be used as evidence against him, tell him of his right to a lawyer and explain that counsel will be provided at public expense if necessary. The law is so stern about this requirement that some police departments have had the necessary statements printed on cards—inevitably called Miranda cards—to be read or handed to suspects *(sample, opposite)*.

PD 47
REV. 12/70

METROPOLITAN POLICE DEPARTMENT
WARNING AS TO YOUR RIGHTS

You are under arrest. Before we ask you any questions, you must understand what your rights are.

You have the right to remain silent. You are not required to say anything to us at any time or to answer any questions. Anything you say can be used against you in court.

You have the right to talk to a lawyer for advice before we question you and to have him with you during questioning.

If you cannot afford a lawyer and want one, a lawyer will be provided for you.

If you want to answer questions now without a lawyer present you will still have the right to stop answering at any time. You also have the right to stop answering at any time until you talk to a lawyer.   P-771

A word of warning

When police make an arrest, they are required to warn a suspect of his constitutional rights at once. Because of this requirement, many police departments order their men to present cards like the one at left, printed with this warning to suspects. Known as Miranda cards, after the main participant in a celebrated Supreme Court case, the cards offer space for a suspect to affirm that he has been informed of his rights.

WAIVER

1. Have you read or had read to you the warning as to your rights? _____

2. Do you understand these rights? _____

3. Do you wish to answer any questions? _____

4. Do you wish to have an attorney present during questioning? _____

5. Signature of defendant on line below.
_____

6. Time _____   Date _____

7. Signature of officer _____

8. Signature of witness _____

The Miranda decision extended to the first stage of criminal proceedings a right that had already been affirmed for later, more critical stages by the famous Gideon case. Clarence Gideon had been tried and found guilty of breaking and entering in Florida in 1961 and, despite his request that he be supplied with a lawyer, was denied one. Gideon was broke, and Florida did not provide counsel for indigent defendants in burglary cases such as his. From his jail cell he appealed to the Supreme Court, charging that his constitutional rights had been violated. The Court agreed. Significantly, in his next trial—with counsel—he was acquitted.

While everyone has a right to a lawyer, the Gideon ruling did not require the states to supply counsel for people who could afford to pay for one. If you have no lawyer of your own, you have a right to keep calling from the station house until you reach a lawyer willing to represent you, for despite what you may have seen on television you are not restricted to one phone call. You may have to spend a few hours—or even the night—behind bars waiting for an attorney to arrive, but such delay may be far better than an inadvertent admission, made without the cautionary presence of counsel, that may lead the police to believe you are linked with a crime—and cause you to spend several days in detention.

What if you *are* guilty of a crime or believe that the police suspect you of one or think that you may be an unwitting accomplice —like the Buffalo pharmaceuticals wholesaler—to something regarded by the law as a crime? Do you go to the police or the district attorney and make a clean breast of things? No, not by yourself. In those circumstances do what you would do if arrested: Get a lawyer, and follow his advice on what steps to take. Volunteering information can be dangerous. The man who, prior to arrest, cries to a police officer, "Yes, yes, I did it!" can have that statement used against him if he is later brought to trial.

The aftermath of arrest

Even before a suspect's lawyer arrives at the station house, the accused criminal is "booked"—that is, the charge against him is entered with other relevant facts in the station house's charge book. He is then fingerprinted and photographed. He must submit to a thorough examination of his clothes and person including, perhaps, a check for injection scars to determine whether he is a narcotics user. Evidence found in such a search can be used against him. If he is subsequently released or acquitted after a trial he has the right, in some states, to demand the return of his fingerprint cards, photograph and other records

of his arrest. The return of these documents in effect removes the record from the criminal files. A suspect cannot, however, demand the return of his records from federal files. The Federal Bureau of Investigation does not return the record of a suspect even if the case against him has been dropped.

At the station house the police often seek evidence against a suspect through the line-up. It is very much like those you have seen in the movies and on television. The suspect is placed in a well-lighted line with other persons, usually other suspects and policemen in plain clothes. A witness to the alleged crime is asked to pick out the suspect. If he does point to the suspect, this identification can be used in court as evidence. It sounds simple, but the line-up contains inherent dangers. For a witness to recall the face of a criminal out of context is sometimes difficult; it has also happened that a witness, having earlier caught a glimpse of someone at the station house, will pluck him out of the line-up as the culprit.

And police do load line-ups—so arrange them that the witness is likely to single out a particular man, the one the police believe committed the crime. An obvious—if blatant—example would be the placing of a black man in a line of white men, or vice versa. As a safeguard against such a stratagem, a suspect has the right to have his lawyer present during the line-up. The lawyer cannot intervene, but his presence tends to inhibit questionable police procedures if only because he can later testify that the line-up was unfair and may be able to prevent use of the evidence it produced.

BEGINNING THE JUDICIAL PROCESS

After arrest and booking, a suspect is usually taken before a judge or magistrate, a step known as the preliminary examination, if the prosecutor feels he has sufficient evidence to make a case. This "prosecu-

A loaded lineup
When displaying suspects for identification by witnesses in station-house lineups, police ordinarily use similar people to avoid influencing the witnesses' choice. But sometimes they do not observe this precaution and place the man they suspect with a group of people who are neither the same size, shape nor color. Guess who the prime suspect is in this loaded lineup?

torial" discretion is absolute; if the prosecutor decides that there is no case, there will be no case, whatever anyone else may think. Only rarely can a prosecutor be forced to proceed with a case if he decides not to —and he does not have to reveal the reasons for his refusal to move against the accused.

But if the case does reach preliminary examination, the suspect must be examined "forthwith." While the interpretation of forthwith varies across the country, most states hold examinations within 24 hours after arrest. Subsequent procedures also vary in detail from state to state, but the pattern is as follows.

At the examination the judge looks at a document called a complaint, which details the charge brought against the suspect by the police or by a civilian complainant. By the time the judge sees this document, it has probably been checked in the district attorney's office to make sure that the charge contains enough facts to support the accusation. The judge must read the charge to the suspect (now known as the defendant by virtue of the preliminary examination) and again advise him of his right to counsel. At this point the judge himself will review the evidence—and if it seems insufficient, he may dismiss the charge. If he does not, the case will be turned over to a prosecutor in some states; in others it will be held for action by a grand jury, a panel of citizens who make the final determination as to whether the defendant must stand trial.

Bail

The defendant does not have to remain in jail while waiting for the decision of the grand jury or the prosecutor. He may obtain his freedom by putting up bail, which is his guarantee—in the form of money or property—that he will show up for the next stage in the legal proceedings. If he does not appear—if he runs away—he forfeits the money or the property and a warrant is issued for his arrest. In most states a defendant has a legal right to bail unless he is charged with a capital offense; for such offenses bail is not granted. In some cases a judge will release a defendant without bail on his "own recognizance," meaning that the judge believes that the accused will voluntarily appear on the date he is told to.

When bail is required, most defendants post it through a businessman known as a bail bondsman. He in effect sells a defendant a bond for the amount of bail set by the court, charging about 10 per cent of the face value of the bond. The bondsman in turn carries a policy with an insurance company against the possibility that the defendant may jump bail—that is, fail to appear at the next legal stage of his case. As further protection against this eventuality, the bonds-man may require his customer to furnish collateral security, such as the deed on his house or the title to his car.

But if a defendant is himself able to offer such security, why the need for a bondsman? The answer is that the courts generally require payment in cash, and few people have the requisite amount of cash readily at hand. A paradox of the bail-bonding business is that the more hardened the criminal—the more times he has been arrested, obtained a bail bond and shown up in court—the better his credit with a bail bondsman. He is, after all, a steady customer.

Because of such problems, many states and the federal government have experimented with other methods of pre-trial release, such as releasing defendants on unsecured bail bonds, for which only a token deposit of 10 per cent of the amount of the bond is required. In 1966 Congress passed the Bail Reform Act, which allows federal judges to release defendants without bond "when detention serves neither the ends of justice nor the public interest."

The grand jury

Eventually, whether a defendant is detained in jail or allowed out on bail, his case may reach a grand jury. Grand juries vary in size from state to state. Members are generally chosen in the same way in which trial jurors are picked *(Chapter 10)*: Names are taken from the voter-registration rolls and drawn from a bowl or selected by some other lotterylike procedure. But the grand jury session is not itself a trial. The proceedings are secret, and the jury assays only evidence presented by the prosecuting attorney without hearing from the defense—neither the defendant nor his lawyer is present.

Although the prosecutor controls the presentation of evidence to the grand jury, the jurors are, in principle, independent. They may ask questions of the prosecutor and witnesses, and they deliberate and vote in secret. If the jury finds the prosecutor's case convincing, the foreman writes "true bill" across the back of the legal paper presenting the prosecutor's charges, and the defendant is formally indicted —he must stand trial. If the jury finds the prosecutor's case unconvincing, it can vote to discharge the defendant. In states that do not use the grand jury system, the prosecutor simply draws up charges in an "information." It, like a grand jury indictment, can move the case to the next step in the proceedings: formal arraignment.

At the arraignment, the judge reads the charges to the defendant and asks him whether he pleads guilty or not guilty. In a capital case, a defendant is not, in many states, permitted to enter a plea of guilty;

an automatic plea of not guilty is entered for him. If the charge does not involve a capital crime, and the defendant pleads not guilty but does not demand a jury trial or a "continuance" to find a lawyer or witnesses of his own, he conceivably could be tried on the spot by the judge alone. Even if the defendant pleads guilty, the judge normally postpones sentencing for 48 hours so that a pre-sentencing report can be drafted and the defendant can prepare a plea for leniency.

Plea-bargaining

Most criminal cases never actually reach the stage of a trial. They are settled before that point either because the defendant pleads guilty or because he agrees to a practice known as "plea-bargaining." Essentially, what happens in plea-bargaining is that a defendant—on the advice of his lawyer and with the consent of the prosecuting attorney—pleads guilty to a lesser charge than that of which he has been accused, and which consequently carries a lesser punishment. Suppose a man is indicted for the major felony of burglary—for which the sentence may be 10 years. After discussion between his attorney and the prosecutor, he might agree to plead guilty to the lesser felony of larceny, for which the sentence may be only two years. The judge, who may or may not have been privy to this bargaining between prosecutor and counsel, then accepts the plea of guilty to the lesser charge and sentences the defendant—occasionally freeing him because the time he has already spent in jail awaiting trial matches the legal sentence for the lesser offense.

Plea-bargaining saves the state the cost of proceeding with a trial. It is also favored on the ground that the courts would be impossibly overworked if every defendant insisted on his right to a trial and pleaded not guilty to the crime charged. Many lawyers and judges, however, retain strong reservations about plea-bargaining. They see in it the danger that an innocent defendant may plead guilty to a lesser charge solely to avoid the risk of conviction for a more serious offense. Moreover, the punishment meted out after the plea-bargaining is sometimes not commensurate with the offense committed; on occasion defendants get off with fairly light sentences for grave offenses. Other legal experts counter that plea-bargaining is a humane procedure, since U.S. laws are sometimes harsh and punishments frequently severe. Some authorities believe that the courts could not function at all without plea-bargaining. "Plea discussions leading to disposition of cases," said Chief Justice Warren Burger, "are indispensable to any rational administration of criminal justice."

For a defendant who has gone this far in a criminal proceeding, there may be a great temptation to bargain—"to cop a plea," in criminal argot. But a plea of guilty means a conviction, and someone convicted of even a lesser felony carries that stigma for a long time.

A fair trial—or trials

The trial procedures in American courts, described in detail in Chapter 10, are the most elaborate of the country's many systems of safeguards against injustice. There may be several trials to settle a single charge, for the most trivial offenses can be appealed to the Supreme Court. The Mapp case, for example, in which the Supreme Court finally strengthened safeguards against unwarranted search, started out as nothing more than a charge of the presence of obscene material in Dollree Mapp's house. (Miss Mapp was nonetheless later proved a criminal and sentenced to 20 years in prison for selling narcotics—but her name will go down in legal history for her part in establishing an essential human right.)

And whether or not a trial has been held, an individual who believes he has been dealt with unjustly has one ancient right that the founding fathers spelled out in the Constitution. This right is habeas corpus (literally, you have the body), which permits a person held in custody to ask a court to order those holding him to deliver him before a judge. The judge must then determine whether the prisoner is being lawfully held. The individual may apply for a writ of habeas corpus—sometimes called the Great Writ—at any stage of his entanglement with the law, from the moment he is arrested to the last day of a prison sentence he has served as a result of a conviction. His lawyer may apply for the writ or he may do so himself; the celebrated case of Clarence Gideon reached the Supreme Court after a writ had been applied for by Gideon from his prison cell.

Habeas corpus serves to prevent the practice of throwing people into jail and detaining them there indefinitely until charges can be found, or manufactured, to be lodged against them. It is also the start of the road to freedom for victims of improperly conducted legal proceedings and wrongful imprisonment. The Great Writ is, in fact, the heart of American justice.

By **JAY BRENNAN,**
MONRAD G. PAULSEN, Consultant

10
The courts

How a lawsuit is
brought, tried,
appealed and decided

One autumn morning in 1970 a Virginia woman sat nervously in the crowded witness room of a courthouse in Washington, D.C. She had just driven 60 miles from her home in answer to a subpoena to testify against two youths who had been charged with mugging and robbing her several weeks earlier near the Capitol building. In the intervening period the youths had been arrested on a warrant issued in her name at the time of the attack; now the wheels of justice were finally turning and her testimony was needed to bring the case to trial.

As hours passed without her name being called—and other witnesses were summoned to take their turns in the courtroom nearby —the woman became increasingly nervous. Like most Americans, she was unfamiliar with the judicial process. But she was especially unnerved to find that among the people in the witness room waiting their turns to testify, was one of the very youths who had attacked her.

Finally, she asked to see the official who had requested her presence. When she found him, he flushed sheepishly and admitted that when her case had been called, the clerk had inexplicably failed to summon her to testify. Without her testimony the case against the youths had been dismissed—the judge routinely canceled the charges for "lack of a complaining witness."

Fortunately, the Virginia woman's experience is not typical. But the overburdened calendars of U.S. courts do occasionally result in such scenes, and these serve to confirm the impression that the courts of the land are part of a cold and alien world. The impression is heightened by the fact that few citizens come into close enough contact with the courts to know how they do work, much less understand how to take advantage of the judicial process when a legal problem arises. One reason for this lack of understanding is that trials are far less common than most people realize. Of the 85,000 civil cases initiated in the federal courts in the course of a typical year only about 10,000 will actually come to trial; the rest will be settled out of court through compromises arranged between the opposing parties. In criminal cases the percentage of out-of-court dispositions is even higher. Ninety-five per cent of these cases never come to trial at all—either for lack of evidence, or because the accused party pleads guilty and thus obviates the necessity of a trial. With so many cases settled out of court, only a small fraction of adult Americans—fewer than 6 per cent over a five-year period—are called for jury duty, and only 8 per cent become involved in court procedures as either litigants or witnesses. As a result, when people do go to court, they are likely to be overawed or even frightened by the prospect.

Elsewhere in this book you have learned of the many different

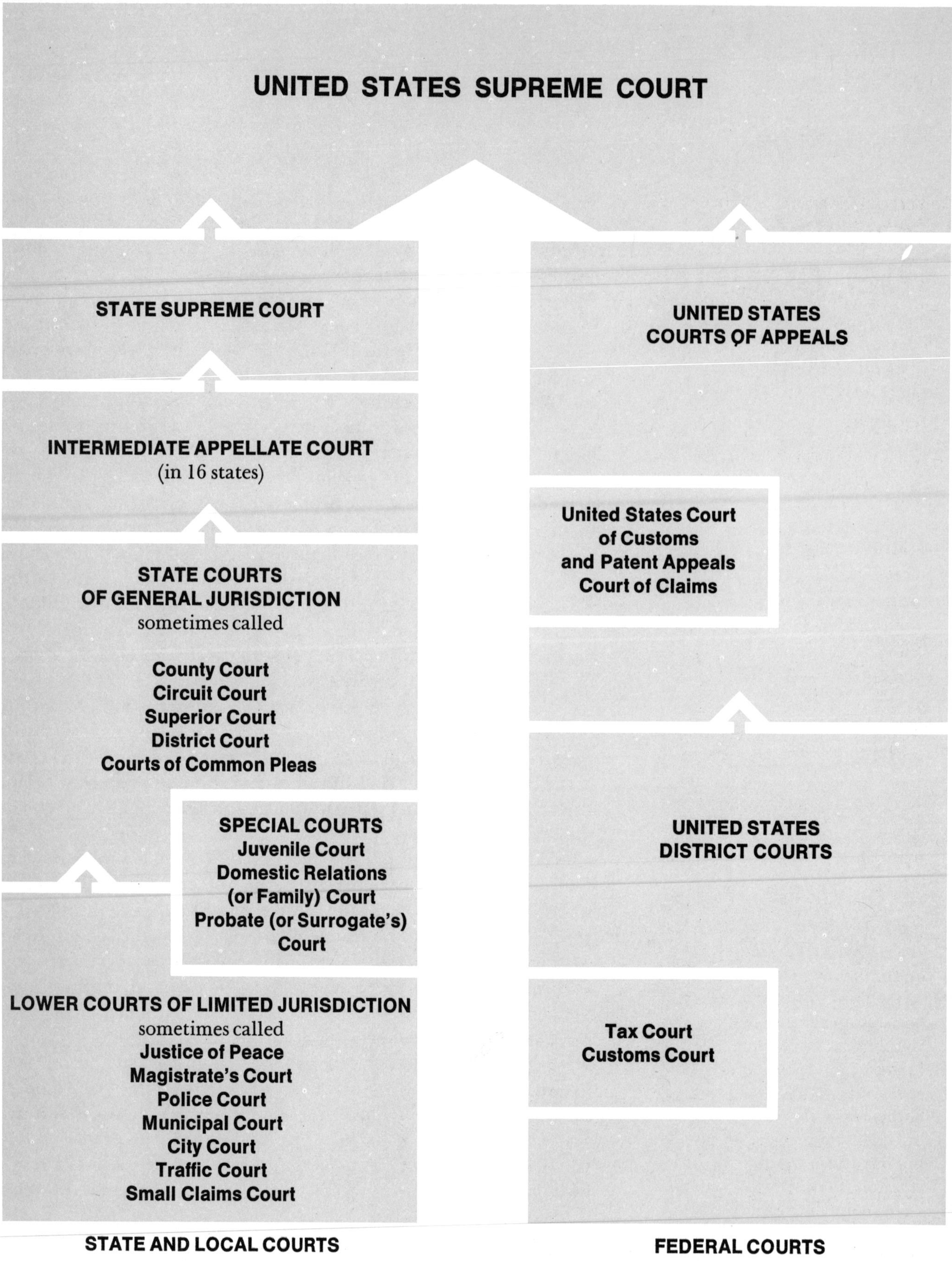

UNITED STATES SUPREME COURT

STATE SUPREME COURT

INTERMEDIATE APPELLATE COURT
(in 16 states)

STATE COURTS
OF GENERAL JURISDICTION
sometimes called

County Court
Circuit Court
Superior Court
District Court
Courts of Common Pleas

SPECIAL COURTS
Juvenile Court
Domestic Relations
(or Family) Court
Probate (or Surrogate's)
Court

LOWER COURTS OF LIMITED JURISDICTION
sometimes called
Justice of Peace
Magistrate's Court
Police Court
Municipal Court
City Court
Traffic Court
Small Claims Court

UNITED STATES
COURTS OF APPEALS

United States Court
of Customs
and Patent Appeals
Court of Claims

UNITED STATES
DISTRICT COURTS

Tax Court
Customs Court

STATE AND LOCAL COURTS   **FEDERAL COURTS**

kinds of legal situations that could require your presence in court, whether as a complainant, a witness or a member of a jury. This knowledge would be incomplete without an understanding of the complex American court system, which transforms legal problems into cases and then converts these cases, by means of hearings and trials, into specific judgments and sentences. No brief description can provide complete understanding, for there are 52 court systems in the United States (50 state systems, the District of Columbia system and the federal system), and none is exactly like another. However, to a large extent each state has tended to copy the others' procedural rules with a few changes; what is stated here is therefore probably true of the state you live in. But there are always exceptions.

MAKING SENSE OF THE COURTS

The chart *(at left)* shows you at a glance how the courts of the land are organized into two parallel systems—one made up of state courts, one of federal—and how each system is constructed pyramid-fashion. The lower courts of limited jurisdiction at the base take up the minor cases; a second layer of trial courts of general jurisdiction on top of this base handles more important or more complicated cases. The third level, topped by the U.S. Supreme Court, consists of appellate courts that listen to appeals sent up from the lower courts. Appeals

A pyramid of courts

The court system in the United States is similar to a pyramid —each level more powerful than the one beneath it. The United States Supreme Court is alone at the top, but the lower courts are set up in two independent but related series, one ruling on state laws, the other on federal. A case may enter the system at any of several levels. If a question involves a state law, it might begin in one of the state's lower courts; but if it is one involving a federal issue, it may originate in U.S. District Court. Special courts have been set up to handle certain types of cases—juvenile lawbreaking, adoption and wills in the state system; patent and import disputes in the federal system. A decision reached in any of these courts may be reviewed by the next higher court. The state Supreme Court (the name by which the top court is known in all but eight states) makes the final decision on matters of state law, but its rulings may be appealed to the federal courts. A civil rights case, for example, might be appealed through state courts, then —on a point of constitutional law—be taken to the U.S. Supreme Court. That body pronounces the last word, final until the law is changed by Congress— or the Court itself reverses its decision.

generally arise because the loser of a case in one of the lower courts believes that the decision reached against him was an inconsistent one —it was contrary to other decisions in similar cases reached by other lower courts in the same jurisdiction. He therefore wants the appeals court to settle, to his advantage, the question that was raised by this seeming inconsistency. At the pinnacle of the entire system, looming over both state and federal courts, is the United States Supreme Court. The Supreme Court reviews decisions that are arrived at in the state courts if the case involves a possible violation of the U.S. Constitution. Its power over the federal courts is even greater, for it can review cases in which any federal law is involved as well as all cases that in any way turn on an interpretation of the U.S. Constitution.

To see in closer detail how a typical system of state courts works, let us take a look at a town located 20 miles outside of Philadelphia: Norristown, Pennsylvania, a city that has a population of some 40,000 people and is the county seat of Montgomery County. The lowest court in Norristown—a state court of limited jurisdiction that handles routine police cases involving most misdemeanors, traffic violations and other violations of municipal ordinances—goes by the name of the District Justice Court. This court also hears civil cases involving small claims; the monetary limit on the cases it handles is $500. Like other courts of limited jurisdiction across the country, it has no provision for jury trials and is presided over by a justice who may or may not be a trained lawyer.

Norristown also has a court on the next-higher level of the judicial pyramid, a state court of general jurisdiction, which is called the Court of Common Pleas. Actually this court is divided into three separate parts. The Civil Court handles all cases of injury to persons and property, cases involving injunctions—a man might want to legally enjoin (that is, forbid) a neighbor from walking across his property, for example—divorce cases and also appeals from the lower District Justice Court. The second segment of the Court of Common Pleas, the Criminal Court, tries such serious cases as drunken driving, drug pushing and burglary. The third part, which is called Orphans Court (the name is an antique bit of Pennsylvania legal nomenclature), handles such domestic matters as adoption, guardianship and the administration of estates. All of the courtrooms of the three parts of the Court of Common Pleas are equipped with jury boxes so that cases may be decided by either a judge or a jury.

If a citizen of Norristown wishes to appeal a decision made in any of these courts to the next higher state tribunal, he has three courts available to him; the one that hears his appeal depends on the nature of the case he brings. There are two intermediate-level appellate courts in Pennsylvania. One, a seven-judge Commonwealth Court, sits in the state capital of Harrisburg and specializes in a certain class of cases, those involving zoning disputes or appeals from decisions that have been made by various state administrative agencies, such as the Public Utilities Commission. The other intermediate-level appellate court, called Superior Court, also has seven judges and sits successively, for a month or two at a time, in Philadelphia, Pittsburgh and Harrisburg. The Superior Court is essentially an appeals court, hearing appeals in both civil and criminal cases that have been through the lower state courts. Sitting above these two intermediate-level courts is the state Supreme Court, another seven-judge panel that also sits in Philadelphia, Pittsburgh and Harrisburg. It reviews cases in which questions of constitutional law come up, and it also hears second appeals—cases that have already been appealed once to one of the lower appellate courts—and first appeals on such grave matters as homicide.

Any citizen of Norristown—or any other town in any state—who finds himself involved in a federal case must bypass all of these state courts and appear in the federal court that serves his district. The state courts handle most of the legal controversies the average citizen is likely to face—such as a damage suit for negligence after an automobile accident, a dispute over the terms of a will, an action for divorce. All of these matters are governed by state law, not federal law. For the U.S. Constitution reserves to the individual states and their citizens the power to decide their own affairs. But there are also federal laws, and it is the province of the federal courts to enforce them. A citizen may become involved with the federal law in any number of ways —for example, by evading his federal income tax, by paying an employee less than the federal guaranteed minimum wage, by interfering with the U.S. mails or with interstate commerce, or by violating another citizen's civil rights.

The U.S. courts can also step in when citizens who are residents of two different states are engaged in a dispute that involves more than $10,000 in damages. Should a citizen living in Norristown, Pennsylvania, for example, be injured in an automobile accident outside Mobile, Alabama, and decide to sue the Alabama driver for $15,000 damages, the Pennsylvanian has the option of bypassing the state courts of both Alabama and Pennsylvania and filing what is known as a "diversity suit" (because the parties are citizens of two diverse states), thereby bringing what is normally a matter for the state courts before a federal court. This court is as close at hand as the nearest Federal Building. In the case of the citizen from Norristown finding a federal court would mean a 20-mile drive to Philadelphia, where a clerk at the local U.S. District Court would inform him of the proper procedures. As is often the case, however, the citizen from Norristown would do well to see his lawyer about the matter and let him decide what course to follow.

HOW TO USE THE COURTS

One of the blessings of the U.S. court system is that it is designed to be of maximum help to everyone. Although lawyers are always useful —and generally are essential—they are not always absolutely necessary. A citizen is permitted to serve as his own counsel. And most large cities have Small Claims Courts (illustrated box, page 287), in which minor civil suits are meant to be settled without a lawyer. The ceiling on the amount of money at stake in Small Claims Court is kept so low that it would not normally pay you to retain a lawyer to handle your case, and the procedures are so simple that any layman who is reasonably alert and self-contained can take care of himself. But there are exceptions even on this level. To see how it is possible to get in over your head in what seems at the start to be a fairly simple case, let us take a look, with a few necessary digressions, at the hypothetical case of a man named Mason.

Mason's problem began with a long-distance move of his home furnishings from one city to another, necessitated by a change in jobs. He retained a firm we might call Intercontinental Movers to transfer his household furnishings. He watched carefully as the men filled up the moving van with the piano, the beds, the crates marked "kitchen," "dining room" and "downstairs playroom." And he paid very special attention as they loaded two prized antique chairs that had been wedding presents from his in-laws. Then, three days later and hundreds of miles away, he watched again as the movers unloaded the van. The piano, beds, marked crates and even the bric-a-brac were intact. But the chairs were missing. Somehow, unaccountably, they had disappeared en route.

Mason wasted no time getting the local office of Intercontinental Movers on the phone and complaining about the loss of the chairs. The girl on the phone was sympathetic but she stalled him at first, claiming that the company would have a search made for the chairs. After several more days had gone by, he called Intercontinental again. A few minutes of conversation was enough to convince him that the movers had no idea what had happened to the chairs and that there was nothing left to do but file a claim for the loss.

"Those chairs were worth at least $500 each," he told the girl —who immediately switched the call to her supervisor. The supervisor took the matter very calmly. He agreed that the chairs seemed to have been lost. But he informed Mason with cool detachment that Intercontinental had no intention of paying him $1,000. Moreover, the supervisor reminded him, Intercontinental had a stated policy —which was written into all their contracts, including the one Mason had signed—limiting its responsibility for any items it moved to "60 cents per pound per article."

"We've checked with the men who moved you," the supervisor went on. "They say those chairs could not have weighed more than 50 pounds each. That means a total weight of 100 pounds and a total responsibility of $60. We'll settle for that—$60."

"The devil you will!" exclaimed Mason. "Those chairs were worth $1,000 when I turned them over to you. You lost them. And I expect the loss to be repaid—at full value. I'll sue you." And he slammed down the phone.

Bringing a suit

The first thing Mason did after that was look for his copy of the contract he had signed with Intercontinental. Sure enough, there was the fateful clause limiting the company's liability to 60 cents per pound. And he knew that the movers had, if anything, overestimated the weight. But he could not accept the logic involved. Mason was no lawyer, but he was a stubborn type and he understood enough about the law of bailment *(Chapter 6)* to know that you cannot always be held to the fine print disclaimers—the kind that a parking lot, for example, includes on the back of your ticket, denying all responsibility for theft or damage while the car is in the lot. And to Mason the lost chairs seemed another example of bailment. He had entrusted his property to Intercontinental. The property was valuable. He was certain, whatever the fine print said, that he had a case.

But Mason was not certain enough of winning his case to rush out to hire a lawyer. For one thing, he did not yet know a lawyer in his new community. Even if he had known whom to go to, the lawyer might charge him $100 to take even this simple case into court. A fair amount of work and time would be involved. If he lost and had to accept the $60, he would be out $40. So he decided to try another tack. He had heard about Small Claims Courts and how easy it was to handle your own case in one of them, so at his first opportunity he dropped by the local courthouse, sought out the clerk of the local court handling small claims and stated his problem. When he got to the part about wanting to sue Intercontinental for $1,000, however, the clerk cut him off and explained that the Small Claims Court's ceiling was $300. However, the clerk suggested Mason could take his suit to the local court of limited jurisdiction, which entertained claims up to $2,500. Even there he could argue his own case, without a lawyer.

"What is that court called?" asked Mason, who knew that in other cities where he had lived previously the Court of Limited Jurisdiction went by all kinds of names: Municipal Court, Magistrate's Court, Justice of the Peace Court.

"General Sessions," the clerk answered. "You'll find the clerk you want to talk to in room 202."

Mason thanked him and went looking for room 202, still determined to seek legal redress for the loss he had suffered.

If you ever happen to have a problem similar to Mason's, you should know that in some cities that have no Small Claims Court, the local court of limited jurisdiction is frequently used as a substitute by people who have fairly minor cases to try. Because the monetary ceilings are higher in these courts, the court costs are also likely to be higher and the procedures that must be followed are usually not so casual as they are in a Small Claims Court. But you can do much of the spadework, if you wish, over the telephone. You should begin by checking the telephone listings for the clerk's office, which will be found in the "courts" section of the county or city government's listings. If you see a listing for a Justice of the Peace Court, General Sessions Court, Municipal, City, Magistrate's or Mayor's Court, you are likely to be on the right track. A call to the clerk's office will probably put you in touch with an assistant who can help you to process your claim with a minimum of technicalities. From this call you should be able to learn where you must go and what you should bring along with you when you come to file your claim—such as the defendant's address, a check or cash to cover the filing fees, the dates of the transactions that led to the suit, and similar information.

Though the cost of filing a case in such a court will be higher than the filing fee for a Small Claims Court, usually it is not an excessive sum. In many localities you can file a suit, have the necessary legal papers served on the defendant (or defendants) to notify him of the action that is being brought against him and have your day in court for as little as $20. The cost will go up if any of the defendants happen to live outside the court's jurisdiction. Most courts charge a set fee for the various steps that are taken in a case—the delivery of notification to the defendants, the formal request that a case be placed on the calendar, the issuing of a subpoena to require a witness to ap-

One of the most useful courts in the entire U.S. judicial system is the Small Claims Court found in most large cities. Established to hear cases involving relatively modest sums of money, these courts make the procedure simple. Here is how a typical Small Claims Court case would proceed.

1 Suppose a dry cleaner burns a hole in your brand-new pair of $30 trousers but offers to pay you only $10 for the damage done.

2 If you decide to sue for the full value of the trousers, check the phone book for the Small Claims Court address and go there.

3 For a small fee the court clerk gives you the forms you need to fill out. One may be the complaint, in which you provide a brief factual description of your grievance. The clerk will often help you compose it.

4 The clerk might assign you a trial date immediately. He will arrange to serve the dry cleaner with a summons informing him of your suit against him and ordering him to appear. If the assigned trial date is inconvenient, you may ask to have it changed. The same option of postponement is open to the dry cleaner.

5 On the day of the trial you and the dry cleaner will appear at the Small Claims Court and present the facts to a judge. No lawyers are present and the discussion of the case is informal and in layman's language, bypassing many of the rules and conventions of normal courtroom procedure. The judge ordinarily wears a business suit instead of a judicial robe, and he is likely to sit at a desk rather than on a platform. The judge will probably decide the case on the spot, but he may prefer to reserve decision for a day or two. In that event you will probably have to call the court clerk to learn the verdict.

pear. When these actions involve travel or the serving of a paper in another locality, the filing fee goes up accordingly.

Another circumstance that raises fees occasionally is the practice, followed in some communities, of using the lower courts as revenue-raising agencies. Naturally such a practice leads to increased fees. It is well to ask about the costs at the time of your initial conversation with the clerk, for they may amount to more than bringing your case to court is worth. Of course, if you think you have an ironclad case and are certain to win, you can assume that these costs will be tacked onto the final judgment against the defendant—and you will eventually get them all back except for your own attorney's fee. If you lose, you must usually pay the court costs—but not any attorney's fee or other litigation costs that were incurred by the defendant.

SERVING THE SUMMONS

When Mason came to file his suit against Intercontinental Movers, the clerk informed him that the total cost of putting his case on the court calendar would be about $23. The next step was to set the judicial process in motion. There are several ways of starting legal action, but all of them are in effect announcements of an intention to sue. In the vast majority of cases the intention to sue is announced by the legal document known as a summons. It is usually accompanied by another document, a written complaint setting out the facts that the plaintiff claims give him a cause for action against the defendant. The summons lists the defendant's correct name and address, and commands him to answer the suit in court. In some state courts this form will be signed by the court clerk. In some lower courts, especially Small Claims Courts, both complaint and summons are contained in a single document; you can file your suit simply by filling in the blanks. You must write down enough of the facts and allegations in your case to demonstrate that you do in fact "have a case"—that is, the court would have enough to go on to rule you the winner provided you proved your facts and allegations to be true. Generally the court clerk can tell you if you have written down enough to fulfill this requirement. Usually he will add to the summons a date when the defendant must "appear"—in reality, file an answer to the suit.

Because a defendant loses his case by default if he does not answer the summons, the law has traditionally gone to great pains to make sure that he actually receives his summons. In time past a process server, who was usually a deputy sheriff, delivered the summons to the defendant in person, placed it in his hands—and sometimes even read it to him for good measure. The little ritual produced some

No. 208. Summons—Small Claims Court.   Published by Eau Claire Book & Stationery Co.

State of Wisconsin   **County Court**   **County**

COURT HOUSE   ——————, Wisconsin

————————

————————

Plaintiff and Address

vs.   SUMMONS
                                SMALL CLAIMS BRANCH
————————

Defendant and Address

THE STATE OF WISCONSIN, to the said defendant; (and each of them:)

You are hereby summoned to appear and plead to the plaintiff's complaint in the above named Court

at its Court Room in the Court House of ——————County, in the City of——————

on the——————day of——————, A. D., 19——, at 9:30 o'clock A.M. A

copy of the complaint is hereto attached. In case of your failure to appear and to plead, a judgment may

be rendered against you in accordance with the demand made by the plaintiff. The nature of the demand

being made upon you is:

————————————————

————————————————

————————————————

(State in terms of Section 299.01)

and the amount of damages, if any, demanded is $————————

Dated this——————day of——————, A. D., 19——

————————————

Clerk of County Court, ——————County, Wis.

By——————
                                              Deputy

Plaintiff's P. O. Address:

————————

————————

Plaintiff's Attorney (if any).

————————
(Name)

————————
(P. O. Address)

Defendant's P. O. Address:

————————

A summons to court

A summons like the one at left is, in most states, the initial step in setting the wheels of justice in motion. A completed summons lists both parties and commands the defendant to appear in court—in this case a Small Claims Court in which citizens present their cases without the aid of a lawyer. On a Small Claims summons, space is provided for filling in the "demand"—the nature of the court action being taken. The specific list of charges is attached to it.

amusing scenes. In efforts to avoid being served, people would jam their hands in their pockets to avoid touching the paper or clap them over their ears to avoid hearing it read. Process servers for their part were given unusual liberties. Short of forcible entry, they were permitted to gain access to the defendant by whatever way seemed best. They would crawl through open windows or trick people into opening their doors by posing as policemen, delivery boys or Western Union messengers.

Nowadays process serving is not quite such a Keystone Kops affair. It may be sufficient to leave a copy of the summons with any responsible adult who lives in the defendant's home or, in many circumstances, simply to send it to him by mail. But this relaxed approach sometimes misfires with harsh and tragic results. Almost any day in any city court there is bound to be at least one wide-eyed man waving a notice of a court-ordered claim to part of his salary and protesting, "But I never even knew I was being sued!" Often the protest is made in imperfect English, suggesting that the man may not have understood the summons. But some unfortunate defendants will truly never have been notified, either through error or through a particularly unscrupulous racket—perpetrated most often against the urban poor—called "sewer service."

Sewer service simply means that a man who has been hired to be a process server takes his fee—and then just throws the summons down a sewer grating. He claims, of course, to have delivered the summons and even signs an affidavit to that effect. On the basis of his affidavit the sheriff's office "certifies" to the court that the summons has indeed been delivered. Thereafter the defendant is said to be "before" the court, with full responsibility for answering the summons and defending his own interests. When he fails to do so, the judgment automatically goes against him. What these victims seldom know, and what harassed court officials seldom tell them, is that they actually have legal relief for their plight. They can sue the process server—or the process-serving agency he works for—for damages suffered because they were not properly served. Further, since the process server has signed an affidavit swearing that each summons was served, he can be prosecuted for perjury.

Responding to a summons

The experience of being at the opposite end of the summons-issuing process is understandably an alarming one to many people. It can come as something of a shock to be handed an ominously formal document entitled SUMMONS by a total stranger—especially if you read the fine print of the legal prose and find a notice that says you are "to appear in person or by attorney at the next term of the Circuit Court, to be held for said County at the courthouse thereof on the first day of October"—and October 1 has already come and gone! Do not be alarmed. Many courts still follow an archaic and confusing custom of dating all summonses with the first date of the court term, regardless of when each summons actually goes into effect. Even if the summons ordering you to appear on October 1 does not arrive until mid-October, you probably have four or five weeks' grace in which to answer it. A call to the court clerk will give you the approximate date of the trial in which you are to be involved. Then you—or your lawyer—should keep checking to find out the exact date. The court clerk can tell you how these dates are announced.

If the summons concerns a matter such as extensive damages in an automobile accident, you should notify your lawyer or your automobile insurance company immediately. Often that telephone call will be the last you will hear of the matter, for the vast majority of such cases are settled out of court in private negotiations. But for your own protection, you should keep in touch with the course of the negotiations—especially if the amount of the claim exceeds the amount of your insurance policy and if there is any likelihood at all that you will be held liable for the damages. For then you could end up with a sizable debt on your hands.

When the summons involves a minor matter, however, such as an unpaid plumber's bill or a suit that has been brought by an irate neighbor for damage done by your children to her prized shrubbery, expert legal advice is not always necessary. In the first place, the summons indicates that the unpaid plumber's bill has probably been turned over to a debt-collecting agency, and the standard strategy of such agencies consists of a loud bark but very little bite. Often they will issue summonses with no intention of suing; the action is simply an attempt to pressure you. If you have failed to pay the plumber's bill because his workmanship was shoddy, and you are absolutely positive you can prove your case in court, tell the people at the collection agency; they will probably stop bothering you.

As for the irate neighbor with the ruined shrubbery, such matters are often handled best by a little direct diplomacy. Perhaps the suit was filed more out of quick anger and hurt feelings than out of any desire to recover money for the lost shrubbery. It is also possible that the neighbor does not really understand the extent of your liability—in most states parents ordinarily cannot be held responsible for damage caused by their children *(Chapter 3)*. Instead of preparing to fight it out, you might visit the neighbor and offer to replace some of her most badly damaged plants. Such an offer in no way jeopardizes your own case if the matter does go to trial, and if she accepts your offer you have avoided an embittering legal confrontation.

While you are conducting these negotiations, however, you should at the same time answer the summons. Determine the approximate trial date, and if it is inconvenient for you—remember, you are still negotiating—ask for a postponement. Generally the court clerk will oblige. Failing to respond to a summons or to appear on the appointed day means, as we have seen, that the judge will hear only the plaintiff's side of things and will automatically award a default judgment in his favor. Though this judgment may be set aside, the excuse offered for nonappearance must be a very good one indeed and the appeal itself must be presented within a fixed time limit. After that date, there is nothing for you to do but pay up.

Suits that reach across state lines

One thing you will discover if, like Mr. Mason, you are the complainant in the matter, is that you need not necessarily sue the defendant in a court that is near where he lives or works. The law used to hold that if the defendant lived in another state or county you had to go there to sue him—or else arrange with a lawyer who practiced in that distant jurisdiction to represent you. But this tradition has gradually been eroded. In recent years, as people have tended to move frequently from one part of the country to another, many of the state legislatures have passed "long arm" statutes that extend the authority of local courts to hear cases against defendants in other areas. As a result, a company or individual with an address in another jurisdiction can normally be sued simply by sending him a copy of the summons by registered mail and notifying the secretary of state in his home state of the suit.

Mason did not face this particular problem and did not need to invoke a long arm statute. Intercontinental Movers had a local office and there was no question of jurisdiction. But it did occur to Mason that the firm, like many moving companies, might be part of a larger interstate combine and that there could be a parent company somewhere. He knew that this parent firm ought to be brought into the suit in order to improve his chances of collecting the court award if he should win his suit. Sure enough, when Mason looked back over the contract and invoice forms he had received from Intercontinental Movers, he saw that it was an affiliate of an out-of-state corporation that called itself simply Intercontinental, Inc.

If Mason had not discovered this fact on his own, it would have been easy for him to find out. For every local office of an out-of-state corporation must list the name and address of its parent company on a roster kept in the state capital by the office of the secretary of state. A letter or phone call to this office would have elicited the information Mason needed and thus enabled him to sue the two firms jointly for the loss of his two chairs.

THE CASE GOES TO COURT

There was no such thing as sewer service in the case of *Mason* v. *Intercontinental Movers and Intercontinental, Inc.* Both firms received their copies of the summons and the complaint promptly, and a local law firm that represented the affiliate was instructed to handle their case when it came up in court.

Mason appeared in the General Sessions courtroom early on the appointed morning and found the scene much less menacing than he had expected. The courtroom was a fairly small place with a raised bench for the judge, but with no jury box or any of the other paraphernalia associated with the courtroom scenes that he had seen so often on television. Promptly at 9 o'clock the judge entered, wearing an ordinary business suit, and took his seat. A clerk began to read the list of cases that were set for disposition that day and, as each case was called, waited for a response. Sometimes the defendants asked that their cases be postponed; often there was no response at all and then the judge called out crisply, "Default." Most of the default judgments were for unpaid bills against which the absent defendants presumably felt they had no defense.

By the time the clerk got to *Mason* v. *Intercontinental Movers and Intercontinental, Inc.*, a number of other cases had been called, so Mason knew what was expected of him. He stood up and said, "The plaintiff is ready." Then, from the lawyers' part of the courtroom, a young, conservatively dressed man rose and said, "The defendants are ready, Your Honor. Mason was momentarily flustered by the fact that he would be contending with an experienced lawyer. But there was nothing to do about it now except take a deep breath and plunge ahead. The judge motioned him to step to the plaintiff's table and told him to proceed with his story. First, a courtroom attendant stepped forward with a Bible, and with his left hand on it and his right hand raised, Mason swore to tell "the whole truth and nothing but the truth, so help me God."

Mason explained that he had chosen Intercontinental Movers to move his furniture by looking in the Yellow Pages of the telephone directory, and he showed the judge a copy of the invoice that Intercontinental had given him when it picked up his furniture; the two chairs were listed on it. Passing the invoice to a clerk, the judge ordered him to label it "Plaintiff's Exhibit One." Then Mason explained that the chairs had been missing when the furniture was unloaded, and he handed the judge a duplicate copy of the invoice, showing that all items had been checked off as delivered except the two chairs. This was marked "Plaintiff's Exhibit Two."

Mason went on to describe the two chairs as wedding gifts from his wife's parents, and he quoted his mother-in-law as saying that the chairs were "genuine antiques" and must have cost "at least $500 each when they were bought."

An objection sustained

At this point, the young lawyer for the defendants rose to interrupt Mason's presentation. "I object, Your Honor," he said; "that is hearsay evidence and as such is inadmissible in this case."

The judge sustained the objection of the defendants' lawyer —hearsay is inadmissible because the source of the information cannot be cross-examined. Mason could introduce into evidence only such facts as he could prove from his own personal experience. Thus barred from using his mother-in-law's evaluation of the lost chairs, Mason did his best to produce his own. He explained that his wife's parents were in the habit of furnishing their home in the best of style, that the two chairs were special favorites of theirs, and that they had parted with them only because they wished their daughter to have something fine in her new home. He described the chairs in some detail —their material, their delicate workmanship and their excellent condition—and stated that in his judgment they were worth at least $500 each when they disappeared. "That is my case, Your Honor," he said in conclusion.

Rising to cross-examine Mason, the lawyer for the defendants began with a question that Mason had anticipated. "Since you seem to be an expert on such matters, Mr. Mason, how much would you say each chair weighed?"

"I never weighed them," Mason replied.

"Well, I can introduce some expert opinion on that point, if necessary, from the men who moved them. They say that such delicate chairs could not have weighed more than 50 pounds each. We are prepared to accept that figure. Are you, sir?"

Mason hesitated for a moment and then answered that 50 pounds, or a total of 100, was probably right.

"In that case, Your Honor, I ask the clerk to pass 'Plaintiff's Exhibit One' back to Mr. Mason and ask him to read aloud for us Paragraph 3(a) on the back of the agreed-upon contract."

Mason took the contract, looked for the paragraph and read it slowly: "The limit of the Mover's financial responsibility is 60 cents per pound per article, unless otherwise agreed upon in writing by all parties concerned."

"And was there any such agreement between you and Intercontinental Movers that was contrary to that paragraph, Mr. Mason?" the lawyer asked.

"No," Mason answered.

"Thank you," the attorney said, and rested his case.

The judge then asked for closing arguments. It was Mason's turn first. He made the point that although he had indeed signed the contract, he felt he should not be bound by such patently unreasonable provisions as those that were contained in the fine print of Paragraph 3(a), particularly since somewhat similar ones in parking-lot tickets had been declared invalid. "I do not see how a responsible firm can lose a customer's valuable property and then escape all liability for that loss by hiding behind such an unfair and dishonest provision," he said. "I ask Your Honor to force the defendants to make full restitution of the valuable property they have admittedly lost."

Then it was the lawyer's turn to make his closing argument. "I submit, Your Honor," he said, "that Paragraph 3(a) is a standard provision that has been approved by no less a body than the Interstate Commerce Commission, which, as Your Honor knows, is charged with monitoring the activities of firms such as those I represent." The lawyer then went on to cite two other cases in which the state appellate courts had enforced the 60-cent limitation, thus establishing a legal precedent. And he asked for a judgment based on this formula for Mason's pair of 50-pound chairs.

The judge sat in silence for a moment, considering the arguments. Then he turned to Mason and explained that although he had demonstrated to a certain degree the value of his property, he had also signed the invoice—and that his signature thereto bound him to its terms, whether he now agreed with them or not. "Judgment for the plaintiff for $60," he ruled. "Call the next case."

THE NEXT STEP: A COURT OF GENERAL JURISDICTION

Mason felt both chagrined and let down by the decision. But, being a stubborn man when principles were at stake, he felt all the more determined to challenge the idea that he should have to accept only $60 for a $1,000 loss. He decided to appeal his case to the next judicial level —but this time with a lawyer to represent him.

Because he was a stranger in town, it took him a few days to locate an attorney *(Chapter 2)*. The lawyer explained that in some states appeals from the lower courts of limited jurisdiction can only be made directly to the appellate courts, and that in such cases the judges will make their decisions solely on the basis of a summary or transcript of the original trial. An appeal in such cases can be successful only if the appellate court finds that the original judge made a legal error in deciding or disposing of the case. There can be no appeal based on the actual facts of the matter. In Mason's new state, however—as in many states—the law provides that a plaintiff who is dissatisfied with a decision reached in a court of limited jurisdiction has the right to ask for a completely new trial in a trial court of general jurisdiction, the next level up on the court pyramid, and to present his case all over again, from scratch.

In any community, the trial court of general jurisdiction is that community's basic, all-purpose court. It hears all major legal controversies and rules on them either through a jury or solely through the decision of a judge. It may be the only court in town in which a jury ever sits. Because a detailed transcript is kept of all testimony for possible later appeals, the lawyers are likely to rise and interpose more objections than in the lower courts, in order to get their arguments on

A jury does not always hear everything. If a dispute arises over whether evidence is admissible, the judge may engage in whispered discussion with the lawyers to settle the matter out of the jury's hearing, so the jurors will not be influenced by evidence that might be inadmissible.

the record. And the presence of a jury adds to the adversary atmosphere. The lawyers are more likely to engage in histrionics in order to impress the jury than they would if a judge were deciding a case alone. A jury also complicates trial procedures to a certain extent. When there is a dispute between the opposing lawyers over whether certain evidence is admissible or inadmissible, the jury may be sent from the courtroom or the judge may occasionally engage in whispered conversations with the lawyers at the bench to settle the matter out of the jury's hearing.

All of this drama is important. In a criminal case a defendant's freedom may be at stake. In a civil case, a large suit for damages may be the issue. The outcome of either type of case depends to a large extent on several interacting factors: on whether the judge or jury has been presented adequate and convincing information on which to base a decision; on how correctly the judge controls the admissibility of the evidence; and if there is a jury, on how astutely the judge instructs its members about the questions of law that are involved. If the judge makes any serious errors along the way, they will show up in the transcript, and they could be the basis for overthrowing the decision if the case is appealed.

A man bound for vacation may still be required to serve as a juror when so ordered by a summons, but judges sometimes grant postponements in such circumstances. And a married woman with young children to care for may be excused from jury service entirely.

The job of the juror

But the jury has a heavy responsibility, too. There are few duties of citizenship that are more important than serving, and those who are called are not excused without a good reason, such as a mother's need to care for small children. The U.S. system of selecting a jury long favored people from the business or professional classes. To serve on a

HOW TO BEHAVE AS A JUROR

Serving on a jury to help decide the guilt or innocence of a fellow citizen is one of the most important civic duties you can perform. To ensure that your verdict is fair and impartial, rules such as the ones outlined in this check list regulate what you may and may not do during the trial; violating them may be considered contempt of court.

1 You must listen carefully to the evidence presented by both sides so that you can remember it when you and the other jurors consider it. You are not allowed to take notes since your notes could be incorrect and therefore might be prejudiced. But if you find that you have forgotten certain facts you need when you reach the jury room, an official transcript of the court proceedings may sometimes be read to you.

2 You cannot search out evidence on your own—say, for example, by making a visit to a scene that is connected with the case on trial. The facts that you might discover during your visit—or think that you discovered there—may have no bearing on the case, and your visit could easily result in a biased judgment. If the judge decides that it would be helpful for the members of the jury to view the scene with their own eyes, he will take the jury there himself.

3 During the trial you must not talk about the case with anyone, including the lawyers, your fellow jurors or even your family. The only time that you are permitted to discuss the case is during deliberations with other jurors in the jury room.

4 The judge will also admonish you to cut yourself off from newspaper, TV or radio accounts of the trial while it is in progress, because they could prejudice your judgment.

jury in many communities one had to be a respected, upstanding citizen, a person of "good moral character" and "good reputation."

The jury lists were compiled from the membership rosters of church groups and fraternal organizations, or from among the friends of the commission that drew up the lists. In many Southern communities, black people were excluded from jury service entirely until the U.S. Supreme Court began overturning convictions that had been reached by all-white panels. But the effort to assure more representative juries is being frustrated at least partly by economic factors that affect poor people most. In many states anyone for whom jury service would pose a financial hardship can be excused—and jury pay is notoriously low. In Mississippi it is only $8 a day. It is not uncommon for juries in some communities to be made up entirely of nonworking middle-class housewives who do not lose out financially by spending their days in a courtroom.

Serving on a jury

Notice of jury service usually arrives by mail in the form of a summons, ordering the recipient to report to the jury room of the courthouse on a particular date. If you are called, be sure to take plenty of reading matter or handwork. The most frequent complaint about jury duty is that there is too much waiting. Each day a certain number of prospective jurors are picked by lot to serve on the cases beginning that day. You may have to report each morning for a week or more before your name finally comes up. When it does, you will be sent to the jury box of a particular courtroom, where the judge and the opposing lawyers who are preparing to try a case will question you in what is called a *voir dire* examination (Old French for "to say the truth"). The purpose of their questioning, which may be pointed, is to expose anything about you, your beliefs or character that might prejudice your judgment in the case about to be tried. If you are personally acquainted with either litigant or have some connection with the lawyers or with the issues in the case, you will undoubtedly be dismissed "for cause." You may also be dismissed for no cause at all by one of the lawyers, each of whom is entitled to a certain number of "peremptory challenges"—for which he is required to give no reason. He may simply not like the fact that you do not belong to the country club and his client does. That difference in itself, he might feel, could lead you to prejudge his client.

If you are seated as a juror, certain behavior will be expected of you *(check list for jurors, opposite)*. You must listen attentively as the witnesses testify, but you will not be permitted to take notes, for they might be inaccurate or biased. A transcript of the entire proceedings will sometimes be furnished to you in the jury room if you need to refresh your memory. Neither will you be permitted to question the witnesses directly, although you may, if you think a crucial question has been left unanswered, pass a note to that effect to the judge. If he thinks the question is proper, he will ask it so that the jury can learn the necessary facts.

Except in cases where jurors might be influenced by reports of the case in the news media, jurors are not locked up at night. Most jurors come and go at the end of the day in the world of ordinary men. As a result, care must be taken not to compromise the jury's integrity. The law is very strict on this score. A juror is forbidden to discuss the case with anyone—not with the lawyers, not with members of his family, not even with other jurors. He may not read newspaper accounts of the case or listen to reports of it on television or radio. Neither may he play amateur detective and visit any scenes involved in the case in an attempt to uncover evidence on his own initiative. Any juror who breaks these rules could be charged with contempt of court and suffer the consequences. A Chicago judge once sentenced a juror to three years in prison for contempt in a case involving the sale of the drug Krebiozen as a cure for cancer. The juror was discovered to have read an article on the drug, watched a film on it at a union convention and discussed the subject with the jury foreman—who reported him. Though an appeal reduced his sentence, the juror was still packed off to prison for 18 months—the most severe punishment ever meted out in such a case by an American court.

After a jury has heard all of the testimony in a case and has listened to the lawyers' closing arguments, it is "charged" by the judge to reach a verdict. It then retires to the jury room. In his charge, the judge will explain the legal points that are at issue in the case, and he may in a subtle way "appoint" the jury foreman by ordering the bailiff to hand the case file to a specific juror. If he does not, the foreman may be elected by the other jurors or he may simply be the juror who sat in the No. 1 chair in the jury box—these practices differ from court to court.

The jury room is usually an antechamber sparsely furnished with an oblong table, 12 chairs and two doors marked "Ladies" and "Gentlemen." Once within it, the jury behaves much more informally than it did in the box. The deliberations generally start with a discussion in which the case is reviewed and each juror expresses his view of the matter. Then there will be a vote—sometimes secret, sometimes not. Unanimity is required in most states. If the result is not unanimous, there will be more discussions, followed by still more votes. Usually these later votes will not be secret so that the jurors can direct their arguments to the holdouts on the panel. One of the extraordinary things about jury duty is that the holdouts need not bow to the will of the majority. If it is a question of conscience or your own sense of reason, you have the right, and the obligation, to vote "No" while all the other 11 jurors vote "Yes"—until you have worked out your doubts. If you cannot work them out, the foreman will report that the jury is hopelessly deadlocked, the judge will declare a mistrial, and the entire trial procedure will begin all over again with a new jury.

Judge or jury?

Mason assumed, as he began to imagine what would happen in the courtroom when his case against the movers was retried, that there would be a jury of sympathetic listeners to hear the evidence and arrive at the decision. And after the experience he had had with the judge in the lower court, he rather hoped there would be, for he felt they might be likely to accept his view of the case.

Either side can demand a trial by jury, but it has traditionally been plaintiffs in civil cases and defendants in criminal cases that have requested a jury. In civil cases, in the past at least, the reasoning seems

A juror in a criminal trial does not have to bow to the will of the majority during the deliberations in the jury room. If everybody except you votes thumbs down, you must stand your ground; the foreman will report that the jury cannot reach a verdict.

to have been that an ordinary citizen—especially when he is a plaintiff suing a corporation for damages—would probably find more generous treatment at the hands of a group of fellow citizens than from a judge who may once have represented corporation interests himself as a practicing lawyer. Defendants in criminal cases, on the other hand, have tended to feel that a group of their peers would be more sympathetic to people who found themselves in trouble with the law than would a judge who over the years had grown rather accustomed to meting out punishment.

Such generalizations are no longer accurate. Defendants in criminal cases have come to realize that an experienced judge may be more lenient than a jury of citizens who have become increasingly fearful of crime in the streets. And plaintiffs in civil cases often forego jury trials because such a trial normally lasts longer—and therefore costs more, both in lawyer's fees and court costs—than one in which a judge renders his own decision.

This reasoning led Mason's lawyer to advise against a jury trial. At the lawyer's insistence, Mason had accumulated some additional evidence concerning the actual value of the two chairs that had been lost. The lawyer felt, therefore, that it should now be easy to convince either a judge or a jury of that fact. It would also be fairly easy to pin down Intercontinental Movers' responsibility for the loss. The only really difficult issue at stake was one of law: Could Mason be forced to accept the 60-cent limitation on the loss? Since that question depended on the interpretation of various legal points and precedents, a judge would have to rule on it anyway.

Mason agreed to a trial before a judge. His lawyer then went about the task of arranging an approximate date for the trial with the clerk of the court of general jurisdiction. He had to send out a new batch of summonses and complaints to advise the defendant companies of the coming trial, and he also had to prepare the two witnesses that he had decided to use to back up Mason's own testimony. These witnesses were Mason's wife, who would testify about the fine condition of the chairs at the time of their loss, and Mason's mother-in-law, who had volunteered to appear and bring with her the original receipt for the chairs, proving that their total value at the time of purchase was indeed $1,000.

The subpoena

While waiting for the trial date, Mason's lawyer took the additional precaution of issuing subpoenas to both Mason's wife and mother-in-law. He also asked them to drop by his office one day for a brief period of preparation, and during this visit he arranged to have sworn depositions taken of the same testimony that they intended to give when they were on the witness stand.

A subpoena is an order to appear in court as a witness at a specified time on a certain day. Sometimes it is labeled *Subpoena ad Testificandum* (subpoena to testify), which means that nothing more than your oral testimony is desired. If the subpoena is labeled *Subpoena Duces Tecum* (subpoena to produce documents), it means that you should have in your possession certain papers that the court will want to see as part of the evidence. Mason's mother-in-law had received a *Subpoena Duces Tecum* to indicate that she should not forget to bring with her the receipt for the chairs, which would be introduced into evidence.

Serving a subpoena on someone who you already know is willing to testify on your behalf may seem superfluous. But there are several good reasons for observing the ritual, even when the witness-to-be is as close to you as your wife or mother-in-law. For one thing, if a witness is subpoenaed but is unable to appear, the trial will be postponed. On the other hand, if no subpoena has been served and the witness does not appear, the trial will simply go on without his helpful testimony. A subpoena is also a protection for the witness. In some cases, for example, he could be required to give rather delicate information concerning a friend's health or marital life, or divulge some fact that would be damaging to a business associate. If this testimony is provided by a witness who is under subpoena, no one can accuse him of supplying the information voluntarily.

In most states a subpoena also entitles a witness to collect a standard fee at the conclusion of a trial—on presentation of the subpoena to a sheriff or marshal. Unless you are testifying as an expert in some aspect of the trial, this fee will not be princely. But such as it is, it is yours. Mississippi pays its witnesses $1.50 a day, plus five cents a mile in travel expenses. At the other end of the scale, the federal courts pay their witnesses $20 a day, plus 10 cents a mile for travel, plus $16 for each night the witness must remain away from home. Other jurisdictions fall somewhere in between. It is perfectly correct to ask for an advance on this fee, if you need it to get to the court. But you should never ask for more than the going rate, for that could be construed as soliciting a bribe.

To ignore a subpoena is to risk contempt of court. Should a genuine emergency arise that prevents you from appearing in court, such as a death in the family, you may call the lawyer who issued the subpoena or the clerk of the court and ask for a postponement or to be ex-

TIPS ON BEING A WITNESS

If you are called as a witness, the effectiveness of your testimony will be influenced by your appearance. The following check list will help you avoid some common mistakes that may damage your credibility.

1 Do not lose your temper when you are cross-examined. Testimony given by a cool, collected witness is more likely to impress the jury as truthful than an angry outburst that might distort the facts.

2 Do not appear inattentive. Answer questions in an alert manner—but after you have thought about what you are going to say. Once voiced, an incorrect answer is a matter of record. If you fail to understand a question, ask to have it explained. The judge will make certain that the questioning attorney makes it clear to you.

3 Do not attempt to sway the court with fancy clothes. An extravagant hat, a low-cut dress or a wild shirt generally creates an unfavorable impression. And a misguided attempt to indicate nonchalance by taking out a cigarette may get you thrown out of court.

4 Do not try to be anything but your normal self. Your testimony will carry more weight if it is presented sincerely. Speak up frankly, openly and politely.

5 Do not allow nervous mannerisms to distract the jury from the testimony you are giving. Avoid, for example, chewing gum or toying with a key chain.

6 Do not try to be funny when you are testifying on the witness stand. A trial is a serious affair, no place for witticisms, flippancy or cockiness. Attempts to draw laughs will do nothing to enhance your credibility as a witness, and they may injure the cause of the person for whom you are testifying.

7 Do not set out to show the lawyers that you are as smart as they are by anticipating their questions. It is almost always a mistake to amplify your answer. Answer only the questions asked, as briefly as possible.

cused. If your request is granted, be sure to get a confirmation of this change in writing—it is possible that your failure to appear could later be challenged.

Depositions

In addition to a subpoena—and sometimes instead of it—you may also receive a letter from one of the lawyers in the case, asking you to appear in his office to provide a "deposition." The lawyer for the opposing side will be present, to question you as he would if you were on the witness stand. The only difference between testifying in court and making a deposition is that usually no objections will be raised against hearsay—hearsay is deleted before the evidence reaches court.

You should not be lulled by the informality surrounding a deposition into believing that your testimony is less important than testimony given in court. You will be sworn in by a stenographer-reporter who is also a notary public, and an exact record will be kept of your testimony. This record will be at the opposing lawyer's elbow during the trial. Inconsistencies between the statements you made in the deposition and what you say at the trial will be used by the opposing lawyer to embarrass you and discredit your testimony. If you gave incorrect information, you can be accused of perjury.

In civil cases depositions carry out a legal process called discovery. Through depositions, each lawyer learns what evidence the opposition is planning to bring out in court. This advance knowledge often permits settlement out of court.

When the day of the trial comes and you are finally to be called to the witness stand, you will naturally want your testimony to express the facts in the most accurate and forceful manner possible. Every trial lawyer has wept inwardly over key witnesses whom he knew to be telling the truth, yet who failed to impress the judge or jury because they faltered. For this reason, lawyers often rehearse their witnesses until they are certain that they understand the kinds of questions they are likely to be asked and how these questions should be handled. If a jury is to be present, the lawyer may also give the witnesses tips on the proper etiquette of conducting themselves on the witness stand so they can make the best and most positive appearance (*check list for witnesses, opposite*).

A TRIAL IN THE COURT OF GENERAL JURISDICTION

Mason was much impressed as he entered the courtroom for the second trial. He sat down with his lawyer, wife and mother-in-law in a space reserved for those whose turn would soon come to appear, as ei-

THE CAST OF THE COURTROOM DRAMA

Real trials are seldom as pulsingly dramatic as the courtroom scenes presented on television, but they involve the same cast of characters, each of whom has a necessary role to play.

The first of these characters, reading clockwise from the left in the drawing below, is the court bailiff. His many duties involve the physical progress of the trial. It is he who opens the door for the judge and asks everyone present to rise when His Honor enters the courtroom. He also holds a Bible and swears in witnesses: "Do you swear to tell the truth, the whole truth and nothing but the truth. . . ." And he ejects unruly people if he is ordered to do so by the judge. The bailiff is a bit player in the drama, so to speak, but an important one.

The clerk manages the paper work. He (or she) hands the judge documents relating to the case, and catalogues exhibits that are presented in evidence. The court reporter does another sort of vital paper work. He keeps a verbatim account of the progress of the trial, stenotyping all the lawyers' questions and all the witnesses' answers. During the jury's de-liberations he is often called on to read critical parts of the testimony to them.

The judge is the director of the drama. He alone runs the show, and has responsibility for explaining the law and ruling which questions, testimony and evidence are, or are not, admissible.

The lawyers draw testimony from the witnesses, who occupy a box directly under the judge's eye. The witnesses play major supporting roles in the cast, for their testimony often proves to be the key element in deciding a case.

The jury, too, has a crucial role. In a criminal case the jurors actually decide—with instructions and advice on the law from the judge—if the defendant is guilty, and of what crime. They also determine who is to win what in a civil suit.

Other stellar roles fall to the defendant and the plaintiff and their lawyers. Generally the lawyers do most of the talking for their clients, but both plaintiff and defendant may play active parts on the witness stand, giving their versions of the conflict that caused the trial to be held in the first place.

ther litigants or witnesses, in one of the several trials scheduled for that morning. Trials in a court of general jurisdiction have more of the drama and legal byplay frequently seen on television than trials in any other sort of court. The familiar trappings of jury box, judge's bench and courtroom attendants are all in evidence (*illustration, opposite*). And everyone rises in solemn silence as the judge enters from his chambers behind the bench to take his place and the clerk intones that the court is now in session.

When Mason's case was finally called, he and his lawyer took their places at a table inside the railing that separated the spectators from the bench. The lawyer for the two Intercontinental firms took his seat at another table opposite them. The jury box was empty, of course, but had there been a jury on the case, this would have been the time for both lawyers to begin their *voir dire* examination of jurors. At this point the judge would also have invoked "the rule." He would have ordered all witnesses, other than the plaintiff and defendants themselves, to leave the courtroom and wait outside until they were summoned. This action prevents any witness from being able to tailor his testimony to fit or dispute the testimony of a previous witness. On this occasion, however, Mason's wife and her mother were permitted to remain in the courtroom, and Mason's lawyer began his presentation. Most of the information was the same as it had been in the original trial, but this time it was presented in more orderly fashion by a trained attorney.

First he outlined the nature of the case against Intercontinental, and then he called Mason to the stand to identify the original invoices, which were once more placed in evidence as Exhibits One and Two. He then called Mason's mother-in-law to the stand, where she was sworn in and, in reply to questions from Mason's lawyer, identified the original receipt she had received when she bought the chairs, which stated their value. This document was introduced into evidence as Plaintiff's Exhibit Three. Mrs. Mason then took the stand to describe, under careful questioning, the condition of the chairs at the time they were lost.

"Would you say that they were excellent examples of 18th Century craftsmanship, Mrs. Mason?"

"Yes," she answered.

"And would you say that their condition at the time of their loss was such that it had not diminished since their original purchase for $500 each?"

"Yes."

The hearing of testimony is the heart of almost every trial, and it follows a standard procedure. First the plaintiff's witnesses are heard and cross-examined. When they are finished the defendant's lawyers generally ask the judge to dismiss the suit—on the ground that the plaintiff has not presented sufficient evidence to prove his case even if the defendant offered no rebuttal. Since this is rarely true, the request is generally denied. Then the defense proceeds to call its witnesses, and they in turn testify and are cross-examined. The plaintiff also has the right at this point to call additional witnesses if the defense has introduced new issues. A final go-round of questioning is designed to clear up any remaining ambiguities in the evidence. At this point both sides almost invariably ask for a "directed verdict." In doing so, each of the opposing lawyers claims that the weight of the evidence is so heavily on his side that no reasonable judge or jury would be able to decide in favor of the other and therefore an immediate decision is proper. Both of these motions are usually denied, as is the first request for dismissal. After some additional legal parrying, the trial moves into its closing phases.

The brief

Occasionally the testimony of witnesses is not the most important element in a trial. Rather, the decision in the case can turn on the interpretation of a subtle point of law; the lawyer's view of this point is presented in the form of a written "brief" or argument. Copies of this brief are handed to both the judge and the opposing lawyer at the start of the trial.

Mason's lawyer had prepared a brief arguing a point of law about the movement of goods, and his argument was to prove decisive in the case. The brief focused on the crucial issue of the 60-cent-per-pound limitation on the liability of the moving company, and it cited the decisions of several courts in similar cases. Although these courts had approved the limitation, the cases before them had all applied to damaged goods rather than lost goods. Furthermore, the brief argued that when goods are lost, the contract covering them should be considered dissolved. In two cases then pending before the state appellate court in which the issue was indeed lost rather than damaged goods, no decision had yet been reached. Consequently the legal question of whether the limitation applied to lost goods was still open. Then, taking a legal long shot, Mason's lawyer introduced a key argument. He maintained that if the state's courts were to enforce such a harsh restriction, it could seriously retard commerce in and out of the state. And by doing so, the state would in effect be regulating interstate commerce—something it did not have a right to do, for the U.S. Constitution stipulates that the power to regulate commerce between states rests solely with the federal government.

At the conclusion of the trial of Mason's case, the judge announced that he would take the case under advisement and render his decision later. This step is customary when the docket is crowded and a judge must hear a number of cases before he can take the time to retire to his chambers and study the stenographic reports of testimony and the briefs. In Mason's case two weeks went by before the judge finally handed down his decision. He ruled in Mason's favor, saying that the 60-cent limitation did not apply since the contract was dissolved when goods received for shipment by movers were lost by them, rather than damaged in transit. The decree carried with it a judgment of $1,000 plus court costs against Intercontinental Movers and its parent organization, Intercontinental, Inc. Not unexpectedly, the lawyer for the two companies lost no time in notifying the trial court of his intention to appeal the decision to the state Supreme Court. For this ruling would establish a precedent for settling other similar claims, and over the years such a precedent, if not overturned, could conceivably cost the moving company a great deal of money in claims for loss that might in the future be brought by other customers.

THE APPEAL

Any dissatisfied litigant may appeal the decision of a lower court—except, of course, the prosecutor in a criminal case in which the defendant has been acquitted, for no one may be tried twice for the same offense. No such restrictions apply in civil cases. Notice of intention to appeal to a higher court may be filed in many states any time within a 30-day period after the contested decision is announced. The appeal must usually be accompanied by a transcript of the testimony given at the original trial, for the appellate court may need the transcript in order to study the entire case. It is typed at the appellant's expense (in an appeal, the complaining party is no longer called a plaintiff but an appellant, and his name comes first). The cost of the transcript can average about $200 a day for each day of the trial. In addition, the lawyer's fees could come to another $1,000 or so. If the appeal is denied, the court costs will also be levied against the appellant, as will the original monetary judgment of the lower court—plus interest accrued through the period of appeal. (The defendant must pay his own lawyer's fees.) Strictly in financial terms, an appeal is not something to be undertaken lightly.

Nevertheless, many disappointed litigants are eager to try, especially if the stakes are high and a failure to appeal is tantamount to giving up without a struggle. Persuaded of the rightness of their cause and convinced that the judges of a higher court may have more sense than the judge or jury of a lower court, they decide to try the next level up. This is their legal right, but of course it is not always successful. Many disappointed litigants think that the lower court has simply misunderstood the facts of the case, and that another go at it will clarify these facts before a new judicial body. However, an appellate court seldom second-guesses a lower court on the facts. Normally, it confines itself to considering whether or not the lower court has correctly applied the law involved. The chances of an appellant's lawyers proving that a substantial legal error was committed on the lower level may be exceedingly slim. Unless the prospective appellant has been convicted of a serious crime and wishes to postpone the day of reckoning by filing appeal after appeal, or has an immense amount of money, or has a crucial principle of business operation at stake, he would do well to pay close heed to the advice of his lawyer when the latter says, "Quit now."

A CONTEST BETWEEN LAWYERS

The managers of Intercontinental, for reasons of their own, did not quit. Although Mason still had a decided interest in the outcome of the case—the $1,000 plus costs was not his until the appeals procedure had run its course—there was no reason for him to attend the final hearing, although he was entitled to do so as a spectator if he wished. All his evidence was on the record; all the facts had been stated. This was now a matter between the lawyers and the judges. In an appellate court, three or more robed judges sit behind a high, imposing bench. The lawyers for each side present their arguments in turn and answer questions from the bench with a minimum of arm-waving histrionics. Indeed an appellate proceeding is decidedly rational and well-mannered compared to a normal trial court proceeding. When the judges are satisfied that they have heard all the arguments they need, they turn immediately to the next case and several months may pass before they finally announce their decision, in the form of a written opinion. In the case of *Intercontinental Movers and Intercontinental, Inc.* v. *Mason,* their opinion upheld the lower court decision.

The case of Mason and his lost chairs would normally have ended right then. In his original brief, however, Mason's lawyer had raised the question of the constitutionality of the 60-cent limitation, and anything concerning the U.S. Constitution is automatically a question of federal law. On this basis, Intercontinental was entitled to appeal its case again, this time to the highest tribunal in the land, the U.S. Supreme Court, and it decided to do so. Again, the odds were not good that this action would have any effect. Each year many disappointed litigants make the pronouncement, "I'll take it all the way to the Supreme Court." And indeed many of them do, although the cost to both parties involved is substantial. But of the 4,000 or so cases that are submitted each year to the U.S. Supreme Court for review—either from lower federal courts or from state appellate courts—only about 150 are overturned. Indeed, in a majority of cases the U.S. Supreme Court simply refuses to consider the case, thereby automatically sustaining the lower court's decision.

The U.S. Supreme Court

The procedure for appealing a case to the U.S. Supreme Court generally begins with a document called a Petition for Certiorari, which is in effect a request to be heard, and which may be either granted or denied. If the petition is denied, the decision of the lower court stands —but this does not necessarily mean that the Court approves the decision. Unlike most other courts, the U.S. Supreme Court has the flexibility to pick and choose among the cases presented to it for review. It can hear what it wants to hear, and it chooses mainly those cases in which it considers the legal issues to be pressing and important to the whole of American society.

One morning, among the hundreds of petitions on which it acted, the Supreme Court issued an order in the case of *Intercontinental Movers and Intercontinental, Inc.* v. *Mason*. The order said simply: "Certiorari denied." Mason's experience had thus established the law in his state, giving a protection that other homeowners, entrusting their household goods to moving companies, might subsequently —and gratefully—use.

By **FRED P. GRAHAM,**
ERNEST C. FRIESEN, Consultant

11
Personal freedoms

The right to vote,
to protest,
to be let alone

Americans grow up convinced that they "know their rights." The phrase itself has a reassuring ring, but its meaning is far from clear. Few people could, if called upon, define the rights U.S. law gives them —and fewer still are aware of the limitations that hedge and restrict these rights. Broadly speaking, there are three kinds of rights:

■ Political—the right to citizenship and its prerogatives, such as the right to vote and to leave and re-enter the U.S. at will.

■ Civil—the right not to be discriminated against—because of race, color, creed or sex—in employment, housing, education and accommodation in public places such as hotels, restaurants and parks.

■ Personal—the right to speak freely, to meet with other people, to be secure in your home, in general to be let alone to work out your way of life free of government interference. And these rights also guarantee that if you should run afoul of the law, you will be dealt with according to certain precise legal procedures.

This listing is, on the face of it, impressive, a charter of individual liberties that anyone under totalitarian rule would envy. Yet the rights Americans assert—particularly the personal rights—are hardly unlimited. Throughout our history a basic conflict has existed between the individual's prerogative to say and do as he pleases and society's need for order. Repeatedly these questions have arisen: What happens if a man exercises his freedom in a way that threatens to disrupt the community at large? Where does the law draw the line? The answers have never been absolute, nor is it likely they ever will be.

Most of your rights as an individual derive from the U.S. Constitution and its amendments, notably the first 10—known as the Bill of Rights—as well as the 13th, 14th, 15th, 19th and 26th *(pages 319-321)*. Ironically, the men who wrote the Constitution in the late 1780s did not think that a Bill of Rights needed to be spelled out; it was their firm belief that individual liberties went without saying. It was only at the insistence of some of the states that the first 10 amendments were formulated.

But setting down rights and applying them in specific situations are, of course, two very different matters. Interpreting the Constitution and its amendments is the responsibility of the Supreme Court, and as the membership of the high tribunal has changed, so have its interpretations. One legal observer puts it this way: "Your rights are what the Supreme Court says they are." He might have added, "at any given time." For despite the fact that guarantees of individual freedoms are permanently embedded in law, passing years and changing circumstances alter views of where those freedoms begin and end.

Inevitably, too, the values placed on different rights have varied.

A right once thought essential dwindles in importance; for example, the Third Amendment allows a homeowner to refuse to house a soldier in peacetime—a matter that greatly concerned Americans two centuries ago but one that is now academic. A long-unchallenged clause in another right becomes suddenly controversial; thus, "the right of the people to bear and keeps arms," granted by the Second Amendment in the interests of a "well-regulated militia," is now a source of contention between foes and friends of gun-control legislation. Other rights take on added import because of technological developments. When the founding fathers wrote the guarantee of free speech into the First Amendment, they could not have foreseen that people would one day speak through radio and television.

Indeed, advances in communications—as well as in all other sophisticated electronic devices—have raised questions about individual rights that are not even remotely touched on in the amendments to the Constitution, but that, according to some legal experts, come logically within their "penumbra," or shadow. One such right is the "right to privacy," the individual's defense against electronic snooping and against the misuse of personal facts about him that are stored in governmental data banks.

In today's era of proliferating machine marvels—and of big government—the individual has become all the more aware of threats to his individuality, and of the need to be alert to infringements on it. As a result, the field of personal rights law is in considerable turmoil. You have only to pick up a daily newspaper to find evidences of alleged encroachments on those rights: a mass arrest of antipollution demonstrators asserting their right to assemble peaceably; a suspension of a student asserting his right to wear a black arm band as a form of free speech; the jailing of a street-corner orator on a charge of inciting to riot. The issues on which such cases hinge are likely to be argued in the courts for years to come, with the Supreme Court as ultimate arbiter—and its interpretations seemingly unpredictable.

The pages that follow are devoted to a discussion of each of the major rights of the individual. Those rights that are more or less settled issues are dealt with first, followed by those that are still subject to controversy and to varying judicial opinions.

YOUR RIGHT TO BE A CITIZEN

Any person who is born in the United States, the Commonwealth of Puerto Rico or the territory of the Virgin Islands—"and subject to the jurisdiction thereof," automatically becomes a citizen when he draws his first breath. The subject-to-jurisdiction clause, which is part of the 14th Amendment, excludes, for example, the offspring of foreign diplomats stationed in the United States.

Children born of Americans abroad also gain their citizenship without difficulty. All that the parents must do is register the infant with a U.S. consulate. Establishing citizenship is more complicated if a child is born abroad of one American parent and one foreign parent. He also acquires citizenship by being registered at birth with a U.S. consulate but will lose it if he does not later fulfill a U.S. residency requirement. Suppose that an American girl marries a Frenchman and settles in Paris. If she wishes her children to be American citizens, she must not only register their births at the consulate but also make sure that each one lives continuously in the U.S. for five years at some period between his 14th and 28th birthdays.

However, a similar residency rule that once applied to foreign-born Americans who became citizens by the naturalization process was struck down in 1964; the Supreme Court said that it created a kind of second-class citizenship. Under the old law, a naturalized American forfeited his citizenship if he returned to the land of his birth for more than three years at a stretch or lived anywhere abroad for more than five years continuously. This rule meant that a naturalized citizen could not retire to the old country and live out his years on Social Security payments—unless he came back to the U.S. for a month or two every three years. Now a naturalized American enjoys unrestricted citizenship, no matter where he lives or for how long.

There are a number of ways in which citizenship can be lost. It can be taken from a naturalized citizen if he obtained citizenship fraudulently, either by lying about past activities that reflect on his moral character or by lying when he renounced his allegiance to his previous country. And both naturalized and native-born Americans have been stripped of citizenship for committing treason, for acquiring citizenship in or taking an oath of allegiance to another country, for serving in the army of a nation hostile to the U.S. or for conspiring to overthrow the U.S. government by violent means.

Your right to vote

All citizens over 18 have the right to vote in federal and state elections. The states could once demand proof of your ability to read and write, but they can no longer use these or any other tests of your knowledge as a means of barring you from voting. Poll taxes, which levied a fee of $1.50 or more for the right to vote and thus tended to keep the poor away from the polling booth, were abolished by the 24th Amendment to the Constitution.

Some states still have special residency rules for voting in state and local elections; these laws require the would-be voter to have lived in the same district for three to six months. Such rules have been attacked, however, in a number of law suits, and they do not apply to federal elections; anyone who has lived in one place for more than 30 days can vote in Presidential elections. Nor can states establish property-owning qualifications for voters. The only exception to this rule has recently been disallowed. It applied to small localities—towns and villages. When such a locality held a special referendum concerning a school budget or a local bond issue—matters that affected the local tax rates—it could previously limit the voting to owners of taxable real estate.

Your right to travel

Before World War I, Americans were as free to travel abroad as they were to roam their own land. Few countries required passports of international travelers except in times of declared war or national emergency. An American could get a U.S. passport from the Department of State if he asked for one, but not many people bothered. Old-timers can still remember the relaxed era when they simply got on a boat in Boston or New York and sailed for Europe without any formalities whatever.

Passports became increasingly convenient to have during the 20s, and since the late 30s a series of acts passed by Congress have made possession of a passport a prerequisite for travel outside the Western Hemisphere. Initially, the State Department had total control over who did or did not receive a passport. If—for any reason that it deemed "contrary to the best interests" of the U.S.—the State Department wanted to prevent someone from traveling abroad, its Passport Office refused to issue him one. But now, as a result of several Supreme Court decisions, every citizen has the right to a passport if he applies for it. In 1964, when two avowed American Communist Party leaders found that their passports had been revoked, the Court reversed this action because, the majority held, freedom of travel "is a constitutional liberty closely related to rights of free speech and association."

However, in another decision a year later the Court held that these rights did not include the right to "gather information." The State Department had denied a passport to an American who wanted to travel to Cuba in order, he said, to satisfy his curiosity about the state of affairs under Fidel Castro's regime. The State Department, for its part, argued that travel to Cuba by U.S. citizens might conceivably involve the U.S. in dangerous international incidents. The Court upheld the Department's authority to place such area restrictions on passports.

YOUR RIGHT TO RELIGIOUS FREEDOM

The first clause of the First Amendment guarantees your right to abide by any religious faith you choose. It gives you an equally firm right to reject all of them. As Supreme Court Justice Robert Jackson once wrote, "The day this country ceases to be free for irreligion, it will cease to be free for religion—except for the sect that can win political power." His view was reaffirmed in another ruling in 1961. A man named Roy Torcaso had been denied the right to become a notary public in Maryland because he refused to make "a declaration of belief in the existence of God," as the state constitution required all public officials to do. Other states had similar requirements; Tennessee even went so far as to demand that the oath-taker affirm his belief in "a future state of rewards and punishments," thus denying public office to many God-fearing people who were not so sure about the hereafter. The Supreme Court struck down such laws on the ground that any "religious test for public office unconstitutionally invades . . . freedom of belief and religion."

Further protection for freedom of belief is provided by a clause in the First Amendment that bans the establishment of a state religion, thus erecting what Thomas Jefferson called "a wall of separation between church and state." In a 1962 decision the Supreme Court disallowed prayers in public schools because, as Justice Hugo Black wrote, "in this country it is no part of the business of government to compose official prayers for any group of American people to recite. . . . This very practice of establishing governmentally composed prayers for religious services . . . caused many of our early colonists to leave England and seek freedom in America." In short, nobody can tell anybody else to pray—or how to pray.

But other Supreme Court decisions in recent decades have proved the wall between church and state to be a rather flexible barrier. In 1947 the Court ruled that communities could provide bus transportation for children going to parochial schools as well as for children attending public schools. Providing such transportation, the Court noted, did not favor religion but merely helped children get to and from school safely. In another case the Court approved a "released-time" plan that permitted public school youngsters in New York to leave their classes for religious instruction one day a week, if they so requested. A similar law in Illinois, however, was ruled unconstitutional, because the children were receiving their released-time religious instruction in public school classrooms.

The Court applies two guidelines in deciding whether a law or a school program unconstitutionally crosses the church-state barrier. First, the law or program must have a secular purpose, neither advancing nor inhibiting religion. Second, it must not involve the government, federal, state or local, in an "excessive entanglement with religion." Thus the Court has ruled that it is proper for local governments to aid children going to church-affiliated schools—paying for their lunches, say, or their textbooks on secular (but not religious) subjects—because such aid does not advance religion but simply promotes the education and welfare of the students. On the other hand, the Court ruled that Pennsylvania and Rhode Island could not give direct financial aid to church-affiliated elementary and secondary schools, helping to pay teachers' salaries and meet other costs, because that would directly involve these states in promoting religious instruction.

YOUR RIGHT TO DUE PROCESS

Some of your most formidable rights come into play if for any reason you become enmeshed with the police. The Constitution and its amendments have more to say on this subject than on any other.

Under the Fourth Amendment neither your person, your house, your papers nor any of your belongings can be subjected to "unreasonable searches and seizures." This means that the police cannot enter and search your living quarters, office or even a hotel room unless they show you a warrant, signed by a judge, that spells out precisely why they want to make the search and what sort of evidence they expect to find. Evidence obtained in any other way may be excluded from use in a subsequent court action against you.

Moreover, you cannot be detained by the police unless they formally charge you with a crime; this right of habeas corpus is Article 1 Section 9 of the Constitution as originally ratified. Another of your bulwarks is the Fifth Amendment, which gives you the right to refuse to answer any question put to you by the police, a prosecutor or a judge if you feel your answer might incriminate you.

These guarantees are all specific, but you have, in addition, a remarkable blanket guarantee against arbitrary arrest and against slipshod judicial proceedings. It is based on the most famous constitutional clause of all, providing that no one may be deprived of life, liberty or property "without due process of law." These words appear not once, but twice, in the Constitution. The Fifth Amendment places

TEXT CONTINUES ON PAGE 322

A CHARTER OF LIBERTIES

The personal freedoms that Americans cherish are spelled out in the first 10 Amendments to the Constitution—known as the Bill of Rights—and extended by later amendments such as those excerpted below.

1 Congress shall make no law respecting an establishment of religion, or prohibiting the free exercise thereof; or abridging the freedom of speech, or of the press; or the right of the people peaceably to assemble, and to petition the Government for a redress of grievances.

2 A well regulated Militia, being necessary to the security of a free State, the right of the people to keep and bear Arms, shall not be infringed.

3 No Soldier shall, in time of peace be quartered in any house, without the consent of the Owner, nor in time of war, but in a manner to be prescribed by law.

4 The right of the people to be secure in their persons, houses, papers, and effects, against unreasonable searches and seizures, shall not be violated, and no Warrants shall issue, but upon probable cause, supported by Oath or affirmation, and particularly describing the place to be searched, and the persons or things to be seized.

5 No person shall be held to answer for a capital, or otherwise infamous crime, unless on a presentment or indictment of a Grand Jury, except in cases arising in the land or naval forces, or in the Militia, when in actual service in time of War or public danger; nor shall any person be subject for the same offense to be twice put in jeopardy of life or limb; nor shall be compelled in any criminal case to be a witness against himself, nor be deprived of life, liberty, or property, without due process of law; nor shall private property be taken for public use, without just compensation.

6 In all criminal prosecutions, the accused shall enjoy the right to a speedy and public trial, by an impartial jury of the State and district wherein the crime shall have been committed, which district shall have been previously ascertained by law, and to be informed of the nature and cause of the accusation; to be confronted with the witnesses against him; to have compulsory process for obtaining witnesses in his favor, and to have the Assistance of Counsel for his defence.

7 In Suits at common law, where the value in controversy shall exceed twenty dollars, the right of trial by jury shall be preserved, and no fact tried by a jury, shall be otherwise re-examined in any Court of the United States, than according to the rules of the common law.

8 Excessive bail shall not be required, nor excessive fines imposed, nor cruel and unusual punishments inflicted.

9 The enumeration in the Constitution, of certain rights, shall not be construed to deny or disparage others retained by the people.

10 The powers not delegated to the United States by the Constitution, nor prohibited by it to the States, are reserved to the States respectively, or to the people.

13 Neither slavery nor involuntary servitude, except as a punishment for a crime . . . shall exist within the United States. . . .

14 All persons born or naturalized in the United States, and subject to the jurisdiction thereof, are citizens. . . . No State shall make or enforce any law which shall abridge the privileges or immunities of citizens of the United States; nor shall any State deprive any person of life, liberty, or property, without due process of law; nor deny to any person within its jurisdiction the equal protection of the laws. . . .

15 The right of citizens of the United States to vote shall not be denied or abridged by the United States or by any State on account of race, color, or previous condition of servitude.

19 The right of citizens of the United States to vote shall not be denied or abridged by the United States or by any State on account of sex.

26 The right of citizens of the United States, who are eighteen years of age or older, to vote shall not be denied or abridged by the United States or by any State on account of age.

THE STILL-VIGOROUS BILL OF RIGHTS

1 The First Amendment guaranteed our ancestors' rights to pray, speak and print what they wished. Like the other amendments making up the Bill of Rights (*quoted on page 319*), the First is as vital today as ever. It provides a frequently contested limitation on governmental interference in private affairs. It has protected antiwar speakers from arrest. It has helped to block official censorship of journals printing documents critical of the government. And to the delight of some and the dismay of others, it has kept public school systems neutral on religion.

2 The abhorrence of professional standing armies motivated the authors of the Bill of Rights to include the Second Amendment, guaranteeing that citizens could "keep and bear arms," in order that an effective citizens' militia could be raised quickly. This amendment was seldom invoked until the 1960s. The rise of armed violence—riots in cities, political assassinations—led many to advocate stringent laws controlling firearms. But sportsmen resurrected the slumbering Second to protect their right to own guns for their own use.

3 Because of the quartering of British troops in American homes the first Congress wrote the Third Amendment, forbidding the government to lodge soldiers in private homes without the homeowner's consent. The amendment has served to strengthen the concept of an army subordinate to civilian authority.

4 No British custom so angered the American colonists as the wholesale use of search warrants to collect evidence of anti-British activities from their homes and persons; it was one of the main causes of the Revolutionary War. To protect citizens from unreasonable search and seizure the Fourth Amendment set stringent limits on the ways police can gather evidence. As now interpreted by the courts, it covers other kinds of privacy as well. It not only protects a man's home from illegal search, but also his barn, garage, car, boat and hotel room. The use of wiretaps, hidden cameras and similar secret recording devices has been declared a violation of the Fourth Amendment, except when the use has been ordered by a court—and then only for a specific purpose and a specifically limited period of time.

5 The Fifth Amendment's most famous provision —that no man can be "compelled in any criminal case to be a witness against himself"—was designed as a bulwark against the police power of the state. Just as officials of the government cannot arbitrarily search your house, neither can they force you to speak during a police investigation or even during a trial. Thus they cannot extort a confession or force you to answer possibly incriminating questions. This amendment receives much publicity when used by people who seem to have something to hide—during the 1950s alleged subversives and purported underworld notables "took the Fifth" before Congressional investigating committees. While it may sometimes help a criminal evade justice, it also gives the innocent a refuge from excessive state power.

6 Cruel and unusual punishments —torture, drawing-and-quartering, near-drowning in a ducking chair—had been common before the Eighth Amendment. It was the last of the protections for personal freedoms written into the Bill of Rights; the Ninth and Tenth Amendments are safeguards of general rights of individuals and states. All have been invoked in recent years—the Eighth by foes of capital punishment, who maintain that death is too severe a penalty for most crimes.

the obligation of due process on the federal government; the 14th Amendment—passed after the Civil War—places the same obligation on the states, and allows federal courts to step in if any state or local governmental body or official disregards it. (This right, which guarantees the application of precisely specified procedures during every step of a criminal action, is discussed in detail in Chapter 9.)

YOUR DEFENSES AGAINST DISCRIMINATION

You have a right to be treated on an equal basis with all other U.S. residents whatever your race, religion, sex or ethnic origin. In recent decades numerous Supreme Court decisions, reinforced by sweeping acts of Congress, have outlawed many forms of discrimination. The anti-discrimination laws now cover virtually all but the most private areas of American life, such as a private club or a man's own living room. They are, of course, still often flouted. But the legal rights of every citizen are clear. Anyone who feels that he has been barred from a restaurant because of his color, or turned down for a job because of his ethnic background—or suffered any other form of discrimination—has two kinds of legal recourse.

First he can bring suit in a federal court (or in state court in many states). If the discrimination is proved, the defendant can be compelled not only to stop discriminating but even to pay substantial damages; the late Nat King Cole, the popular black singer, won several such damage awards from hotels that had refused to accommodate him because of his color. The second kind of help against discrimination is provided by government agencies set up to enforce civil rights. Most states now have a human rights commission, and one major federal agency in the field is the Equal Employment Opportunities Commission. It is generally simpler to file a complaint with one of these agencies than to bring an independent suit in court, and the results are similar: The discrimination is ordered stopped, and in some instances monetary damages are awarded.

The crucial point in both types of legal proceeding is, of course, to prove the presence of discrimination. This is particularly difficult to establish in housing. Landlords and real estate brokers are aware that discrimination is illegal; some try to dodge the law by resorting to subterfuge. They seldom come right out and say, for example, "We don't rent to Negroes." Instead they might claim that an apartment is already rented, or that it is not ready to be shown. They also sometimes try to discourage apartment- or home-seekers by quoting a higher-than-normal rent or sale price.

A way has been devised to deal with such situations and to provide the legal groundwork for a claim of discrimination. The rejected apartment applicant, for example, sends two friends (one to act as witness if the matter should get to court) to see the same real estate agent. The friends, of course, are selected on the basis of being more acceptable racially or ethnically, to the agent in question. If they are willingly shown the apartment that was supposedly not yet ready to be shown or are quoted a lower rental, the rejected applicant has grounds for a suit under the Federal Housing Act of 1968. Sometimes the prospect of having the deception aired in court—or merely publicized in a local newspaper—will cause the real estate agent to settle the matter to the original applicant's satisfaction.

THE LIBERTIES—AND LIMITS—OF FREE SPEECH

Few guarantees are dearer to Americans than the right to say what they like about anybody and anything. And few have been more hotly debated in recent years. The first part of the First Amendment declares that "Congress shall make no law . . . abridging the freedom of speech or of the press; or the right of the people peaceably to assemble. . . . " You can stand up in a civic meeting and denounce your city council over an irksome parking ordinance, or you can lead a demonstration demanding the impeachment of the President. You can write out your ideas, print them and hand them around freely on the streets without a license.

It was under the protective umbrella of the First Amendment that the Black Panther leader Eldridge Cleaver took public platforms in various cities to suggest, presumably rhetorically, that the White House should be burned down. The late American Nazi leader George Lincoln Rockwell held frequent turbulent rallies extolling Hitler's regime. Many people were outraged, but Cleaver and Rockwell were both exercising precious rights given all of us in the Constitution.

The individual's right of free expression often conflicts not only with the beliefs of society as a whole but also with the rights of society. And so legal limits have been drawn around certain forms of expression. These limits do not deny you the right to say, write, symbolize or even act out what you think, but they sometimes prescribe where and how you may say it. The law also forbids you to say things that have immediate and obvious harmful consequences; the classic illustration, cited by Justice Oliver Wendell Holmes, is that no one is entitled falsely to shout "Fire!" in a crowded theater. And there are other limits, such as laws against libel, slander and obscenity.

Your right to speak and write as you please does not include the right to make false and reckless accusations that harm the reputations

If you call a man a crook in private, that might be intemperate but would not be legally defamatory. But if you wrote it on a postcard, where a postman might read it, the slur would be legally "published" and you would be guilty of libel.

of innocent people. However intangible a man's reputation may be, it is the foundation of his relationship to society; if a piece of the foundation is chipped away by lies, he is hurt just as surely as if he had lost a leg because of someone's negligence. A person who is defamed is, like a victim of negligence, entitled to bring suit in court, and to have the defamation judged in terms of its economic damage to him.

There used to be a clear distinction between the two kinds of defamation, slander and libel. The first was spoken, the latter either printed or pictured. Because spoken words are "written on the wind," while printed and pictured lies endure and may circulate indefinitely, libel was considered the more serious of the two. But this distinction has become blurred since the advent of motion pictures, radio and television. Defamatory remarks made in these media can be disseminated so widely that they may have as enduring an impact as if they were written; as a result, the law now views them as libel, even though they are spoken rather than written.

The difference between slander and libel now depends on circumstances. If someone rose in a town meeting—or even telephoned a gossipy friend—and falsely accused the local bank treasurer of being an embezzler, the charge would probably be slander. On the other hand, if he said the same thing on radio or on television he would be committing libel—just as he would have if he had written the false accusation in a book, in a letter to a newspaper or, for that matter, on a postcard or a public wall. Postcards, not being sealed, can be read by anyone as they pass through the mail; thus anything written on them is published, in the sense of having been made public. Anything written on a public wall is also published. A tavern in California once had to pay damages to a respectable married woman whose name and telephone number—plus crude suggestions that she was sexually available—had been written on its men's room wall.

The recourse against slander is far more limited than against libel. Only four sorts of defamatory remarks constitute slander and provide grounds for a suit: (1) falsely accusing a person of having a loathsome illness, such as a venereal disease; (2) falsely accusing a person of a serious crime, such as murder or fraud; (3) falsely accusing a woman of being unchaste; (4) falsely damaging a person's professional reputation or job standing. Calling a surgeon a butcher would qualify as slanderous, but calling a surly butcher a bastard would not. If an angry neighbor comes up to you on a public street and only vents his spleen in vituperative phrases—even very rough ones—you do not have grounds for legal action. Epithets like son of a bitch are no longer regarded as slanderous (or, in fact, defamatory) because they are so commonly used that they have lost their meaning.

In private, of course, you can call a person almost anything you like. Had the treasurer of the bank been called an embezzler to his face when he and his accuser were alone, the accusation would have been intemperate, but it would not have been illegal. Nor can action be taken over accusations made in sealed letters. They are private communications and you can say anything you choose in them—if, that is, you are careful. In one case a man wrote a savage letter calling another a cheat and all-around crook. But he placed this message in the wrong envelope and it was delivered to a third person, who read it. The court held that if the man the letter was intended for had received it, there would have been no case; the lie would have been private. But since a third party got the letter by mistake, it was published, and its writer was guilty of libel.

Conversely, the most public kinds of false accusations are seldom illegal. The laws of slander and libel rarely apply to people in the public eye unless the false statement is made maliciously. Generally, you can say pretty much what you like about your senator, your local park superintendent or a television personality you despise, and get away with it. Public figures are fair game simply because they happen to be public figures. On the other hand, the law offers some comfort to officeholders. While you can say what you like about them, they —so long as they speak in their official capacities—can say what they like about you. Even village functionaries are generally immune to defamation suits when acting as officials. Free discussion of issues, and even of personalities, is considered so vital to the democratic political process that the courts almost always forgive the rough and sometimes slanderous talk that goes with it. The law holds that officials cannot efficiently carry out their duties to the public if they must live in constant fear of being sued for what they say.

Your right to express and learn about ideas offensive to particular people has in recent years been extended to include ideas that might offend large segments of society. Censorship of various kinds, which—in the name of protecting society against obscenity—restricted what artists and writers could produce and what audiences could see and read, has been largely eliminated. Obscenity is still illegal; laws prohibit the sale of obscene material to juveniles, ban its public display, and limit its shipment by mail. But what constitutes obscenity has been redefined to permit maximum freedom of expression.

For any work to be considered obscene, said the Supreme Court, three elements must coalesce: (1) the dominant theme of the material must appeal to prurient interest in sex; (2) the material must be patently offensive because it affronts contemporary community standards relating to sexual matters; and (3) the material must be utterly without redeeming social value. Unless obscene material meets all of these tests, states and local communities cannot outlaw it. The third requirement, particularly, protects the dissemination of almost all material except the most crassly debased commercial pornography.

Free expression versus public order

A fiery speaker incites a crowd to destructive violence. Demonstrators tie up traffic, obstructing the movements of hundreds of motorists. The operator of a sound truck drives through the streets broadcasting messages with a din that almost deafens everyone within earshot. Each of these people is exercising his First Amendment right to free speech or free assembly. Yet his actions may disturb the peace or endanger public order. Where does the law draw the line?

No question has been asked of the Supreme Court so often or in so many different ways. As a rule, the answer has been in favor of individual liberties—unless that exercise places society in grave and immediate danger. Some forms of expression clearly do endanger society, and legal limits have been drawn around them. The limits affect where and how you may speak, where and how you may assemble to demonstrate your ideas, what forms of expression you may adopt and what kind of written material you may circulate on the streets.

Speech itself has few limitations if you do not incite your audience to violence. Any speaker who deliberately plays upon the emotions of a crowd, stirring it to a violent reaction, can be arrested by the police under laws against incitement-to-riot. A classic case of this sort came before the Supreme Court in 1951. In Syracuse, New York, a man named Feiner gathered a crowd of about 80 listeners on a street corner and lit into the U.S. civil rights situation. In the course of his remarks he called the city's mayor a "champagne-sipping bum," the President a "bum" and American Legionnaires "Nazi Gestapo agents." The epithets upset some of Feiner's listeners and they grew restless. There was what police on the scene later described as "angry muttering and pushing." A listener even warned one policeman that if he did not take Feiner away, the crowd would. The police sensed that a breach of the peace was imminent and asked Feiner to move on. When he refused, they arrested him for disorderly conduct. He was convicted and given a 30-day term in the county penitentiary. The Supreme Court upheld the conviction.

However, the Court's decisions since the Feiner case have tended to take the side of the speaker rather than that of the crowd. The fundamental legal principle remains: A man cannot wantonly and maliciously, with total disregard for human safety, stir a crowd to violent action. But the Court has made clear that it will not approve of a "heckler's veto" of free speech, and that the first obligation of the police is not to silence the speaker but to control the unruly crowd. The arrest of a speaker can only come as a last resort, when it is certain that there is no other way to prevent violence.

Your right of free speech applies also to written material. The First Amendment guarantee that gives newspapers and other periodicals the right to publish without interference gives you as a private citizen the same right. Whatever the law permits you to say out loud you can also say in writing—and you can also print it and distribute it without asking anyone's permission. You can give your material away on the streets to anyone who will take it, or you can sell it. Further, if people accept your material and then litter the streets with it, you cannot be held responsible for the mess. The Supreme Court has ruled that antilittering ordinances may not be used to suppress the free distribution of noncommercial literature. If your community wants to keep the streets clean, it must either sweep up after you or go after the people who threw your literature away.

If your freedom to write and print as you please is sacrosanct, so

Publishing and littering
Antilittering laws, the Supreme Court has held, cannot be used to thwart your constitutional right to publish and distribute your opinions. If people accept your printed material and then strew it on the street, you cannot be held responsible for the mess. If the police want to do anything about it, they must arrest the litterbugs.

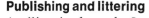

Putting limits on "speech plus"

The First Amendment's guarantee of free speech does not allow a man to use a loudspeaker without restriction. In most localities, laws govern when and where loudspeakers may be used—and how loud they can be turned up. The Supreme Court has backed these limitations on amplified speech—the simplest form of what lawyers call "speech plus"—on the ground that while free speech is a basic right, it need not be exercised in a way that blasts the ears off the entire community.

is your right to join any group or organization you wish. Your right to "free association" is an extension of your right to free speech, for in choosing to join a group you are expressing your private likes and beliefs. Further, your membership can usually be kept secret; the group you join need not reveal the names of its members. In 1958 Alabama tried to compel the National Association for the Advancement of Colored People to disclose its local membership lists. The NAACP refused, and the Supreme Court upheld the refusal.

The limits on speech plus

Recent decades have seen an increased use of various forms of free speech that lawyers have come to call speech plus. Amplified speech —the use of loudspeakers—is the most obvious form of speech plus, but the concept has also been extended to cover protest marches, mass demonstrations and picketing. The law draws tighter limits around these forms of speech than it does around pure speech, since the potential for disturbing public order is much greater.

The problems concerning amplified speech are relatively simple. Few people would disagree with a comment once made by Supreme Court Justice Felix Frankfurter, "Modern devices for amplifying the range and volume of the voice, or its recording, afford easy, too easy, opportunities for aural aggression." Thus most communities have laws controlling amplified speech. You must have a permit to use a loudspeaker out of doors, and you may have to agree to keep the sound below a certain decibel level and to turn it off altogether at certain hours as well as in specified areas where a highly concentrated population may be annoyed by the din.

A far more fluid legal situation exists with regard to protest marches, demonstrations and picket lines. Perhaps the most vital decision in this field was a ruling that public property can be used for demonstrations. As the Supreme Court put it: "Wherever the title of streets and parks may rest, they have immemorially been held in trust for the use of the public and, time out of mind, have been used for purposes of assembling, communicating thoughts between citizens, and discussing public questions. Such use of the streets and public places has, from ancient times, been a part of the privileges, immunities, rights and liberties of citizens."

There is, however, a legal catch to this broad permission, for it depends on the number of marchers or demonstrators involved. If a relatively few people want to assemble in a public park to protest or to pass out leaflets, they have an absolute right to do so, and they need no permit. The only legal limit on them is that they must not interfere with the movement of other citizens. But what happens if a large number of protest marchers decide to demonstrate on the streets? In an age of instant traffic jams, this sort of action almost inevitably interferes seriously with the freedom of movement of other citizens. And so the laws require sizable groups of demonstrators to obtain a permit from the local police. The permit's purpose is not to license the demonstration; the right to demonstrate cannot be denied. Rather, the process of getting the permit gives the police a chance to tell the leaders of the proposed demonstration what days, hours and places would be best for the gathering and least likely to dislocate traffic. It also gives the police a chance to reroute traffic, close off certain streets and generally make the demonstration as interference-free as possible. As a Supreme Court decision of 1965 put it, "Control of travel on the streets is a clear example of governmental responsibility. . . . One would not be justified in ignoring the familiar red light because this was thought to be a means of social protest. Nor could one . . . insist upon a street meeting in the middle of Times Square at the rush hour as a form of freedom of speech or assembly."

But while the police and city governments do possess this regulatory power, the Supreme Court forbade them to exercise it arbitrarily. The police cannot deny one group the right to march down a certain street, then allow another group to march down the same street. Loosely phrased ordinances that give a city government wide latitude to issue or withhold permits have been declared unconstitutional. In 1969 the Court so labeled a Birmingham, Alabama, law that said that permits could be withheld if the city fathers thought "the public welfare, peace, safety, health, decency, good order, morals or convenience" would be offended by the proposed demonstration.

Under some circumstances a rally or march can be held, or a picket line established, on private as well as public property. Disgruntled strikers seeking higher wages can, for example, picket a supermarket right in the supermarket plaza; the plaza, although owned by the supermarket, is commonly used as a public area. So long as the pickets do not block the entrance to the store or annoy and obstruct passers-by —those actions are illegal—they have a right to picket there. A similar right extends to people who demonstrate outside a factory that they believe is polluting the air. The grounds around the factory may be private property, but the demonstrators still have the legal right to be there—again, if they do not block exits, entrances and other means of access to the plant.

Civil disobedience

When such peaceful protests have failed, many people have attempted to apply their right, specified in the First Amendment, by participating in acts of civil disobedience—deliberately violating a law as a means of expressing their need for redress. The technique is an old one. For refusing to pay what he considered to be an unjust tax, the writer Henry David Thoreau was jailed in his home town of Concord, Massachusetts, in 1849. (The delightful, if undocumented, story goes that his colleague Ralph Waldo Emerson came by the jailhouse, saw Thoreau through the barred window and said, "What are you doing in there, David?" To which Thoreau replied, "What are you doing out there, Waldo?")

In our own time, Dr. Martin Luther King, following Thoreau's tactics for protesting unjust laws, disobeyed a number of laws he thought improper, and he too spent a good deal of time in jail. For both Thoreau and King knew—and accepted the fact—that if the citizen of conscience disobeys the law he must expect to be punished for it. An ecology-conscious group, for example, can legally demonstrate against an industrial polluter; its members can march to the gates of the factory and express grievances there freely, but if they enter the factory and refuse to leave, then they have trespassed on private property and are liable to prosecution. Students protesting a university's involvement in military research have a right to do so, but if they seize the administration building or try to bar faculty members and other students from entering offices and classrooms, they can be prosecuted for trespassing. In both instances the demonstrators have the same legal rights as any other citizens who are arrested, but they must also, like any other lawbreakers, face the consequences. The Supreme Court's attitude toward this sort of civil disobedience was once summed up by Justice Felix Frankfurter as follows: "If one man can be allowed to determine for himself what is law, every man can. That means first chaos, then tyranny."

STUDENT RIGHTS

The rising tide of dissent by college and high school students in recent years has stirred a special interest in their personal rights—and led to a widening of their freedoms. School administrations once assumed that they had almost unlimited power to make their own rules and to discipline any students who transgressed them. In cases of trouble the courts invariably backed up the school authorities. But in many recent cases the courts have ruled that schools do not have absolute authority to make and enforce their own rules, and that students do not forfeit their constitutional privileges of free speech and assembly just because they are in school.

The courts have held, for example, that the grounds of a public school and the campus of a state-supported college are as much public property as a public park, and that students therefore have the right to assemble on these grounds and hold protest meetings there—peaceful ones, at least. Private schools and colleges—institutions not supported by public funds—once had a stronger legal claim to exert authority over their students. They could, for example, search the rooms of students living on campus for evidence of misconduct. Now, however, school authorities must have either the resident's permission or a warrant to enter a dormitory room.

The courts have also held that no educational institution can draw up and enforce rules that are "arbitrary and capricious." One rule that many students would so describe is the ban often imposed against long hair on male students. Several school boards suspended students who flouted the ban, and their parents in turn went to court, claiming that such a regulation is, in fact, "arbitrary and capricious." In some cases the school won, in others the students. The decision hinges on one key question: Did the long hair disrupt the learning process in school? In a Texas case, the school board was able to convince the court that the youth's long hair did cause commotions in class and study hall. But in a Wisconsin case, the court found that long hair had caused no educational or disciplinary problems; the school's rule, the judge declared, infringed "personal freedom protected by the United States Constitution."

As opposed to arbitrary and capricious rules, the courts have held that an educational institution has a right to enforce rules that promote education. Legally, schools, colleges and universities are "special purpose institutions," and if students behave in a fashion that frustrates the special purpose, they can be punished. Recent court decisions have forbidden college students to blockade a university's administration building and to stage a noisy sit-in that disrupts classes by shouting. On the other hand, other court decisions have affirmed the right of students to distribute antiwar literature near a Marine recruiting booth, participate in a nonviolent demonstration protesting against bad food in the college cafeteria and march along a public highway to present to a university president a petition outlining student grievances. Moreover, no student can legally be punished for simply being caught up in a violent student demonstration; the college administration must prove that he helped to incite or actively participated in the violence.

Students at colleges or universities who are accused of serious breaches of discipline are generally entitled to a fair hearing before an impartial board of inquiry. The due process involved in such cases requires the college authorities to inform the student in writing of precisely what rule he has broken, and when and where, and of the evidence the college has against him. The authorities must give the student an adequate amount of time to prepare his defense. At the hearing before the board of inquiry he has the right to present his own evidence and witnesses and to hear all of the evidence against him. The board of inquiry's decision must be based on substantial evidence, and the student can appeal its decision in a court.

Some of the legal rights and recourses that the courts have granted to students in public institutions have not been applied to students in private colleges and universities, but at least one case indicates that similar rights may be extended to such students. Four students were expelled from Franklin University, a private institution in Columbus, Ohio, for failing to measure up to a newly enacted set of academic standards. They sued for reinstatement, lost in the lower court, but won in an appellate court, which ruled that Franklin had "abused its discretion" in too quickly and arbitrarily applying its new academic standards. Many of the newly won rights of students—particularly those granting them their own choice of hair style and clothing

The clash over crash helmets

The perennial conflict between personal freedom and the need for public order and safety broke out anew when a number of states passed laws requiring motorcycle riders to wear helmets.
Some riders challenged these laws as an infringement on their right to dress as they wished—an extension of the constitutional right of free expression. But courts have held that in this instance public safety outweighs individual freedom. If a helmetless rider were struck by a rock, he might lose control of his machine and injure or kill other people. Since he has no right to imperil others, helmets remain the rule.

—are a form of "symbolic free speech." What is worn, as well as what is said, can express an opinion. And the freedoms granted students apply outside the classroom as well.

Symbols of protest

The wearing of a button or a black arm band to express political sentiment is a right ordinarily protected by the First Amendment. Some schools have laid down rules forbidding students to wear such controversial symbols of protest on the ground that the sight of them would cause commotions, and possibly even fights, in the school. In one case that was contested up to a federal court of appeals the court upheld the school; but in a similar case that went all the way to the Supreme Court in 1969, the high court found in favor of the wearers. It struck down a ban placed on black arm bands by school authorities in Des Moines, Iowa, concluding.that the authorities had failed to prove that the wearing of the arm bands had caused or would cause disruption. The majority opinion of the Court noted that the arm bands in this case were "a silent, passive expression of opinion, unaccompanied by any disorder or disturbance" and thus were permissible.

The form a symbolic act may take is not always predictable. A couple in an elegant neighborhood of Rye, New York, for example, decided on principle to protest a local ordinance against hanging laundry in the front yard. They strung up a ragged batch of old clothing and left it there until they were given a summons for violating the ordinance. When the case came to court, the judge held that the couple had overstepped the bounds of free speech with their symbolic demonstration, because the ordinance was a reasonable one passed in the interests of making the community more pleasant for everyone.

Perhaps the most controversial acts of symbolic expression have involved the American flag. People have refused on both political and religious grounds to salute it, war protesters have flown it upside down and angry militants have burned it. Since desecration of the flag is outlawed in all 50 states and by federal law, its uses and misuses have led to many court cases. But there is still no clear-cut definition of what constitutes desecration. A New York art dealer was fined $500 and sentenced to 60 days·in jail for displaying a flag "in the form of the male sexual organ," and the Supreme Court upheld his conviction. Another New Yorker, a black man, flew into a rage at the reported assassination of a civil rights worker in Mississippi, took a flag into the street, shouted "We don't need no damn flag!" and burned it. A municipal court convicted him of malicious mischief. The Supreme Court overturned this conviction—but not on the

Short skirts and the law

A legal test of the right to wear a miniskirt was launched in a New York court when a woman lawyer, dressed in a fashionably brief costume, arrived to defend a client. The judge barred her from the courtroom, declaring that her high hem affronted the dignity of the court. But, as in the case of the motorcyclists and their crash helmets, the lawyer argued that her right to dress as she chose came under the constitutional right of free expression, and in this case a higher court agreed with her.

ground that flag desecration was permissible; the Court ruled that the man had been found guilty as much for what he said as for what he did, and that his words were protected by the First Amendment.

The right to refuse to salute the flag has been upheld and so has the right to fly foreign flags, even those of hostile nations. People who have been arrested for flaunting Russian, Chinese, North Korean, North Vietnamese or Cuban flags have been permitted to keep them aloft. Such acts of dissent have been adjudged permissible forms of symbolic free speech.

YOUR RIGHT TO PRIVACY

The founding fathers attempted to guarantee that most personal of all rights—the right to be let alone—when they passed the Third and Fourth Amendments. Later laws and court decisions have broadened some of these protections, yet have not been entirely able to keep up with advances in technology that make it easy to discover and disseminate information you consider nobody's business but your own.

Within your own home, your rights to privacy are fairly clear. You can refuse entrance to almost anyone, even government officials. Civilians who force their way in are trespassing, of course, and the law will throw them out for you. The Third Amendment says that soldiers cannot stay in your house without your permission, and the Fourth Amendment guarantees your "person, houses, papers, and effects, against unreasonable searches and seizures" by government officers, including the police. Before they can legally disturb your privacy, they must have a formal warrant, issued by a judge, that accurately describes what they are looking for.

The definition of what constitutes a house, safe against unreasonable search and seizure, is quite broad. The Supreme Court has ruled that it is almost any private place where you hang your hat, even briefly. Apartments qualify, and so do hotel rooms where you may stay for only a few hours. Not even the owner has the right to let the police into a guest's room. One guest slapped a suit on a California hotel in 1960 when the hotel clerk unlocked the man's door to allow the police to search his room. The Supreme Court acknowledged that when a guest registers in a hotel he gives his implied permission for maids, repairmen and other hotel employees, including the house detective, to enter his room as required; but this, the Court concluded, did not give the police, too, the right to walk in, even if the clerk willingly unlocked the door for them.

The Court applied the same principle to boardinghouses in a case in which an owner, assuming that he had property rights to a tenant's room, let the police in to search it without a warrant. The Court found against the owner. By the same token, your employer cannot grant the police permission to make an unwarranted search of your office desk. If you leave something exposed on top of your desk, it is fair game for anyone who sees it; but if you shut things away in your desk drawers you are entitled to the same privacy you would have in your home. Even a telephone booth can become your temporary home. Once you have dropped your dime into the slot, you have paid your rent for the little cubicle, and you are entitled to as much privacy inside it as you would be in any other residence.

Once you venture outside your "home," your privacy becomes vulnerable, although you still possess a number of protections. All states give you the power to control the use of your name and photograph for commercial purposes, for example. New York was first to pass such a privacy law, in the wake of protests over an indignity suffered in 1902 by a young woman named Roberson. A firm called the Rochester Folding Box Company used a pirated picture of her to advertise its brand of flour, compounding the injury by printing the slogan "The Flour of the Family" under the picture. The unauthorized use of her likeness—and the awful pun—made Miss Roberson wince, and she sued for invasion of privacy. The court was sympathetic but ruled that there was no such legally protected right. The ensuing public outcry led to passage of the New York law, making it both a misdemeanor and a ground for a damage suit to use a person's name or likeness, without written sanction, for trade purposes. But where the right of privacy clashes with the right of the public to know, privacy generally loses. One case involved a former child prodigy who had slipped into drab obscurity. When a magazine published an account of his life, he sued, claiming that his privacy had been invaded. He lost; the Supreme Court held that the public had a right to know what had happened to a person who had once been a public figure.

If you do something that turns you into a person of public interest, you must usually take the consequences as far as publicity is concerned. People who deliberately make themselves public figures —government officials, actors—lose most of the normal rights to privacy. No court is likely to restrain a photographer who sneaks pictures of a publicity-hungry starlet sunbathing nude. But even ordinary private people can be made public figures by events beyond their control. Suppose you happen to be present at a big fire and a news photographer snaps your picture; the newspaper has the right to print it whether you like the idea or not. In such a case, the right of the press to report the news takes precedence over your right to privacy.

A telephone booth becomes your temporary home, the Supreme Court has said, the moment you drop your dime in the slot. Since you have paid your rent, you are entitled to complete privacy, free of police snooping, just as you would be in your own house.

Even when the right of the public to know is not being served, you may not be able to prevent others from observing—and reporting on—your personal affairs. Your only recourse against the snooping of a private detective, for example, is to sue for damages on the grounds that the unofficial probing unfairly hurt your reputation or caused you mental anguish. One case that came to court involved a private detective who had been hired by an insurance company to shadow a man. He did his job so crudely that both the subject and his friends became aware of it. The man sued the insurance company because its sleuth's "rough and open" shadowing had hurt the plaintiff's reputation. The court agreed. But the opinion of the judge made it clear that a private detective has the right to operate if he does his job properly. He can follow a man around the clock and even photograph him—if he does it so discreetly that the subject and his associates are unaware of the surveillance.

Electronic snooping

Discreet surveillance is now so simple that many of the basic safeguards for privacy have become at least partly ineffective. Long-range cameras, secret wiretaps and hidden radio transmitters enable snoopers, private or official, to penetrate even the constitutionally guarded precincts of the home—without giving anyone a chance to demand a warrant. A group of lobbyists in Washington were surprised to discover that their conversation was being picked up by a miniaturized microphone-transmitter planted in the olive of a martini. The CIA is said to have a device that picks up a conversation in a closed room from hundreds of yards away by focusing on the minute vibrations of the room's window.

The use of such devices is not necessarily illegal. You are presently allowed to record any of your own conversations, regardless of whether other participants know their words are being recorded. You can tape everything that goes on in your office while you are there, and you can carry a hidden recorder to someone else's office. But you can go no further. It is a crime to eavesdrop on conversations that do not include you. If you do so, you break the law (and you also become liable for damages for invasion of privacy). Moreover, this area of privacy is being expanded, with further limits being placed on the use of recording devices.

These restrictions apply generally to private individuals. The police are not so limited. If they obtain a court order in advance, they can listen in on all the conversations of a suspect. Evidence they obtain in this way can serve as valid evidence in court. And in a few instances, recorded evidence obtained without benefit of advance court approval has been accepted during trials.

The legal problem first arose in 1862, when California outlawed the tapping of telegraph wires. The Supreme Court considered the issue in 1928, in a celebrated case of a West Coast bootlegger named Olmstead. The police had obtained evidence of his infractions of the Prohibition law by tapping his telephone, and Olmstead claimed that such evidence could not be used in his trial since the wiretap violated his Fourth Amendment protection against police search without a warrant. The Supreme Court disagreed, ruling that the police had not invaded Olmstead's house but had only tampered with the telephone wire outside the house. Yet in later cases the Court has sometimes ruled for, sometimes against, such forms of surveillance. In one case a conviction was reversed because evidence had been gained with a "spike mike" stuck into the wall of a house. And in 1963 Justice William Brennan said, "Electronic aids add a whole new dimension to eavesdropping. They make it more penetrating, more truly obnoxious to a free society. Electronic surveillance, in fact, makes the police omniscient; and police omniscience is one of the most effective tools of tyranny." But only a few years afterward the Supreme Court took a different tack when it approved tape-recorded evidence that was obtained by a police agent interviewing a suspect. This kind of eavesdropping is not really eavesdropping, the Court held, because the device "was carried in and out by an agent who was there with petitioner's assent, and it neither saw nor heard more than the agent himself." Thus, if an investigator from the Internal Revenue Service enters your home at your invitation and sits down to discuss a problem concerning your taxes, he may be able to record your conversation without telling you. Unknown to you, he could have a hidden tape recorder in his brief case or even his coat pocket—some tape recorders are smaller than a pack of cigarettes—that would record every word you say as possible evidence in a later tax case against you.

Lobbyists who gathered at a Washington bar one day discovered a new form of assault on their right to privacy. Their conversation was being recorded by a miniature microphone-transmitter planted in the olive of a martini.

The specter of the computer

A potentially far greater danger to individual privacy is posed by another modern electronic miracle, the computer. Electronic data banks of both government and private agencies have amassed detailed descriptions of most Americans, their beliefs and habits and daily activities. The half dozen largest credit bureaus in the U.S.—those companies that keep track of how you pay your bills—maintain computerized files on approximately 50 per cent of all Americans. The FBI has electronic files on many millions of citizens—exactly how

The inescapable school record
School records can haunt you all your life. If as a boy you were marked unruly for beaning your teacher with an apple, that unpleasant characterization may pop up in later years when you apply for a job or a mortgage. Many schools have long opened their files to the police, employers and welfare workers; and in the age of computers these records are easier to get at, stored in data banks that will yield up your personal history at the push of a button.

many it will not say—while the Internal Revenue Service has fed information on every taxpayer into a single massive computer setup in Martinsburg, West Virginia *(Chapter 8).* Unless you have been living in a cave and subsisting on nuts and berries for the last couple of decades, there is almost certainly a computerized dossier on you at Martinsburg. And if you are a modern American who uses credit cards, has a couple of department store charge accounts and has a mortgage on your house, there are probably a half dozen or more such dossiers concerning you on tape in other computers.

For many years, of course, banks, credit agencies, Internal Revenue and other government agencies have kept records on people. But these records used to be tucked in folders that in turn were hidden away in file cabinets, and these cabinets were widely separated. Imagine a typical mobile American. He was born in Tucson and went to high school there, compiling a fair record. Then he went to college in Arkansas and had a minor brush with the police there as the result of a prank. He got his first job in St. Louis and, trying to feed a new wife and family on a puny starting salary, had some trouble paying his bills. Then a better job opportunity arose in Philadelphia and he moved there, negotiating a mortgage to buy a house and otherwise using credit to purchase needed items, from furniture to food.

In the old days all such records would have stayed behind. That merely fair high school record would be locked away in a dusty school archive in Tucson, the police record would be a long-forgotten item buried in some Arkansas courthouse, the bill-paying trouble in St. Louis would be similarly hidden in a yellowing folder in the basement of a Missouri bank—and so on. Nobody could possibly retrieve all this buried information and assemble it in one place, thus drawing a misleadingly unflattering portrait.

But if this information had been placed on tape in computers —as is being done more and more nowadays—it could be retrieved almost instantly, with the push of a button. What is more, computers often flesh out their files by automatically swapping information among themselves. "We now live in an age of the total documentary portrait," according to Dr. Alan F. Westin, who directed a National Science Foundation study of the threats to privacy posed by computerized data banks. One example of such data-bank-to-data-bank interchange: The FBI obtains about 25,000 credit reports from credit bureau dossiers every year and feeds this information into its own data banks. As Dr. Westin points out, "Every individual has a life-long record somewhere, and we are being judged on those records more than on a face-to-face basis."

A crucial problem with such electronic dossiers is that you have very little legal control over what goes into your documentary portrait or what the operators of the data banks do with it. Facts that you do not mind sharing with an institution such as your insurance company may become fair game for any government bureaucrat who asks for them. Then the information may be passed along from his data bank to other fact-hungry computers.

Public schools probably compile the most intimate of all data portraits, points out Arthur R. Miller of the University of Michigan, and yet, in most communities, the students have no control over how or by whom this information may be used. As a rule, the child described in these school records is not permitted to see them, and neither are his parents. On the other hand, many schools willingly open the records to truant officers, local and federal police agencies, sociologists, welfare workers and potential employers. Many of the records are computerized, and they find their way into data banks, where it is almost impossible to discover who makes use of them. Thus, a 20-year-old applying for his first job might be turned down because a teacher had noted on his record 10 years before that he was "unruly" and had a "short attention span."

Even the innocent exercise of your freedom to travel may expose you to unwelcome scrutiny. A major airline acknowledged in 1968 that it keeps a computer dossier on all of its passengers, fed constantly by its electronic reservation and ticketing service. The airline said that 10 to 15 federal, state, local and "other" investigators had used this data bank daily to find out who traveled where, the telephone number from which he made his reservation, his seat number on the airplane, the names of his traveling companions and what he ate for lunch. Such information—coupled with data retrieved from car rental agencies, credit card companies, and hotel and theater reservation systems—could paint a flash portrait of the unwitting traveler that is open to many unwarranted inferences. You might unknowingly fly cross-country seated next to a notorious gangster, for example. By retrieving this fact from a computer memory bank, the authorities could conceivably draw the wholly false conclusion that you and your seat partner were cronies. Yet you might never even learn that your activities had become a part of someone's permanent files.

Such inaccurate or misleading information is a part of many dossiers. The FBI admits that its files often contain "raw"—unevaluated —material that ranges from the trivial to the downright false. Much of the information in credit files is also unchecked gossip. Taken all together, this collection of raw information can draw a totally misleading profile of a man's life. Technology has simply raced ahead of the law by permitting masses of private information to become stored for instant retrieval in computers. The only federal law that protects your reputation against harm from data banks applies to commercial credit services. Under the Fair Credit Reporting Act, which took effect in 1971, you can demand to see a credit agency's file on you, correct all misinformation it contains and require that the corrections be sent to previous recipients of reports on you *(Chapter 7)*.

Another, if halting, step toward legal control of computers has been taken by several states. These new laws deal with the police records on the eight million Americans arrested on some ground or other every year. Most of these records involve people arrested by mistake

Guilt by computer association
At least one major airline uses a computer to record your identity and that of your seatmate on a flight—and allows police and the FBI access to this information. If you happened to sit next to a gangster, a law enforcement agency might conclude that you and he were cronies, and your brief, innocent contact with him could return to plague you.

or charged with minor crimes for which they were never prosecuted. A college student, for example, may be a bystander at a mass rally when it erupts into a riot. The police arrest 60 students, the uninvolved youth among them. He is taken to the police station, fingerprinted, photographed and arraigned before a judge. When he explains his role, the charges are dropped and he goes free. But his arrest record remains behind. Such records, even those of mistaken arrests, become "rap" sheets. In many areas the police give credit agencies and would-be employers access to these rap sheets, and most police departments routinely forward them, with picture and fingerprints, to the FBI's crime information center in Washington, D.C. There the file remains, ready for instant retrieval unless the police who sent it request that the report be destroyed. Federal agencies, including the Civil Service Commission, have access to reports in the FBI files. Thus a person who once was mistakenly arrested may forever find himself mysteriously turned away when he seeks a job.

To prevent such injustices, 10 states—Alaska, Arizona, California, Indiana, Kansas, Michigan, Minnesota, Missouri, New Jersey and Utah—have passed "expungement" laws, which provide for the erasure of police records on certain offenses once the state concludes that there is no overriding public reason for keeping them. It is generally quite simple to initiate the procedure—a letter to the attorney general sets the machinery in motion in many of the states. But so many limitations surround expungement—in Minnesota, for example, the only police record that can be erased is one on a first offender in a drug case—that these laws are seldom taken advantage of.

The semipublic circulation of rap sheets has also been challenged, and at least one use of them was forbidden by a federal court in Los Angeles. An aerospace company refused to hire a job-seeker because on checking police arrest records it found he had been arrested 14 times. He had never been convicted or even tried for a crime, and he sued the company for violating his civil rights by prying into his inconclusive arrest record. The court upheld him and ordered the company to stop examining arrest records, as distinct from conviction records, when it considered applicants for nonsensitive jobs.

The founding fathers would have approved. They were wary, from bitter personal experience, of intrusions on an individual's privacy. And they built into the basic law of the land safeguards that, extended and broadened, can protect the rights of Americans even in a day of computer data banks and martini-olive eavesdropping devices.

By **DON A. SCHANCHE**
PAGE KEETON, Consultant

12 Wills and estates

What you can (and cannot) do with what you leave behind

While the law watches over you every day you live, its concern is never more punctilious during your lifetime than it is afterward. The moment that you have died, the law steps in to supervise the distribution of your estate, all the worldly goods you leave behind—money in your bank accounts, stocks, life insurance, house, automobile, even clothing. None of it will belong to you any more, for you can't take it with you. And to whom it should then belong is controlled by an ancient and often confusing body of legal doctrine. Your own wishes will be observed, up to a point, if you plan your estate carefully. But if you fail to make a careful plan in advance, the sometimes strange operations of these inheritance laws may fritter away a large part of the estate, for taxes and legal charges that might have been avoided with proper planning can take a big bite. And whatever is left over can be kept from those whom you intended to provide for and may be turned over to others whom you had no intention of benefiting.

Planning for death is one legal step that many people put off. Dying is unpleasant to think about. And estates are often regarded as chiefly a problem for the rich. But your estate may be larger and more complicated than you realize. If you total up the value of all your possessions, the sum may surprise you. It is not unusual for a man in modest circumstances to leave behind $100,000 or more. Whatever the sum, it is worth distributing with care, and with due regard for the laws of your state.

The traditional way to control the distribution of such assets is by making out a will, a legal document specifying who is to get what. These orders are not executed automatically after a person dies. The will must first receive court approval through a process called probate. It almost always requires a lawyer and involves some legal costs. But in most cases probate is fairly fast and simple, and the court routinely directs that the provisions of the will be carried out. Under some circumstances, however, stipulations in a will may be altered or canceled by the court. And if there is no will, the probate court must divide up the estate according to rigid rules laid down by state laws, and can pay no attention to the desires of the deceased.

Not everything a man leaves behind him goes through probate. Life insurance, for example, is usually made out to a specific beneficiary; the proceeds are paid directly and automatically to that beneficiary upon the policyholder's death without any need for a will or probate. Similar direct disposition of other property—bank accounts, stocks, a home—is also possible with a number of legal devices. The property can be held in the name of several people, so that when one dies ownership is automatically transferred to the others. Or it can be

Intestacy laws are on the books to establish precedence for the heirs of someone who died without a will. But sometimes these laws turn over an estate to forgotten relatives—even if one or two are bums.

given away in advance of death—either completely, as outright gifts, or with strings attached—through trust agreements, which may permit the original owner to control and sometimes even use the property until he dies. Such devices may have advantages. They generally eliminate any question over who is to receive the property; they may reduce delays and legal fees; and in some cases they may save on taxes. But they also have disadvantages. They can tie up property the original owner may need while he lives; and instead of reducing his taxes they may prevent him from taking advantage of tax-saving arrangements that could otherwise have been used.

The choices are so complicated—and the harm caused by a wrong choice so severe—that even a man with modest assets needs the help of a lawyer, preferably one who has specialized in a field of law that is called estate planning. The lawyer may recommend that some things be jointly owned and others be placed in trusts of one kind or another. But no matter what other arrangements he sets up, he will almost certainly insist on drafting a will.

To see what happens when there is no will, consider the case of the Markses. Mr. Marks, 34, his wife and their three small children lived in a $32,000 house in a pleasant suburb. As sales manager for a chemical company, Marks earned $26,000 a year, owned two automobiles, had about $10,000 invested in stocks and a few thousand more in his checking and savings accounts. He justifiably felt that he and his family were in pretty good shape.

Marks was, but his family was not. For he had never made out a will. He always assumed he would get around to that before anything catastrophic happened to him, and that even if something did happen, his wife would automatically inherit all of his property. He was wrong. One rainy night, driving home to the suburbs from a late sales conference in the city, Marks's car skidded off the road and struck a tree, killing him instantly.

After the funeral, when the shock of his death had partially worn off, Mrs. Marks received another shock. Because her husband had not made a will, he had died "intestate"—that is, he had left behind no legal testimony to guide the state in the distribution of his property. And in the absence of such testimony, the state—like all 49 others in the nation—was obliged to take over the management of Marks's estate and distribute its assets according to the intestacy laws. No amount of pleading as to the deceased person's real intentions can alter or affect the application of a state's intestacy statutes.

In Mrs. Marks's case, the laws stipulated that the widow of a man who dies intestate receives one third of her husband's estate, while the remaining two thirds go to the children. This arrangement seems fair enough, but the way it works out becomes complicated when the children are minors. Each child's share remains under the control of the court until he comes of age; in the meantime the court delegates some of its responsibility to a legal guardian, who can use the children's inheritances for their support. In this case the court appointed Mrs. Marks guardian of her own children—but she had to petition the court to be appointed, post a bond to guarantee that she would not misuse the children's funds, and continue over the years to file frequent, detailed reports accounting for every penny of the children's money she spent. The only part of her husband's estate that she could use freely, for any purpose she chose, was the one third that the intestacy laws granted to her.

How much simpler the Marks family's life would have been had there been a will. Marks could have left his entire estate to his wife, giving her the legal right to use as much of it as she needed for herself and the children—without the necessity of posting bonds or making a financial accounting to anyone. His failure to take a simple legal step forced her to go through a number of irksome and unnecessarily costly steps in order to care for her family.

Actually, Mrs. Marks was relatively lucky. Sometimes state intestacy laws turn over an estate to some forgotten relatives—even if one or two are bums—and leave deserving members of a family without the funds they need. When one wealthy man died intestate, a shiftless nephew he detested wound up with the estate. The man's wife had already died, and the only child was her daughter by a previous husband. Under the state's intestacy laws, the nephew was next in line; the girl, dearly loved by her stepfather, was left without a cent. Another man who married a wealthy woman decided he need not worry about her or their children's financial security and failed to make a will. He forgot about his own impecunious parents, however. When he died intestate, his estate went to his wife and children—who did not need it. His parents, who did need support but did not qualify under the state's intestacy laws, received nothing.

Intestacy laws may seem unnecessarily harsh or cruel. They are not meant to be. They are on the books to establish a reasonable

The widow of a man who dies without a will may have to petition the court to be appointed guardian of her own children, post a bond to guarantee that she will not misuse their funds, and account for every penny of this money.

order of precedence for the heirs of someone who dies without making a will and also to stipulate a fair portion for each heir. If such laws did not exist, the estates of those who die intestate might be tied up for years in bitter legal wrangling among relatives.

While most men recognize the need for a will, many women do not. Even if a woman is married and depends entirely on her husband for the support of their family, she may have property of her own—a bank account, securities and jewelry. And if she dies without a will, these assets may not automatically go to her husband. Part of her property usually goes to her children, and if they are minors, the intestacy laws create the same problems of guardianship that arise when a father dies without a will. Her parents might also be entitled to a share of her estate whether they actually need it or not. One childless couple, for example, had lived in a house belonging to the wife. When she died, leaving no will, the husband was astonished to discover that his in-laws, with whom he had never gotten along, were legally entitled to a share of the house. In order to give them their share, he had to sell his home and split the proceeds with them.

Such a case is rare. Wives generally outlive their husbands. But their longevity means that almost certainly they will have substantial estates to leave behind them, consisting largely of what they have inherited from their husbands. To ensure proper, legal disposition of such property, a woman needs a will.

There is also another, very modern, reason for a woman to make her own will: Marriage has become a considerably less permanent institution than it used to be. Take the case of Nancy, who packed up and separated from her husband after enduring several years of his drinking and philandering. She went to live with her parents in another state and never saw her husband again. On her own she built up a successful decorating business and was able to accumulate a modest estate. But when she died at the age of 55, she left no will. Under the laws of intestacy of her state, half the assets she had accumulated went to the husband she had not even heard from for nearly 30 years. Her aged parents, who had become dependent on her, had to make do with what was left. Although divorce generally cancels out any legal obligations that may previously have existed between the two people, a separation does not.

His-and-her wills

When both partners in a marriage make wills, they have a choice of different types. Many couples who are getting along well and assume that this happy condition will continue throughout their lives choose "reciprocal," or "mutual" wills. These are separate documents that are made out, signed and witnessed independently of each other; but they are complementary, each leaving one spouse's estate to the other. Another type of husband-wife will is the joint will, a somewhat more complex legal instrument. It is a single document that serves as the will of both parties. A major drawback to both kinds of his-and-her wills, however, is the chance that there will be later difficulty in changing them to suit altered circumstances. Once both parties have agreed on the distribution of their joint assets to certain heirs, and one party dies, the survivor may not be free to amend the agreement. Suppose, for example, Bob and Mary draw up a joint will combining their estates and leaving equal shares of this combined estate to their two children. Bob dies first. Their daughter Jane then marries a wealthy man and no longer needs her full share of the estate. But there is nothing that her mother can do to change the will to leave the bulk of the family estate to her other daughter, who could well use the money. Because the will was signed by both Mary, and her late husband, she remains bound by that agreement.

Who can make a will?

Despite the fact that making a will is a good idea, it should be pointed out that not everyone can legally do so. Children, for example, have no say in the disposition of their property. A testator (or testatrix, if female) must be at least 21 years old (18 in some states), before his or her will can be honored in court. Many states make an exception to the rule and allow anyone serving in the armed forces the right to make a will regardless of his age.

While no states have upper limits on the age at which a testator may legally make a will, all require that he be "of sound mind" and not subject to "undue influence." Just exactly what sound mind means has been the subject of numerous court battles. Heirs who feel they have been shortchanged by a will frequently conclude that rich old Uncle Charlie could not possibly have been of sound mind when he drafted it. Such claims are difficult to prove. The laws in most states simply require a testator to be rational enough to realize what he is doing, to understand what property he owns and to remember who the members of his immediate family are, even if he does not wish to leave them anything. The laws say nothing about his intelligence, his living habits, his beliefs or his tastes. If he clearly states his intent to dispose of his property in some fashion, the court usually upholds him, as one did in the case of a wealthy man who left his entire estate to his pets. His relatives contested the will, claiming the

When a man left his fortune to his cats and dogs, relatives fought the will, claiming he was irrational—he had dined at table with his pets. The court ruled that the man was as entitled to pick his heirs in death as his companions in life.

old man was obviously irrational—he had made a habit of dining at the same table with his cats and dogs. The court upheld the will, however, ruling that the deceased had as much right to choose his heirs in death as he had to choose his companions in life.

Miffed heirs often decide to contest a will on the grounds that the person who made it was "acting under the influence" of someone else—a nurse, say, or a secretary or friend. But undue influence is also extremely difficult to prove; while the courts realize that a person of advanced age might easily have been subjected to certain emotional influences as a result of close personal ties, they have been reluctant to discredit such influences as necessarily "undue" or "improper." The only times courts have thrown out wills because of undue influence have been in cases in which it could be shown that the influence was so powerful that it rendered the testator totally incapable of exercising his own independent judgment.

Take the case of a millionaire Texas widower who left the bulk of his estate to an attractive young secretary, the constant companion of his later years. The millionaire's children contested the will, charging that the secretary had actually been their father's mistress and had used this relationship to persuade him to change his will in her favor. The judge agreed. But he also decided that, however mercenary the woman's motives may have been, there was no proof that she had made use of any influence other than her attention and affection. There was also no evidence that the deceased had been unaware of what he was doing at the time he revised his will. It was upheld.

Don't do it yourself

Once you decide to make a will, do not grab a pen and try to draw it up yourself. For the provisions that should be included depend on the size and nature of your estate, the number of heirs involved and their relationship to you, the specific conditions that you may wish to apply and the complicated laws governing wills, property and taxes in the state in which you live. No layman can fully understand all of these possible options or their legal consequences.

The fact that you should not draw up your own will does not mean you cannot. So long as a homemade will meets the legal requirements of the state in which it is filed—including signatures from the correct number of witnesses—the courts will usually uphold it. In some states a handwritten, or "holographic," will, if it has been properly executed and can be proved to be in the deceased's own handwriting, will be accepted even if it has not been witnessed. Courts have accepted wills that were done in pen, pencil, crayon and even paint, so long as the writing was legible. And in some special cases, a will need not even be written, but can be stated orally. This kind of will, which lawyers refer to as a nuncupative will, is sometimes used by servicemen who are on active combat duty or by persons who are near death as the result of an accident or serious illness. Such oral wills must also be properly witnessed and then put into written form by the witnesses as soon as possible. Even so, they can be used to convey only the deceased's personal property, not real property such as a house or piece of land.

PLANNING YOUR ESTATE

But there is more to your estate than a will. To provide most efficiently for your heirs, you will probably need the assistance of a lawyer who has had experience not only in drafting wills but in the broader field of estate planning as well. Estate planning is the legal specialty that covers the entire scope of problems involved in managing and distributing one's property, including wills, trusts, gifts, taxes and investments. The first thing an estate-planning specialist will probably ask you to do is to draw up a detailed list evaluating all of your assets. The first things you will probably think of are stocks, bonds and bank accounts. But there are also your home, furnishings, appliances, clothing, books, automobile and such other personal property as sporting equipment, a stamp collection or a work of art. And you might not think to add to this list life insurance policies, pensions or the profit-sharing plan provided by your company. These last assets are seldom disposed of in a will, but they are nonetheless part of your estate, and they are vital segments of your total plan.

Next your lawyer will ask you to draw up a second list, naming all of the relatives, dependents, friends, charities or institutions you wish to include as beneficiaries of your estate. Make sure you list the exact legal names, correct addresses and any relationship to you of the persons named so that the courts will later have no trouble distin-

Your estate may be larger than you realize. You will probably think first of stocks and bank accounts. But there are also your home, furnishings, clothing, car, sporting equipment. And you might not think to add to this list life insurance policies and pension.

guishing them from possible other claimants with similar names. Next to each designated beneficiary, you should enter the amount of money, the percentage of your estate or the specific items in your inventory that you plan to leave to that particular person or institution. Some of these beneficiaries and the property you intend for them to receive will be stipulated in your will. Others may already be named as direct beneficiaries of your insurance or annuity funds. You may wish to take care of still others by making gifts of one form or another while you are still alive; such transfers need not be listed in your will, although in some circumstances it may be advisable to mention them. Once your lawyer has all the information he needs, he can assist you in drawing up an overall plan that will help to assure that your wishes will be carried out after your death with a minimum of delay and administrative costs.

Property problems
One thing your lawyer may explain to you at the start, and in terms of your own particular financial situation, is that the law views an estate as divided into two kinds of property—real property (real estate) and personal property, such as money, investments, automobiles, jewelry and other objects of value. In general, anything that is not real property is considered personal property. The transfers of the two types are even given different names in a will. When you leave someone personal property, you "bequeath" it, and what he receives is a "bequest." When you leave real property, you "devise" it, and what he receives is also called a devise. State laws may allow more freedom with bequests than with devises.

There are a number of ways to devise real property—as well as a number of legal restrictions on what you can do with it. You may discover, for example, that your estate would benefit if you owned some of your property—personal and real—not by yourself but jointly with someone else. There are several different kinds of joint ownership: "tenancy in common," "joint tenancy with the right of survivorship" and "tenancy by the entirety." The second—joint tenancy—is far and away the most widely used.

The first type—tenancy in common—is a useful way of sharing ownership among two or more people so that each part-owner retains control of his share. Suppose two friends buy some land in a resort area as an investment, splitting the purchase fifty-fifty. They would probably choose to become tenants in common, for then each holds a separate half-interest in the property. In most states each of these separate interests is like any other wholly owned property. Unlike property held in other forms of joint ownership, each share of property owned by tenants in common becomes part of its owner's personal estate. Thus, each owner can sell or give his interest in the property to another person, or dispose of it upon his death through his own will without affecting the interest of the other party.

The second type of joint ownership arrangement is a favorite means of arranging for disposition of property without the need of a will or probate. When a married couple buy a house, for instance, they will probably take ownership as joint tenants with right of survivorship. Joint tenancy means that if either spouse dies, ownership of the entire property will pass immediately to the survivor, regardless of the terms of the deceased's will or of the laws of intestacy if he or she happens to die without a will. The property then does not become involved in probate procedures and it is not tied up during settlement of the estate. Legally the property is considered to be wholly owned by both parties simultaneously, and either one of them has total control over it at any time. A joint bank account with right of survivorship, for example, usually allows either person to withdraw the entire contents of the account without the consent of the other.

While anyone may hold any kind of property as a joint tenant with the right of survivorship, this form of ownership is most commonly used by married couples. Joint tenancy is sometimes used by young couples who mistakenly feel they do not need wills. They put all their assets—investments and bank accounts as well as their homes —into joint ownership. While this practice eliminates problems with wills and avoids probate costs, it may cause more trouble than it saves, for if both spouses die suddenly, the intestacy laws then apply. Joint tenancy also raises estate tax questions that may impose unnecessary tax costs on your estate.

The third form of joint ownership, tenancy by the entirety, is available in some states but is restricted to married couples and can be used only as a means of owning real estate. The husband and wife become legally one person, so that the death of one of the parties does not affect the legal title of the property, and it automatically comes under sole control of the survivor, regardless of the provisions of a will. But for all practical purposes, neither can sell the property without the consent of the other.

In eight Western and Southern states (Arizona, California, Idaho, Louisiana, Nevada, New Mexico, Texas and Washington), there is still another form of joint ownership, called community property. The laws on community property differ widely among these states, but in general, they assume that all property acquired by the joint efforts of a husband and wife during marriage belongs to both in equal shares. Each has a right to only half of the jointly owned property and can dispose in his or her will of only his or her half. However, any property acquired by gift or inheritance by either individual is the sole property of that spouse.

Of all forms of real property, none receives more attention from the law than the home, or as lawyers sometimes call it, the homestead. In most states a man does not have complete freedom to dispose of his home upon his death. Since a surviving wife and children must be assured of continued shelter, many states have laws requiring ownership of the home to pass directly to the wife upon the death of her husband, regardless of what he may have stated to the contrary in his will. Other states give the wife and children the right to occupy the family homestead at least temporarily after the father's death, regardless of his will. Only a few states fail to give the widow any rights at all to the home. Under these homestead laws, the house cannot be seized or sold to pay off any debts of the deceased.

Inheritance rights

In addition to laws governing how certain kinds of property can be transferred, most states also stipulate who must receive certain shares in the total estate. These laws protect a spouse and children from being entirely cut out of an inheritance inadvertently—or deliberately. Suppose a husband decides for reasons of his own to leave his wife nothing at all. Since the husband usually owns the bulk of the property in any family, most states protect the widow against being cut short by granting her the right to renounce the will and to claim part of her husband's estate, regardless of the terms of his will. These dower rights for widows date back to the Middle Ages, when it was common practice for a widow to receive one third of her husband's real property for the rest of her lifetime. While modern laws differ from state to state, and some states no longer use the term dower, most guarantee a widow at least a portion of her husband's probate estate. (Similarly, many states grant surviving husbands a share of the wife's estate, originally called curtesy.)

Suppose, for example, that Mr. Clark dies and leaves a will in which he gives his wife only 10 per cent of his estate. If he had left no will, Mrs. Clark would have been entitled to at least a third of his estate. Under the dower laws, Mrs. Clark has a "right of election"; that is, she can elect to take the 10 per cent stipulated by her husband or ignore her husband's will and receive a portion of his estate that equals or approximates—depending on the state—the amount she would have received had he died intestate. The intestacy laws can also be invoked in many states if the husband fails even to mention his wife in his will, much less grant her an adequate sum. The law politely assumes that such a failure to mention a wife was not intentional, but rather an oversight. And it can be an innocent oversight, of course, with no intention on the man's part to disinherit his spouse. It is conceivable, for example, that he made out the will when he was still a bachelor, and never got around to revising it after he married.

Children have no rights to a deceased parent's estate comparable to dower or curtesy, but most states guarantee them some consideration. A father who wishes to disinherit his children must generally do so specifically, and by name, in his will, for in some states the law assumes that the father did not necessarily intend to disinherit his children even if the will does not mention them. One man whose closest heir was an only daughter intentionally made no mention of her in his will because he felt that she had already been quite adequately provided for. Instead, he provided in his will that his estate be divided among friends and distant relatives who were in need of financial assistance. The law in his state, however, assumes that the omission in a will of mention of a direct descendant constitutes an oversight rather than an intentional act. The court consequently ordered that the man's entire estate go to his daughter, and the friends and other relatives he had hoped to aid received nothing.

A son or daughter who is not mentioned in a will is known in legal terms as a pretermitted—that is, disregarded—child. Some states grant such children the same share of the parent's estate that they would have received had the parent died intestate, unless there is proof that their omission from the will was intentional. Other states grant such rights only to pretermitted children who were born after the will was made, on the assumption that anyone who does not mention children living when the will was made has done so intentionally and meant to disinherit them. In states that follow this rule, the wishes of the deceased are usually carried out. All the more reason for consulting a lawyer to find out the law of your state.

The law is so solicitous about making certain that close relatives are not inadvertently disinherited that intentionally disinheriting them is extremely difficult. Unless a wife has signed a document expressly waiving her dower rights, the courts will normally see that she receives a share of the estate. And it is difficult for a father to disinherit his children except by inserting a clause in the will indicating that he is aware of what he is doing and stating a clear and reasonable excuse, such as "I have made no provision in this will for my son because he is already adequately provided for through a trust created by his grandfather." In such cases, the courts are careful to carry out the father's wishes and will uphold the will.

Four types of legacies

In addition to these restrictions as to what you may or may not be able to accomplish with a will, the law also stipulates priorities that establish the order in which your heirs may benefit from the proceeds of your estate.

Every inheritance, whether bequest (personal property) or devise (real estate), is known as a legacy. There are four major types of legacies, and they are listed here in the order in which they are generally stated in a will—the same order, it should be noted, in which the heirs usually receive their shares of the estate.

■ *A specific legacy* consists of a particular item of personal property that you leave to a named beneficiary—a silver bracelet to your niece Ellen. Once this object is stipulated as a specific legacy, it must be given to the stated beneficiary after your death. It cannot be sold by the executor of your estate, for example, in an effort to raise cash for other bequests.

■ *A general legacy* is a gift of a sum of money to a named individual. It is paid out of the general assets of the probate estate—everything except the specific legacies—but is reduced by debts and expenses. The cash for general legacies comes from bank accounts and money raised by selling property that is not disposed of as specific legacies. If the total general assets prove to be insufficient to cover all the general legacies listed in the will, each general legacy is reduced proportionately so that everyone receives a fair share.

■ *A demonstrative legacy* is a bequest of a sum of money to be paid from a specific source, such as the sale of a stipulated piece of real estate or a certain number of securities, and is given priority over a general legacy to the extent of the value of the specific source. If the source available to cover the bequest does not produce the specified sum, the difference is made up from general assets.

■ *A residuary legacy* consists of whatever personal property is left in the estate after all debts, medical bills, taxes, administrative expenses and the costs of the funeral have been settled and all other legacies have been paid out.

Any items of personal property that you do not specifically mention or dispose of in your will automatically become part of the residuary legacy. In many cases, this may represent the bulk of an estate. But you should remember that the other legacies have first legal priority when the will is filed. The residuary legacy is paid out last. So if there is any chance that the assets of your estate may decline in value over the years, it would be wise not to stipulate that your wife and children are to be taken care of solely from the residue.

When stating bequests in your will, you need a great deal of foresight to avoid difficulty when the will is probated, perhaps many years later. Be sure to use full legal names rather than any shortened version or nickname. Do not refer to an heir as Jack, for example, if his legal name is John. And if he is a relative, stipulate the relationship —"my cousin, John Jones." It is also a good precaution to include addresses, for if more than one John Jones shows up to claim a bequest made to someone of that name, the court could use some help in determining who is the intended legatee. Courts have been known to disallow bequests that became bogged down in confusion—and any cause for confusion over the will could lead to its being contested.

Trying to control the future

Some people who are accustomed to having their own way during their lives try to perpetuate their control over events as they contemplate death. They try to influence their heirs' behavior by attaching conditions to bequests. One uncle, for example, left a large sum of money to a nephew on condition that the young man give up smoking. The nephew contested this clause, arguing that his uncle had no right to control his personal habits. The court, however, ruled that the uncle's request was not illegal or unreasonable, and that the young man would have to choose between his cigarettes and the money. He chose the money.

While courts generally respect a testator's conditions about such habits as smoking or drinking, they are reluctant to uphold stipulations that go beyond matters of life style, and they generally cancel provisions judged to be "contrary to public policy." A condition that a son or daughter never marry, for example, is usually ruled invalid. Nor can wills be used to break up an existing marriage. For example, parents who disapprove of a son-in-law may not leave money to their daughter with a stipulation that she divorce her husband. Such conditions are never recognized by a court. On the other hand, courts generally do allow husbands or wives to leave property to their widows or widowers on condition that they do not remarry.

Sometimes a person making a will sets up a condition unintentionally. In one strange case a benefactor left a yearly income to the wife of another man for "as long as she is above ground," meaning of course, as long as she lived. After the woman died, her husband had

Left a legacy by his uncle on condition he quit smoking, a young man challenged this effort to control his habits as unreasonable. But the court ordered the nephew to choose between cigarettes and cash. He chose the cash.

her body installed in a glass case and literally kept her above ground for another 30 years, all the while collecting the yearly income from his late wife's benefactor.

Choosing an executor

While planning the provisions of your will, you should also be giving some thought to how it is to be administered. For the will merely gives legal instructions for the disposition of your property. Someone must see to it that these instructions are carried out. He is the "executor," normally chosen by you and named in your will. If you make no will, however, the probate court will appoint an "administrator," who is paid from your estate as he distributes it according to the state's laws of intestacy. If you make a will but do not name an executor, the court again will appoint someone, possibly someone you do not know —or trust. You may choose more than one executor, if you wish, or name an alternate in case your first choice has moved to a distant city or dies before you do.

Anyone of legal age can serve as executor: your wife, your brother, your lawyer, a bank, a friend. Before you choose, however, consider the duties involved. Your executor will be responsible for supervising the liquidation and settlement of your estate as well as for administering and taking care of it until it has been fully distributed. He should be someone familiar with your own financial affairs and your business, if you have one. He should be known to and trusted by your family so that they can rely on him to protect their interests after your death. He should be young enough to survive you and likely to remain in your locality. And finally, he must be willing to accept what may turn out to be a considerable responsibility.

If your executor is not a lawyer, he will very likely need a lawyer's help. In some cases, your lawyer might be a good choice as your executor. For while he may not be so close to the family as others you could name, he would possess compensating advantages as an executor. Having helped to plan your estate and draw up your will, he probably understands your intentions concerning its disposition. A trust department of a bank offers many of the same advantages your lawyer does, and if the estate is a substantial one, involving trusts, real estate and other sources of income, the bank is particularly well qualified to manage such matters.

Many people combine the advantages of a professional executor —a lawyer or a bank—with those of a family executor by appointing several coexecutors. You could name your wife, or some friend close to the family, plus a lawyer who would handle most of the legal details. If you have extensive investments you might choose an investment counselor to take care of these matters. And if you have a business of your own, you might want to name a responsible associate as a coexecutor. No matter whom you choose, he should be prepared to devote a good deal of time and energy to his duties, for some settlements can take anywhere from a few months to a year, depending on the size and complexity of the estate. In the event of complications or disputes among the heirs, the process can sometimes drag on for years. The experience of your executor will determine the need—and expense—for legal assistance. A lawyer or banker will charge your estate for his services as executor, either on the basis of the time he spends or on a percentage of the value of the estate. Be sure to ask what the fee will be.

Your wife, brother, son, cousin or a friend could perform the same services free, of course, and often one of them can serve quite well. But there are some arguments against choosing a nonprofessional as sole executor. He will probably have to call upon a lawyer anyway to guide your will through probate channels and carry out the various legal functions of an executor *(box, page 363)*. Since the job can be long and tedious, he may come to hate it and give it less attention than it needs. Also, choosing a close relative to serve as executor may lead to family squabbles over the handling of the assets in the estate. If you do name a relative or friend as executor, there is an important point to remember: Unless you state otherwise, he will be required to post a bond with the court and put up a certain sum of money as "surety." The bond and surety, based on the total value of your estate, serve as a guarantee that the executor will protect the estate and carry out your instructions honestly and according to the law. If you do not wish to put your executor to the expense of making such a pledge, you must state in the will that you want him to serve "without bond." Banks and trust companies, because of their financial stability and reputation, are generally not required to post bond when serving as executor of an estate.

The executor manages only the financial aspects of your estate. If you have minor children, their care must be provided for, too. The surviving parent is normally recognized by the court as the natural guardian of the children, responsible for their upbringing. But only a legal guardian—someone specified by name in the will or appointed by the court—can look after whatever property they may have. The distinction is between the natural guardian of their persons and the legal guardian of their property.

If both parents die, the legal guardian assumes responsibility for

After your signature on your will comes a statement by witnesses that they have signed at your request and in your presence, that they saw you sign and that you appeared to be of sound mind and body and acting under your own volition.

both the persons and the property of minor children. If you do not name such a guardian in your will, the court must make this choice for you. The courts usually appoint a close relative as guardian, if at all possible, but he might not be the person you would have chosen. Suppose the court picked your brother, as your closest surviving relative. He might seem a logical choice to a judge but not necessarily to you if your sister-in-law, who would provide day-to-day care for your children, was someone you thought too harsh and demanding.

The best procedure is to name your spouse the legal guardian of your minor children and, in case your spouse does not survive you, to make a trusted relative or friend an alternate guardian. Don't forget that if a man's will fails to specify his children's legal guardian, the court will have to appoint one.

Since the guardian of your children may have to post a bond and file regular reports with the court, you may want to eliminate these problems for the person you choose. If you believe your wife can manage financial affairs for herself and the children, the simplest solution is to leave all of your property to her, and none to the children (remembering to indicate in your will why you are disinheriting them). Then they will have no legacies and she will not need to post a bond or file reports. Still another way to solve this problem—one that is commonly used when the estate is sizable—is to leave property to your children in the form of a trust, to be administered for them by your wife or anyone else you name as trustee (page 368).

WHAT A WILL SAYS

Putting into legally valid form all these complex instructions—the property to be left, the heirs you wish to give it to, the kinds of legacies you wish to bequeath, any conditions or stipulations you want to make, and the appointment of executors and guardians—calls for a lawyer. The format of a will is not mysterious, and indeed you can find printed forms and models in books. They are dangerous to use. Every person's estate is unique, and taxes, probate procedures and local laws vary so widely from state to state that you need a lawyer's help to make your will conform to your own particular situation.

The document he draws up begins with an "opening statement," a section that gives your name and full address and includes a sentence to the effect that you are making your last will and testament and are revoking all previous wills you may already have made. This language is used to convince a probate court that you knew what you were doing and that the instructions you gave took legal precedence over all others you might have given previously.

The next section would stipulate the distribution of your various devises and bequests, including whatever specific, general, demonstrative and residuary legacies you may have decided on.

An "administrative section" usually follows. It names your executor or executrix and a legal guardian if you have young children; and it stipulates whatever legal powers or limitations you wish to place on these persons (such as a phrase, for example, that the executor is to be permitted to serve without bond). This section would also normally contain a statement indicating your desire that your debts, including funeral expenses, be paid as soon as possible so that the slate will be wiped clean.

The final part of the will is a statement—to be followed by your signature—giving the date and testifying that you are indeed subscribing your name to the document. This should always come at the end of the will. (If a will contains more than one page, the previous pages should be numbered, dated and initialed by you as legal proof that no pages have been substituted.) If you supplement your will by adding fresh information after you have affixed your signature, the court may not accept it.

Your signature is followed by the attestation clause, which is a declaration by witnesses that they have signed at your request and in your presence, and that they have witnessed your signature to the will. They further attest that in their opinion you appeared to be of sound mind and body and acting under your own volition. They also state that, still in your presence and in the presence of one another, they have signed their names to the document. In other words, you and your witnesses must all state that everybody watched everybody else sign his name. Most states require at least two witnesses to a will, though it is common practice at most signings to have three witnesses present. While they need not read the will or know its contents, you should tell them, formally and clearly, that you are knowingly and willingly signing your last will and testament. If any question should come up later in probate court, these witnesses should be prepared to swear to its validity.

Some of this may seem like hocus-pocus, but it is legally important. Take the case of Elwood, who asked two friends if they would witness the will of his sister Johanna, who was confined to a wheel chair. He drove them to her house and had them wait in the sitting room while he wheeled her in. He then told his sister to "sign this paper," and she did. Next he told the witnesses to sign, and they did. When Johanna died, her will left her entire estate to good old Elwood. But when the will came to the probate court it was rejected. For when the witnesses were questioned under oath during the probate hearing, they said that Johanna had not demonstrated that she knew what she was signing. They further testified that she was not informed in their presence, nor were they themselves told at the time, that "this paper" was in fact her will.

Because similar questions may be asked about your will during the probate process, you need to be sure the witnesses will be available to answer them. The witnesses usually note their addresses on the document so that they can be tracked down more easily. Ideally, they should be younger than you are—so they will still be around if needed—and relatively permanent in their residence. A witness to a will should not be a legatee in that will. If a beneficiary is a witness the will might not be invalidated, but a bequest to him might be canceled. Even if the spouse of a beneficiary serves as a witness, the inheritance may be endangered.

Keeping your will up to date

You might think, once your will has been drawn up, signed and witnessed, that you can forget about it. But wills grow old, like the people who make them. The conditions that existed when you drew up your will can change considerably in later years. Births, deaths, marriages and divorces may alter the relationship between you and some of your heirs. A well-planned will should anticipate that you and your wife may have additional children. If it does not, it should be revised after their birth to include some provision that covers them. Otherwise, the law might award them their intestate share of your estate whether this was your intention or not. There may also be grandchildren to take care of. If any of your heirs die before you do, you will probably want to revise your will to shift their legacies to others. And you may decide for some reason that you want to increase or decrease a legacy or even exclude a legatee you had originally named. If a daughter marries a wealthy man, for example, she may no longer require the amount you had originally stipulated; your schoolteacher son might need the money far more. Or you may find in your retirement years that it is necessary to sell some of the securities that you had left to your best friend in your will.

You should certainly review your will if you move to another state. For the laws in this state may differ significantly from those where you were living when you made out your will. For example, you might find that the state you have moved to grants greater dower rights to your wife, and therefore a lesser legacy you left her under the laws of your former state is no longer sufficient and can be at-

Some people have tried to cut heirs out of their wills by literally snipping out the paragraphs containing their legacies.

tacked in court. You would then want to redraft your will to avoid the court action and to reapportion the distribution of your estate to your other beneficiaries. If you do move, seek out a lawyer in your new community and check your new status.

Moving also means that you are farther away from your witnesses, and from your original executor or guardian. If your executor or guardian happens to be a bank, you have a special problem, since banks cannot always serve in states in which they are not incorporated. Some states also have restrictions on the individuals who may serve as executors. Illinois, for example, requires executors to be Illinois residents. And if either your executor or guardian should die before you, you must of course change your will to incorporate your new selection, if you have not anticipated this possibility and already named an alternate executor.

If you do decide for any reason to revise your will, you should first discuss the revision with your lawyer. For you must be careful to fulfill most of the same requirements you faced when you drew up the original will. The revision itself is done in the form of a "codicil," a supplement that must be signed, dated and witnessed like the will itself—although not necessarily by the same witnesses. There is no limit to the number of codicils that may be made to a will, so long as each is properly executed. If the codicils become too numerous or confusing, however, it might be wise to start all over and draw up a new will.

When you make a new will, it should contain a clause stating that you hereby "revoke" the old one, making it "null and void," since without such a statement, the new will might not replace the old. The old will should be destroyed in the presence of the witnesses to the new one. Simple as this process is, many people try other methods of revoking a will, often with disastrous results. One man simply scrawled on the bottom of a carbon copy of his will: "This will is void." The court refused to accept this procedure and declared that his old will was valid. An old will can be revoked by intentionally burning it. Merely crossing out a provision of a will may not legally revoke it. Some people have even tried to cut heirs out of an estate by literally taking scissors and snipping out the paragraphs containing their legacies. What constitutes a total or partial revocation of a will varies from state to state.

THE PROCESS OF PROBATE

Many of these requirements seem to be meaningless legalistic formalities. They have a purpose, however—to make sure that no one has pulled any tricks to deny the intended beneficiaries their due. When a testator dies, his will must be presented for probate, a precise legal process in which a court decides whether the will is valid, reviews its provisions and orders ultimate disposition of the assets of the estate. The courts that handle probate procedures go by many names. In California, they are Superior Courts; in New York, Surrogate Courts; in Illinois, Circuit Courts; in Texas, County Courts. In Ohio, Massachusetts and Michigan, they are actually referred to as Probate Courts.

In order to get probate started, a will must first be proved authentic by at least one of the witnesses who signed it. (In some states, two witnesses are necessary.) Normally the witness certifies the will's authenticity by signing an affidavit. He need not appear personally in court unless some further question arises that such an affidavit cannot competently answer—for example, someone contesting the will may claim that the deceased was not really of sound mind when he signed.

Once the will is proved authentic, it is formally "admitted" by the court, which then issues a certificate to the executor of the estate authorizing him to begin carrying out his duties. The executor's first concern is usually to see that the family and dependents of the deceased have enough money to live on until the estate is finally settled. This point in the probate process is generally reached quickly, but until it is, no assets in the estate can be touched. If delay does occur, a family may be hard-pressed for living expenses, particularly when a breadwinner dies. The way to avoid such a problem is to provide funds that need not go through probate. A life insurance policy naming the wife as beneficiary, for example, can pay a lump sum almost immediately after the husband's death. Even better is a separate bank account in the wife's name. A joint checking or savings account does not serve as well, for it may be sequestered (i.e., temporarily locked up) by tax authorities.

In addition to looking after the deceased's family, one of the executor's first duties in some states is to publish a notice of the death in the local newspapers, requesting all creditors of the deceased to submit their claims. In most of these states such claims must be filed within a given period of time, about six months to a year. The reason for this limit is that debts generally take precedence over the inheritance rights of the heirs (except for a wife's dower rights). Thus, the court will not allow the assets of an estate to be distributed to the heirs until all debts are paid. Most states classify these claims according to certain priorities. The funeral bill is often first on the list. Other high priority debts are federal and state taxes.

The executor must file with the probate court an inventory of all the assets of the estate, along with an evaluation of each item. If the as-

THE EXECUTOR'S DUTIES

A will explains what a person wants done with his assets after he dies. Carrying out these instructions becomes the responsibility of the executor of the estate.

1 Engage a lawyer to file the will with the local court that handles probate.

2 With the lawyer's help, petition the court to admit the will to probate and to authorize your appointment as executor. Submit the original of the will to the court and supply the addresses of persons who witnessed it to satisfy the court that it is valid.

3 List the assets of the estate: any cash on hand and in bank accounts, real and personal property, and stocks and bonds. Obtain enough copies of the death certificate to present one to each bank in which the deceased had an account and one to each corporation in which he owned stocks or bonds.

4 Evaluate the immediate financial needs of the family and other dependents of the deceased and, with the court's permission, use the assets of the estate to ensure their support until the estate is settled.

5 If required in your state, publish a notice in the local papers asking all creditors of the deceased to present their claims. All valid debts of the deceased must be paid before bequests can be made to the heirs.

6 Notify the local post office of the death and arrange to have bills and income accruing to the estate sent to you.

7 Collect all monies owed the estate, such as the deceased's outstanding salary and death benefits due his estate from the company that employed him at the time of his death. In the event that you are unable to collect any substantial sums that are owed the estate, obtain approval from the probate court and file suit for payment.

8 Notify insurance companies and Social Security of the death and request that payment be made to the beneficiaries.

9 Locate the safe-deposit box and remove the contents—in the presence of witnesses and a state tax officer to avoid any implication of tax evasion. Take possession of any assets found in the safe-deposit box and include them in the total estate.

10 Inform yourself of the status of real estate taxes and mortgages, and keep payments up to date. Check the amount of insurance carried on property and increase coverage on anything inadequately insured. Pay rent on any lease the deceased may have had until you can arrange to terminate it.

11 Itemize for the probate court all the assets of the estate, together with an evaluation of each item in the inventory, including all furniture and household possessions. You will be expected to make a final statement listing these assets just before the settlement and distribution of the estate to the heirs.

12 Take over active management of the assets of the estate. Study the condition of the property, make repairs where needed, and attempt to sell property as necessary. Inform yourself fully about the conditions affecting the estate's enterprises and determine policy to follow as to management, liquidation, merger or sale of business. Examine investments with a view to retaining or selling them, taking acccount of market conditions and the possibility of tax gains or losses when the estate is ultimately settled. In these matters you are allowed to draw on the advice of experts to a "reasonable and prudent" extent.

13 Within nine months of the date of death submit an estate tax return to the Internal Revenue Service if the assets total more than $60,000. If required in the state in which the deceased resided, you must also file a return with the state tax office.

14 File interim federal and state tax returns on income received by the estate.

15 After federal and state death tax claims have been settled and the one-year period allowed for creditors' claims has expired, distribute the remainder of the estate to the legatees in accordance with the will and obtain final receipts from each.

16 Prepare and submit to the beneficiaries and to the court a detailed accounting of the assets collected, the disbursements made and the net balance distributed to the heirs. If in doubt about the meaning of the terms of the will, submit the problem to the court.

sets total more than $60,000, the executor must file an estate tax return with the U.S. Treasury Department and, if required by local law, with the state tax office as well. At the same time, as the manager of the estate and guardian of its assets until he can get them distributed, the executor must also file federal and state income tax returns on income that is accruing to the estate, pay local property taxes for any real estate that may be held as part of the estate and pay the court the standard fees for its probate service.

Once these steps have been completed, the executor requests an "order of distribution" from the court authorizing him to transfer the assets of the estate to the beneficiaries according to the stipulations of the will. As a part of the probate process, he may be required to publish a notice in the local paper over a period of several weeks stating that the probate proceedings are going on.

Certain notices may also have to be mailed to members of the family and known beneficiaries. These notices give anyone who wishes to contest the will or any aspect of the administration of the estate an opportunity to file objections with the probate court. Such objections are seldom upheld if the will is well-drawn, but ineptly drafted wills can set off court battles that may tie up the settlement of an estate for several years. To prevent this sort of entanglement, Clark Gable had his will stipulate that any legatee who attempted to contest any of its provisions would receive "One ($1.00) Dollar only," and forfeit his right to any other bequest made to him. However, most courts would consider such a provision contrary to public policy, as it discourages inquiry into the true intentions of the testator.

If no objections are filed, and the probate judge has approved the executor's reports, the executor can then begin to distribute the legacies in the order in which they were made in the will. After all the assets have been distributed, the executor makes a final accounting to the court, showing that his duties have been completed. The court then gives the executor his "final discharge" and the administration and probate of the estate are done.

Reducing the probate estate

As you can see, probate procedures can take up a good deal of time, during which your heirs must wait patiently to receive your bequests. Depending on the details of your will, the process can also cost a good deal of money that would ordinarily go to your heirs. For the estate must pay the standard court costs for probating the will and any fees required for executors and lawyers. If there is any dispute over the value of any of the property involved, expert advice from an appraiser may be needed, and his fee, too, comes out of the estate. One cynical gentleman with rather complicated assets willed his entire estate to his lawyer and the tax collector. "I know," he explained, "that they are going to get it all anyway."

The situation in most cases is not nearly that bleak. But enough of your estate does get siphoned off in fees and costs as it goes through probate to make it worth your while to consider various other ways of distributing some assets. Certain kinds are usually immune from probate in any event. The most important one is life insurance, which is often the largest single item in an estate: It does not become part of your probate estate unless you name your estate itself as the beneficiary, instead of naming an individual. Similarly, company, union or veterans' death benefits do not go through probate so long as a specific individual is named as beneficiary. As a result of such arrangements, a good portion of your estate may already be immune to the costs and complications of probate.

To dispose of other assets without probate, two major legal means are available. One is joint ownership. The other is gifts, either outright or in the form of trusts. Once assets belong legally to someone else, they are no longer considered part of your estate by the law—even though you may retain some control over them.

While these methods can protect against the costs and possible delays of the probate procedure, each brings in special problems of its own. Not all trusts and joint ownership arrangements will bypass probate; you must use the right ones. Some trusts protect against death taxes, but others do not. And joint ownership may affect tax liability. Keeping federal and state death taxes to a minimum is one of the principal problems of the expert estate planner: Your taxable estate may be much larger than your probate estate, since the former includes life insurance proceeds—and possibly a share of all joint property—while the latter does not.

The federal estate tax is a tax on the transfer of property from the estate of the deceased. It is called an estate tax because it is calculated on the size of the entire estate after expenses such as funeral costs and executors' fees have been deducted. Some states have estate taxes of their own. Most states, however, have a different kind of death duty either alone or in addition to the estate tax: It is the inheritance tax, which is a tax on the share of the estate that goes to each beneficiary and is measured solely by the value of each separate inheritance. The inheritance tax is usually scaled according to the relationship of the heir to the deceased, the widow having the lowest tax rate and an unrelated friend the highest. Although state taxes cannot be ignored in estate planning, the federal tax is generally the more important to consider. For any estate worth more than $60,000 the federal government requires a tax return listing the estate's total assets to be filed within nine months after death, regardless of whether any tax is actually owed. The reason this $60,000 figure is used is that everyone automatically receives a standard $60,000 exemption when calculating his federal estate tax liability. If the total property amounts to less than $60,000, no federal estate tax is due. Most state inheritance and estate tax laws also allow exemptions. The federal laws also offer a number of other deductions from the total gross estate tax bill, including legitimate debts owed by the deceased, loans or mortgages outstanding against his property, legal and administrative fees involved in settling his estate, plus any money left to charity.

The marital deduction

By far the most important deduction for most estates is the marital deduction. Under this provision, up to one half the estate may be transferred to a surviving spouse free of the federal estate tax. For example, a husband whose wife survives him can leave an estate of $120,000 on which no federal taxes at all need be paid. One half would be counted as a marital deduction, the remaining $60,000 would represent the standard exemption.

Even such a large deduction may not be enough to eliminate all taxes on the estate a widow receives, particularly if the life insurance benefits are substantial. And the tax liability can be needlessly increased if she and her husband had had an arrangement of joint ownership of property. While one form of joint ownership—joint tenancy with right of survivorship—avoids probate, it places the value of the property in the taxable estate of the spouse who originally bought the property; when that spouse dies, tax must be paid on it. If the property was jointly owned—with both spouses putting up part of the money—careful records should be kept. Otherwise, it might be difficult to prove the property did not belong entirely to the husband. A widow's inheritance might then be reduced by taxes paid on property that was really hers all along. For this reason, it is advisable not only to keep detailed records but to maintain separate bank accounts.

Give it away while you can

One of the best ways to reduce the costs both of probate and of taxes is to give some of your assets away before you die. Then you no longer own those assets; they cannot be part of your estate, and they are of no interest to the probate court or to the death tax collector. While monetary gifts may be of interest to the gift tax collector, the tax rate on gifts is much lower than death tax rates, and outright gifts may be financially advantageous, especially for single people who will not be able to take advantage of the marital deduction. The trick, of course, is to hold onto enough money or property to meet your financial needs for the remainder of your own life. Since none of us know exactly how many years we have ahead of us, it is difficult to figure out how much will be enough. Fortunately, the federal gift tax laws are designed (for the government's purposes, not yours) to keep you from giving your property or money away at too rapid a rate. Under these laws, you may, in any one year and for as many years as you wish, give up to $3,000 each to as many different people as you like, tax free—if the gifts are outright, no strings attached. Any amount over $3,000 to one person in one year must be reported to the government on a gift tax return. A couple may make joint gifts of up to $6,000, with the husband and wife each claiming a $3,000 "exclusion." In this way parents can present $6,000 a year to each of their children tax free.

In addition to the annual exclusion for each recipient, you also have a $30,000 lifetime exemption as a donor. The exemption allows you to make tax-free gifts of more than $3,000 each a year—up to a point. Suppose you give each of two children a gift of $4,000 every year. Of that amount, $3,000 of each gift is covered by the exclusion. The additional $1,000 (or a total of $2,000 a year for both children) would be charged against your $30,000 lifetime exemption. At this rate, your exemption would run out after 15 years, and any gift over $3,000 per year after that would be taxable.

If a person has the means, he can also settle a good deal of money on his wife with yearly gifts. For the law provides still another tax break. Gift tax laws include a marital deduction similar to that used in estate tax computations. One half the value of any gift from husband to wife (or vice versa) each year is tax free. Thus a husband can give his wife $6,000 a year as long as he wants to (or can afford to) without paying any gift tax on it. For half of it is covered by the marital deduction, and the remaining $3,000 is covered by the individual gift exclusion. If a husband wishes to give $9,000 a year to his wife, $4,500 of it would be deductible under the gift tax marital deduction, and $3,000 of it would be deductible under the individual gift exclusion. This would leave only $1,500 each year to be applied to the $30,000 lifetime exemption. Thus, supposing this man made no other gifts to anyone, he could give his wife $9,000 a year for 20 years before using up his lifetime exemption.

But the law is on the watch for wary donors who try to dodge

One way to reduce estate taxes is to give assets away before you die. According to federal laws you may give $3,000 a year to different people. In addition, a $30,000 "exemption" allows you to make tax-free gifts over a lifetime of more than $3,000.

death taxes at the last minute. An elderly man, for example, may hang on to most of his assets until shortly before his death and then try to give them all away, hoping to pass on his property to his heirs without shrinkage from taxes. Tax laws, however, do not recognize gifts that have obviously been made "in contemplation of death." Gifts made less than three years before a person's death create a presumption that death was anticipated, and these gifts may be considered part of the estate for tax purposes—and taxed accordingly. If a donor dies suddenly at a fairly early age, however, his gifts will probably be given the benefit of the doubt. And gifts will be recognized as such if they are clearly part of a regular plan going back several years before the three-year limitation. Gifts that take effect only upon one's death, however, are taxed as part of the estate.

Trusts

Many of the advantages of outright gifts can be retained without relinquishing all control over the assets you give away—provided you give them through the legal machinery known as a trust. To most people the word has overtones of great wealth, and it is true that trusts are widely used by the rich because a trust can save on taxes, avoid probate and even allow you posthumous control of your assets. But a trust can also be useful for someone of moderate means. Although the actual setting up and administration of a trust can be quite complicated, the basic principle is simple: You turn a certain amount of your property over to an individual or to an institution, to be held "in trust" and administered by "trustees" for the benefit of someone else, the "beneficiary." There are two basic kinds of trusts: A "testamentary" trust which goes into effect upon your death, and an *inter vivos* (living) trust into which assets can be placed while you are still alive. Only the living trust, however, escapes probate, since only this kind turns over the property before you die.

The most common living trust is the revocable type, which can, in some cases, leave you in complete control of its assets as long as you live. You can amend it or revoke it at any time. In its simplest form it is a bank savings account made out in your name as the only trustee and listing someone else (usually a wife or child) as the beneficiary. The money in the account remains yours to do with as you wish during your lifetime; after your death it automatically becomes the property of the beneficiary, regardless of any provision in a will or any need for probate proceedings.

Because the assets in a revocable trust remain under your control, they are not an outright gift and are not exempt from estate taxes. Upon death, they are counted as part of the taxable estate.

For a tax-free, as well as a probate-free, trust, you need one that is irrevocable. But not necessarily totally irrevocable—under some special circumstances you can cancel or change it, but only with the consent of the person or persons you have named as beneficiaries of the trust. While an irrevocable trust generally ties up assets for a long time, you need not surrender total control over them. You can name yourself as one of several trustees and thus continue to have a voice in managing the assets and administering them for the benefit of those who are to be the beneficiaries. You cannot, of course, use part of such a trust for your own benefit, nor can you have any say in decisions that affect the amount received by the beneficiaries.

The other basic kind of trust, the testamentary trust, does not provide a way of escaping probate or death taxes, but it is a very useful legal device nonetheless because it does provide a way to safeguard an inheritance long after the heir has received it. Suppose that you wish to leave your wife the bulk of your estate, but you realize that she is not particularly adept or even interested in handling a large sum of money. Suppose also that you wish to leave a sum to each of your children, but because they are not yet mature enough to use it wisely, you would like to delay their receipt of the money for a time. A testamentary trust can solve both problems.

In setting up such a trust, you must name a trustee in your will who will administer its assets, and you must direct your executor to turn these assets over to the trust. You can even make life insurance policies payable to the trust. In the will, you can instruct the trustee on the management of the assets, although when modest trusts are managed by banks, the assets are usually converted to cash and invested in stocks and bonds. You can direct the trustee to pay all the income from investments to the beneficiary, or you can instruct the trustees to reinvest part of this income and to pay the beneficiary only a certain sum of money each year. Furthermore, you can authorize them to "invade principal" if need be.

For example, if you leave your wife $100,000 in trust, the income from the principal might amount to $7,000 a year. If you think your wife can continue to live in her customary manner on this amount, you can direct that she receive only that income. If her needs are greater, however, you can direct the trustee to give her an additional amount from the principal, in hopes that she will not outlive the declining principal. The trustee can also be given authority to use part or even all of the principal for the beneficiary if an emergency arises. In the case of minor children, the trust can be set up so that when

One father set up a trust fund solely for the schooling of an errant son. The youth shrewdly managed to pile up four years of college, five of graduate school, then signed on for further courses until he used up the entire trust fund.

they reach college age, the principal can be used to pay their tuition and expenses. Or they can receive the entire principal upon reaching 21, or some other age specified in the trust. In this way, although the person who set up the trust is dead, his estate is under controls that he stipulated and its funds are distributed according to his wishes.

Sometimes these best-laid plans can backfire. One father, for example, concerned about an errant son, decided to set up a trust that would do nothing more for the boy than provide for his schooling. Once he was armed with a proper education, the father felt, the boy would have to continue on his own. The trust, therefore, was to cease payments to the son and divert the money to charity as soon as the boy completed his education. The son, although shiftless, was shrewd. He managed to stay on at the university through four years of college and five years of graduate school, and then signed up for further courses until he had used up the entire principal.

But there are other cases in which a trust would be better than a legacy. Take the example of Mrs. Butler, 43, who was left a $100,000 inheritance in her husband's will. This seemed to be ample money to support her and her two teen-age children. But Mrs. Butler soon remarried, choosing a family friend who was just launching a new electronics company of his own. He borrowed $20,000 of her inheritance to help him get started. It proved to be a bad year for electronics, however, and Mrs. Butler soon found herself lending him another $20,000 to keep the business going. It continued to flounder, and rather than lose her investment entirely—and perhaps her new husband as well —she continued to advance money. Unfortunately the business finally collapsed and Mrs. Butler found that most of her inheritance had gone down the drain with it. By this time, her children were ready for college, but she no longer had sufficient funds to help them pay their tuition. Had her late husband been able to foresee the pressures on his widow, he could have put the $100,000 into a trust fund for her and their children, with most of it earmarked for the children in the event that she remarried.

THE LETTER OF LAST INSTRUCTIONS

Whatever steps you take to complete your estate plan—making a will, distributing gifts, setting up trusts—there is one more document you should draw up before you can really sit back and assume that your affairs are in order. This document is a "letter of last instructions," which provides the information your family, executor and friends need to know about the arrangements you have made.

One important function of this letter is to inform all those concerned where to find your will. A word of warning is in order here. Many people place their wills in a safe deposit box. In some states, however, the law requires that a safe deposit box be sealed immediately upon the owner's death so that no one can tamper with its contents; it can be opened only under court supervision. Obtaining authorization from the court to open the box may require several days, and during this time nothing can be done to process the will.

Some people hide their wills at home in a strongbox. But it is far safer and more convenient to leave your will with your lawyer or your bank, both of which have safes for such documents. In this way the will is safeguarded but can be made available when needed. You can always keep a carbon copy of it at home, and you might also want to give a copy to your executor.

The letter of last instructions should also inform your family where to get money for their immediate needs. Perhaps the life insurance payment will cover this requirement, but the letter should explain where to find the policy. The letter should include an updated list of all your assets, and where and how to locate them. It also should give instructions as to your burial. If you wish to leave your body or some of its organs to a medical facility, the letter of last instructions is the place to say so.

And just as you should keep your will up-to-date in order to avoid any confusion, your letter of last instructions should be gone over from time to time and revised to take care of changed facts or circumstances. You should keep it in a safe but easily reachable place at home, perhaps in your desk drawer. You should tell your wife or another close relative or friend where to find it, and it is also a good idea to give a copy to your executor. For the letter, like a thoughtfully drafted will and well-planned gifts, trusts and insurance, can do much to help your family through a difficult time.

By **BERKELEY RICE**
A. JAMES CASNER, Consultant

GLOSSARY

ABSTRACT OF TITLE—A condensed history of the ownership of a parcel of real estate.

ACCESSORY—A person who does not take part in the actual commission of a crime, but who contributes to it by participating in its preparation or by later concealing the crime or the criminal.

ACCOMPLICE—A person who knowingly and voluntarily helps another person commit a crime.

ACKNOWLEDGMENT—A statement, made under oath before a notary public or a court clerk, affirming that a document, such as a deed or will, has been the free act of the person making the statement.

ACT OF GOD—An occurrence resulting from the vagaries of nature rather than from any human activity; thus, no one can be held criminally or financially liable for damages caused thereby.

ACTIONABLE—Furnishing the legal grounds for a court action.

ADMISSIBLE—Referring to evidence or testimony that is acceptable by a court.

ADVERSARY SYSTEM—The court procedure whereby each of the opposing parties presents his side of a case and tries to rebut arguments and challenge evidence presented by the other party.

AFFIDAVIT—A written statement of facts, made voluntarily and sworn to before an authorized official, such as a notary public.

AGENT—A person who has agreed to act on behalf of another person, called the principal, in one or more transactions.

AGGRAVATED ASSAULT—Intentional violence against a person, usually with a dangerous instrument or when some other crime is also intended.

ALIBI—(Latin for "elsewhere"). The claim of an accused person that he was not at the scene of the crime when it was committed and hence could not have committed it.

ALIMONY—(from the Latin *alimonia*, "sustenance"). Money or property paid by one spouse for the support and maintenance of the other spouse during a legal separation or after a final divorce decree.

ALLEGATION—An assertion that a party to a legal action expects to prove in court.

AMICUS CURIAE—(Latin for "friend of the court"). One who volunteers information on a point of law in a court case in which he is not directly involved.

APPEAL—A request, by a defeated party in a court action, that a higher court review the decision because of legal errors made during the court action.

ARRAIGNMENT—The formal procedure in which a suspect is called before a court, hears the charges against him, and is required to plead guilty or not guilty. It is at this point that the suspect's status changes to that of defendant.

ARREARS—Overdue payments on a debt.

ARREST—The physical detention of a person, usually to answer a criminal charge lodged against him.

ASSAULT—An unlawful threat to inflict physical harm on a person.

ASSIGNMENT—A transfer of property, or of some right to it, from one person (the "assignor") to another (the "assignee").

ATTACHMENT—The legal seizure of property, by an officer of the court, usually to discharge debts owed by the property owner; also, the legal seizure of a person to ensure his appearance in court.

BAIL—A sum of money determined by a judge and given to the court as security in exchange for the temporary release from custody of a suspect or defendant, usually in a criminal case.

BAIL BOND—A formal document, signed by a person temporarily released from custody, pledging to appear in court on a certain day or forfeit the money or property that secures the bond.

BAILIFF—Most commonly, an official responsible for keeping order in the courtroom.

BAILMENT—The temporary handing over by one person to another of an item of personal property. Often such a transfer is made in exchange for some service to be performed on that item, such as leaving a coat to be dry-cleaned.

BANKRUPT—A person who is unable to pay his debts and uses the provisions of the Federal Bankruptcy Act to distribute his assets to his creditors.

BAR—The section of a courtroom occupied by attorneys and their clients, set off from spectators and prospective witnesses in the courtroom by a bar, or railing. A convicted person stands "at the bar" for sentencing. Also, a collective term for lawyers.

BATTERY—The unlawful and intentional striking of a person or touching him in a menacing manner. Often coupled with *assault*.

BENCH WARRANT—A court order for the arrest of someone guilty of a crime or of contempt of court.

BEQUEST—A gift of personal property in a will.

BILL OF PARTICULARS—A statement written by a plaintiff's lawyer expanding on the specific reasons for which a legal action has been brought; also, a written response by the defendant's lawyer.

BINDER—In real estate, a document in which the seller and buyer of a piece of property proclaim their common intention to effect a sale and purchase of the property; in insurance, a memorandum from the insurer giving temporary coverage to the insured.

BONA FIDE—(Latin for "in good faith"). Referring to an action taken, openly and sincerely, in innocence of any fraud that might be involved.

BOND—A signed promise guaranteeing payment of a specified sum of money to a person, business or institution at an appointed time.

BREACH—Violation of a law, legal right, contract or obligation, either by commission or omission.

BREACH OF PROMISE—Usually, failure to carry out a pledge to marry.

BRIEF—A written summary of arguments to be presented by a lawyer in a court case; also a summary of a case that is presented to an appellate court.

BURGLARY—The crime of breaking and entering into property owned by another person with the intention of committing another crime such as larceny.

CAVEAT EMPTOR—(Latin for "let the buyer beware"). A once universally accepted maxim warning a purchaser to examine the quality and condition of his purchase, because he buys at his own risk.

CHAIN OF TITLE—A list of owners of a parcel of real estate, traced from the original to the current owner.

CHALLENGE—An objection by an attorney to a prospective juror in a trial. Each attorney is allowed a certain number of challenges for which he need give no reason (these are "peremptory challenges"). There is no limit to the number of challenges for which an attorney must show that the prospective juror's judgment would be biased (these are "challenges for cause").

CHANGE OF VENUE—The transfer of a case from one county or district to another for trial.

CHARGE—The accusation for which a person is arraigned and put on trial; also, a final address by a judge to a jury in which he sums up the case and instructs the jurors as to the law.

CHATTEL—An item of personal property.

CHILD SUPPORT—Payments to provide for the cost of raising a child of estranged or divorced parents.

CIRCUMSTANTIAL EVIDENCE—Known facts, bearing on the question at hand, from which a reasonable person can draw conclusions as to the existence or veracity of other facts.

CIVIL ACTION—A legal proceeding in which a party seeks some remedy such as an injunction or monetary damages. This is distinguished from a *criminal action*, in which a fine or imprisonment is sought.

CIVIL LAW SYSTEM—The system of law, based on statutes or codes rather than on cases, that is in existence in many non-English-speaking countries, and is distinguished from the *common law* system.

CLEMENCY—A judicial or executive act of mercy that grants a milder punishment to a defendant who has been found guilty.

CLOSING—The completion of a transaction, most commonly one in which ownership of a parcel of real estate is transferred from seller to buyer.

CODICIL—A document that contains additions or amendments to a will.

COLLATERAL SECURITY—Property pledged to ensure the payment of a debt.

COLLUSION—An agreement by two or more persons to defraud or deceive.

COMMON LAW—The body of law that derives its authority not from statutes but from time-honored customs and from court decisions based on them.

COMMON LAW SYSTEM—The system of law based on customs and cases rather than on codes and statutes. This system is in effect in most English-speaking countries (see *civil law system*).

COMMUNITY PROPERTY—A principle of ownership, in existence in eight states, establishing that property acquired during a marriage by husband and wife, or either, is owned equally by both. This excludes inheritances by either spouse during the marriage.

COMPETENCY—The fitness of a witness to give testimony in a trial; the fitness of documentary evidence to be accepted. Competency is determined by the judge, while the "credibility" of a witness or document is determined by the jury.

COMPLAINT—In a civil action, a document stating the cause of an action that has been brought and the damages that are being sought, in order to inform the defendant of the reasons for the plaintiff's suit. In criminal law, a charge presented to a magistrate in which one person accuses another of a crime.

CONDEMNATION—The taking of private property for public use with compensation to the owner (see *eminent domain*).

CONDONATION—Forgiveness by one spouse of the other's breach of the marriage contract, which, with restoration by the wronged spouse of the other's marital rights, stops any possible divorce action.

CONNIVANCE—The advance consent by one person to the unlawful conduct of another, such as the consent by one spouse to the adultery of the other.

CONSANGUINITY—Blood relationship.

CONSENT DECREE—A court-approved agreement between parties to an action to settle out of court.

CONSORTIUM—The reciprocal conjugal rights and duties of husband and wife, including affection, aid and comfort, support and sexual intercourse.

CONSPIRACY—An agreement by two or more people to commit a crime.

CONTEMPT OF COURT—Willful disobedience of an order of the court. Also, conduct that brings the court or the law itself into disrespect.

CONTINUANCE—The postponement of court proceedings in a pending action from one day or one court term to another.

CONTRACT—Promises made by two or more parties either to cease performing an act or to carry out an act or a promise that creates or modifies obligations and rights, the breach of which can be the basis for a court action.

CONVEYANCE—A transfer of property from one person to another.

COPYRIGHT—The exclusive right granted by federal law and international convention to the creator of a literary or artistic work for the publication, reproduction and sale of the work. In the U.S. the right lasts for 28 years and may be renewed.

CORONER—An official empowered in some states to conduct an investigation, sometimes with the aid of a jury, into a death that has taken place under violent or suspicious circumstances.

CORPUS DELICTI—(Latin for "body of the crime"). The material object upon which a crime has been committed, such as the body of a murder victim or the ruins of a building that was bombed.

CO-SIGNER—A person who, by his signature on a promissory note or other such document, guarantees payment of a debt and is liable for the debt if the original signer defaults.

COUNT—A single item in an *information* or *indictment,* and one which is sufficient cause for legal action against an accused person.

CRIMINAL ACTION—A legal proceeding in which imprisonment or a fine is sought as punishment for performance of an act deemed injurious to society as a whole. In such an action the role of plaintiff is filled by the state, and the case is tried by a public prosecutor.

CROSS-EXAMINATION—The questioning in court of a witness for one side by the attorney representing the other side in order to test the accuracy and truthfulness of the testimony the witness is giving.

CUSTODY—The physical supervision of a person; also, the day-to-day supervision of a minor.

DAMAGES—Monetary compensation awarded by a court for loss or injury to one's person, property or reputation. "Punitive" or "exemplary" damages are awarded to a plaintiff in a damage suit over and above the actual compensation for his injury. They are intended to punish the offender and to deter a repetition of the offense.

DECLARATORY JUDGMENT—A court decision, without an accompanying order, concerning the rights of the parties to an action, or concerning a question of law.

DECREE—A court ruling on the respective rights of the parties to an action.

DEED—A formal document, transferring ownership of real property from one person to another.

DEFAMATION—False and malicious statements either written (see *libel*) or spoken (see *slander*) that injure someone's reputation.

DEFAULT—Failure to fulfill a legal obligation.

DEFAULT JUDGMENT—A court decision for the plaintiff when the defendant fails to appear or answer a complaint within the prescribed time period.

DEFENDANT—The person against whom either a *civil action* or *criminal action* is brought.

DELINQUENT—A minor who commits a crime, or is incorrigible or beyond parental control. Also refers to a debt or claim that has not been paid by the appointed time.

DEPOSITION—Testimony given by a witness under oath outside the courtroom but in the course of a judicial proceeding.

DEVISE—To make a gift of real estate by a will; also the gift itself.

DIRECT EXAMINATION—The questioning of a witness called by one side in a trial by the attorney representing that side.

DISORDERLY CONDUCT—Behavior that disturbs the public peace or sense of morality.

DISPOSITION—The giving up of property, as in the distribution of the assets of an estate to the heirs.

DOCKET—The list and dates of cases to be tried during a court term.

DOMICILE—A person's permanent and principal home, to which he always expects to return.

DOUBLE JEOPARDY—A second prosecution for the same offense. Prohibited by the U.S. Constitution.

DOWER—Classically, the portion of a man's real property that his wife is entitled to claim on his death. This concept is being replaced by the right of election (against the will), which guarantees a wife a portion of all property—real and personal—that had belonged to her deceased husband.

DUE PROCESS OF LAW—The right, guaranteed equally to all persons by the U.S. and state constitutions, that no one may be deprived of life, liberty or property without scrupulous legal safeguards.

DURESS—The use of force or threats against a person or his family to compel him to do something that he would not freely do.

EARNEST—A token payment of money or a partial delivery of goods that serves to bind a contract.

EASEMENT—The right one person has to use the land of another person for a specific purpose.

EMANCIPATION—A parent's free surrender of control over a minor child and recognition that the child may keep his own earnings and choose his own home.

EMINENT DOMAIN—The right of the federal government or a state to acquire private property for public use, after compensation to the owner (see *condemnation*).

ENCROACHMENT—A structure or planting that extends across a property line, intruding upon the neighboring property.

ENCUMBRANCE—A legal claim against a parcel of real estate that reduces the rights of the owner to less than complete ownership (see *lien, mortgage*). Also, a claim against personal property, such as a car.

ENTICEMENT—Coaxing or seducing a person to commit an unlawful or wrongful act.

ENTRAPMENT—The act by a police officer of inducing a person to commit a crime in order to arrest him for that crime. The arrested person cannot be convicted if he did not have it in mind to commit the crime before being induced to do so by the officer.

ESCROW—The keeping by a third person of a deed, property or money given to him by one party to a transaction, to be turned over by him to the other party upon fulfillment of a specified condition.

ESTATE—Any property or rights to property, real or personal, owned by a person.

ESTOPPEL—(Medieval French for "cork or obstruction"). An obstacle that legally precludes someone from alleging or denying a fact. Such an obstacle may be his own previous statements or conduct to the contrary.

EVICTION—The expulsion of a person from real property, usually after a court judgment.

EVIDENCE—Testimony or material objects introduced at a trial for the purpose of convincing the judge or jury of the truth of a fact. Corroborating evidence is additional evidence that differs from evidence offered earlier in a court case, but tends to confirm the previous evidence.

EX PARTE—(Latin for "one-sided"). A court order issued upon the application of one party to an action.

EX POST FACTO—(Latin for "after the fact"). Most often refers, in a criminal action, to a law passed after something has occurred or has been done that retroactively changes the legal consequences of that occurrence or action. The U.S. Constitution forbids such laws.

EXECUTOR—The person or institution named in a will to carry out its provisions.

EXTENUATING CIRCUMSTANCES—Facts surrounding an illegal act that make it less reprehensible than it would otherwise be, or that may lessen the punishment of the perpetrator if he is found guilty.

EXTORTION—The unlawful exaction of a payment of money or other object of value from another.

EXTRADITION—The surrender by one state or country to another, on demand, of a person accused or convicted of a crime in the latter.

FALSE ARREST—Any unlawful detention of a person in jail or elsewhere.

FALSE PRETENSE—Intentional misrepresentation of fact in order to defraud someone of property.

FEE SIMPLE—Ownership rights to real estate that grant the property absolutely to the owner and his heirs forever.

FELONY—The most serious category of criminal offense, which is defined by the punishment given —in most states either imprisonment for more than a year, a fine, or both.

FIDUCIARY—A person such as an executor, guardian or trustee whom the law holds to an especially high and exacting standard of fairness in dealing with those who are committed to his guidance: He must always act for their primary benefit.

FORECLOSURE—Termination of ownership of a parcel of real property and of all rights to it by one who owns a *mortgage*.

FOREMAN—The informal chairman of a jury, either elected by the other jurors or appointed by the court. It is his duty to report the jury's verdict to the court.

FORGERY—The fraudulent writing or alteration in writing of such legal documents as checks.

FRAUD—An intentionally false representation of fact intended to deceive someone to his detriment.

GARNISHMENT—A proceeding by which a creditor is permitted to obtain money owed him by taking possession of the debtor's funds, property or salary before they come into the debtor's possession.

GUARDIAN—Someone appointed to protect and manage the person, estate or legal affairs of an individual who has been adjudged by a court to be partially or totally incapable of handling some or all of his own affairs.

HABEAS CORPUS— (Latin for "you have the body"). A court order that requires an official holding a person in custody to bring him into court and show cause for his detention.

HEARSAY—Evidence offered by a witness concerning what someone else has said. With certain exceptions, hearsay evidence is not admissible in court.

HEIR—Someone designated to receive the property of a deceased person.

HOLOGRAPHIC WILL—A will written entirely in the handwriting of the deceased and generally not executed or witnessed in the usual way. Holographic wills are generally accepted in a few states, and accepted elsewhere when written by mariners at sea or by soldiers in wartime.

HOMICIDE—The killing of one person by another. It is not necessarily a criminal offense, as in the case of accidental homicide, which is the inadvertent taking of a life, and justifiable homicide, which is legally sanctioned in such circumstances as necessity or duty.

IMPANEL—To select the jurors for the trial of a particular case.

IMPLIED CONTRACT—An unwritten agreement in which a legally binding promise is implied from the conduct of the parties or is imposed by law.

INCOMPETENCY PROCEEDING—A court hearing to decide whether an individual is capable of functioning on his own in society or whether he should be supervised by a guardian.

INDICTMENT—A formal written charge accusing an individual of an offense and indicating that he must stand trial. It is issued by a group of citizens, impaneled by a court, called a *grand jury*.

INFORMATION—A written accusation of a crime presented to a court by a prosecutor.

INJUNCTION—An order issued by a court at the request of one party prohibiting another party from performing an act that infringes on the complainant's rights. Such an order may also be issued to compel the performance of an act.

INQUEST—Most commonly, an inquiry into the manner of death of anyone who has died suddenly or in prison. It is usually conducted by a coroner.

INSANITY—In the legal as opposed to the medical definition, the mental incapacity that prevents a person from being held responsible for his acts. The definition varies from one area of the law to another.

INTERLOCUTORY DECREE—A temporary ruling by a court, prior to its final decision, settling some point of fact or law in a suit.

INTESTATE—Referring to a person who has died without making a will that disposes of his estate.

JURISPRUDENCE—The philosophy or science of law.

JURIST—One who is skilled in the law, usually having written learnedly on legal subjects.

JURY—A group of citizens that hears evidence on a case and reaches a decision on it. A "grand jury" decides whether there is sufficient evidence of wrongdoing to bring someone to trial on criminal charges (see *indictment*). A "petit jury" reaches verdicts on criminal charges and decides civil suits. A jury whose members cannot arrive at a verdict is called a "hung jury."

LARCENY—The unlawful taking and carrying away of another's personal property. There are two types: "petty" larceny and "grand" larceny, the difference, which varies from state to state, being in the monetary value of the goods stolen.

LEASE—A written contract giving one person (the "lessee") the right to use land or property belonging to another person (the "lessor"), in return for rent or other compensation.

LEGACY—Either personal or real property left by its owner (the "legator") to someone else (the "legatee") in a will (see *bequest, devise*).

LETTERS TESTAMENTARY—Written authorization from a court empowering the person responsible for carrying out provisions of a will (see *executor*) to undertake his duties (see also *probate*).

LIBEL—A defamatory statement about a person, expressed in writing or pictures, that holds him up to public ridicule or otherwise harms his reputation (see *defamation, slander*).

LIEN—A claim made on a property in order to secure the payment of a debt (see *encumbrance*).

LITIGANT—A person engaged in a lawsuit.

LITIGATION—The carrying on of a lawsuit or legal proceeding for the purpose of enforcing a right.

MALICE—The spiteful intent and the will to commit a wrongful act.

MANSLAUGHTER—The unlawful killing of another person, but without malice. Manslaughter may be voluntary, in the heat of passion, or involuntary, as an unintended byproduct of some other careless or unlawful act.

MINOR—A person below the legal age of adulthood.

MISDEMEANOR—A crime less serious than a felony and hence carrying a lesser penalty. In most states, misdemeanors are defined by punishments of a fine or a prison term of one year or less.

MISTRIAL—A trial that is invalid because the jury is deadlocked or because some procedural error has been made during its course.

MORTGAGE—A pledge of property that accompanies a loan of money and that acts as security for repayment of the loan and attendant interest.

MURDER—The unlawful killing of a person with malice, either express or implied.

NECESSARIES—Those items, such as food, clothing and shelter, that are in keeping with a person's station in life that constitute support.

NEGLIGENCE—The performance of an act that causes harm and that a reasonable and prudent person would not do. Also, the failure to perform an act that such a person should have performed. "Comparative" negligence, a doctrine in effect in some states, is the failure of both parties to an accident to exercise the reasonable care that would have avoided the accident, damages being assessed against the relatively more negligent party.

"Contributory" negligence, a doctrine in effect in most states, is any lack of reasonable care by an injured party that contributes to his own injury and thereby precludes him from suing for damages. "Criminal" negligence is any lack of reasonable care that endangers another person's life or safety. "Gross" negligence is the commission of an injurious act with reckless and wanton disregard of human life or safety.

NOLO CONTENDERE—(Latin for "I do not wish to contest"). A plea by a defendant in a criminal action indicating that he will accept the court's verdict without presenting evidence to rebut the charge. It generally has the same legal effect as a plea of guilty.

NONAGE—Under the age established by law that constitutes majority.

NUISANCE—Anything that disturbs the enjoyment of life or property. A "private" nuisance, such as a defective chimney pouring smoke on a neighboring home, is one directed at a single individual or a limited number of individuals; a "public" nuisance, such as a gambling house, is one that may offend the public at large.

PATENT—A grant by the federal government to an inventor of the exclusive right to make, use and sell his invention for 17 years.

PERJURY—A willful statement made under oath in a judicial proceeding and known by the person making the statement to be false.

PERSONAL PROPERTY—Movable items such as clothes, jewelry, cash, stocks and bonds, as distinguished from *real property*.

PLAINTIFF—The complaining party in a *civil action*.

POWER OF ATTORNEY—A written authorization by one person to permit another person to act as his agent or attorney.

PRECEDENT—A court decision that sets an example by which later cases of a similar sort may be decided.

PRETERMITTED—Referring to an offspring who is unmentioned in a will.

PRIVILEGED COMMUNICATION—An exchange of certain information between two persons in a relationship that requires trust and confidentiality. Among others, communications between attorney and client, husband and wife or priest and penitent are considered to be privileged; neither party can be forced to testify against the other in court and reveal such secret information.

PROBATE—The judicial process that first verifies a will as being a deceased person's true last testament, and then ensures that the terms of the will are carried out exactly.

PROMISSORY NOTE—A written and signed promise by one person to pay another person named or the "bearer" a certain sum of money on demand or on a date specified in the document.

PROSECUTOR—The public official whose duty it is to bring court action against persons accused of crimes.

PUBLIC DEFENDER—An official designated by the court to defend an accused person who lacks the means to pay for his own defense.

REAL PROPERTY—Land and any structures on it (see *personal property*).

REBUTTAL—The refutation of a charge or evidence by the presentation of evidence to the contrary.

RECEIVER—A person appointed by a court to hold property that is the subject of litigation and to manage or dispose of it at the court's direction.

RECESS—A short period of time during which a court suspends business without adjourning.

REFEREE—A person appointed by a court to take testimony in a civil case and to report to the court.

RETAINER—A fee paid in advance by a client to an attorney to secure his services.

ROBBERY—The forcible taking of personal property or money from someone by the use of violence or the threat of violence.

SEARCH WARRANT—A court order in writing permitting a police officer to search specified premises for specified evidence of a suspected crime and to seize the evidence if he finds it.

SLANDER—Defamatory statements spoken, rather than written, about a person that holds him up to public ridicule or otherwise harms his reputation (see *defamation, libel*).

STATUTE OF LIMITATIONS—A law setting a time limit beyond which a legal action cannot be brought.

STIPULATION—A fact agreed to by both sides in a case in order to speed up a trial.

SUBORNATION OF PERJURY—The offense of instigating or procuring another person for the purpose of offering false testimony (see *perjury*).

SUBPOENA—An order issued by a court commanding the appearance of a witness to give testimony at a court proceeding. This is sometimes called a Subpoena ad Testificandum. A court order commanding that material evidence, such as documents, be produced is called a Subpoena Duces Tecum (Latin for "bring with you").

SUMMONS—A document notifying a person that a legal action has been brought against him, and advising him of the results of failure to appear in court on or before a specific date.

TESTAMENT—A will. Formerly, the term was applied solely to the disposition of personal property.

TESTIFY—To give oral evidence in a case, under oath, for the purpose of proving or establishing a fact, usually at a court trial.

TITLE SEARCH—An examination of public records to ascertain the history of ownership of a property.

TORT—A wrongful act that injures another's person, property or reputation. Also, the violation by one person of a duty or obligation he owes another that thereby harms the latter. The injured party is entitled to sue the wrongdoer for damages.

TRIAL—A judicial examination, in accordance with the law of the land, of either a civil or criminal case before a court that has jurisdiction over the case.

TRUST—A legal organ created for the purpose of holding property, and, in turn, committed to the charge of someone else, a "trustee." The trustee must administer the trust for the benefit of either the property owner or other parties designated by him, the "beneficiaries."

USURY—The intentional exaction of an interest higher than the rate permitted by law.

VENIRE—A group of citizens, called veniremen, summoned for jury duty. Juries for particular cases are chosen from this group.

VERDICT—The decision of a jury, in either a civil or criminal case, as to the issue which has been submitted to it. In some instances a jury will produce a "directed" verdict; this is a decision made at the order of the judge when he finds that the evidence in a case and the law concerning it so strongly favor one party to a court action that no reasonable jury could find in the other party's favor.

VOIR DIRE—(French for "to say the truth"). The preliminary questioning of a witness to see if he is qualified to testify, or of a potential juror to see if he is qualified to serve on a jury.

WILL—A legal document providing for the disposition of a person's property after his death. Formerly the term applied only to the disposition of real estate as apart from personal property.

WRIT—A court order requiring the performance of an act. Among the more common types of writ are a "writ of certiorari," an order from a higher to a lower court requiring it to submit its record of a case so that the higher court can determine whether to review the judgment of the lower court; and a "writ of mandamus," an order from a higher to a lower court or a government official, commanding the performance of a specified act, or the restoration to a complainant of a right of which he has been illegally or unjustly deprived.

ACKNOWLEDGMENTS

Portions of this book were contributed by Paul Trachtman and Anthony Wolff.

For their valuable assistance and contributions in the preparation of this book, the editors wish to thank the following: Betty Bay, Executive Office of the President, Office of Consumer Affairs, Washington, D.C.; Kenneth Bialo, Attorney at Law, New York City; Robert H. Blumberg, Attorney at Law, New York City; Stanley Boriss, Attorney at Law, New York City; Nathaniel E. Butler, Educational Director, National Conference of Commissioners on Uniform State Laws, Chicago; Stephen A. Carb, Attorney at Law, New York City; Thomas A. Carlson, Assistant Attorney for the State of Michigan, Lansing, Michigan; Mrs. Peter Castalde, Accountant, New York City; Susan Costello, New York City; H. E. Dillmore, Pittsburgh, Pennsylvania; Dennis Dunn, American Civil Liberties Union, New York City; James P. Economos, Director, Traffic Court Program, American Bar Association, Chicago; James J. Egan, Attorney at Law, New York City; Harriet Wilson Ellis, American Bar Association, Chicago; Betty Elton, Acting Executive Secretary, The American College of Probate Counsel, Los Angeles; Susan J. First, General Counsel, New York City Department of Consumer Affairs, New York City; Professor Harry Foster, School of Law, New York University, New York City; Ursula M. Gallagher, Children's Bureau, Office of Child Development, Department of Health, Education and Welfare, Washington, D.C.; Suzanne Gottlieb, District Attorney's Office, County of Manhattan, New York City; Robert C. Griffin, Assistant to the Director, Traffic Court Program, American Bar Association, Chicago; James Hamilton, Attorney at Law, Boston, Massachusetts; Melitta Hartung, American Automobile Association, Washington, D.C.; Alan J. Hruska, Attorney at Law, New York City; C. Sumner Katz, Vice President, Insurance Company of North America, Philadelphia; James Kielty, Supervisor, Road Safety Information, National Safety Council, Chicago; James J. Lack, New York State Consumer Protection Board, New York City; Charles H. Lake, Attorney at Law, Louisville, Kentucky; Barnett Levy, Assistant Attorney General for the State of New York, New York City; Michael A. Liethen, Director, Legal Rights Program, National Student Association, Washington, D.C.; Thomas McFerrin, Assistant Attorney General for the State of Louisiana, Baton Rouge, Louisiana; Vincent McInerney, Attorney at Law, Hollis, New York; John L. McKinzey, St. Paul, Minnesota; Edward O'Hare, Insurance Information Institute, New York City; Joseph T. Pizzullo, Law Librarian, Trenton, New Jersey; Rodney Robertson, Attorney at Law, Boston, Massachusetts; Sanford Rosen, Attorney at Law, New York City; Flora Schnall, Attorney at Law, New York City; Marc Seltzer, Attorney at Law, New York City; E. Donald Shapiro, Director, Practising Law Institute, New York City; Robert Shnayerson, New York City; Maxine Virtue, Assistant Attorney General for the State of Michigan, Lansing, Michigan; Norman Wachtel, Attorney at Law, New York City; Ron Weger, Weger Governmental Systems, Lansing, Michigan; Philip Wittenber, Attorney at Law, New York City; Paul A. Wolkin, Assistant Director, The American Law Institute, Philadelphia, Pennsylvania; Carl Zuckerman, New York City Department of Social Services, New York City. Many of the legal forms used as illustrations for this book are reprinted by permission of Julius Blumberg Inc., New York City.

BIBLIOGRAPHY

Some of the sources consulted in the preparation of this book include: *Digest of Motor Laws, 1971,* the American Automobile Association; *The Legal Profession in the United States,* The American Bar Foundation; *The Mentally Disabled and the Law,* The American Bar Foundation, Frank T. Lindman and Donald S. McIntyre, editors; *Business Law,* Ronald A. Anderson and Walter A. Kumpf; *What Lawyers Really Do,* Bernard Asbell; *How to Comply with the Fair Credit Reporting Act,* Associated Credit Bureaus; *Ballentine's Law Dictionary* (third ed.), James A. Ballentine, edited by William S.

Anderson; *Business Law*, Louis O. Bergh and Thomas Conyngton; *Perspectives in Constitutional Law*, Charles Black; *Black's Law Dictionary*, Henry Campbell Black, revised fourth ed. by West Publishing Co. Editorial Staff; *What You Ought to Know about Truth in Lending*, Board of Governors of the Federal Reserve System; *Tax Savings Through Estate Planning*, William J. Bowe; *Preventive Law*, Louis M. Brown; *Laws Concerning Religion in the United States*, Abraham Burstein; *A Summary of the Uniform Consumer Credit Code*, Nathaniel E. Butler; *Cases and Text on Property*, A. James Casner and W. Barton Leach; *Estate Planning*, Volumes I, II, III, A. James Casner; *Lawyers for People of Moderate Means*, Barlow F. Christensen; *The Law of Domestic Relations in the United States*, Homer H. Clark Jr.; *The Supreme Court and the Electoral Process*, Richard Claude; *The Rule of Law in the United States*, The Committee to Co-operate with the International Commission of Jurists; *Business Law*, Andrew J. Coppola and Harry Katz; *The Book of States, 1970-71*, The Council of State Governments; *Basic Business Law*, David S. Craig and Rate A. Howell; *Under 21, A Young People's Guide to Legal Rights*, Michael Dorman; *Bender's Uniform Commercial Code: Sales & Bulk Transfers*, Richard W. Dussenberg and Lawrence W. King; *Ehrlich's Blackstone*, J. W. Ehrlich; *Privacy, The Right to Be Let Alone*, Morris Ernst and Alan U. Schwartz; *The Law and the Impaired Older Person; Protection or Punishment*, Gertrude H. Hall, editor; *Consumer Credit Handbook*, Frederick M. Hart and William F. Willier; *Principles of Real Estate Law*, Edna L. Hebard and Gerald S. Meisel; *The Common Law*, Oliver Wendell Holmes; *A Guide to Court Systems*, Institute of Judicial Administration; *Criminal Law and Its Processes, Cases and Materials*, Sanford H. Kadish and Monrad G. Paulsen; *Women and the Law; The Unfinished Revolution*, Leo Kanowitz; *Constitutional Law, Cases and Materials*, Paul G. Kauper; *Consumer Credit, Cases and Notes*, Homer Kripke; *Federal Estate and Gift Taxes*, Charles L. B. Laundes and Robert Kramer; *Legislative Approaches to the Problems of the Elderly: A Handbook of Model State Statutes*, Legal Research and Services for the Elderly; *Introduction to Jurisprudence*, Dennis Lloyd; *Growing Up Clean in America* and *Power and Put-On*, Joseph S. Lobenthal Jr.; *Contingent Fees for Legal Services*, F. B. MacKinnon; *Ancient Law, Its Connection with the Early History of Society and Its Relation to Modern Ideas*, Sir Henry Sumner Maine; *The Innocent Consumer vs. The Exploiters*, Sidney Margolis; *Martindale-Hubbell Law Directory, Volume V, Law Digests, Court Calendars and Uniform Acts, 1970; Assault on Privacy*, Arthur R. Miller; *Oxford History of the American People*, Samuel Eliot Morison; *What to Do with Your Bad Car*, Ralph Nader, Lowell Dodge, Ralf Hotchkiss; *Credit Manual of Commercial Laws, 1969*, National Association of Credit Bureaus; *Uniform Probate Code*, National Conference of Commissioners on Uniform State Laws; *Student Legal Rights, What They Are and How to Protect Them*, Michael Nussbaum; *The Complete Jefferson*, Saul K. Padover, editor; *Cases and Other Materials on Domestic Relations*, Monrad G. Paulsen, Walter Wadlington, Julius Goebel Jr.; *Rights and Writers*, and *Your Marriage and The Law*, Harriet F. Pilpel and Theodora S. Zavin; *The Law of Torts*, William L. Prosser; *Law Dictionary*, Max Radin; *The Legal Adviser on Home Ownership*, Jerome G. Rose; *Cases and Materials on the Law of Torts*, Warren A. Seavey, Page Keeton and Robert Keeton; *Freedom to Travel*, Special Committee to Study Passport Procedures of the Association of the Bar of the City of New York; *Court and Constitution in the Twentieth Century*, 2 vols., William F. Swindler; *Bankruptcy Hearings, 1969*, House Committee on the Judiciary, United States Congress; *Commercial Credit Bureau Hearings, 1968*, House Committee on Government Operations, United States Congress; *The Impact of Credit Cards on Small Business*, House Select Committee on Small Business, United States Congress; *The Credit Industry*, Senate Committee on the Judiciary, United States Congress; *Developments in Aging, 1968*, Senate Special Committee on the Aging, United States Congress; *Invasions of Privacy*, Hearings Before the Subcommittee on Administrative Practice and Procedure, Senate Committee on the Judiciary, United States Congress; *Privacy and Freedom*, Alan F. Westin.

INDEX